PR

everything

"A wonderful read. Anyone who wants to know where blogs come from—and why they matter—should read this book. Rosenberg, who's been doing new media from its very start, as well as writing about it, is the perfect person to tell this story."

—**Josh Quittner**, editor at large for *Time*

"The more you know about the blog world, the more illuminating *Say Everything* will be. Scott Rosenberg has put recent history into a perspective that makes me look at today's websites—and tomorrow's—in a new way."

—**James Fallows**, national correspondent for *Atlantic Monthly*

"Engaging and important, *Say Everything* tells the story of the people and the movement with the strange name that has changed our world."

—**Jeff Jarvis**, creator of BuzzMachine.com and author of *What Would Google Do?*

"Scott Rosenberg provides an excellent fifteen-year history of the 'voice of the person' on the Web, from Talking Points Memo to Twitter, and profiles both idealistic pioneers and scrappy entrepreneurs. He offers a cogent look at not only what's new but also what's next."

—**Greg Mitchell**, editor of *Editor & Publisher*

"Scott Rosenberg deftly recounts blogging's raucous rise with a storyteller's skill, a journalist's care, and a blogger's verve."

—**David Weinberger**, coauthor of *The Cluetrain Manifesto* and fellow at Harvard's Berkman Center for Internet & Society

ALSO BY SCOTT ROSENBERG

Dreaming in Code:

Two Dozen Programmers, Three Years, 4,732 Bugs,

and One Quest for Transcendent Software

say everything

HOW BLOGGING BEGAN, WHAT IT'S BECOMING, AND WHY IT MATTERS

scott rosenberg

THREE RIVERS PRESS
NEW YORK

Originally published in hardcover in the United States by Crown Publishers, an
imprint of the Crown Publishing Group, a division of Random House, Inc.,
New York, in 2009.

Library of Congress Cataloging-in-Publication Data is available upon request.

ISBN 978-0-307-45137-8

Printed in the United States of America

Design by Maria Elias

10 9 8 7 6 5 4 3 2 1

First Paperback Edition

For Dayna

CONTENTS

INTRODUCTION: WHAT'S NEW   1

PART ONE
PIONEERS

CHAPTER 1
PUTTING EVERYTHING OUT THERE
Justin Hall   17

CHAPTER 2
THE UNEDITED VOICE OF A PERSON
Dave Winer   46

CHAPTER 3
THEY SHALL KNOW YOU THROUGH YOUR LINKS
Jorn Barger, filters   74

PART TWO

SCALING UP

CHAPTER 4

THE BLOGGER CATAPULT

Evan Williams, Meg Hourihan 101

CHAPTER 5

THE RISE OF POLITICAL BLOGGING

Josh Marshall 131

CHAPTER 6

BLOGGING FOR BUCKS

Robert Scoble, Nick Denton, Jason Calacanis 165

CHAPTER 7

THE EXPLODING BLOGOSPHERE

Boing Boing 198

CHAPTER 8

THE PERILS OF KEEPING IT REAL

Heather Armstrong 229

PART THREE

WHAT HAVE BLOGS WROUGHT?

CHAPTER 9

JOURNALISTS VS. BLOGGERS 269

CHAPTER 10

WHEN EVERYONE HAS A BLOG 301

CHAPTER 11
FRAGMENTS FOR THE FUTURE   328

EPILOGUE: TWILIGHT OF THE CYNICS   352

Author's Note and Acknowledgments   361

Notes   363

Index   395

Pointer to the Online Postscript   405

INTRODUCTION: WHAT'S NEW

O
n the morning of September 11, 2001, James Marino sat at his desk at 568 Broadway, looking out a tall window that revealed a panorama of the lower Manhattan skyline. He'd come to the office early to work on his side business—a website called Broadwaystars.com. The site collected tidbits of news and gossip about the New York theater scene and served them up blog-style, time-stamped, with new items at the top. At 8:49 a.m. he'd posted a passel of links: An AIDS benefit recap. Declining box office numbers from *Variety*. The impending release of a cast album for a show by *Rent*'s Jonathan Larson titled *tick, tick . . . BOOM!*

Marino clicked *post* and looked up from his monitor. He froze a moment, stared, then started typing again:

Something very terrible just happened at the World Trade Center. I think a plane crashed into the northwestern tower. It is horrible and stunning to look at.—james

posted at 9/11/2001 08:56:32 AM

Like so many other New Yorkers that morning, Marino kept watching. He also kept typing:

> Oh my god. I just saw the other building blow up. A second plane approaching from the opposite direction (south to north) crashed into the south-east tower.
>
> posted at 9/11/2001 09:06:06 AM

> My office is on the 10th floor of a Soho building with large southern facing windows, so I have a full view of downtown. From my vantage, I see a huge hole where the first plane entered the north west tower from north to south. The south east tower was hit from the south to north. It is being reported that a plane or planes were hijacked and flown into the towers with passengers in them.
>
> posted at 9/11/2001 09:06:06 AM

Marino had worked for four years at Lehman Brothers in the World Trade Center complex; he'd been there in 1993 when a car bomb exploded in the basement garage.

> one tower just collapsed (south east) i am weeping. . . . . i cant tell you how i feel
>
> posted at 9/11/2001 10:02:52 AM

> The second building just exploded and collaped. This is just beyond anything that I can even conceive. I feel so much anger and helplessness.
>
> posted at 9/11/2001 10:33:07 AM

Eventually, Marino left his desk and made his way uptown to his brother's West Side apartment, then finally home to Westchester. That evening he posted again:

> I think I lost about 100 friends today. I can't count them. I keep breaking down. I don't think that I have ever been so sad and cried so much. I don't know if I will ever be the same. But I am home now. Thank you to everyone for the notes.
>
> posted at 9/11/2001 07:31:01 PM

Most New Yorkers have indelible memories of the minutes and hours after the planes hit that day. Those memories are recorded on countless Web pages, in emails and forum postings and uploaded photos. But much of that record made its way onto the Web after the fact, by hours or days or weeks. In the chaos on the ground, a lot of people were focused on getting to safety, or their eyes were glued to TV news, or their Internet connections were disrupted by the crushing network overload.

The Broadwaystars.com posts recorded the 9/11 events as they piled up, one fraught moment on top of the previous one. Though they broke from what Marino calls the site's typical "gossipy, snarky" tone, they were not carefully composed or particularly eloquent. Instead, they offered a witness's raw feed, unmediated by anchorperson or interviewer—a naked vantage on a cataclysm.

Marino wrote what he saw. And if you scroll down the page he wrote, you see that at 8:49 a.m. the world was one way, and at 8:50 a.m. it was another.

As the day's disasters unfolded, most Americans got their news from TV, with its ceaseless loop of billowing smoke and cratering towers. TV broadcast the big picture, but it couldn't tell you whether your friend who worked at the World Trade Center had made it out in time, or whether your sister or uncle had made it home safely. The telephone systems failed almost immediately. The websites of the big news operations quickly overloaded, too. But email still worked, and smaller websites managed to stay up. The Internet's arteries clogged, but people found ways to communicate through its capillaries.

Marino's 8:56 post was among the first to hit the Web that day; it might well have been the very first. (The first AP story went over the wire at 8:55 a.m., but most websites took a few minutes to get it up. At 8:58 a.m., Metafilter, a popular group blog, posted a link to a one-line news bulletin on the front page of the CNN website, but CNN did not yet have a full story posted.)

Later that morning, a gaming journalist and Web celebrity named Justin Hall—who'd been chronicling his life in an open Web diary since 1994—posted:

> at these times there's two types of media valuable -
> email
> friends from japan and london writing - are you okay? and
> the only way to reach people - small packet transit.
> and the TV
> rebirth of the broadcast media. The only pipes big
> enough still to bring us the pictures and moving pictures
> of buildings collapsing.

In San Francisco, Evan Williams, who ran a service called Blogger that helped thousands of people—including Marino—run their weblogs, wanted to do something useful, so he got to work building a page that automatically collated postings about the attacks from Blogger users across the Web and listed them in chronological order. Marino's post headed the list.

In Woodside, a rustic enclave of homes for Silicon Valley's stock-option millionaires, a software developer named Dave Winer had started his day early, posting links and headlines to his blog, Scripting News. Winer didn't have a TV set, but around 9:00 a.m. (6:00 a.m. on the West Coast) he received an email from a fellow blogger named Bill Seitz, alerting' him to the news and suggesting he look at the Empire State Building webcam, which offered real-time snapshots from the venerable skyscraper's observation deck. Seitz captured an image right after the collapse of the South Tower and posted it to his own blog at 10:17 a.m.; at 10:57 a.m., he posted a second image under the words "No more WTC."

Winer's father, Leon Winer, was a professor at Pace University, and it occurred to Winer that Pace was near the World Trade Center. When he couldn't get through by phone, he posted a photo of his dad at the top of Scripting News and asked for help or info. Leon, it turned out, hadn't made it farther than Grand Central that morning before the subway system shut down; then he'd had to walk miles across the 59th Street Bridge and through Queens before finally getting a bus home—all of which Winer reported to his readers.

That afternoon Winer got an email from *New York Times* reporter Amy Harmon, who was researching a story on how people used the Web during the disaster. She wanted to know about "the impulse to collect and share news and reaction and how the Net facilitates that." At first Winer couldn't get through to her by phone. Instead, he posted his answer to her question:

> I see this as an opportunity to cover a big news story, it's largely the same reason the NY Times home page is all about this. We want to figure out what happened, what it means, and where we go from here. The world changed today. It's still very fresh.

In September 2001, conventional wisdom held that Web content was "dead." Vast fortunes had been poured onto the Web during the late-1990s dotcom bubble; a lucky few had made a killing, but once the stock-market game of musical chairs ended, most media companies took heavy losses. In perhaps the single worst-timed deal in history, Time Warner had traded more than half its value for America Online at the very moment that the online stock balloon was pumped up with helium and about to pop.

Now the media barons were nursing their wounds, cursing the Internet, and concluding that it had all been a bad dream. While the Web wasn't going to go away, they decided that it wasn't going to change everything, either. The path was clear for them to return to a familiar world of mass publishing and broadcasting, "eyeball collection" and advertising sales. At the same time, the collapse of the Internet bubble had dragged lots of new ventures and ideas down with it. Williams's company, Blogger, had seen steady growth in users, and yet, earlier that year, had been forced to lay off all its employees and persevere as a one-person operation. The small Web publishers that hadn't fallen off a cliff were hanging on by their fingernails. That was how we found ourselves at Salon.com, the magazine site I'd helped start in 1995. Enthralled as I remained by the new medium, I couldn't help thinking, *Maybe it wasn't so smart to give up that newspaper job after all.*

As a business, publishing stuff on the Web had fallen on very hard times. Yet that wasn't stopping people from publishing more stuff on the Web. The profit motive, apparently, wasn't the only force at work here. And when the planes hit the towers, money was the last thing on most people's minds. They first wanted to know what had happened to the people they knew and loved; later they wanted to understand what had happened and why.

According to the most thorough study of media consumption on and after 9/11, use of the Internet actually *dropped* for a while after the initial news spread. The crisis didn't introduce the Internet to a vast new population or represent a "breakthrough moment" in which large numbers of people abandoned other media for online sources of information, the report concluded. Yet those who did turn to the Web sensed a breakthrough nonetheless: at that moment of crisis, many of us looked to the Web for a sense of connection and a dose of truth. The surrogate lamentations of the broadcast media's talking heads sounded manufactured and inadequate; people felt the urgent necessity to express themselves and be heard as singular individuals. Those who posted felt the gravity of the moment and the certainty that stepping forward to record their thoughts had unquantifiable but unmistakable value.

"Only through the human stories of escape or loss have I really felt the disaster," wrote Nick Denton, a journalist turned Internet entrepreneur, in the *Guardian* on September 20, 2001. "And some of the best eyewitness accounts and personal diaries of the aftermath have been published on weblogs. These stories, some laced with anecdotes of drunken binges and random flings, have a rude honesty that does not make its way through the mainstream media's good-taste filter."

David Weinberger, an author and Web consultant, wrote in his email newsletter: "When the *Maine* was sunk a hundred years ago, messages scatted over telegraph wires to feed the next edition of the newspaper. When the *Arizona* was sunk at Pearl Harbor, the radio announced the wreckage. When Kennedy was shot, television newscasters wept and we learned to sit on our couches while waiting for more bad news. Now, for the first time, the nation and the world could talk with itself, doing what humans do when the innocent suffer: cry, comfort, inform, and, most important, tell the story together."

In his *Guardian* article, Denton wrote, "In weblogs, the Web has become a mature medium." A column headline on CNET similarly declared that blogging had "come of age." Such statements may be hard to believe today, years later, when blogs—frequently updated websites typically filled with links, news, or personal stories—are still widely reviled as a medium for immature ranting. In fact, within a year of writing those words, Denton himself went on to found Gawker Media, a network of rant-heavy gossip blogs powered by adolescent attitude.

In retrospect, 9/11 hardly marked any sort of maturity for blogging. Instead, it marked the moment that the rest of the media woke up and noticed what the Web had birthed. Something strange and novel had landed on the doorstep: the latest monster baby from the Net. Newspapers and radio and cable news began to take note and tell people about it. That in turn sent more visitors to the bloggers' sites, and inspired a whole new wave of bloggers to begin posting.

Many of these newcomers faced the post-9/11 world with militant anger and proudly dubbed themselves "warbloggers." As they learned how to post and link, they felt they were exploring virgin territory, and it was, for them, as it has been for each successive new generation of blogging novices. But blogging had already been around for years. In a sense, it had been around since the birth of the Web itself.

From the instant people started publishing Web pages, they faced a problem unique to their new medium. How do you help readers understand what's new? Newspapers and magazines are date-stamped bundles of information; each new edition supersedes the previous one. TV and radio offer their reports in real-time streams, a continuum of "now." But Web pages are just files of data sitting on servers. They can be left untouched or changed at will at any time.

And that's just what the print-world refugees who began to colonize the new medium proceeded to do in the Web's infancy. When new material was ready for publication, it simply replaced the old. This, they quickly realized, meant they were throwing out yesterday's news, with no archive or record of their first draft of history. So instead they started scattering the home pages of their sites with bright little "NEW" icons to direct visitors' eyes to the latest updates. But "new" is a relative concept. At what point did "new" stop being new? And how could you separate what was new to someone who checked out your site once a day from what was new to the hourly visitor?

Telling people what's new proved unexpectedly confounding in the early days of Web publishing. Yet a simple solution lay close at hand, embedded in the medium's DNA by its creator.

Tim Berners-Lee—a British software engineer at CERN, the Geneva particle-physics lab—devised the World Wide Web and built the very first website at the address http://info.cern.ch in 1990. He dreamed that his invention, a method for linking pages, would knit together the primarily academic information then scattered across the larger Internet and foster intellectual collaboration. As he proselytized for his new creation, enthusiasts at other universities would crank up their own Web servers, begin publishing sites, and email Berners-Lee to tell him about the cool things they'd done. Each time the network gained a new node in this way, Berners-Lee would insert a listing for it—and a link to it—from a page on his info.cern site.

This "W3 Servers" page had a simple scheme: newcomers would be added to the top of the list. This proved convenient for the return visitor, who could immediately see the latest information without having to scroll down the page.

In choosing to organize the new links this way, Berners-Lee was borrowing from computer science the concept of the "stack." Stacks are data structures in which each new addition is piled on the top, pushing down previous items; outputs get taken from the top, too. Stacks are therefore said to work on a "last in, first out" principle: the last thing that you add becomes the first thing you remove. Similarly, a stack of news and information is a page in which the last thing that the publisher added is the first thing that you see. Such a design was present at the Web's creation, and would keep reasserting itself like a genetic trait, turning up at critical points in the Web's development.

Journalists instinctively resisted this approach. They were used to ordering information according to an editorial process, rather than handing the ordering over to a set of rules. "We'll tell you what's important," they said, "not the clock." Their preference was understandable. But the model of the news stack spread anyway. Its method of making sense of the new was native to the online world, not imported from print, and today we see it as a universal building block of the medium.

Only a handful of pioneering programmers ever made much use of Berners-Lee's servers page. But the next proto-blog to come along reached a wider audience. In 1992, Marc Andreessen, a computer-science student at the National Center for Supercomputing Applications (NCSA) at the University of Illinois, discovered Berners-Lee's invention. He fell in love with the Web, and decided that what it really needed was pictures. He and a handful of classmates quickly wrote Mosaic, a program that let the user browse Web pages containing both text and images. Berners-Lee's text-only browser had been created primarily for Steve Jobs's Next operating system; Andreessen and company offered Mosaic to everyday people who used Windows and Macintosh machines. They believed, Andreessen says today, that "everybody should be using the Web," and they were impatient with Berners-Lee's more academic approach. Their program proved an instant hit.

Once people downloaded Mosaic, they began hunting for diverting stuff to look at. Andreessen obliged. Beginning early in 1993 with Mosaic's initial release, he personally assembled the NCSA What's New page. "Any page anyone put up on any topic, we would highlight," Andreessen recalls. Like Berners-Lee before him, Andreessen added new links at the top of the list, since that was the spot people would see first. When Mosaic turned into Netscape, the browser was tweaked to help users who had slow dial-up connections. The top of the page would display first, even before the rest had loaded, which meant that the new items would always be visible the fastest. Every Netscape browser also came with a built-in button that linked directly to What's New. That made the page a welcoming gateway to the Web for its first generation of users—and a subliminal introduction to the simple utility of a reverse-chronological list.

As the Web's popularity exploded, businesses started erecting "virtual storefronts" that attempted to mimic physical layouts, with gimmicky graphics for ticket counters and help desks and front porches. Publishers began constructing flashy front pages for their sites with elaborate "hotlinked" images. They were all caught up in the misconception that the key to helping people find their way across the Web was to give them pictures to click on—to offer users metaphors from the physical world.

But the reverse-chronological list never entirely vanished. As the 1990s advanced, it kept reasserting itself, becoming the basis for the form that today is familiar from a million blogs: a stream of link-laden posts with the latest on top. Over time, as blogging spread from a handful of Web designers and software developers to writers and political activists and then on to the general public, this form has grown flexible and capacious enough to encompass virtually anything that anyone might wish to express.

In this way, the rise of blogs has gone a long way toward making good on the promise of the Web's first inventors: that their creation would welcome contributions from every corner of the globe and open a floodgate of human creativity. Berners-Lee's first browser was a tool for reading *and* writing: "The initial WorldWideWeb program opened with an almost blank page, ready for the jottings of the user," he wrote in his memoir. As the Web extended its reach first to offices and then to homes, across the United States and around the world, it became theoretically possible for millions of people to publish millions of thoughts for millions of other people to read. The Web implicitly invited people to say anything—and everything.

But would they? The primordial Web was largely a repository for research and cool science experiments. Berners-Lee's and Andreessen's lists both grew up inside academe and were heavy on technical reports. People first understood the Web as a treasury of static knowledge and a showcase for the occasional geeky stunt (like the Trojan Room coffeepot camera from the Cambridge University computer lab, or the "fishcam" that Netscape programmer Lou Montulli created in 1994). The Web browsers that followed Berners-Lee's weren't two-way; it was a lot harder to write the program code for a tool that could both read and write, and everyone was racing to release new browsers at the breakneck pace of "Netscape time." The writing part could wait. That meant that the first Web experience for most newcomers was an act of media consumption: "browsing" or "surfing." Basically, reading.

So it was never a sure bet that the Web would evolve beyond its scholarly roots into something more personal—a sort of conversational water cooler and confessional. The first publishers of Web pages outside of the academy were a motley, self-selected population of fringe types: software programmers, science-fiction fans, 'zine publishers, and misfit journalists. They created a profusion of what the industry now calls "user-generated content"; observers of their efforts were often dismissive.

"By many measures," Michael Hiltzik wrote in the *Los Angeles Times* in 1997, "the Web reached the vast-wasteland stage faster than any other communication medium in human history." Michael Kinsley, the celebrated editor and columnist, famously told the *Washington Post* in 1995 that most of the Web was "crap." He elaborated in 1997: "The first time you go on the Web you think, 'Wow!' and the third time you go on, you think, 'There's nothing to see here.' My point was that if the Web was going to make it, it was going to have to pass higher standards." Indeed, the initial flowering of forum postings and personal home pages was crude, sometimes cheesy. Those visitors from the mainstream press who parachuted in to see what all the fuss was about took a quick look and decided it was one big amateur hour. Once the pros arrived and showed the world how it was done, surely all that crap would shrivel and vanish. Their misunderstanding set the stage for an angry debate about quality and accuracy and literary standards and business models that is alive today—and that has always been a little beside the point.

In those days, media companies venturing forth on the Web would declare their faith in "interactivity," by which they usually meant "cool buttons you can play with on the screen." And people who were actually using the Internet would say no, sorry, "interactivity" means being able to send an email or post your thoughts to a discussion. It's just a clumsy word for communication. That communication—each reader's ability to be a writer as well—was not some bell or whistle. *It was the whole point of the Web*, the defining trait of the new medium—like motion in movies, or sound in radio, or narrow columns of text in newspapers.

Only when blogs took off did this insight begin to spread beyond the most idealistic quarters of the Net. At the start of the first decade of the new century, easier tools for creating blogs and free services for hosting them removed many of the technical and economic barriers, and masses of newcomers swarmed in: college kids and retirees, diarists and polemicists, political junkies and sports fans, music lovers and investors, preachers and professors, knitters and gun nuts, doctors and librarians. The one trait they all shared was the passion behind their postings. They were indeed amateurs, in the original sense of the term: they wrote out of love. That love led them toward new rewards and into new perils.

As I write this at the end of that decade, the Web world is transfixed by a new generation of social-networking software. Facebook, MySpace, and their cohorts have taken some of the energy behind blogging and enhanced it with new tools for sharing and communicating among friends. People are flocking to these services, and as they do, they face unfamiliar quandaries: How much of your life should you expose to the Web? What line should you draw between job and home, colleagues and friends? At what point does sharing edge into Too Much Information? Is there any healthy way to keep up with the snowballing volume of Web stuff?

The experiences of the early bloggers prefigured every one of the dilemmas that we are encountering today, as we move more and more of our lives online and as new technologies—broadband to the home, wireless, digital cameras, cell phones and other handheld devices, YouTube video—keep extending the Web's reach. Blogging, the first form of social media to be widely adopted beyond the world of technology enthusiasts, gave us a template for all the other forms that would follow. Through its lens, people could see the Web for the first time as something they were collectively building. It gave a multitude of formerly private people a public voice. It handed them a blank page and said: Learn. Learn what happens when you take strangers into your confidence. Learn what happens when you betray a confidence. See how it works when you find a lover online. See what happens when you tell the world that you've broken up. Find a job with your blog. Get fired from your job because of something you wrote on your blog. Expose media misinformation. Spread some misinformation of your own.

Then take everything that you've learned and post it.

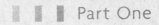 Part One

PIONEERS

Chapter 1

PUTTING EVERYTHING OUT THERE
JUSTIN HALL

In 1994, Justin Hall invented oversharing. Of course, we didn't have a name yet for the compulsion to tell the online world too much about yourself. Back then, Hall was just an eccentric nineteen-year-old college student who recorded minutiae of his life on his personal website; no one knew that the self-revelation he found so addictive would one day become a temptation for millions.

Beginning at the dawn of the Web, Hall parked himself at the intersection of the Bay Area's remnant counterculture and Silicon Valley's accelerating economy and started writing down everything he saw. His website, at www.links.net, became a comprehensive personal gazette and archive, full of ephemeral details and intimate epiphanies, portraits of the Web's young builders and nude pictures of himself.

Hall, who is fair and thin and lanky—he looks a bit like one of Tolkien's elves—has the affable grin of someone who is fully at ease with strangers. If you took away his nonconformist streak, he could make a great salesman. You could even see him running for office and winning, in some alternate dimension where no one cared that he'd littered the public record with radical opinions and accounts of his illegal drug use, or that he frequently undermined his considerable charisma by intentionally irritating people. He often begins public speaking engagements by stepping to the podium, facing his audience, and silently beaming as the seconds tick by and the crowd begins to wonder what's going on. He seems perfectly comfortable making other people uncomfortable.

For more than a decade, Hall's site had presented an open window onto his life. "It's so much fun," he'd say, "putting everything out there." January 2005 seemed no different. He kicked off the new year with a blunt four-word post: "I really enjoy urinating." He told the story of a mustache-growing competition with a friend. He mentioned meeting "a smart, motivated gal" who wanted to collaborate on a story involving angels.

Then, in the middle of the month, the window slammed shut. All signs of the layers upon layers of Hall's personal history stretching back to 1994 were gone. In their place was a little search box and a fifteen-minute video titled *Dark Night*.

The video, which is still available on YouTube, opens with Hall's face, half in shadow, filling the frame. He begins: "What if inti—" Then he cuts himself off as his bleary eyes widen. He looks away, lets out an exasperated breath, and starts over:

> So what if intimacy happens in quiet moments and if you're so busy talking and searching and looking and crying and yelling and—then you won't ever find it.

A subtitle appears below Hall's face: "I sort of had a breakdown in January 2005."

Hall was an accomplished storyteller in his own callow, motormouthed way. But this story emerged only fitfully, in raw fragments. Hall, it seemed, had met a woman. One who "opened me up like crazy." He'd fallen head over heels. Bliss! But the new relationship had clashed, somehow, with his confessional writing on the Web. His new beloved, Hall hinted, didn't relish the glare.

What if a deeply connective personal activity you do, that's like religion, that you practice with yourself, that's a dialogue with the divine, turns out to drive people away from you? . . . I published my life on the fucking internet. And it doesn't make people wanna be with me. It makes people not trust me. And I don't know what the fuck to do about it . . .

Dark Night played out its psychodramatics with *Blair Witch*–style lighting and confessional ferocity, like an Ingmar Bergman therapy scene reshot by a geeky art student. The video was awkward, sometimes embarrassing, and more than a little unnerving. It made you fear for Hall's mental state—you wanted to pick up the phone and talk him down from the ledge. Still, for all its raw atmospherics, it was hardly naïve. Hall had been creating autobiographical media all his life, and most recently he'd been studying filmmaking at USC. *Dark Night* was, in its own ragged way, a calculated work, not some piece of "turn on the camera, then forget about it" vérité.

It wasn't the soul-baring that made *Dark Night* a shocker. Rather, it was the prospect that Justin Hall's soul-baring days might be at an end. On the subject of self-exposure, Hall had always been an absolutist. When he began writing on the Web, the word *transparency* hadn't yet been drafted into service in its contemporary meaning: openness, no secrets, all questions answered. But transparency had been Hall's guiding principle from the start. He had turned his website into a glass house.

Only now, it seemed, he no longer wanted to live there.

In 1988, when Hall was thirteen, he got his first glimpse of the Internet. He'd already been online a few years, dialing up private bulletin-board services (BBSes) from his mom's computer in their Chicago home, looking for videogame tips, and sticking around to enjoy the camaraderie. The

fun of tapping into a national BBS based in California ended quickly
when his mother looked at the phone bill; from then on, hometown
boards would have to do.

Hall's father was gone. An alcoholic, he'd killed himself when Justin
was eight, a story Justin would later tell, prominently and unflinchingly,
on his site. His mother, a successful lawyer, worked long hours and trav-
eled a lot, so he was, as he put it, "raised by a series of nannies." In 1988 a
new one arrived, a medical student at Northwestern who saw Justin's
enthusiasm for going online and showed the youngster the nascent Internet, then a university-only enclave. (This was well before the Web's easy-
to-use interface tamed the technical difficulties of using the Internet for
the masses; it took geek tenacity just to connect.) "It wasn't just a bunch
of fifteen-year-olds in Chicago on their computers," Hall says. "It was
people all over the country. And the scope of what the people were talking about was fantastic." His gaze was drawn to Usenet, the collection of
Internet-based forums that, in the pre-Web days, offered the most
reward to an adolescent looking for online kicks. "People were getting
nerdy there," Hall recalls, "about this specific Frank Zappa record, or this
specific transgender bent, or this specific drug experience. I was
extremely turned on."

Hall called the university and tried to get an Internet account for
himself. Sorry, he was told, we don't just give them out. What does a
teenager do in such circumstances? A teenager borrows a friend's password. But the Northwestern system administrators eventually figured
out what Hall was up to and kicked him off.

Hall finally got his own Internet account when he went off to
Swarthmore in September 1993. The dorm rooms there had just been
networked; for Hall, this meant "up-all-night information." That December, John Markoff, the *New York Times* technology reporter, wrote an
introduction to the new World Wide Web and the Mosaic browser,
describing them to his readers as "a map to the buried treasures of the
Information Age." Hall read the article—on paper—and then went and
downloaded Mosaic. "It was hugely exciting. Now you can use a mouse

to get to all this information! Now you can put pictures and text on the same page!"

At that early date, the experts, and the money, agreed that the future of online communication was in the hands of the "big three" commercial online services (America Online, Compuserve, Prodigy); technology giants, such as Microsoft, Apple, and IBM; and cable companies like Time Warner, which were sinking fortunes into interactive TV. The Internet had been a backwater accessible only to eggheads and nerds; it was hard to get on to, hard to use, and its nether regions, like Usenet, were uncensored and untamed. The whole thing was simply not ready for prime time.

That was precisely what attracted Justin Hall. "The big online services always felt like a magazine stand at a grocery store, whereas Usenet felt like Telegraph Avenue in Berkeley," he remembers. "Then when I saw the Web I knew I had to try it, because the quality of pages that I saw made me think it couldn't be expensive or hard to put them up."

On January 22, 1994, Hall put up his first Web page. He published it by downloading a free server program and running it on his Macintosh Powerbook 180 laptop plugged into Swarthmore's campus network. Like so much of the early Web, "Justin's Home Page" warned visitors that it was "under construction," and most of its information was about its own technology—including a list of the tools Hall had used to put it together. But if you scrolled down a bit you'd find, nestled under the header "Some Personal Shit," a photo of the long-haired Hall smirking next to Ollie North. Also a couple of links to bootleg recordings of two bands, Jane's Addiction and Porno for Pyros. And, finally, a strange black-and-white UPI photo of Gary Grant popping a tab of LSD into his grinning-wide mouth.

Writing about yourself was not unknown on the Web, even at that point, and neither was cataloging your offbeat obsessions. Hall says that in his early postings he took inspiration from a site created by a programmer at the University of Pennsylvania, Ranjit Bhatnagar. Beginning in November 1993, "Ranjit's HTTP playground" provided offbeat links, along with a "lunch server." Each day, Bhatnagar would carefully record what he'd had for lunch. The page was, of course, in reverse chronological order. Although the "lunch server" was as much a pun as anything else, it foreshadowed a future in which people would use blogs to record all manner of quotidian data points.

If Hall was not the very first person to build a funky personal site, he was the first to find a wide audience. His site, which he soon renamed Justin's Links from the Underground, gained speedy notoriety. This was partly because it provided valuable "what's new?"–style listings with an emphasis on the unconventional, including an inevitably popular list of sex-related links (most of which look charmingly tame compared to today's pornographic Web). Hall took pride in his link-connoisseurship; he wouldn't link to the front page of sites that had already made it on the NCSA What's New page, but he might point his readers to some note-worthy tidbit he'd found a few levels down on one of those sites.

Hall promoted his new site, submitting it to anyone and everyone who was maintaining lists of websites. Links from the Underground's popularity also owed something to all that up-all-night energy Hall invested in frequent site updates. But mostly, people flocked to Links from the Underground for its lively personality. It may at times have been sophomoric, self-indulgent, or gross, but it was never boring.

In 1994 the Web party was just starting up, but it was evident to Hall that he'd have an easier time joining it in the San Francisco Bay Area than in Chicago or Pennsylvania. Once, back in Hall's high school days, his eye had been caught by an ad, shouting in neon across the full length of the side of a bus, for a new magazine called *Wired*. He picked up a copy at Tower Records and fell in love. "I'd been working at a software store, so I knew all about computer magazines, but this one had *people* on the cover. So the first day I got it I actually called and left a voice mail for [editor] Louis Rossetto. 'Your magazine is awesome. My name is Justin, I live in Chicago, and I can connect you to the hacker pirate underground scene and the BBSes.'"

"Oddly," Hall deadpans, "he never called me back."

At Swarthmore, Hall once again took aim at *Wired*; he set his heart on a summer internship at the magazine's San Francisco office. He phoned each department at the magazine in turn. "It was like, give me the custodial department—I'll empty trash cans! I just wanna be around. And they're like, no. No, no, no." Finally he asked for the online department, which was then in the early stages of planning a commercial website called Hotwired. The woman he got on the line, Julie Petersen, suggested he email her with the address of his website; he said, "Why don't you look at it right now?" She typed in the URL, and then he heard her laugh—she'd found the photo of Cary Grant dropping acid. He got his interview, and later his internship.

When the Hotwired crew gathered for an introductory Thai dinner, Hall found himself seated next to the editor of the site, Howard Rheingold, the veteran of the venerable WELL online forum and author of *The Virtual Community*. Rheingold turned to the teenager next to him and asked, "What brings you to Hotwired?"

Hall looked him in the eye solemnly and replied, "The opportunity to work with you."

Later Rheingold wrote, "Either the guy was such a brazen suckup as to be a genius of the genre, or he was a wiseass who was laying on the irony, or he just said the first thing that came into his mind. In any case, I went for the straightforward audacity of it. He sure blew my icebreaker to oblivion."

At Hotwired, Justin Hall found a community of partners in audacity. No longer a lone webhead, he was now surrounded by other ardent geeks. Yet even in such company he was a rarity: at the ripe age of nineteen, he was already a Web veteran. He had plenty of hands on experience in building a widely visited site—but none in navigating the labyrinth of the business world.

Hotwired's birth was difficult. As the October 1994 launch neared, Rossetto began to realize how important the site would be for the future of the magazine, and he seized control of the project from Rheingold and Jonathan Steuer, *Wired* magazine's original online leader. Rheingold had imagined a "global jam session," but Rossetto wanted something less funky and more flashy. To Rheingold, the Web was about community; Rossetto saw it as a brand extension. Hotwired would feature the Web's first banner ads, and Rossetto decided to require visitors to register before accessing its pages, to gather demographic data for the advertisers. The young idealists at Hotwired, including Hall, saw the registration requirement as an abomination. In their view, Rossetto was selling out the Web's populist patrimony for a mess of marketing pottage. He dismissed their perspective as one big stoner pipe dream and declared that "the era of public-access Internet has come to an end." Despite the proclamation, Justin's Links, a one-person operation with zero commercial ambition, remained better known and (at times) attracted more visitors than Hotwired did during its first year.

At that point in the Web's evolution, if you wanted to post a personal website, it was understood that it would take the form of Your Home Page—a little personal bio, maybe links to some stuff you'd written, maybe some more links to other sites you liked, perhaps a photo of you or your cat. That's pretty much where Hall had started, too. But as he steadily added pages of autobiographical anecdotes, portraits of relatives and friends, photos, personal artwork, and observations about the Web itself, his site quickly grew into something more ambitious and unique. Justin loved to link, not just to point to interesting pages he'd found on other people's sites, but to build elaborate cross-references into his own storytelling.

Hypertext—the academic term that described the sort of writing-with-clickable-links that the Web relied on—had long been a plaything for experimental fiction authors, for dabblers in a popular Macintosh program called Hypercard, and for authors of the short-lived interactive CD-ROM genre. Now the Web was popularizing hypertext, and Justin Hall was determined to use it as its theorists had imagined—not just as a convenient way to hop from one website to another, but as a subtle and potent tool for creating webs of meaning. "I really thought I could create this structure that would reflect everything, absorb everything, re-create the patterns of my mind," he says.

Indeed, as Hall feverishly dumped the contents of his life into Links from the Underground, the site began to look like the inside of a brain—a neural network of cross-referenced memories and hotlinked dreams. That made it feel novel, and fun, and truly "webby." But it was also kind of a mess. If you wanted to get lost inside Justin's head, it was great, but it was hard to get your own head around it. As Hall began to attract repeat visitors, they had a tough time figuring out where to look for the latest material.

Hypertext was alluring, but hypertext overload was off-putting. Most of us apprehend stories more easily in time than in space. We're accustomed to a beginning, middle, and end—not necessarily in that order, but with some order that the storyteller has mapped for us. By late 1995, Justin's Links from the Underground remained phenomenally popular, but it was beginning to feel like an overgrown garden.

Hall was long gone from Hotwired by then—he'd returned to Swarthmore after six months. But he was far from the last "iconoclastic smartass" (Rheingold's phrase) to grace its payroll. In the summer of 1995, Carl Steadman was working as the site's production director, and Joey Anuff was his assistant. Both young men were full of ideas and strong opinions about how the Web really worked. They were also frustrated by the inexplicable failure of Wired's honchos to listen to those ideas and opinions. So that August, working after hours from the back corner of the Hotwired office, they began putting their ideas into practice with a new side project called Suck.com—conceived as a sort of *Mad* magazine for a new generation of cubicle laborers to consume at their desks.

In several ways, Suck.com was the opposite of Links from the Underground. Where Hall set out to tell all under his real name, Suck's writers lobbed their spitballs from pseudonymous cover. (Even most of their Hotwired colleagues were in the dark about their identity at first.) Where Hall's links aimed to create personal meaning, Suck used links with panache, sarcastically, as a literary device—hypertext as a new outlet for double entendre. Where Hall was full of the young Web's utopian fervor— its "Prodigious Personal Publishing Potential," as one of his pages put it— Steadman and Anuff shot darts at each new hype balloon. They cast themselves as Menckenesque cynics, wedding the analytical vocabulary of the literary theory they'd studied in college to a late-night-TV comedy irony that said, "The world is corrupt, and so are we." "At Suck," their introductory manifesto read, "we abide by the principle which dictates that somebody will always position himself or herself to systematically harvest anything of value in this world for the sake of money, power and/or ego-fulfillment. We aim to be that somebody." Their timing was good: Suck started up on the immediate heels of Netscape's August 1995 public stock offering, which kicked off the first cycle of Internet-investment mania.

All these traits helped turn Suck into a Web-underground sensation (though by contemporary standards its traffic numbers were minuscule). But Steadman and Anuff's most influential innovation was their simplest. At the time, most ambitious sites had adopted a magazine format—first Hotwired, quickly joined by a succession of sites like Urban Desires, Feed, Word, Salon, Slate, and many others. They all had front pages that served as tables of contents and linked to article pages; they all updated their sites at stately intervals with "issues" consisting of new tables of contents and new batches of articles. Steadman's job involved analyzing the Hotwired server logs to understand how visitors were using the site, so he quickly saw what each novice Web publisher would learn in turn: people flocked to a website only when they knew they were going to find something new. If you published a new issue on Monday, traffic spiked, then dipped for the rest of the week. So Suck's founders tossed the whole issue concept overboard and posted a new essay on its front page every weekday. In the process they demonstrated to everyone else on the Web that the medium would work not through regularly spaced issues, but through as fast a stream of updates as you were capable of creating. Websites, it became clear, were less about subscription than about addiction.

By the end of 1995, Steadman and Anuff had tired of their grueling schedule of overnighters, and Rossetto had finally traced the source of this new underground Web sensation back to his own server room. So he bought it from Steadman and Anuff for $30,000 and some stock, gave them new titles, and sent them forth to turn Suck into a business.

Wired held an anniversary party in January 1996. Justin Hall showed up, looking for old friends and free food, and ran into the Suck duo. They were "probably the folks in the room closest to my personal publishin' with distinctive tude outlook," as he wrote in his account of the party— but they taunted him. Justin had been a Web pioneer, but now he had "too many links till you get to the links." Suck had demonstrated the Web's true pace. Why wasn't Justin updating Links from the Underground *every day*?

Hall accepted the challenge. He had always stored his personal stories on his server in a folder named "/vita" that in turn contained nested subfolders (all of which would then turn up in a page's Web address— for instance, "http://www.links.net/vita/fam/mom/"). Now he added a new folder, "/daze," to hold date-stamped journal entries. Each day's entry would appear on the links.net home page, then get archived in /daze. The first entry, for January 10, explained:

> daily thoughts, a useful notion
> I met again the two guys who run suck.com
>   again last night
> at a Wired anniversary party
>
> both pleasant misanthropists
> typical, Joey said he used to love my pages
> but now there's too many layers to my links
>
> at suck, you get sucked immediately, no
>   layers to content.

they're urging folks to make it their
  homepage
(it changes daily)

sounds like a good idea to me,
I think I'm gonna have a little somethin' new
at the top of www.links.net
every day.

This new, linear incarnation of Justin's Links turned the site into more of a conventional diary—albeit one that continually linked back into the thickets of Hall's "/vita" folder. The Web already had a small but growing population of diarists—people like Alexis Massie of the Web 'zine After-Dinner and Carolyn Burke, a Canadian whose online diary, begun in January 1995, is usually credited as the first. But the work of these diarists typically turned inward; its purpose was primarily personal. Justin, thanks to his early start, his service as a hub of valuable links, and his own spasms of self-promotion, was already a public figure. His daily updates served a dual purpose: his readers kept up with his life, but they also got a fly-on-the-wall view of the burgeoning Bay Area Web community, because he'd placed himself at its center. After his stint at *Wired*, he'd been shuttling back and forth between Swarthmore and San Francisco. He found a home at Cyborganic, a hangout in the South of Market warehouse district for the Web industry's freakier elements, and began furiously building Web pages about all the characters he encountered there.

At the start of 1996, the Web was entering its first conflict with the American political system. Newt Gingrich's Republicans had taken over Congress, fueled by the emotions of the so-called culture wars. And it was an election year. So it was hardly surprising that the anarchic new medium quickly sparked an allergic reaction on Capitol Hill. Unlike the commercial online services, there was nobody in charge of the Web, no one to keep it safe for the children. Skeptics in business and government had warned that the Web's openness would cause trouble and provoke a backlash of censorship. And, as if to illustrate their point on cue, Justin Hall had stepped right out of the national id. With his outlandish hair (he'd taken to bundling it in a knot that towered eight inches above his head), his trippy Technicolor outfits (heavily influenced by the style of his mentor, Rheingold), and his cringe-inducingly frank posts, he embodied everything that middle Americans might fear about inviting the Web into their homes.

The politicians who passed the Communications Decency Act in February 1996—which criminalized the transmission to minors of "obscene or indecent" material, or descriptions of sexual acts—said they were targeting commercial pornographers. But at that point in the Web's evolution, there weren't a whole lot of commercial pornographers to be found—probably because there was no obvious and simple way for them to make any money. What you could readily find was "the sexy stuff" to which Justin's site had always linked.

The courts eventually struck down the CDA, leaving Justin and every other Web publisher free to keep "putting everything out there"— but not before the conflict had inspired a deluge of Web pages espousing freedom of expression. Like many other Web devotees that month, Hall posted an impassioned critique of the law:

> am I afraid that my 5 year old nephew elias will find something on the internet he might be too young to see?

> at 8, was I too young to have my real time father commit suicide?

> outrageous sex and violence surrounds us. I was surely damaged by his death, but I can not imagine it hidden from me. . . .

> you can't make people shut up. they will find a way to say what they want to, if they really need to. that's what's wonderful about the internet. they can say it, and you don't have to read it.

if you try to make them shut up, you will spend a lot of
energy trying to stop other people from doing their thing.

instead, spend your energy doing your thing.

knowing that I can't expect to stop someone else's stupid shit,
I wanted to provide a positive alternative. Perhaps if folks are
after sex and images of naked folks, if they see something
relatively healthy and comfortable, they won't feel so weird
about themselves or those issues. I should be arrested!

On the words "something relatively healthy and comfortable," Hall
linked to a page of "nekkid" photos of himself—examples, he wrote, of
"healthy nudity."

Before the Web, the only people you'd find exposing themselves in
public were small children, prank-happy fraternity flashers, the occasional actual pervert—and let's not forget the performance artists. The
CDA fight took place against the backdrop of a series of previous conflicts between provocateur performers and the government—notably
the so-called NEA Four, sexually frank performance artists whose small
grants from the National Endowment for the Arts were vetoed by
appointees of the first Bush administration in 1990. These artists and
their peers had learned firsthand some of the possibilities and dangers of
uncompromising personal storytelling in public. But Hall and all the
other early Web self-chroniclers who exposed themselves online had a
big advantage over these predecessors: their websites cost only a few dollars; to reach a public online, who needed a grant?

On the surface, Hall's exhibitionist antics recalled the work of the
infamous Karen Finley—who drove conservatives nuts by smearing
chocolate on her nude body on stage. But Finley, for all her notoriety, had
a social critic's agenda and a dark vision of the human penchant for inflict-
ing pain. Hall was more of a young naif, a digital Candide recording his
experiences getting knocked about by the realities of the Web business.

That made Justin's Links feel a bit like an adolescent monologue by Spalding Gray transposed to the Web. Gray, the raconteur who sat at a desk with a glass of water and told wry stories from his life, was at the peak of his popularity at the time Hall began posting, but Hall was only slightly familiar with Gray's work—he'd once watched the movie of Gray's monologue *Swimming to Cambodia*. The parallels between the two men are purely coincidental, yet they're striking nonetheless: As with Gray (whose mother had killed herself), Hall's calling to public autobiography was driven in part by the trauma of a parental suicide. Gray was known for performing a piece titled *Interviewing the Audience*, in which he'd invite theatergoers onstage and coax their tales out of them. Similarly, Hall had always dedicated a big chunk of his time and pages to teaching and proselytizing for his faith in self-expression on the Web.

At the start, the way Justin saw it, he was a collector of links. He particularly loved sharing links to "weird shit"—underground art, sex and drugs and rock 'n' roll, stuff he wanted people to see and feared might not make it through more respectable filters. "But it became pretty clear to me that you would only get a certain amount of weird shit if you tried to write it all yourself," he recalls. "The best weird shit comes from other people—because it's weird to you." So instead of trying to build more "weird shit" sites of his own, Hall decided—in the "teach a man to fish" tradition—that it would be easier and smarter to show other people how to do it.

Teaching people to make Web pages also gave Hall a way to correct a "conversational imbalance" and deflect the focus from himself—a focus he'd hungrily sought, but was beginning to find monotonous. ("There was always a German camera crew following Justin around," one former colleague remembers.) "At some point I was like, this is great—thank you for paying attention to me. Now let's stop talking about me. What about you?" he recalls.

In the earliest days of Justin's Links, people started emailing Hall with questions about HTML, the simple text-formatting code used to build Web pages. To save time he wrote and posted a quick tutorial. Later a little icon appeared at the bottom of every page on links.net: "Publish

Yo' Self," it read, and linked to a page headlined: "You are about to be let in on the big Web secret: HTML is easy as hell!"

A famous magazine cover from the early days of the British punk rock scene in the 1970s featured some crude fingerboard sketches labeled, This is an A chord. This is an E chord. "NOW FORM A BAND." In the same spirit, Hall told his readers, in effect, "This is an <a> link. This is a <p> tag. Now post your page!"

The missionary ideal increasingly drove Hall's work. When the filmmaker Doug Block began interviewing Hall in 1996, collecting material for a documentary about personal Web pages, Hall grabbed the camera, turned it on Block, and challenged him to start his own website. At the end of the Swarthmore term in spring 1996, Hall posted a notice telling his readers to "put me up for a night in your town and I'll teach you how to build Web pages." He spent the summer traveling by bus, from Pennsylvania down through the deep South, into Texas and up into Kansas, talking at community centers and coffeeshops and churches, preaching the profane gospel of HTML.

Block's camera caught him talking to reporters at the *Wichita Eagle*, spewing at hyperspeed: "I really feel like this is a wonderful blessing, a wonderful power that's been given to me, and so I want to share this with as many people as I can. . . . Every high school's got a poet. Whether it's a rich high school or a poor high school, they got somebody who's into writing, who's into getting people to tell their stories. You give 'em access to this technology, and all of a sudden they're telling stories in Israel, they're telling stories in Japan, they're telling stories to people in their town that they never could have been able to talk to. And that—that's a revolution."

At the apex of his Web-pioneer celebrity, Justin Hall was a human transmitter, beaming forth on all possible frequencies. The words gushed out of him in public. Stories spilled out onto his website. Even his outrageous look—with hair emerging from his pate in a column and then spilling down again, like a freeze-frame image of a fountain—seemed to reflect the flow of everything Justin from his head to the world. Whether all this hyperactivity represented fecundity or incontinence, it plainly could not last forever.

At the end of the summer of 1996, Hall cut his Johnny Appleseed tour short to take a job at Howard Rheingold's new Electric Minds site, an effort to unite professional journalism with community discussion groups. EMinds didn't last more than about six months, but it was long enough for Hall to develop wrist pain from repetitive strain injury. Too much all-night typing will do that. He took a break from the Web, traveling to Honduras the next summer, writing out diaries in longhand. He returned to Swarthmore to stick it out through graduation in spring of 1998. Now what?

If Hall's story was a classic *bildungsroman*, a young person's passage from innocence to experience, then he was about to begin his *wanderjahre*, the years of rootless travel and questing for purpose. In 1998 it was easy for a champion of what Louis Rossetto had dismissed as the "Public Access Internet" to feel defeated. Hall still updated his /daze entry every day. But the dotcom boom was roaring, pumping the NASDAQ index full of helium, and the Web, it was generally understood, was fulfilling its destiny by becoming a giant shopping mall. As part of Hall's Swarthmore course work, he had written (and, of course, posted) an epic poem titled "The Wyrd of Wired"; it looked back on the early Hotwired crew as visionary populist fighters locked in battle with Rossetto, the sneaker-wearing, marketing-minded "young prince of media." Now the corporate vision seemed to be winning out. Where could Hall fit in?

During his entire in San Francisco a succession of editors had tried to channel Hall's energies in slightly more conventional directions. At Hotwired, editor Gary Wolf found that Justin was uninterested in simple editorial assignments. At Electric Minds, Rheingold, who'd say Justin was his "guru" (and that he was Justin's), tried to get him to write a column. "I couldn't discipline myself to write regularly, reliably, stuff for other people, because I was so immersed in the nonfiction-i-lating of my own life," he says now. Hall got a steady stream of column invitations as main-stream editors started looking for material about the Web; each time it was the same routine. He'd write his first installment, on how and why to publish on the Internet. And that was that. "Because then, what was I gonna write next? 'My mom hasn't been calling me back'? Or, 'I met this girl I like'? That's the stuff I was writing about on my website."

For a time, Hall found a home at ZDTV, a cable channel dedicated to technology and the Internet. He'd do brief segments about Web publish-ing and cool sites. The people were smart, the pay was nice, and, unsur-prisingly, the camera loved him. Alas, a national cable operation reached a different demographic from Justin's Links. When the ZDTV manage-ment discovered that their young on-air talent had a website packed with sexual indiscretions, they asked him whether he would be willing to take down the "mature" parts of his site. But how could you crawl those thousands of pages and bowdlerize them? And even if you could, what would you have left when you were done? The sex and drugs, the nude pictures and the four-letter words, were the heart of links.net; stripping them out was unimaginable—like banning wine in France, or performing Wagner without tubas.

As Hall tells it, his departure from ZDTV was precipitated by an outraged letter from a puritanical viewer who'd stumbled on his site. (It read something like, "Don't you know that this Justin Hall character is a *homosexual freak pornographer* who uses *drugs and profanity?*") A former colleague recalls a different story involving a mishap during a live on-air demo: Hall accidentally clicked on the wrong window, "and his site came up with a picture of Justin in all his naked, dangly glory." Hall remembers that incident happening to someone else at ZDTV who was browsing Justin's links after he'd already left the network. Whatever actually hap-pened, Hall's TV days were over.

Shortly after his graduation, Hall's Macintosh laptop was stolen from him at gunpoint on the street in Oakland. When he replaced it with a new Windows PC, he became reimmersed in the world of videogames he'd inhabited before the Web. (Then, as now, more games were avail-

able for Windows than for Macintosh computers.) Hey, he thought, I
don't have to write exclusively about myself—I can become a gaming
journalist! He found a gig with a gamers' website and settled into the life
of a twentysomething former Web celebrity.

In truth, Hall's site did contain a vast amount of material that was in
at best questionable taste. And he continued to add more. In 2002, in
Japan, where he'd moved with a new sweetheart, he posted a page
recording a medical incident of some sensitivity:

> "You know how cats' dicks swell up after sex?"
>
> She shook her head and pursed her lips.
>
> "When you hear caterwauling, the long slow painful
> meowling of some cats in the neighborhood during sex, it's
> because the male cat's dick has swollen up something large
> so he can't get out while the sperms are busy working.
> That's pain for both of them I believe, so they yeowl."
>
> "So . . . "
>
> "Maybe I have cat dick."

Five closeup photos followed—a time-lapse sequence of an increasingly
swollen foreskin that looked in need of medical attention.

Such material provided confirmation for those who held the view
that personal sites like Hall's were simply narcissistic self-indulgences.
And it was sometimes hard to argue with that view. Yet Hall never lacked
for readers. When the Web first took off, Gary Wolf once wrote, "hordes
of voyeurs discovered legions of exhibitionists." However much Hall
might have indulged himself, he always managed to interest others—
whether they genuinely cared what was happening to him, or were just
gawking at how far his next stunt might go.

In popular parlance, *narcissism* is simply a synonym for *selfishness*. Psychologists have a more detailed set of criteria that define narcissism as a specific personality disorder. Clinically, a narcissist is a person who is unable to relate to others as independent actors with legitimate needs; other people are simply props in some grand narrative of the self. There were times, particularly early on, when Justin Hall's work seemed to fit that bill—when, for instance, he'd hook up with young women at Swarthmore, then post detailed pages about his dalliances, with little regard for his partners' privacy. At one point someone wrote the question "What does everyone think of Justin?" on a women's-room wall in Swarthmore's science library. Answers included: "Cult of personality." "Megalomaniac." "Entrepreneur." "Weirdo." "Needs attention because he wasn't breastfed."

You didn't have to work hard to psychoanalyze Hall; he'd preempt you at every turn, talking about how "neither one of my parents was an enormously present force," ruminating about how his father's suicide influenced his storytelling mania, questioning his own motives. He was accustomed to charges of exhibitionism, and in his open, cheery way, he pondered them at length on his site. Over time, he grew more considerate about sucking other people into his vortex of publicity. In the end, if you were fair to Hall, it was hard to make the narcissism charge stick. He was always too permeable to the rest of the world, too willing to listen to anyone else's story, too energetic about encouraging other people to tell their stories. His self-centeredness didn't exclude others. And he always kept a sense of humor close: for a while in 1996 his home page led with the headline ONE DUDE'S EGO RUN AMOK.

Calling Hall a narcissist was understandable, though. For many observers, the label was just shorthand for the disorientation and discomfort they felt as they watched Hall dump an extraordinary volume of personal detail into global view. Hall's actions said, *I'm doing this because I can do it*. They also said, *Soon*, everyone *will be doing it*.

Surely that couldn't be right! That wasn't what all this technology was for. Most people don't want to expose themselves so fully to the world. Hall was an exceptional case.

And of course he was. His mania for revelation was extreme. For one thing, he was testing the novel capabilities of the Web itself, like a driver gunning a new sports car. The medium was in its adolescence, and so was he, and there were so many possible identities to explore, so many experiments to perform, so much fun to be had, so many agonizing choices to be weighed over all-nighters and weed. All of which looked ridiculous to the adults on the Web scene, who were typically looking for "growth opportunities" and worrying about "business models." In retrospect, though, it's remarkable how much about the Web those adults got wrong, and how much Hall got right.

In June 1995 and again in 1996, Hall came to speak at a conference called New Directions for News, organized by the Newspaper Association of America and the Rand Corporation. Doug Block's *Home Page* documentary captures a moment from one of these events. The few attendees—mostly serious-faced, gray-haired men in suits—scratch their chins and take notes impassively as Hall clicks links on a laptop at the podium, points at a projection screen behind him, and rattles through a tour of his website in machine-gun staccato: "Swarthmore. Hotwired. San Francisco. Jail. Cyborganic. Howard Rheingold. Web, music, spirit, dreams, painting, speaking. This right here is the most hit-resonating part of my page. This is the story of my relationship with this woman—it's a mutha, it's a doozy."

Hair flying and eyes blazing, Hall must have come off like a dancing Martian. And his stunned listeners, in turn, were having their very own Mr. Jones moments: something *was* happening, and they sure didn't know what it was.

Of course Hall posted the text of his talks at these events on a page labeled "NewD irections" (he couldn't resist turning a typo into a dumb dirty joke).

> If everyone was to tell their stories on the web, we would have an endless human storybook, with alternating perspectives . . . when I meet big honchos, important people

involved in the web, I ask them if they have a web page,
and they point me to their magazine. I don't really care
about the magazine's top five hotsites for the week, I
want to know what that guy thinks is cool. How did he get
to be on top? Who is there with him? Tell me about yourselves. Otherwise, I'm gonna get bored and look for
someone who's telling me something heartfelt, not something market driven.

Journalism, Hall declared, was going to change. "The need for staff
and overhead" was dwindling. The "journalism of the future" was on its
way: "Give someone a digital camera, a laptop, and a cellular phone, and
you've got an on-the-spot multimedia storyteller from anywhere in the
world." Reporters would leave their jobs to go solo on the Web. Profits
would come not from "mass market media" but from "millions of minuscule fees." "The best content comes from people who love what they are
doing," Hall said.

At the time, most of this sounded impractical, insane. A decade later
it would be the conventional wisdom of a whole movement of media
insurgents.

It was always easy to see Justin Hall as a crazy kid and lovable eccentric,
to enjoy his ramblings and ravings and then go on with one's business. He
practically begged not to be taken too seriously, what with his erratic cos-
tume changes, his rappy spontaneous style, and his sometimes gauzy
techno-utopianism. As the mass media slowly cottoned to the Web and
started looking for spokespeople, Hall was eminently bookable for TV
sound bites, but his eccentricity also reassured observers that the Web
would remain a fringe medium, too weird to matter much.

Yet everything about Justin Hall turns out to be more complex than
it appears. Remember, for instance, his tactic of silently smiling at an

audience before a talk? It turns out to have its own backstory. Hall says
he got the idea from Osama bin Laden, of all people. He'd read an
account of how the al-Qaeda leader would sometimes pause in silence
for whole minutes when answering interviewers' questions. "I thought,
this is a really interesting technique to seize attention, and I began experimenting with it," Hall says. "A whole group of people is assembled in a
room to hear a talk or participate in a discussion. And you start off by
having an unacknowledged moment of silence. People don't know what
to do. Sometimes people call out my name, like, have I had some kind of
an episode?"

Hall's high-wattage smile has always thrown people. Howard Rheingold says: "You can't tell whether he's kidding or he's sincere. He's actually mostly sincere. But that shit-eating grin on his face makes you think
he's putting you on."

For years Hall played a bit of a fool's role, playfully provoking people,
smiling even as he pissed them off. He was the clown of the Web's class of
1994, who, it often seemed, was never going to graduate. After his stint as
a gaming correspondent, first in California and then in Japan, he enrolled
at the USC film school's Interactive Media program. There he found controversy quickly: he started posting short student films on the Web, and
that broke the school's rules. USC claimed copyright over all the students'
work. And, oh, if you posted your film online, you couldn't enter it to win
a prize at Cannes.

"I got into a long discussion with the head of the school," he remembers. "I said, you know what? Ten of your students are going to get into
Cannes in the next ten years. And that leaves ten thousand students who
could be experimenting with the future, building a following, doing their
thing."

In January 2005, Hall still had his following, though it was much
smaller than in his nineties heyday. So when he abruptly replaced his
mountain of self-chronicling Web pages with a single tormented video—
a *cri de coeur* unleavened by smiles or jokes—people noticed. The *San
Francisco Chronicle* even put a story on its front page: TIME TO GET A

LIFE—PIONEER BLOGGER JUSTIN HALL BOWS OUT AT 31. (Actually, Hall had just turned thirty that December.) But neither the *Chronicle* audience nor Hall's own readers got a clear picture of why Hall was shutting down his venerable online confessional.

The tale began on January 7, late on a Friday evening, when Hall posted notes on a first date under a header that read "wordless." He marveled at the "immediate deep intimacy" he'd found with his new partner: "Something deep in me was being fed, and it made my hunger greater. . . . Much of the 20 hours was speechless staring at each other from two inches away giggling, laughing, smiling 'til our faces hurt."

Underneath Hall's ecstatic words, his readers began posting their comments:

> ANYONE I KNOW??
> . . . you? Speechless? ya right. :p
> Lol J. - Justin got laid! That's about it.

Late on Saturday night, an anonymous reader posting simply as "Q" wrote:

> In the beginning I admired Justin, but recently have grown disillusioned with his perpetual adolescence. Every so often Justin is "In Love!!," and it is always lighting speed and recklessly intimate. The first few posts with Jane and Amy sounded exactly the same. . . .
>
> Intimacy isn't when you have a deep conversation with a near-stranger or when you recklessly bare your soul on a first meeting. Intimacy is definitely not making bad porn with strangers in latex bodybags. These things are just games people play with trust, like those games in high school where you have to fall backwards and you have to trust someone to catch you and it feels somewhat exhilarating.

While playing such games shows you the excitement and intensity that a feeling like "trust" can produce, and is a nice preview of it, it's not the real thing. The real thing happens when there is a real reason to believe you can bare your soul to this person. For instance, that they've been there for 1000 days already. That they did the right thing when you bared one small detail, and then one medium-sized detail, and after a year, you *really* trust them with the big details. . . .

Justin has no respect for the boundaries in life that allow you to become very close with one person (or several), and comparatively less close with the rest, and thus create intimacy. . . . Justin throwing around intimacy shows that he doesn't know what it's worth.

On Sunday morning, Hall responded to Q:

You make stirring points. I can't help but think I've been skimming the surface on intimacy some, as you intimate.

But there is much unpublished. The broader narrative of search is clear; the motivations and affectations are incompletely stated. My relationships have a resonant depth for me. At times I feel something sorely lacking; don't all humans have those moments? I have no long view of a single face, and perhaps I could know something more meaningful from more interpersonal patience. I've been looking for that partner; the lesson, seems to be . . . Sit still boy!

A day later, the whole decade-old apparatus of the links.net site—the vast cross-referenced tissue of links and photos and words splaying out the contents of Justin Hall's brain on the Web like paint on a Jackson Pollock canvas—disappeared from view. First there was simply an empty search box. (Hall hadn't actually deleted any of his pages; he'd just removed the home-page links that let you navigate to them. If you wanted to find your way in, all you had to do was enter keywords in the search box.) A few days later, the *Dark Night* video appeared above the box. A couple of weeks later, both were replaced by a little red heart plastered over with a swarm of question marks.

Hall's date had been at USC with a woman named Merci Victoria Grace Hammon. Hall told her he had a website. "Everyone has a website," she recalls, "so I didn't think too much of it." But when she looked at the comments on his post about her date, she recoiled. "It was like Justin was maintaining a celebrity gossip blog about himself. Who needs that kind of cruelty in their lives?" She told him he couldn't write about her on his website.

"She saw it and said, 'This is ugly,'" Hall recalls. "'I don't want people auditing our love in public.'"

Over the years he'd learned to write more circumspectly about other people. The ascent of Google had made it possible for potential employers, current mates, or other interested parties to unearth all the stray comments he'd made about college classmates and partners in flings. And because links.net was an old and heavily linked-to site, Hall's mentions often turned up at the very top of a Google vanity search. So he'd tried to narrow the circle of his posts—to reduce the potential for collateral damage. He'd determined to write only about his own feelings and views and use fewer real names of third parties.

But Hammon's request represented a tougher choice. This relationship, Hall felt, was a big deal. Not writing about it would mean not writing about a central experience in his own life.

"When I was nineteen, I'm like, I'm gonna write in real time for the rest of my life, chronicling my life, and I'll be a new kind of writer. I would be living what I was writing. And what I discovered is, it's very hard to maintain relationships and write in public. I decided in the end that I would rather have relationships."

The anguish recorded in *Dark Night* shows Hall in the process of making that choice. The video was Hall's goodbye-to-all-that note.

Hammon says she didn't realize at the time that Hall was known for writing about his private life. "I just knew that I didn't want to subject myself to that kind of public criticism." She will sometimes meet long-time readers of Hall's site and find that they think they know him better than she does, and "that it's their duty (or joy) to warn me about him." But she says she has not gone back and read any of the contents of Justin's links.net site: "If Justin wants to share something about his past with me, then he will. Otherwise I don't need to delve into his history. I love and accept him for who he is now."

A month after that first-date post, Hall and Hammon moved in together. A year later, they started a game company together. In June 2008 they got married. The Internet was not invited.

Writers who tell stories about themselves, their families, and friends always walk a tightrope: you fall off one side if you stop telling the truth; you fall off the other if you hurt people you care about, or use them as fodder for your career. Dishonesty to the left, selfishness to the right. Over the past decade, confessional autobiography has become a popular literary trend, and as a result the bookstores are filled with examples of both kinds of failure. Instances of the balance and grace that success requires are comparatively rare. Until recently, however, the difficulty of this high-wire act was of concern only to literary critics and autobiographical monologuists. Most of us lacked the opportunity to share our intimate stories beyond the circle of our intimates themselves.

The Web changed all that. Today the hesitancy many older Web users felt about exposing personal details online has been replaced by the reckless abandon of young people weaned on MySpace and Facebook. This has left a lot of grownups shaking their heads in "kids these days" style. "Don't they get it? Can't they see how that topless spring-break photo is going to haunt them? Don't they know those tales of bong-induced epiphanies won't go over well with that hiring manager?"

It's possible, of course, that future generations will simply give up on privacy—that the Web user of the future, surrounded by cell-phone snapshots and surveillance cameras, will assume that everything will turn up in the public record anyway. Perhaps everyone else will be equally tarnished by revelations of impropriety, which will evoke dwindling levels of outrage, and no one will worry about hiding anything.

But the story of Justin Hall, the Web's original oversharing champion, suggests a different outcome to the transition we're living through today. The struggle to draw a line between the self and the world isn't some novelty imposed on us by technology; it's part of human development— an effort we all face from the moment our infant selves begin to notice there's a world *out there*, beyond our bodies. The Web has just made the process of drawing this line more nettlesome. In the end we're each going to find the compromise between sharing and discretion that's right for ourselves. If we're lucky, it will take less than the decade it took Hall.

There is an "endearing habit" Justin Hall has, as Howard Rheingold describes it, of "shoving you aside, sitting down at your computer, and reconfiguring everything for your own good": changing the settings of your Web browser or your word-processing program, arranging your desktop using helpful features you didn't know about. "You can call this a lack of boundaries, and it is, but that's such a value judgment," Rheingold says. "You could also say, 'Here's a very open person. He's not only open about himself, he's open about you—he's open about whoever he's near!' And he'll sit down at your computer and change your defaults."

In a sense, Hall changed the defaults of the Web itself. In its formative stages, he turned it into an arena for youthful self-exposure. He put on a defiantly outrageous show, attracted a following, and demonstrated how easy it was to do both. He took a medium that had been conceived as a repository for scholarship and scaled it down to personal size. Then he took his confessions and intimacies and blasted them out to the whole world.

The Web was what made all this possible, but Justin Hall made it the norm, the expected—the default. Then, years later, he discovered, as he put it in *Dark Night*, "I can't seem to be an adult and feed the Web my intimacy and be with the people that I want to be with."

As long as there is a Web, it will offer youthful seekers a seductively grand public stage for playing out their quests for connection and identity and meaning. But why would anyone think it could stop them from growing up?

Chapter 2

THE UNEDITED VOICE
OF A PERSON

DAVE WINER

n October 1994, spam was still a canned pork by-product, and email was a promising novelty. Only in the computer business could you catch a glimpse of email's future, as a new kind of communication channel that promised you direct access to an industry's power centers. All you needed was the right people's addresses.

So, when a San Francisco multimedia developer named Marc Canter wanted to publicize a product launch party, he thought, *I need a good email list.* He turned to a friend, software entrepreneur Dave Winer. Winer was a garrulous industry veteran and knew a lot of people. He dug into his Rolodex and old conference programs and assembled a list of about a thousand email addresses of influential people in the personal computer and software world. He sent Canter's invitation to them all on October 7, 1994, and followed up after the event with another message—a short piece by Canter on media coverage of the multimedia industry.

A few days later, Winer was driving up I-280 to San Francisco when it hit him: Why not use the same list to promote his own ideas? He turned his car around, drove home, and started cranking out short essays.

He began with an open letter to an IBM executive. Then he sent out some thoughts on the handheld computing market. Somebody wrote back with a counterargument, and he recirculated that back to his list. Then he mailed out an essay titled "Bill Gates vs. the Internet":

> The users outfoxed us again. It happens every fifteen years or so in this business. We lost our grounding, the users rebelled, and a new incarnation of the software business has been created.
>
> What is it? The Internet, of course. It's a very magic thing whose potential has barely been explored. New stuff is happening almost on a daily basis. There's a rebellious spirit to it. . . .
>
> While the software industry was looking one way (obsession with Bill Gates), the users went the other. They stopped waiting for Bill and the rest of us.
>
> Now the tail is wagging the dog! The old software industry is struggling (even flailing) to not be random idiots.

The Internet hadn't been created by any of the giant companies that dominated the industry. And its rise was going to humble those companies:

> Bill can bring Apple to its knees. He may have Novell pinned down. Microsoft is a very impressive company. But Marvel [the code name for Microsoft's then-gestating proprietary online service] can't compete with the Internet. Once the users take control, they never give it back. They allow a new industry to form, let the old one wither and fade, even die, and then repeat the process all over again. It happened in the transition from mainframes to minis, in the transition from minis to PCs. And it's happening again.

Nine days later, Microsoft's founder sent Winer an email responding to his criticism. Winer's unguarded, rambling manner was less like a trade-magazine column than like a late-night discussion among friends, and Gates's reply was equally unpolished:

> Your mail is stimulating because the Internet is a very important "external" development but why the demagoguery? . . . I am not sure this industry gets its best discussion when it takes a serious issue and turns it into an attack on one person complete with insults. Perhaps you have read some of the more extreme things written about me. In terms of your own work with Microsoft and me personally do you feel wronged in some way?

"He responded in a very Bill Gates way," Winer commented later. "It was shrill, it was whiny, it was rebellious. . . . He just didn't accept the basic premise of what I had said. It was Bill Gates exactly as Bill Gates is, without any PR interference." Winer took Gates's message and promptly sent it back out to his full list.

Gates was making himself surprisingly accessible via email that year. In January 1994, just as Justin Hall was building his first home page, *The New Yorker* published an article by John Seabrook titled "Email from Bill," in which the reporter recounted the then-uncommon experience of getting to know a famous interview subject by exchanging electronic messages. Seabrook found that "billg" the email persona was in many ways more engaging than Bill Gates in person.

Still, getting a reply from the software industry's most powerful CEO wasn't all that surprising if you were on assignment for *The New Yorker*. All Winer had going for him was an informal email list. Gates's response to Winer's criticism on Winer's own turf sent a signal to the tech industry that Winer's mailing list was a forum of consequence; it also validated the very idea of the Net's new quick-and-dirty model for business communication. Forget about layers of PR people and vetting by lawyers and the slow roll-out of carefully tested messages. Participants in the marketplace could now talk directly with each other. Journalists weren't excluded—but they no longer sat in the middle of the conversation with their fingers on the microphone switch, choosing what people at each end would hear.

All of this made Dave Winer extremely happy. Winer had plenty of company within his industry in his enthusiasm for the Internet—but his ardor had a personal edge. For him, the Net was not just the Next Big Thing as a technical playground and an unprecedented business opportunity. He saw its advent as the healing of a wound, the redressing of an ancient wrong, a righting of the scales of justice.

For years, Winer had believed that the technology industry got a bum deal from its media coverage—and that he'd gotten a bad deal, too. His company, Userland, produced software tools for Apple's Macintosh platform—a scripting environment called Frontier that allowed programmers to write short programs and snippets of code for automating repetitive tasks. Frontier was popular among Mac experts who found uses for it in publishing and education. (For instance, in the newsroom I then worked in at the *San Francisco Examiner*, we used Frontier to run an entire Mac network dedicated to photo production and graphics.) Winer knew that the Mac software world was full of lively, if struggling, small companies like his own. But the trade journals dismissed the whole market as a moribund backwater. To Winer, that was not just a practical hurdle for selling software; it was downright disrespectful.

The longer he worked in the tech industry, the more Winer became convinced that most of the media simply did a lousy job covering it. The trade publications were corrupt; the mainstream reporters were clueless. In the trades, the journalists sometimes knew their subject, but the publications cared only about selling ads. Winer tells an anecdote from his days as a software CEO in the 1980s: The editor and publisher of a well-known trade magazine were visiting his offices; when the editor stepped out to the bathroom, the publisher told Winer he would guarantee coverage of Winer's products if Winer ponied up some cash. In the mainstream press, tech-company advertisers couldn't call the shots so nakedly, but the writers were often out of their depth. At best they got details wrong, and at worst they presented a record of events that bore no resemblance to the events he'd observed. "Ask any expert who's been interviewed on a subject of any subtlety or complexity," Winer once wrote. "The reporter always mangles it."

So Winer reveled in the new direct email line he had established with his colleagues and peers, and in his ability to circumvent the media. He started writing several times a week, and his list, christened DaveNet, grew quickly. Each message you got from DaveNet showed you the email addresses for a different, randomly selected batch of ten other recipients; it was like your own little table at a giant dinner party (and every now and then, there he was, "billg@microsoft.com," right across from you). You could start a conversation thread by doing a "reply all" to that little group (which always included Winer), but unlike on a typical Internet mailing list, DaveNet didn't let individual users reply to the whole list. Instead, Winer would sometimes choose interesting responses he'd received and send them back to the entire group.

The discussion quickly zeroed in on one subject: the World Wide Web. Winer began to get his head around the new medium in early November 1994, when he pitched in to help the striking members of the Newspaper Guild at the *San Francisco Chronicle* and *San Francisco Examiner*. The guild journalists (I was one of them) were posting articles on a website that had been thrown together overnight, the San Francisco Free Press; Winer wrote some scripts that helped automate the work. Suddenly his Frontier tools had a new purpose in life. The strike ended after two weeks, but Winer deployed similar scripts to build his own website, which went live at the start of the new year. For the moment the DaveNet email list remained Winer's main soapbox; on the website he kept an archive of DaveNet essays and tested new software. But he could see that the Web had thrilling possibilities.

"When I first understood how the Web worked, I had this epiphany, this awakening," Winer recalls. "Omigod, this stuff actually is easy, simple.

Everything that I had learned worked in this space. And everything that I wanted to do could be done."

Winer stood at a career crossroads: he had decided to give up on the software industry after a bruising experience with Apple, which had incorporated into the Macintosh operating system software tools that competed with Frontier. Although he felt his product was superior, he saw no way to beat Apple; it owned the platform. He would fold his software-development tent, focus on DaveNet, and become a writer. But the Internet was a new software platform that no one—neither Apple nor Microsoft nor anyone else—controlled, and that got Winer excited about software all over again. Now he had a mission: "Everyone gets their own personal website," he wrote. "I want to help you do this." In February 1995 he sent out a DaveNet essay titled "Billions of Websites." At the time the number sounded ludicrous, even to Internet optimists, but Winer was serious:

> Every new website begets more websites. If I have one, I want my friend to have one, so I can point to it. And so they can point to my site. Someday I'll be able to walk a network of friendships, automatically knowing that each of us has mutual friends. It'll be cool. . . . The breadth of the web is limited only by the available space on hard disks, and the availability of human thoughts and feelings to fill that space. . . . Every writer can participate in the web. Someday, very soon, I believe, every writer will. . . . But the clean-up act, the new leader of the online busi-ness, will be the one who makes it really easy for anyone to publish a website on their server.

In early 1995 Winer was hardly alone in getting worked up about the Web's potential. But he was unusual in that he combined two roles that hadn't coexisted before: he was both a writer with an audience and a software developer with a handy set of tools. As he started trying to realize his billion-websites vision, he quickly dove into the spiral of work that characterized his career: build a little piece of something in code, write about it, try it out with some users, write about what happens, work on it some more. Borrowing a term from the technology pioneer Douglas Engelbart, he called this process "bootstrapping." He was as unafraid to present unfinished programs to his customers (often for free) as he was to email hastily written essays to his readers. Broken code could be fixed; errors in writing could be followed up with apologies and corrections. "We make shitty software," he told his readers:

> We know our software sucks. But it's shipping! Next time we'll do better, but even then it will be shitty. The only software that's perfect is one you're dreaming about. Real software crashes, loses data, is hard to learn and hard to use. But it's a process. We'll make it less shitty.

Programming was old-hat for Winer, but a writing career was altogether new. At the Bronx High School of Science in the early 1970s he'd put out five issues of an underground newspaper, dedicated to organizing Vietnam War protests and Earth Day events. Later he'd spent a lot of time in the early days of Compuserve on its CB Simulator chat service. But he'd never thought of himself as a writer before. He'd never kept a journal or written fiction. Now DaveNet was a standing invitation for him to ruminate, and he soon widened his focus, writing not only about software and the Web but about the San Francisco 49ers, and his new pied-à-terre in San Francisco, and his thoughts about gender relations, and the songs that formed the soundtrack to his work—from "Que Sera Sera" to "Respect."

Not everyone who'd signed on for tech-industry commentary was thrilled. In a February 1995 DaveNet message titled "A Tough Customer," Winer republished an email from a reader:

> How about just sending me the *important* DaveNet messages? I really don't care about your new house, the fog,

football, or whether you and the folks at HotWired are going to be chummy. Too much ego, too little substance. But when you have something to say, I'd love to hear. I just don't need the fan club stuff. Would you be interested if everyone you knew sent out their daily schedules to you?

Winer wrote that he decided to treat the message as a "resignation" from his list, but the criticism rankled.

My father used to say the same kind of thing when I was a kid and did something creative or funny. He'd ask me, in all seriousness, what if everyone did that?

As a kid, I didn't have the words to answer him. Now I do.

It would be great!

Imagine being able to find out what's *really* going on in anyone's life. What if everyone wrote about their issues. We could all learn from each other. Friendship would mean a lot more. We could grow more quickly, accomplish more in our lives, live more richly, have more fun.

If there was one thing that was sure to press Winer's buttons, it was suggesting that he pipe down. There was no way he was going to shut up; instead, he urged everyone else to chime in.

Defiantly and at times euphorically, Winer just kept widening DaveNet's scope. Before long, in between the industry analysis and the software debates and the kibitzing about Apple's increasingly dire fortunes, he was also writing about Internet censorship, turning forty, an eleven-day class in massage, and the phone message from someone he'd had a date with the previous week. He proposed that people stop saying, "Hi, how are you?" when they met, and instead try saying, "Hi, I forgive you." He shared his discovery that "there are two fundamental opposing forces in the world, love and fear." Subscribe to DaveNet, it was becoming clear, and you were going to get a cross-section of a human mind. Some readers told Winer they enjoyed these forays into personal philosophy; others saw glib pop-psych naïveté, and winced.

Either way, Winer was beginning to reach a wider audience. Hotwired invited him to publish some of his DaveNet pieces on its site, and he began doing so in June 1995, while still sending them out to his email list and posting them on his own site. Contributing to Hotwired gave Winer some of the professional recognition as a writer that he had admitted craving in one of his early columns. It also meant he would be edited for the first time.

In the beginning, things worked out well. He was often paired with a young editor named June Cohen, a Stanford grad who ran Hotwired's "Net Surf" feature, a compilation of interesting links from around the Web (in the tradition of the NCSA What's New page). Cohen was experienced in editing columnists and humor writers; she saw her job to be helping Winer sound more like Winer, and they generally saw eye to eye. But sometimes Winer was edited by other people, and as his nearly yearlong tenure at Hotwired went on, he began to bridle at their changes to his copy. Increasingly he dealt with editors who weren't on his wavelength— people with backgrounds in the technology trade press who, he felt, were trying to make his writing sound more generic.

In May 1996 he wrote his last column for Hotwired. "I knew I had to leave," he says, "when I read one of my own columns and felt I needed to write a rebuttal to it."

For people who knew Dave Winer—and he'd become a well-known figure in Silicon Valley and San Francisco technology circles—it didn't come as much of a surprise that he'd had a hard time getting along with his editors. Getting along with anyone at times seemed a perplexing challenge for him. Six foot two, with an expansive belly and a beard he'd added over the past couple of years, Winer could be an overbearing presence when he decided to speak out in public.

In October 1996, for instance, Winer sat in a crowd of the industry elite at the Agenda technology conference in Phoenix, listening to an interview with Larry Ellison, the arrogant billionaire founder of Oracle. Ellison had decided that the future of the industry lay with something he was calling the network computer, a stripped-down machine that would connect you to the Web, but not do much else on its own. The crowd was skeptical, and Stewart Alsop, the moderator, was trying to get Ellison to come down to earth and provide more details about his product, which was then "vaporware"—all talk, nothing shipping.

Winer walked to the mike and challenged Ellison and his vision of the future: Why, he asked, would users want what Ellison was selling? Ellison told him, in effect, to shut up and sit down.

The dismissive response ought to have gotten Winer's back up, but instead he wrote an appreciative DaveNet piece praising Ellison as a "straight shooter," "bold and truthful in his assertions" and "too honest" to sugarcoat his message. For Winer, the value of abrasive honesty trumped even the indignity of having been publicly rebuked—perhaps because it was one of his own signature traits. In confronting Ellison—as he had confronted others in similar incidents—Winer proudly assumed the role of truth-teller. He cherished the right to damn the niceties and speak his mind. He accepted that he'd probably tick a lot of people off. But if sometimes he could speak his truth, get other people to listen—and earn or keep their respect, too? That would be heaven.

"All my life, I've placed the highest value, derived the most happiness, from simply being heard," Winer wrote in his first column for Hotwired.

> It's a precious commodity in a world that seems to always say "shut up" or "go away." People don't want to hear other people. When people shout, they're really

> saying "listen to me!" It can be a struggle to keep quiet
> and give other people the space to say something, espe-
> cially to feel safe saying something real, something that
> reflects how they really feel.

He was writing about his pride at being chosen for *Newsweek*'s 1995 list of the fifty "Most Influential People to Watch in Cyberspace." He was being acknowledged as a speaker worth hearing, and the world seemed to be listening. But, deliberately or not, he was also painting a self-portrait of his struggle to "keep quiet" and let others speak—a constant battle whose outcome always seemed balanced on a beard-hair.

As Winer began revealing more of his personality to his readers on DaveNet, he came into focus as a uniquely unstable compound of bicoastal stereotypes—the blissed-out California hippie and the argumentative New York Jew. From moment to moment, you never knew which Dave you were going to get. Over time this volatility caused some in the industry to give him a wide berth. Others stuck around for the show—and for what they could learn from him. Whatever people might say behind Winer's back, few would deny that he had a reliable record of finding, and fostering, the sort of innovative Big New Things that Silicon Valley has always craved.

On January 12, 1996, Suck editor Carl Steadman posted a satire of DaveNet, stringing together a collection of Winer's casual mannerisms and verbal tics:

> I'm zooooooooooming!

> The big picture: I'm filled with contradictions. So what?
> Yeah!

> I'm going for it!

> Let's have fun!

Winer appreciated the parody as a homage, and thanked Suck in a brief DaveNet message that jokingly recycled even more of his verbal tics: "Wow." "Check it out." "Cooooooooooooooooooool." But much of the time, criticism instead exposed Winer's thin skin. Whenever writers called him "cantankerous" or "irascible," which they did regularly, he'd bristle. And each of his objections to these labels simply confirmed them.

Any public career online is going to attract a certain volume of drive-by flak; potentially useful criticism is likely to be hopelessly tangled together with personal invective. Winer took nearly every putdown to heart. One of his last columns for Hotwired explored the psychology of mailing-list flame wars—those inextinguishable verbal conflicts that often derailed and paralyzed email lists. When mailing lists work, he wrote, they foster collaboration and understanding, but when they don't, they're "like unhappy families" stuck in loops of projection and blame:

> I'm right, therefore you're wrong. This is the argument we had in the family I grew up in. I think this is the big argument of humanity. . . .

> Instead of participating, someday make an effort to observe an email flamefest and stay uninvolved. Imagine people actually saying those things to other people, face to face.

> Clue: This is the stuff that people are thinking, but don't dare say.

> Internet mailing lists are like sewers, carrying the refuse that we can't share with other people who could hit us, fire us, or abandon us. But on the Net, we can broadcast our pain to the world, using a virtual person, a total projection, as a symbol for our discontent. Here's someone who's wrong. Everyone look! . . .

> The only way to find out what's going on inside another person is to listen to them. Their words may be confused, but you can be sure of one thing: they're trying to say something. Everyone—young or old, educated or not, woman or man, rich or poor—everyone has something to say. And some reason for believing they're right.
>
> The key is to ignore it when they say you're wrong. I know it's hard to do! But when they say you're wrong, they're just telling you why they've decided not to listen to you.

DaveNet mailings often came with multiple PSes. At the bottom of this one, Winer tacked on an idea:

> PPS: A flame-reduction suggestion: Offer each side a place to state their point of view on the Web. Let them add to it whenever they want. The Web may be better suited for debate than mailing lists are.

Winer, of course, already had a digital soapbox. But what about everybody else? Where were those billions of websites?

In February 1996, Winer, like many other writers online, felt impelled to take up arms against the Communications Decency Act's effort to censor "indecent" content on the Web. He conceived of a project called "24 Hours of Democracy," which invited people to write short essays about what freedom meant to them. The vehicle for planning the project in the weeks beforehand was a mailing list.

"We couldn't get any work done," Winer recalls. "Everything started a flame. Everything you posted caused somebody to be paranoid about it and get personal with whoever it was. There was no chance of communicating. Yet we still needed to communicate." Disgusted, Winer eventually unsubscribed from the list.

In the end, the project succeeded despite the turmoil, inspiring contributions from hundreds of people, mostly posting on their own sites. To showcase the outpouring of essays, Winer built a special Web page listing links to each new addition so people could follow the flow of material; following the leads of Tim Berners-Lee and Marc Andreessen, he'd add the latest news and links to the most recent contributions at the top of the list. He called it the project's "news page."

The 24 Hours project was a one-off, but its news page had given Winer the idea of creating a similar page for the community of developers that had gathered around his Frontier scripting software. So, on April 27, 1996, Winer started one. "Frontier News & Updates" was just that—information about new releases, links to software documentation, reports of bugs. From the start, though, Winer threw in links to DaveNet essays. And around September he started widening the scope of the news page links. He'd point readers to a technology column in Hotwired about email software, or analyses of Apple's woes, or news of releases from other companies. And he'd list sites that had adopted Frontier: Winston Salem Online, the 18th World Aerobatic Championships, the Bangkok Post.

Frontier News & Updates was what today is called a "vertical blog," a page that provides commentary and collects links of interest to some specialized community on a particular subject. Winer found the format so useful that he built into Frontier a tool for publishing such news pages, the Frontier NewsPage Suite, which he released in January 1997. In addition to streamlining the process of posting new items, the NewsPage Suite made it easy to post selected incoming email messages directly to your website, opening up a feedback loop. Sometime in February, Winer changed the name of the original Frontier News page to Scripting News, and as the year progressed he continued to expand its scope. DaveNet remained his outlet for extended essays, but Scripting News became a home for links, offhand observations, and ephemera. Over time the choices grew quirkier: Over here was a page where someone had posted the lyrics to "Okie from Muskogee." Over there was annoy.com, "the most annoying website!" The hodgepodge was perplexing to some readers; it took a long time for the logic to emerge. In 1998 a software developer named Eric Sink sent Winer a note:

> Your website has finally started to make sense to me. I've been reading it for a long time. At first I was irked by the fact that you keep including tidbits of questionable relevance. At some point I realized that the whole point of scripting.com is a daily listing of whatever the heck *Dave* thinks is relevant.

Web surfers from outside of the software development world who stumbled upon Scripting News in those early days also found it a little opaque. For one thing, the news page label was confusing: wasn't that, like, CNN.com? For another, in an era when Web designers had fallen in love with increasingly elaborate devices, including frames and image backgrounds and other gimmicks that emphasized the cool things you could do in a browser, the look of Scripting News was crude and down-to-business. Early on, Winer posted an open invitation for web-designer readers to post their own remixed designs of the site, and many responded, but he stuck with his home-grown original. It was just a column of text and links—but it loaded fast, and it repaid frequent visits with a stream of updates. Like many visitors who arrived that year, I was sometimes left scratching my head trying to figure out what it was supposed to be. But I found myself coming back often.

So did a growing number of other people. Winer found he had a significant "flow" at Scripting News, a volume of traffic that meant that, when he linked to another site, that site gained a sudden influx of new visitors. He shared his flow generously, linking broadly and promiscuously, to his friends and people who said positive things about him, but also to people who were angry with him, or with whom he was angry. As the months flew by, Winer posted more and more to Scripting News; it would sometimes have dozens of new items on a single day.

At the same time, Winer and his colleagues at a rejuvenated Userland were furiously shipping updates and new software, first for Frontier and later for new weblog publishing tools. You could follow the progress of each new release on Scripting News. Winer conducted his business in full public view: sometimes he would think out loud in public about what direction to take his products; at other times he'd tease readers about something big coming down the pipes, and then unveil it with a fanfare.

Winer wouldn't always tell you what he thought about what he was linking to; sometimes he'd pass along a headline without comment. And sometimes he'd admit ignorance and post a link anyway: he'd stumble on some new site and say, "What exactly is X-ACT?" "Interesting! What is Alexa?" He'd propose business partnerships right there on his weblog: "Anyone want to work with us on this? Excite? Yahoo? Netscape? Microsoft? dave@scripting.com." And sometimes he'd post a thought and, later, thinking better of it, edit or delete what he'd written. (The practice was controversial, leading critics to charge that Winer would post a flame and then tone it down after the fact, making responses people had published elsewhere look like overreactions. Winer says he has always reviewed each day's Scripting posts at the end of the day, reordering and occasionally rewriting posts; after that he doesn't touch anything.)

For readers used to the conventions of old-fashioned journalism, there was something at once invigorating and unsettling about the way Winer mixed his roles as a widely read pundit and an ambitious entrepreneur. There was no question that Scripting News gave you a fascinating as-it-happened portrait of the work of writing software for the Web in the 1990s—the arguments over technical standards, the shifting sands of the "browser wars" between Microsoft and Netscape, the dream of providing tools that millions of people might use, the reality of bugs and server crashes and network-service interruptions. It also served as a very effective public advertisement for Winer's software. What in an earlier era might have been decried as conflict of interest looked, from a different angle, like an effective instance of what the software industry called "eating your own dog food"—using your own products, both to shake out bugs and to show off their capabilities. Before long, a small handful of technically adventurous writers adopted the Frontier NewsPage Suite and began playing around with their own sites in the Scripting News vein.

But the Frontier software was far too complex for most people to install and use. Those nontechnical users were nonetheless beginning to fill up the Web with pages of TV-show trivia, pet photos, political rants, and whatever else was on their minds. They relied on a number of services, like Geocities and Tripod, that had arrived on the scene, promising to take the pain out of Web publishing. That promise was fulfilled—in part. It *had* become easy for anyone to post a plain Web page. But just try updating it! This first iteration of simple tools for what the Web industry would later call "user-generated content" failed miserably at making it possible for people to organize the material they posted and keep things current. They hadn't solved the "what's new" problem. As a result, it wasn't long before individual pages deteriorated into unnavigable chaos, and entire online neighborhoods became blighted with broken pages and out-of-date information.

Winer believed in the billions-of-websites future he'd predicted. "Web authoring can be as easy as email," he wrote. "I know this can be done." But in order to make that happen, he saw that you needed to do more than help users post pages; you had to give them the keys to what the software industry called a content management system, or CMS—a tool for editing and publishing text (plus photos, art, video, and other files) stored in a database. At the time, content management systems were expensive software packages deployed by large commercial publishers, like newspapers and magazines, that needed easily updated Web pages. The systems not only provided structure for the material on a website, but also organized the workflow for the writers, editors, and designers to move individual pieces of content down a production line toward publication. In 1997 or 1998, the idea of handing individual users their own CMSes sounded like overkill. But as the movement that would later be known as blogging began to gain popularity, that's exactly what it accomplished. Just as personal computers were scaled-down versions of room-sized mainframe computers, the programs that would evolve for publishing weblogs were basically CMSes trimmed down for individuals.

Winer and his company devoted several years to cranking out different versions of weblog publishing tools, in a market that was gradually becoming more competitive. After the NewsPage Suite came Manila, a program for small groups or communities of associated weblogs, released in 1999. Fast on Manila's heels came EditThisPage.com and Weblogs.com, two similar free services that let anyone start up a weblog that would be hosted on Winer's company's servers. Later came another program called Radio Userland. Each had some useful innovations; each had some barriers for the novice to overcome.

What they all shared was a structure rooted in Winer's definition of a weblog as "the unedited voice of a person." Most CMSes incorporated a process for editorial review of content before publication. Winer's products set a norm for weblog publishing tools by leaving this feature out. He was making software for self-determination.

For Winer, such autonomy was the "essential element" of weblog writing: "Almost all the other elements can be missing, and the rules can be violated . . . as long as the voice of a person comes through, it's a weblog." A weblog was a place where you got to say your piece your own way. Where nobody else's voice could drown yours out. And where no one could make you shut up. All previous forms of online communication—the discussion-group hubbub of early communities like the WELL, the early dial-up bulletin boards, Usenet, and the teeming world of mailing lists—placed participants on an equal footing. Good moderators could inhibit dysfunctional behavior, but never eliminate it entirely, and sometimes useful conversations were swamped by noise or non sequiturs. Your "eureka!" posting exposing the secrets of the universe as revealed to you in a 3:00 a.m. flash might be immediately buried by a spirited argument about the superiority of Macs over Windows PCs. If you wanted control over what you were saying and also over the environment in which you were heard, none of these formats would do. Weblogs cleared a space in the hubbub for a lone voice. What about "interactivity"? Though it would be a few years before weblogs routinely allowed visitors to comment on posts, readers could always email the author. Winer would regularly republish interesting responses, as he had with Bill Gates's email in 1994, but he carefully filtered them. Feedback might pour in—but the author was in firm control of it, choosing what to publish and what to ignore.

If your weblog gave you a soapbox with a microphone that no one else could turn off, you were free to use it however you wished. Winer used his as an outlet for his vision of a future in which millions of people could tell their own stories, and no one could stop them. He also used it for more mundane material, like complaints about his Internet service provider or praise for Dell for speeding up the delivery of a new laptop. This jumble of big ideas and little reports could be jarring, and sometimes Winer's readers would criticize him for that. But the model of the weblog as a general miscellany—mixing the professional and the personal, the philosophical and the ephemeral—grew familiar before too long. Not everyone who started a weblog imitated the style of Scripting News, but enough did to establish its stubborn eclecticism as a standard. You were the sole arbiter of relevance; if a reader didn't like your choices, well, there were plenty of other sites to read.

Over time, Winer saw the fulfillment of his first hope for weblogs—that they'd become easy enough for millions of people to speak directly with one another, "routing around" media gatekeepers and pesky editors. But the other part of his vision, that weblogs might reduce friction online? That proved more elusive.

The idea of Winer's original "flame-reduction suggestion" was that once we all came to understand that our voices could not be squelched, we would stop trying to shout each other down. Winer has always attracted personal conflicts as if according to some law of physics, so his interest in lowering the overall volume level was natural. But in his corner of the Internet, even as weblogging began to take hold, the shouting matches showed a dismaying stamina. In October 1998 he'd opened up a discussion group for Userland products, a Web forum that became a watering hole for blogging enthusiasts, a support forum for users of Winer's products, and a space to comment on Scripting News. For the first few months he found it an "incredibly collegial community," but then things began to go downhill.

One of the fiercest arguments in the Userland discussion group came in September 1999, in the middle of a debate over a flash-in-the-pan Web company called Third Voice. Third Voice's gimmick was to enable its users to post comments and annotations on any website they landed on. These comments existed in a sort of transparent layer over the sites—like sticky notes pasted to the screen, visible only to Third Voice participants—and site owners had no control over them. This design got a lot of people worked up, including Winer. In the Userland group, a developer named Rogers Cadenhead posted a message arguing that Third Voice's new twist was consistent with the true spirit of the Web, which was all about giving users more control over what they read, how they read it, and how it looked—its "presentation."

In response, Winer wrote:

> If any Third Voice users are tuned in, check out Rogers' home page. See the little boy? Want to have sex with him?

> I wonder if Rogers would object to your comments on his site? After all, he doesn't own the presentation.

The post contained a link to Cadenhead's personal home page, which featured a photo of him as a kid. Cadenhead replied with self-control and a light touch:

> I would certainly object—no one should desire to have sex with me at any age, and if you need reasons I'll post a

current photograph or ask my wife to participate in this discussion.

I don't own the distasteful comments of a Third Voice user any more than I own the tacky comment you just made here. They are hosted on servers I do not control and published by other people.

If Third Voice becomes the forum of choice for chatty pedophiles, I'll certainly recommend against using the plug-in the same way I recommend against public AOL chatrooms.

I won't, though, object on the grounds that Third Voice has no right to offer public annotation in the context of my Web site to users who opt to see it.

Others were less measured in their response to Winer. Peter Merholz, a well-known Web designer with his own weblog, wrote, "Where are those 'shut-the-fuck-up' bullets when you need them?" Winer admitted he was being deliberately provocative to make a point, but he stood his ground. In a follow-up message, Cadenhead wrote, "So much for my theory you made the sex-with-boys remark in the heat of the moment. You should get your hindsight checked."

When I interviewed Winer for this book, I told him I thought I'd have found his comment offensive if I were Cadenhead. He replied that it should have been obvious he was trying to "focus people on the danger of Third Voice," of "random people being able to deface websites," and that his critics' outrage was contrived, anyway, since the little boy in the picture, young Cadenhead, was a "fictitious person," no longer in danger of actual molestation. Still, he said, if a similar controversy arose today, he'd just keep quiet.

The Third Voice debate subsided, but other quarrels kept flaring. In

September 2000 Winer shut down the Userland Discussion Group with a plaintive note:

> I'm still spending a lot of time responding to messages that put me in a defensive corner . . . if you have a complaint, find some other space, and we'll do the best we can. . . . Also, please don't send me email apologizing or flaming or further embroiling me in your needs or emotions. I've given all I can to this. I want a vacation from this discussion group, and sending me private email is probably the worst thing you could do. Please.

Later, Winer said he figured it was time for the discussion-group regulars to go off and start their own blogs.

At the same time that he was coping with complaints on his discussion group, Winer also found himself making tough calls as the proprietor of a growing free blog service at EditThisPage.com and Weblogs.com. He was a longtime outspoken advocate of free speech; now he had to deal with users who would, inevitably, seek to test his commitment to those principles.

In March 2000 this inevitability materialized in the person of Greg Knauss, an occasional contributor to Suck who'd maintained his own personal website for years and had been fascinated and infuriated by Winer for almost as long. "I admire his intellect," Knauss says, "and am frustrated to the point of tears by his almost pathological hypocrisy." Knauss felt, basically, that Winer dished it out but couldn't take it. So he decided to set up a "Dave test case"; he'd open an account on EditThisPage.com, call his new blog "Winerlog," and use Winer's own service to start making fun of him. Knauss says he explicitly set out to "push Winer's buttons," in order to "throw some of his various contradictions into sharp relief."

Winer passed Knauss's test: he didn't delete Winerlog. In fact, as with the Suck parody years before, he even linked to it from Scripting News, albeit with a touch of sarcasm. Experiment completed, Knauss stopped posting after a couple of weeks. But that wasn't the end of Winerlog; somebody else who went by the pseudonym Zaphod asked Knauss for the password, he provided it, and the blog was revived, in a considerably nastier vein, with apparently more than one contributor. Winer would sometimes come close to shutting it down—there was one incident, in May 2000, when the site's parodies of Userland's promotional graphics nearly pushed him over the edge—but the site lived on for years.

The technology Winer championed had now turned into an instrument of torment for him. The Winerloggers were demons flying out of his own creation to peck at him and plague his days. As they dug under his skin, he struggled to stick to his principles. Winer was regularly accused of being a utopian, but this was more like a small hell.

In our interviews, I asked Winer why he thought he kept getting into fights with people. "If there's a pattern, it's that I'm gullible," he answered. "I have a very limited sense of irony. I tend to take people at face value, and people take advantage of that." While he thinks he's less vulnerable today, he worries that he has also given something up. "I think that's where creativity comes from, the fact that you're not always second-guessing yourself. When you put brakes on, you've really lost a lot."

When he isn't being deliberately provoked or provocative, Dave Winer is often a charismatic speaker. He can warmly engage an audience, presenting himself humbly and really listening to what other people are telling him. In 2007 he was demoing a modest, free web-software project to a few dozen guests (including me) at a Yahoo office in downtown San Francisco. When somebody demanded that he add a new feature, he paused a second, and it looked as though he was thinking through a hundred reasons to say no. Then he looked down and said, "I've learned not to argue with users. Basically the answer is yes. It took me years to learn that."

When he writes about himself, Winer can sometimes display the self-awareness of someone who has done time in therapy and gotten results from it. In 2007 he described an incident in which he'd posted a note on the Web to an Internet telephony entrepreneur named Jeff Pulver. Pulver was calling himself an "iPhone Refusenik"; he disliked the way Apple's trendy cell phone prevented you from choosing your own service provider. "He should get an iPhone," Winer wrote. "You should always do what you least want to do as long as it's safe. How you learn." Pulver took Winer's advice and thanked him publicly for the suggestion. Winer blogged about his surprise: "People aren't supposed to listen to what I say," he wrote. "That's not part of my movie, whose plot is that I spread the truth and no one hears me."

Dave Winer, Spreader of Truth: it is a self-assigned role that Winer sometimes can evaluate from a distance, with a chuckle. At other times he has embodied it self-righteously, and those seem to be the occasions that spark the bitterest quarrels. Winer says he doesn't enjoy such fights; I think he *is* telling the truth about that. Yet the squabbles reappear through his career in a repetitive loop. Each time one breaks out, some of his readers shrug it off; others decide he is a jerk and move on. Friends tangle with him one year, stop talking with him the next, then renew the friendship a year later.

The part of truth-teller is seductive: you get to say exactly what's on your mind, and you've got advance protection from any blowback. When people applaud, you can feel good, and when they get mad, you can tell yourself, "They can't handle the truth." But telling-it-like-it-is can easily tempt you over the edge into meanness. When you believe you're speaking truth to power, sensitivity to other people's feelings becomes a dispensable luxury. The archetype is Dr. Stockmann, the protagonist of Ibsen's *An Enemy of the People*, who shouts the truth about his town's corruption from the rooftops. Although his uncompromising stance turns his whole community against him, the satisfaction of being right serves as a potent consolation for being made a pariah. And the further he is ostracized, the more fiercely he believes that "the strongest man in the world is he who stands most alone."

Dave Winer's indomitable Ibsenesque self-sufficiency has kept him going for a decade and a half's worth of DaveNet and Scripting News and a stream of other experiments and innovations in online communication. In addition to providing the world with a protean demonstration of the possibilities of the blog form, he was largely responsible for the popularity of RSS, a technology format that turned blogs into feeds of discrete posts that you could subscribe to or remix; he pioneered podcasting, the informal audio-blog form; and as the 2000s wore on, he gravitated toward political blogging and tinkered with new ideas in the universe of social software. Through it all, two constants have held. Winer has never wavered from his technological goal of providing or promoting the tools that allow individual voices to be heard without editing or interference. And he has never completely tamed his impulse to blurt out his take on the truth, even when he knows it might come off as rude.

In the summer of 2007 he sat in a Seattle auditorium, at a geek gathering called Gnomedex. Onstage, an entrepreneur named Jason Calacanis was giving a talk on "the Internet's environmental crisis," reviewing the sorry record of how each new technology that becomes useful and popular ends up swamped by "overzealous marketers" and spam. Calacanis had recently launched a new venture—a "human-powered" Web search site called Mahalo that, he argued, would be immune to spam and the sort of deceptive manipulation of links that plagued Google and similar automated systems.

Gnomedex participants viewed their conference as a place for discussing ideas rather than promoting products. So when it started to look like Calacanis's talk was turning into a pitch for his new company, some listeners began chattering and trading irritated instant messages on their laptops. In the back row, Winer couldn't contain himself. He and Calacanis were on-and-off friendly, and they had even been collaborating on planning their own conference. But now, Winer thought, Calacanis was blatantly shilling for his company in what Winer thought should be a self-promotion-free zone. Winer called out, "What about *conference* spam?"

Calacanis looked stunned for a moment at the heckle. Winer restated his complaint. Unlike Larry Ellison a decade before, Calacanis didn't just tell Winer to shut up. Instead, he forced a smile, rolled his eyes, muttered, "Dave always has an opinion, which I appreciate," and moved on.

In a world without weblogs, that might have been that. But after the talk—with the two men seated at their laptops in the same row, only a few feet away from each other—they each wrote posts about the event on their own blogs, sparking an escalatingly angry online contretemps.

Winer had always griped about the way tech-industry conference presentations so often became pitches for companies. As he put it, "I hate speeches that are ads." He had had a right, he felt—really, a duty—to pipe up, to bring the "backchannel" murmuring to the fore.

Calacanis posted his own response:

> What perplexes me is why Dave would yell at me. We're friends Dave, right? Sort of? If you disagreed with my format why not talk to me after the event and say "hey, I felt it was a little commercial, you might want to tone that down."

By this point the fracas had attracted a crowd of online rubberneckers, and even earned some news coverage in outlets like Wired News. The two men circled each other warily on their blogs. Winer offered a public apology of sorts—"I wish I hadn't done it. It'll never happen again. That's a promise"—and for a time it looked like they might both move on.

Then, six days after the event, Winer posted again:

> Today I got a brief note from Jason Calacanis requesting that I not mention him on my weblog. This requires a public response. The answer is no. Jason, you just crossed a sacred line. I decide what belongs on this blog.

Knowingly or not, Calacanis had waved a red cape at Winer's most bullishly stubborn principles. Winer couldn't stop posting on the matter.

> A sure way to become a former friend, is to say that I
> have an obligation to express my opinion privately. . . .
> When I'm exposed to something that's wrong, you can
> count on me to say so. Without that, this blog is nothing.
> And I don't sell anyone the right to tell me what I can
> and can't write about. And friendship is the worst excuse
> possible to say why I shouldn't write something.

In some ways the whole dustup was a trivial matter. People get heckled all the time. Conferences are filled with self-promoting CEOs. I saw the exchange at Gnomedex, and it seemed to me that both Winer and Calacanis were wrong *and* right—two men with robust egos, each of whom could have easily shrugged off the incident, both choosing instead to escalate it to a shouting match, one resolute in defense of a deep principle, the other aghast at a breach of simple courtesy.

The dispute did make one thing abundantly clear. Both of these antagonists were popular veteran bloggers who had "a place to state their point of view on the Web" and could "add to it whenever they want," just as Winer's "flame-reduction suggestion" had proposed a decade before. Yet that capability had done little or nothing to tamp down a flammable confrontation. If anything, the opportunity the blogs provided for the open-ended pursuit of debating points, for picking at little scabs of disagreement till they ran bloody, ensured that the fight would spiral down to a finale of bitterness and estrangement.

This wasn't how it was supposed to turn out.

At a time when the prediction seemed laughable, Dave Winer had accurately foreseen that, one day, masses of people—inspired more by their own passions than expectation of profit—would speak for themselves on their own personal websites. Then, being the bootstrapper he was, he publicly demonstrated how blogging might work by doing it himself. His vision of easy, abundant, and free self-expression—a picture that so many had dismissed as impractical and utopian and overblown—

had become reality. There were even some areas where reality had surpassed it.

But there had also been another dream: that once we each had our own soapbox, we'd be able to bypass the unproductive strife that paralyzed so many online communities, escape the destructive loops of flame wars, evade the noise of commercialization and the curse of spam, and make our way to some better model for the civilized exchange of ideas. Occasionally, now, we catch a glimmer of that in the welter of today's sprawling weblog world. More often, though, we pull up a chair to gawk at some tussle.

"What happened to the paradise I was writing about then?" Winer asks. "It sure didn't turn out that way."

Our Web-enabled ability to publish anything and everything without asking for permission has opened all sorts of possibilities, but it has hardly sated our human desire to have the last word. In the heat of argument, we now find ourselves tempted to keep rehashing points of contention or, worse, to attack our opponents, until all that's left is the hostility itself. And the medium and its tools provide no brakes on that temptation. Whatever else the spread of blogging might accomplish, it was futile to think it could somehow liberate us from pettiness and discord. Sometimes the unedited voices of people might harmonize; but they're just as likely to holler.

Chapter 3

THEY SHALL KNOW YOU THROUGH YOUR LINKS

JORN BARGER, FILTERS

ecause the World Wide Web works via computer, the people who encountered it for the first time in the mid-1990s often viewed it as a realm of technically forbidding complexity, a geeky maze that you'd need an engineering degree to negotiate. But the first wave of do-it-yourself publishers quickly saw that doing simple things on the Web was, in fact, pretty simple. Justin Hall had observed that HTML was "easy as hell," and if you weren't scared off by a little jargon or a touch of code, you could master it quickly—as promised by the titles of the era's best-selling manuals, like *Teach Yourself HTML in Seven Days*. Throw in a little bit of knowledge about how to move files from one computer to another, and you could be publishing a Web page without further ado.

The early Web, in other words, was a lot of human effort held together by a relatively small amount of technical glue. (The Internet protocols that the Web built upon were more complex; the great thing about the Web was that you didn't have to know much about them in order to use it.) But as the Web grew in size and complexity, programmers returned in force, redeploying computing power to help people make better use of the new medium. They created Web spiders that crawled from link to link, cataloging the contents of the Web for search engines like Infoseek and Altavista. These "bots"—computer programs that moved around the Web, obeying their programmed instructions— were the first harbingers of a larger vision that technopundits expounded: before long, "personal agents" would sift your email and tend your appointment calendar, shopping bots would make your purchases for you, and other programs might prowl the Web finding things for you to read.

For decades, artificial-intelligence researchers had been promising that we could program computers to make smart decisions for us, independent of our intervention. In the mid-1990s they began to wonder whether the nascent Web could ultimately become the environment for the fulfillment of that dream. It seemed plausible. But for the moment, aside from the search engines, any significant work on the Web was still being done by people. And the most significant job of all, it became clear, was helping users stay abreast of the exponential growth of the new medium.

In 1996 I interviewed William Gibson, the science-fiction writer who, more than anyone else, had helped the world imagine a future where people spent as much time in computer-generated "cyberspace" as in the "meatspace" of our flesh-and-blood bodies. Gibson had just recently started exploring the Web as he built a site for his latest book. He told me that he loved what he was seeing: "It feels to me like we've got a global ham television broadcast license, and we can only send post-cards—but that's still pretty cool. You can just put this stuff out there, and people all over the world can go and get it. And you can go and get theirs. I find it really quite sweet." But he saw that the limitlessness of the Web would quickly grow overwhelming: "Pretty soon I think there'll be people who make a living pre-surfing it for you. There's a real need for that—otherwise it becomes this monster time-sink. You can just sit there forever. Looking. Looking. And maybe not finding anything."

Someday, maybe, as some programmers dreamed, a bot would be able to do your "pre-surfing" for you, pointing you toward the most useful or diverting material. But for the moment the job still belonged to human beings.

Ironically, one of the pioneers of the "pre-surfing" that we now know as weblogging—and the man who gave it that name—was himself an acolyte in the field of artificial intelligence. Jorn Barger had grown up in what he called a "fifties hipster household" in the countercultural enclave of Yellow Springs, Ohio, home of Antioch College. In the seventies he "worked on self-discovery the way lots of people did," as he put it. He was an obsessive polymath with a knack for computer programming and, later, a passion for James Joyce. "Joyce modestly bragged of having a grocer's assistant's mind," Barger says. "When confronted with disorder, he classified it into categories, and this has always also been my impulse. I was a big fan of *Roget's Thesaurus* in high school."

Barger's classification impulse drove him, beginning in 1970, to take on an ambitious life-project: he set out to "do psychology scientifically." Driven by an inchoate insight that the entire span of human behavior could ultimately be described and graphed, he set out to pinion the spectrum of human thought and emotion in a descriptive schema. For his raw data, he turned not to the field of actual lives, but rather to the corpus of literary fiction. "Literature," he believed, "is descriptive psychology." He began by building a file of index cards, each one recording some description of human behavior drawn from the stories of the authors he loved—like Vladimir Nabokov, Robert Stone, Thomas Pynchon, Walker Percy. Later he began devising a notational system he called "Anti-Math," a theoretical framework for recording the structures of story plots. He rolled all his ideas together and found a playful name for them that one-upped the artificial-intelligence gurus: what he was pursuing was "robot wisdom."

Like many young men of the era, Barger had what he described as an "epiphany" when he first encountered video games like Asteroids and Missile Command. But his breakthrough realization wasn't along the lines of *I'd better get a lot of quarters so I can keep playing*. Instead he taught himself programming on the Apple II and other popular personal computers of the day, and took jobs coding microcomputer versions of arcade games, because he thought the experience would serve his intellectual agenda. People had a hard time understanding his Anti-Math system; maybe, he thought, they would catch on faster if he presented it in video-game style, animated "with colored shapes on a video screen."

Anti-Math led Barger to the field of artificial intelligence, which was booming in the 1980s. He quickly decided that its leaders were doing everything backwards in their attempt to create computers that could think like people: they were focused on the software and programming end of the problem. He felt that would take care of itself once we solved the hard part: mapping out a thorough model of human psychology itself. Fortunately he'd already been working on that project for years. Previous attempts had foundered on the sheer size of the undertaking; Barger's idea was to go further down the road he'd taken with his index cards, to mine literature for the patterns and structures that programmers could eventually use to endow computers with working artificial intelligence.

> If you enumerate all the interesting categories of "human histories" on index cards, all the stories of emotion, every plausible configuration of events you'll ever need in an interactive fiction (elf meets orc, villain plots counterattack, boy kisses girl), and lay them out on the floor (of a gym, figure . . . it's gonna be a lot of cards!), so that as far as possible the most similar ones are closest together . . . what's the overall pattern?

In the archives of Barger's website you can find some fragmentary remnants of his work in this area, including "Anti-Math" and "Solace: a textbook of romantic psychology," which collects thousands of literary quotations on love and organizes them into a taxonomy of amatory wisdom. The goal of "Solace," Barger wrote, was "a new paradigm for the social sciences, making possible computer simulations of human behavior."

Barger had admired the work of Roger Schank, a scholar who studied the place of narrative in human psychology, and when Schank relocated to Northwestern University in Chicago, where Barger lived, the young man sent Schank a letter begging for a job, offering to "sharpen pencils" for a chance to work with him. For several years Barger worked at Schank's Institute for the Learning Sciences, but he was fired in 1992— according to Barger, because he asked for a forum to present his ideas, which challenged Schank's. Around the same time, Barger became immersed in Usenet—the proliferation of newsgroups that, in the days before the Web, were the Internet's most open environment for discussion and debate. If Barger couldn't get a hearing for his ideas at Northwestern, Usenet offered plenty of listeners for any idea, the more unconventional the better. Over the years Barger contributed nearly ten thousand postings—on Joyce and his other favorites, of course, but also on everything from a history of flaming to a frequently-asked-questions page on ASCII art (illustrations made out of the standard alphabet and typewriter symbols) to a memorial haiku contest for Bill Bixby. On Usenet he also got into a lot of arguments; he found that he'd become, in his words, a "lightning rod for a-holes."

When the Web came along, it sucked much of the energy out of Usenet. But Barger wasn't spending much time on the Web himself; his old computer couldn't display the graphics. In 1997 he finally got a new Mac and could see what was causing all the excitement. "By that point," he later wrote, "the Web had grown into a vast impenetrable treasure cave, generally in pitch blackness. I desperately wanted someone to 'turn on the lights' so I could see what was where, what treasures were there for my enjoyment." Barger had always seen himself as a collector and classifier, "finding good stuff and arranging it so that others can share it," as he put it. On Usenet he'd launched several experiments that involved curating "keeper" posts and organizing "best" messages. Looking out at the burgeoning Web, he saw a similar opportunity.

On December 17, 1997, Barger published the first post on a new site inspired by Winer's Scripting News and powered by Winer's Frontier

NewsPage publishing software. He wanted to give his project a catchy name, but the "news page" label often used by adopters of Winer's software didn't appeal to him: "At first I didn't intend to do 'news' at all, so I needed a different term." He went to Altavista—in those pre-Google days, the most useful search engine—and started plugging in different combinations of "web," "link," "list," "log," and similar terms to see what might be available. Ultimately he settled on "weblog." The word already had some currency as a name for the often gigantic log files that Web server programs generated—detailed records of every request for a Web page made by individual browsers. But only system administrators concerned themselves with such files, and the likelihood of confusion was small.

The term "weblog" was inspired: it had resonances—a nautical air, a *Star Trek* echo—that would help it, over the next year and a half, win out over the other labels that vied to describe the new phenomenon of personal sites with links and commentary in reverse chronological order. In christening his new site the Robot Wisdom WebLog, Barger introduced one eccentric twist: "I capitalised the L (WebLog) because the syllable 'blog' seemed so hideous."

Barger may have coined the term "weblog," but he was hardly the first collector of links. In the early days of the Web, everyone promised to find you "the good stuff" online. The slogan "More signal—less noise" had become a rallying cry for link recommenders like Hotwired or the Netsurfer Digest email newsletter. In radio, the "signal-to-noise ratio" measured the strength of a broadcast: too little signal and all you had was static. Modern radios use a variety of filters to boost their signal-to-noise ratios. So the word "filter" gradually came to describe what early webloggers saw as their job: sifting the Web's heap of informational ore for gems.

In 1995, Michael Sippey, a young product manager at a software startup company, began publishing Stating the Obvious, a series of weekly essays about the Internet and the technology industry. Similar to Dave Winer's DaveNet, he'd email you his essays if you wanted, or you could read them on the Web at theobvious.com. "It was a way for me to play," Sippey says. "The way I figure out what I think about something is that I write about it." Sippey's following grew, and in early 1997, right about the time Winer renamed his Frontier news page Scripting News, Sippey began collecting interesting links on theobvious.com under the header "Filter." "It was just a way for me to keep track, a way for me to pull my notes together and share," he recalls. At first Sippey's links were posted off to the side of his main page; later they were collected in once-a-week "Filtered for Purity" posts. In its early incarnations, the Obvious Filter didn't look or work exactly like a modern blog, but it helped establish the idea of the blogger as a human filter of the Web's overwhelming bounty.

Both Scripting News and the Obvious Filter predated the launch of Barger's Robot Wisdom WebLog. The same was true for Slashdot, a software-oriented bulletin board created in September 1997 by Rob Malda, a computer science student at Hope College in Michigan, who went by the handle "CmdrTaco." Slashdot posted "news for nerds" multiple times a day, with excerpts from and links to breaking news coverage of the tech industry organized in a reverse-chronological list. Barger was indisputably first with the term "weblog," but he had no clear claim to the "first blogger" title. There was too much "prior art," as the patent system calls it—too many examples of people doing something similar, earlier.

That didn't stop several media outlets from leaping in 2007 to declare that blogging had hit a tenth-anniversary milestone, and that Robot Wisdom was the first blog. These articles drew people out of the woodwork to declare that the publications were wrong and to claim for themselves the "first blogger" mantle. So many sites recognizable in hindsight as weblogs had preceded Barger's—not only the best-known ones, but more obscure participants like Steve Bogart, who started his NowThis.com in early 1997, and Harold Stusnick's Offhand Remarks, begun in September 1997, and Blues News, a gamers' site with a bloglike format from July 1996. What about Justin Hall, who was posting daily in January 1996? Or Howard Rheingold's Web pages of personal links, with the newest on top, begun in April 1995?

And then, of course, if you were really serious about identifying the first blogger, you could always look further back, before the Web itself. That's exactly what many commentators did as they tried to grant blogging an ever lengthier pedigree. Desktop publishing was giving Joe Average a soapbox before anyone had ever seen the letters "HTTP." Maybe the first blogger was really someone on public-access cable TV (like Wayne and Garth!), or amateur "ham" radio. Surely it was I. F. Stone, the original one-man publishing gadfly. Perhaps Dickens, the great serialist, would be a blogger today. Really, if you looked back at the pamphleteers of the American Revolution, or the British coffeehouse culture of the eighteenth century, weren't they blogging? And, you know, what about Samuel Pepys? Perhaps the first blogger could be found scratching at the walls of a cave in the Dordogne—so many stags lined up, with the newest on top!

The efforts to identify a "first blog" are comical, and ultimately futile, because blogging was not invented; it evolved. But the press relies on anniversary dates to fill in coverage that it missed the first time around. Blogging arose in relative obscurity—it got no headlines as it emerged— so the decade milestone declarations were an inevitable catch-up effort as the media tried to account for the prevalence of blogs in the new century.

Robot Wisdom earned its historical place by introducing the word *weblog*, but it was also influential through the sheer force of Barger's unbridled eccentricity. He was no confessional diarist; you weren't going to hear from him about who he was sleeping with or what he had for lunch. But if you followed Robot Wisdom you would very quickly get a sense of his passions and delights. You'd know that he loved Joyce (early on he started a "This Day in Joyce History" feature) and also singer-songwriter Kate Bush. That he religiously kept up with mainstream literary outlets as well as the underground press. That he followed Web design and science, and also politics and movies, but in each realm cut his own path according to specific passions.

One of Barger's early enthusiasms was for the work of Ana Voog, a musician and performance artist who—like the more famous Jennifer Ringley of Jennicam—turned a video camera on herself and streamed it out to the Web, 24/7. The brief "camgirl" craze that followed had a prurient tinge, but Voog didn't tart herself up; she presented herself online as a sort of experiment in transparency, and nudity was just a natural part of the deal. Barger appreciated the purity of this aesthetic, and credits Voog (along with Joyce) for inspiring his prime directive: never censor yourself. "I try to make it my ethic that whenever I see something that I enjoy, I don't filter. You know, if it's some silly thing about a TV commercial, I won't say, well, that's too frivolous."

Filter the Web, not yourself. The organizing principle of Barger's weblog wasn't a novelty; he was simply applying the venerable idea of critical sensibility to the Web. For a long while, his email signature line read, "I edit the Net." Self-motivated and proudly unconventional, Barger wasn't trying to target a particular audience or formulate a mix. He was collecting his own treasures and laying them out for you to admire.

It's difficult now, a decade later, to recall how disorienting it was at first to stumble on Barger's wild link-collecting enterprise. Web users were far more familiar with other kinds of one-person websites, built on recognizable models inherited from the traditional media world.

On January 17, 1998, shortly after Barger's weblog launched, Matt Drudge, the operator of a one-man politics-and-entertainment gossip site called the Drudge Report, posted a report that *Newsweek* had killed a story about sexual shenanigans in the White House. It was thereby that the American public first heard the name Monica Lewinsky from a young man operating solo from his apartment in Los Angeles. Because

Drudge's site was already widely read by journalists and news addicts, this immediately put the Clinton scandal into play in the wider news arena.

Matt Drudge was neither a confessional diarist nor a curator of unusual links. He was an old-fashioned gossip columnist, a self-appointed Walter Winchell for the Web. He'd started distributing an email newsletter soon after his father, concerned about his aimlessness, bought him a Packard Bell PC in 1994. Drudge worked in Hollywood, at the gift shop at CBS Studios, and he shared tidbits of celebrity gossip and right-wing political news with his subscribers. His success at unearthing small scoops got his work picked up by America Online and Wired News; he also built his own bare-bones website and gradually transferred his efforts to it. Drudge had already won some Beltway notoriety in 1997, when he fought a highly publicized $30-million libel suit by Clinton White House aide Sidney Blumenthal over a false report that Blumenthal abused his wife. The 1998 Lewinsky story instantly kicked the Drudge Report to a new, higher level of influence and fame.

When pundits launch their expeditions to find the "first" blogger, they often haul in Drudge's name. That's understandable, but a mistake. His site, with its tabloid headlines and wire-report typography, has become an institution in the American media, and today he is routinely awarded labels like "the Walter Cronkite of his era" and even "the most powerful journalist in America." Drudge controls a powerful fire hose of traffic; he has "flow" like a tsunami, and a Drudge Report link is worth big money to many a news site. But there simply isn't enough Drudge in the Drudge Report to consider his site a weblog.

From the famous Oval Office oral sex act all the way to the John Edwards four-hundred-dollar-haircut story in the 2008 election, Drudge has built his career on trumpeting the private foibles of public figures. Yet he is a reclusive figure himself, to an almost pathological degree. I was hardly surprised to receive no response from Drudge to my requests for an interview for this book. But it was amusing to read, in a probing *New York* magazine profile by Philip Weiss (for which Drudge also refused to talk), that the closest thing Drudge ever had to an associate, conservative writer Andrew Breitbart, claimed that "I haven't talked to him in over a year." Weiss wrote: "[Drudge] has utterly compartmentalized his life, separating the personal and the public. Acquaintances describe very brief, formal encounters, and even friends of Drudge's, if there is such a category, generally communicate with him by IM."

Drudge's end-run around the traditional media with the Lewinsky scoop was a major lesson for the press that the rules of their game were breaking down—and that one young guy with few dollars and no credentials could rewrite them. But when blogs began to win mainstream notice a couple of years later, Drudge resisted the suggestion that the Report was a blog, too. And he was right: all he shared with them was his autonomy as a self-publisher. His notoriously disorganized website did not follow the blogs' new-stuff-on-top design. He offered tons of links, but precious little commentary or annotation. You certainly couldn't get any sense of Matt Drudge as a person from his site—beyond seeing that he had become extremely accomplished at quickly posting insidery scoops about political and entertainment figures ahead of his mainstream competition. He served his readers primarily as "a gateway for conventional journalism," as one media watcher put it. He cherished his outsider's stance, but the fedora he habitually wore proclaimed that he coveted the old-fashioned role of hardbitten journalistic insider. His nearly unreadable 2000 autobiography, *The Drudge Manifesto*, records both his ambition to become a "player" and his satisfaction at having achieved that status.

The Drudge Report's product didn't look like traditional media, and it wasn't staffed like a traditional newsroom, but its modus operandi was conventional at heart. Like most broadcasters and editors, Drudge staked out some general turf and then selected items based on broad appeal to his readers. In effect, he said to his visitors, "These are things that I think would be of interest to as many of you as possible." It's a practical plan for success, and it has worked for Drudge; lucrative advertising on his low-cost site eventually financed his move from the low-rent L.A. apartment to a fancy Miami condo, and in 2008 it's estimated that the site grosses over $1 million a year, nearly all of it profit.

But the blogging ethos—shared by Hall and Winer and Sippey and Barger and all the other early weblog enthusiasts who would soon follow their leads—was different. These under-the-radar upstarts said, "Here are things that are of interest *to me*. Maybe you'll like them, too." Clutching their self-determination defiantly, they checked out of the race for traffic and influence in the existing media world. Instead they set out to construct a new, alternate universe—one in which some of the laws of the old world still held, but others were suspended or upended.

In 1998, webloggers as we know them today first became conscious of themselves as a group—as practitioners of a defined form who constituted a distinct community. They were more than isolated geeks, but not yet a trend or a movement. To most of them, the little virtual scene they were creating together felt like a small circle of friends.

Jesse James Garrett was working in Long Beach, California, as an editor at a corporate website. He had lots of little gaps in his workday, time to surf and find links to interesting new stuff and email them, with comments, to his friends. In early 1998 he decided it would make more sense to post those annotated links on the Web, and—inspired by Michael Sippey's Filter and by Suck—he started a project on his website that he called Infosift. "I wanted to see if I could transform what had been an act of consumption in these dead times at my desk—If I could turn reading the Internet into making the Internet," Garrett says.

As Garrett's surfing breaks continued through the summer and fall of 1998, he began to notice that he was regularly stumbling on other sites that were organized just like Infosift—there was Scripting News, and Robot Wisdom, of course, but there were also other new weblogs sprouting across the landscape, some running on Winer's NewsPage software, others using some kind of home-built jury-rigged software platform, others with the HTML coded entirely by hand. One of the sites Garrett discovered was CamWorld, started by Web developer Cameron Barrett in June 1997. Barrett was teaching an introductory Web class at the local community college in Michigan, and he decided that he'd just put all his course materials on his website, along with links he thought his students might find useful. At around the same time, he'd come across Scripting News and liked what he saw, so he modeled his site on Winer's. He picked his name as a jokingly egotistical parody of *Macworld*; only later did he realize that it gave people the wrong impression: they thought he was compiling reviews of photographic equipment or information on "cam" sites like Jennicam.

In November 1998, Garrett began exchanging emails with Barrett about these weblog-like sites they were each discovering, and he let drop that he had begun assembling a short list of them—bookmarks for his own use when he searched for new links for Infosift. Barrett asked to see it, and Garrett sent it off—a dozen URLs that, he cautioned Barrett, he hadn't had time to filter for quality yet. Barrett took Garrett's list, added some links of his own, and posted them all on CamWorld. It became the first instance of what we now call a "blogroll"—a list of simpatico sites that a blogger acknowledges as a sort of posse or tribe.

Garrett seems to have compiled the first-ever list of weblogs, but Barrett was the first to post it, and that was what made the Garrett-to-Barrett handoff significant. "Cameron had the insight that the list was more valuable if it was public," Garrett says. Once there was a public list, people wanted to be on it—both for the recognition that inclusion would confer and for the actual click-through traffic it might direct. The list began growing quickly, as people who maintained sites that updated frequently, with links ordered in reverse, found it and emailed Barrett, asking to be added.

"There were all these isolated pockets, like tide pools," Garrett says. "Late in 1998 it really started to dawn on me that something bigger was happening. This same form had developed in isolation—it was like convergent evolution. When different animals evolve toward the same solution to a problem, what that means is there's something about the environment that's shaping that evolution. In this case the environment was the Web itself."

Some of the sites Barrett compiled—those that had been inspired by Barger's Robot Wisdom—called themselves "weblogs." Some of them—those inspired by Winer's Scripting News—adopted the name "news pages." Others identified themselves as "filters" or "link lists." At first it was easy to tell which sites belonged on the CamWorld list—Garrett had started simply by looking for "sites like mine." But the list didn't mean anything unless it had some boundaries; sooner or later somebody was going to have to be excluded. The general rule among the early blogrolls was to stick to amateur, one-person sites that posted lists of annotated links. Most of the time that meant excluding popular group sites like Slashdot; established tech-news email newsletters that pointed readers to interesting links (like Ric Ford's Macintouch, Keith Dawson's Tasty Bits from the Technology Front, and Adam Engst's TidBITS); and weblog-style features on newspaper sites, like the *San Jose Mercury News*' tech-news roundup, Good Morning Silicon Valley.

The other group that tended to get left out of the first blogrolls was the community of Web diarists and journal keepers, from Justin Hall to popular diarists like Alexis Massie, and publishers of personal 'zine-style sites like Derek Powazek, whose Fray.com was a well-tended Web community dedicated to true-life stories. The traits that set the newer sites apart from these predecessors, the distinctive markings that Garrett recognized as "sites like mine," included the increasingly common reverse chronological organization and the central role of links, but also a focus outward toward information on the wider Web, rather than inward on personal experience.

Garrett describes the transition as one from a static to a dynamic form. "At first, if you were doing any kind of personal website, I think people approached it as a hobby like woodworking: you were gonna craft this beautiful little object. People would build these shrines to their interests—everything you need to know about *Babylon 5*. When you crossed the threshold to weblogs, that represents our realization that this is a dynamic medium. It's not about pushing an object into the world, it's about opening a channel between yourself and the world."

Those channels multiplied quickly, not only through the sense of excitement shared by participants in the new scene, who felt that they were onto something important, but also through the links they provided to one another. In 1998 and well into 1999, it remained possible for anyone with a little time on his hands and a list of links like the one on CamWorld to keep up with the entire weblog world every day. An ethos of giving credit took hold: if you were going to add a link to your weblog that you found on someone else's, you would note its origin, typically with a "via" link pointing back to the source.

"Via" links were both a courtesy and a concrete way of sharing traffic through frequent cross-links. Each time you clicked on a link and hopped from weblog to weblog, the author of the weblog that you landed upon would find out where you came from by looking at his server's logs. He wouldn't know who you were, but based on your click, he'd know whose link you'd followed, and thereby who was linking to him. These referrer-log references were like electronic calling cards that your Web browser automatically dropped on the doorstep of sites you visited. Each one provided the address of the site you came from—thereby alerting the recipient to new posts that linked to his site and perhaps said something friendly, or nasty. That helped knit together a new social Web of friendships and rivalries.

In 1998, Rebecca Blood, a Web designer working at the University of Washington in Seattle, happened upon both Scripting News and Cam-World and through them the small community of early webloggers. She'd been in the habit of sending a daily email with links to a group of friends; in April 1999 she decided to start posting them on a new weblog instead. She started Rebecca's Pocket carefully, with no fanfare or announcement, but a week after its launch, on April 30, she found that Jesse James Garrett had reposted one of her April 27 links—to an offbeat wire story, "Japan Sumo Association to crack down on obesity." Garrett added the comment "File under 'unclear on the concept,'" and appended the link "(Found in Rebecca's pocket.)." Garrett had discovered the otherwise obscure Rebecca's Pocket because Blood had clicked on her own link to his site, thereby showing up in his referrer logs. One thing led to another, and within a few weeks the two were dating. They married in 2001.

Blood wrote the first history of weblogs, a 2000 essay that captured the idealism of the era in which she and Garrett were introduced by their log files. She described webloggers as participants in a new form of media criticism, whose links and pointers could expose flaws in the work of professional journalists and add context that readers might have missed. She also described how the daily exercise of posting to her weblog helped her discover what her true interests were: Where did all these links to archaeology articles come from? Oh, right, she'd actually been interested in the subject as a child, but had never pursued it. And she found that the act of writing for public consumption bolstered her confidence in the value of her perspective.

For Blood, weblogs could be tools for both personal and social change. "By writing a few lines each day," she wrote, "weblog editors begin to redefine media as a public, participatory endeavor."

It was, perhaps, too much significance to hang on "a few lines a day," and there were plenty of skeptics ready to prick the balloon of the new weblog community's sense of its own importance. In May 1999, as the first coverage of weblogging began appearing in the media, Leslie Harpold—who, as a founder of Smug.com, represented a previous wave of personal-publishing enthusiasts—published a short piece titled "Logrolling," in which she counseled the aspiring weblogger: "Don't do it! . . . What makes a select few Web logs good is that they are select and few. . . . If Web Logs become as ubiquitous as the cargo pant, the stylishness and cachet will be wholly depleted and it will be gone faster than the wrap sandwich." In June, another 'zine editor named Ben Brown took a more gleefully vicious line on weblogs in his Teethmag.com "Open Letter to All You Webloggers": "There can't be that much lint in all your navels at the same time. . . . It's the same old shit in the same old package. . . . Sorry, buddy—you're just a dork who can't come up with anything more than a paragraph or two to say every day. You're not a designer, you're not a writer, and you're not an editor! . . . Please, for my sake, and for the sake of the Internet, stop talking about yourselves like you're some kind of fucking innovators. There have been link lists since the beginning of the web, and you ain't nothing special."

Maybe they weren't all great innovators, but to them, what they were doing felt special. Aside from Dave Winer and Jorn Barger, nearly all of the people who started weblogs in 1997, 1998, and early 1999 were young laborers in the booming Web industry. In their day jobs they built boring sites for companies, managed office computer networks, or wrote snippets of program code. On their own time they posted little bits of themselves and their perspectives to their weblogs. Like participants in any small scene, they wrote their links primarily to amuse and impress one another. All of which would be unremarkable—except that this experience gave them a taste of a particular kind of satisfaction that was new and unique to the Web.

People had always written journals for themselves—all it took was time and the effort of writing. But publishing for any size audience demanded more: even a little newsletter or 'zine on paper required supplies and postage. The rise of the Internet opened new doors; suddenly, for the minimal price of some server space and a dial-up connection (and later, even less), you could publish your words for an audience that was potentially in the millions. In practice, the emphasis here was on the "potentially." Most of the early weblogs saw precious little traffic. It was theoretically possible for a particularly noteworthy or funny or outré post to get picked up and linked to from enough other websites to grant unknown Web writers their proverbial fifteen minutes of fame. But the reality of most webloggers' everyday experience was, as the quip went, being "famous for fifteen people."

Laboring in such relative obscurity didn't dishearten them. They were generally satisfied to select their tasty link treats, craft snappy or sarcastic headlines, and share them within the small circles of their blogrolls and with whatever other "lurker" readers they'd attracted. Most of them were not gauging success or failure on their hit counts. At the time, none of them ran advertising, so tracking traffic numbers didn't matter as much, anyway.

It was this experience—of not hungering for a big score, of being okay with writing for a small community—that remained utterly incomprehensible to virtually all of the professional journalists who were just beginning to turn their attention to the subject. What was the point of making media, writing Web pages and sharing links, if you weren't going to be widely read? (It was a bit ironic to encounter this attitude from newspaper reporters and broadcast journalists, because those same journalists often looked down their noses at the way newfangled professional Web publications like Salon.com, where I worked, paid attention to "hit counts"—granular reports of how many readers viewed each article. Web writers and editors, the old-timers sniffed, were going to become mere slaves to their traffic reports! On the Web, apparently, you were damned if you cared about traffic, and damned if you didn't.)

The old-school reporters—whose industries, after all, were driven by circulation figures and ratings—were imprisoned by perspectives shaped by careers in for-profit mass communication. The idea of putting long-term effort into writing for a handful of readers simply made no sense to them. Wasn't it just a hobby, and didn't that make it essentially insignificant and inconsequential? Once you realized that your weblog wasn't going to make you rich or famous, wouldn't you just give up?

Jorn Barger kept up an impressive output on his Robot Wisdom WebLog in 1998 and 1999. Early on, at a time when many of the new webloggers were posting only once or twice a day, he rewarded frequent visitors with a flood of updates. Eventually he took to dividing up his posts between an infrequent, longer format—for him, that meant a couple of sentences, even a paragraph or two—and briefer links annotated by just a few words. Over time, he dropped the long form, and favored an ever-more-telegraphic style, with a column of brief links centered between the left and right margins. He called this "optimizing the linktext"; the weblog read like a series of koans addressing a mesmerizing sequence of arcana. You could pick out sets of three at random and be amazed.

Competent synopsis of Wm Blake's life and legacy (IrishTimes)

Detailed critique of AOL's WebTV-competitor (SJMerc)

Industrial chemistry of nanotube fibers (BBC)

or

Popocatepetl has been very active lately (live Mexican webcam)

Mysterious correlation between immune system and promiscuity in primates (UniSci)

Sensitive update on Linda 'Deep Throat' Lovelace (NYPress)

Robot Wisdom's bounty, in both quantity and quality, flowed from the hours Barger could dedicate to it. Job-free, he led a hand-to-mouth existence. "I live on bread and water," he told one interviewer, "so as not to submit to the idiots." But as the rest of the weblog world began to grow and evolve, Barger found it harder to fit in. Simultaneously, even his low-budget lifestyle grew difficult to sustain financially. Beginning around 2000, his posting became less frequent. In December 2001 he went silent for a couple of months. He had explained to his readers that he'd run out of money, and asked for contributions and suggestions: "I have a gigantic psychological block against Mammon-in-general, and no long-term ideas how to overcome it. Alternative currency? Retreat to a cave?"

The following years were marked by further hiatuses, culminating in a period in 2005 when the Robot Wisdom domain went dead. In *Wired*, Paul Boutin reported that he'd encountered Barger "homeless and broke" on the street in San Francisco, hiding behind his back a panhandling sign that read "Coined the term 'weblog,' never made a dime." Barger declared that the story was "a libelous fiction." He wasn't living on the street, but rather staying on the sofa of Andrew Orlowski, a British technology journalist in the Bay Area who'd written an admiring piece about Robot Wisdom in 2002. The sign was a joke that Barger had used once to try to strike up conversations, Orlowski says, explaining, "He's shy. I don't think he's ever been homeless, though. He can live on a dollar a day."

Eccentricity, reclusiveness, and money troubles could be reason enough for a weblog's slow fade-out. But in Barger's case there was another factor at work. On December 26, 1999, he'd posted a link to what he described as a "long, extremely lucid (and appalling) history of Jewish fundamentalism, by Israel Shahak," along with lengthy excerpts. Shahak was an outspoken and controversial critic of Zionism. It was hardly unusual for Barger, or anyone else on the Web, to link to outspoken, controversial figures. But in January a writer named Leonard Grossman published a long essay on his own website raising questions about Barger's post:

> It contained strangely concatenated political and historical arguments with irrelevant but inflammatory quotations purportedly taken from the Talmud and other sources of Jewish law (Halacha). It presented questionable interpretations of current practices among Orthodox Jews in Israel. All of these were drawn from the text

of the article, but in a way that heightened their inflam-
matory nature.

Grossman didn't draw any conclusions about Barger's motives, but he wrote, "How did I know something was wrong? I trusted my stomach. Something just did not seem right." Grossman also offered references that refuted some of the details in the passages Barger had excerpted, and discussed whether webloggers had a duty to vet material they were posting. It was a verbose but sober critique—more the sort of thing you might find in an academic journal than on the flame-infested forums of the Net. But, given Barger's place in the weblog world, Grossman's piece got widely linked and discussed.

Barger did not take his new notoriety well. In a comment on one message board discussing the controversy, he wrote:

> Webloggers gamble their reputation with every link they offer. If they link to a page that consists entirely of character assassination, they lose my respect. (Grossman's page is entirely character assassination.)

Given Grossman's careful analysis, measured tone, and caution to avoid ad hominem criticism of Barger himself, the response came off as thin-skinned. It was, in fact, Barger's own reputation that was beginning to fray.

I'd long been a regular reader of Robot Wisdom, and I remember skimming over this controversy at the time, thinking that it confirmed my sense of Barger as a bit of a loose cannon (along with my despair that the Web could ever be a home to reasoned debate about Israel). As a nonobservant American Jew with my own long-standing questions and doubts about Israel and its part in the continuing agony of the Middle East, I had no problem with Barger, or anyone else, criticizing the Israeli government or its policies. (Salon, where I then worked as managing editor, was regularly accused of anti-Semitism for publishing criticism of Israel that I usually found legitimate.) But I wanted to feel I could trust the motivations and intellectual honesty of the webloggers to whom I was handing a little of my attention each day. I continued to read Robot Wisdom, as I think most of Barger's regular readers did. But I was now a bit more on guard.

Later in 2000, Barger's weblog output began to include more links that attacked Israel. He seemed determined to demonstrate that he was not going to cave to criticism; backing down would be tantamount to "censoring" himself. Still, I kept reading him. But eventually, it seemed to me, Barger moved from criticizing the state of Israel to attacking Jews. In December 2000 he linked to an article in the London *Times* with the comment "Is Judaism simply a religion of lawless racists?" When he faced an inevitable storm of criticism, he defended himself by pointing to the question mark and declaring that his critics were trying to intimidate him. Then he posted another question: "Are Jews incapable of polite discourse?"

At this point, one could reasonably ask—being sure to include the question mark: Was Barger an anti-Semite?

He was a strange and complex guy. I couldn't say for sure. Andrew Orlowski says Barger "doesn't have a hateful bone in his body." That may well be true. As I read his posts in 2000, I simply felt that a bond between blogger and reader had broken. My Web time was too precious to entrust to someone whose motivations I questioned with his every choice of link. Sadly, I removed Robot Wisdom from my bookmark list.

On those occasions when I revisited the site, I felt I'd made the right choice. In 2008 you could find the following line at the top of Barger's page:

judaism is racism is incompatible with humanity

The early webloggers of 1998 and 1999, human filters of the Web, had the idea that you could, and would, get to know them through their choice of links. They wouldn't have to compose lengthy life stories online; they would write their own intellectual autobiographies, one link at a time.

In an autobiographical page published in 2006, Barger pinpointed his post about Shahak in December 1999 as the turning point for the popularity of Robot Wisdom. (By this time he'd adopted a style of short lines with frequent breaks that recalled Justin Hall's diary pages.)

> my independence consistently
> rubbed people the wrong way
>
> and the more articulate i got
> the more extreme
> became my isolation . . .
>
> the blog was an attempt
> to bridge that rift
> a window of opportunity
> when quality web-content
> was hard to find
>
> and so long as
> my conventional tastes
> sufficiently balanced my heresies
> my blog audience grew
>
> but once i'd linked
> shahak
> and other critics of israel
> the balance catastrophically
> and vituperatively
> shifted
>
> hardly anyone dared link me anymore

In one sense, Barger was right: webloggers did stop linking to him as they began to sense something troubling in his posts and links about Israel and Jews. But I don't think it was because they didn't "dare" to do so. I think they understood that in the world of weblogs, you were what you linked to. And many of them decided that Barger's site, once a cornucopia of offbeat delights, had become objectionable. Neither in unison nor in concert, but at roughly the same time, they de-linked him.

To Barger, this rejection must have felt like a confirmation that he was simply too much of a heretic for the conformists of the Web world. It was as if he had consulted that deck of index cards he'd assembled, his compendium of patterns of human behavior drawn from literature, and found the one that he believed matched what had happened to him. He was the ostracized freethinker, an enemy of the people shunned by the close-minded herd. He didn't seem to entertain the possibility that he had simply "gambled his reputation with his links," and lost.

■ ■ ■ Part Two

SCALING UP

Chapter 4

THE BLOGGER CATAPULT
EVAN WILLIAMS, MEG HOURIHAN

▌n May 1999, Peter Merholz, a puckish, brainy Web designer in the Bay Area, posted a little note in the side margin of Peterme.com, the weblog he'd been writing for a year:

> For What It's Worth
>
> I've decided to pronounce the word "weblog" as wee'-blog. Or "blog" for short.

The observation didn't even merit a full weblog posting; Merholz used his left-hand column for ephemera and tossed-off asides, and, since he was "feeling silly," that's where he put it. It was a lark, a riff making fun of the term *weblog*, which at that point was only just gaining currency among Web insiders.

The coinage didn't exactly spread like wildfire. But the cozy circle of veteran webloggers picked up Merholz's joke and repeated it to one another. It was compact and funny, and even its awkwardness—Jorn Barger had considered the syllable "hideous"—worked to its advantage.

Blog wore its lack of a marketing pedigree proudly; no corporate committee could possibly have signed off on a term that sounded, as Merholz approvingly observed, "roughly onomatopoeic of vomiting." To Merholz, that was only accurate, since "these sites (mine included!) tend to be a kind of information upchucking." And because the word was new and up for grabs, you could bend it to your grammatical needs; it could do service as both noun and verb.

Still, *blog* would probably have languished as an obscure neologism if it hadn't been for its embrace by an equally obscure team of twenty-something Web geeks in San Francisco laboring in a South of Market basement. Evan Williams and Meg Hourihan had started their company, Pyra, at the beginning of 1999, with the goal of producing novel, ambitious software for group collaboration. In August 1999 they unveiled a little side project called Blogger. The fruit of a week's worth of programming labor, Blogger was a free tool for automating the updating of personal weblogs. It took off almost immediately, and its success made the "blog" label stick.

Blogger was neither the first such tool nor the most sophisticated nor, at the time, the easiest to use. But it was the one that ultimately transformed blogging from an arcane pastime for Web insiders into a mass-market, anyone-can-play phenomenon. In the technology industry this sort of success is sometimes described as "deploying to scale" or "scaling up" or simply "scaling." It took years to happen for Blogger. But the scale that Blogger ultimately reached, via a boom-and-bust-and-boom-again saga that mirrored the convulsions of the entire Web industry, was millions of users—an outcome that at its conception looked improbable if not downright impossible, even to its creators.

This was partly because the Web industry of the time was infatuated with the "e-commerce plays" and big "content" investments that were widely viewed as the future of the medium. But it was also because, ironically, Blogger itself wasn't originally designed and positioned for the average Web user at all. Blogger was intended for specialists: HTML jockeys and font nerds and design devotees—people who thought of themselves as "Web geeks." People like Evan Williams and Meg Hourihan.

By the time he moved to California in 1997, Evan Williams had already started two companies—and folded them. At the age of twenty-five, this entrepreneurship was his defining trait, and one that he used as his calling card. Growing up as a geeky kid on a farm in Nebraska, he'd always known he would start "my own thing." His father used an IBM PC to manage the farm, and he'd taken a high school programming class, but the computer bug didn't bite hard until he'd dropped out of college in 1992 and begun looking for his first entrepreneurial opportunity. He found it in CD-ROMs, which, in those pre-Web days, were the Next Big Thing in electronic publishing. With some money from his dad, Williams's new firm, Plexus Tech, started releasing products in 1993.

The first was a pair of CD-ROM guides to Nebraska's beloved Huskers football team. "That seemed like a great idea," Williams recalls, "but the overlap of people who had computers with CD-ROM drives and the Husker football crowd just wasn't that great." His 1994 video guide to getting onto the Internet was a bit more successful.

As the Net boom arrived in Nebraska, Plexus shifted its business to Web hosting and services, and Williams began to learn to program. "We wanted to create software, but we didn't know what we were doing. We were just trying to pay the bills and think of projects. We didn't finish very many." Slowly but steadily, Plexus ran out of money. A second company—named Evhead after Williams's boyhood nickname—met the same fate. "I was really beaten down," Williams says. "I'd lost a lot of my father's money. It was painful." He decided it was time to give up on Nebraska—"there was no one around for me to learn from"—and light out for the West Coast.

In 1997, Williams took a job with O'Reilly, the technology-books publisher in Sebastopol, California, an hour north of San Francisco. Writing code for the O'Reilly website was Williams's "first real job," and it gave him a chance to "see how a company is run, and how you work in an office."

Williams only lasted a few months at O'Reilly. The job had gotten him out of Nebraska and helped him meet people in the industry. But now it was time to pick up where he'd left off and plot his next venture. He moved to San Francisco, began taking on some freelance work, and tried to network. It wasn't hard to get started: during the late-nineties Web boom, the contracts for software developers were bountiful. So were the parties.

At the start of July 1998, Williams showed up for an industry mixer at a bar in San Francisco's South of Market warehouse district and found himself sitting in a curved booth with a quartet of young women. He introduced himself to the one next to him. Meg Hourihan was her name. She was a consultant doing insurance software. Hey, he was a consultant, too—doing independent web development! Web development? Cool—that was what she really wanted to be doing, she told him. He showed her the new keyboard attachment for his Palm Pilot. She talked about how the suits she consulted for just didn't get the Web.

At some point the women all stood up and left and got into a cab. Then they looked at each other and one of them said, "We struck out! Nothing happened! We're supposed to be meeting people! We didn't meet any guys!"

"That guy Ev was kind of cute," another said. "Let's go bring him along." She went back into the bar, pulled Williams out, and told him he was going on to the next stop with them. He wedged into the back of the taxi, once again next to Meg. It was at the next bar, somewhere in the Marina, that the two really began to talk. "He was the first person I met who really seemed to love the Web the way I did," Hourihan remembers.

Hourihan loved the Web as only an English major with a geeky streak could—but she also had a pragmatic head for business. She'd parlayed her Microsoft Word skills into a job doing desktop publishing at a Boston investment firm in the early nineties. When the company decided to experiment with posting prospectuses on the newfangled World Wide Web, she jumped at the chance to learn Web publishing. She down-loaded and printed an HTML primer, taught herself the tags, and posted the first few prospectuses online. The work quickly turned monotonous, though, and she moved on, to a tech-support job with a consultancy in Marin County. Her brief Web experience was enough to make her the in-house expert in the new field, and before long she was jetting around to client meetings, telling insurance-company VPs that in the future people would simply buy policies directly on the Web, and receiving blank stares of incomprehension back from them. "It was a crazy job," Hourihan says now. "I didn't know anything—I was twenty-five years old. But I knew I didn't see the sense in buying something from a person when I could do it from a machine and not have to face the salespeople's wheeling and dealing."

So Ev and Meg sat together that night for a good long while and talked about the Web. At the end, they exchanged email addresses. Soon they began dating. Meg had quit her job—she was tired of traveling and eager to begin doing her thing on the Web. But she wasn't ready to strike out entirely on her own. So she signed on with a small Web consulting outfit in San Francisco where she thought she might get to work on projects that interested her. But the little company was in the middle of being acquired by a big company called Proxicom, and Hourihan quickly found herself miserable. When she tried to speak up on a conference call and was told to keep quiet, she knew it was over: "I went to Montessori school from a very young age, and I am just not a good follower, not a good employee." A manager had once told her, "You've got a lot of poten-tial, but you need to learn to suffer fools better."

It was fall 1998, and dotcom mania had taken over the Bay Area. By rights, two ambitious young Web types could have grabbed jobs at com-panies that were about to go public and begin counting their stock options. Ev and Meg had other ideas. As Hourihan posted a couple of years later on her blog, Megnut:

> A friend told me this story: he met a web designer at a
> party the other night, he says, "oh, do you have a per-
> sonal site?" Her answer, "no." And I realized there are

dot-com people and there are web people. Dot-com people work for start-ups injected with large Silicon Valley coin, they have options, they talk options, they dream options. They have IPOs. They're richer after four months of "web" work than many web people who've been doing it since the beginning. They don't have personal sites. They don't want personal sites. They don't get personal sites. They don't get personal. Web people can tell you the first site they ever saw, they can tell you the moment they knew: This, This Is It, I Will Do This. And they pour themselves into the web, with stories, with designs, with pictures. They create things worth looking at, worth reading, worth coveting, worth envying, worth loving.

Meg and Ev both wanted to make worthy things. They eyed the lookalike e-commerce shops and the ballooning consultancies and all the other enterprises of the new gold rush, and said to each other, "I don't want to work at any of those places." Their romantic relationship had quickly fizzled, but they still enjoyed each other's company, and they shared a youthful enthusiasm for the startup-company life. When Ev told Meg about his idea for developing a Web-based project management tool, her eyes lit up. She quit Proxicom, even though her friends told her she was crazy to give up the stock options. "I said, 'I don't care—this is stupid, it isn't interesting or fun to me.'" And Pyra Labs was born.

In starting their new business, Williams and Hourihan shared a couple of assumptions. First, they wouldn't subscribe to the prevalent get-rich-quick dotcom model, which involved acquiring a vast base of users and then selling stock to the public without worrying about how you were actually going to bring in revenue. Williams already knew firsthand the pain of running out of cash. Pyra would be a real, honest business, with a plan for profit from the start. In an essay published on his personal site in November 1998, under the tongue-in-cheek headline, "New Evidence Suggests Startling Reason Many Internet Startups Fail,"

Williams wrote, "The real reason most Internet start-ups fail is because . . . they do stupid things!" Things like paying millions of dollars for TV ads during the Super Bowl, a profoundly inefficient means of driving people to visit your website. Pyra's founders were determined to eschew such stupidity. They did not believe that "if you build it, they will come" constituted a business plan.

Williams and Hourihan's other assumption was that the future belonged to software tools that worked across the Web and inside the Web browser. Services like Hotmail and Yahoo Mail had already shown how this worked for email: to use them, you didn't need to download an email program, install it, and run it in a separate window—you just signed up on a website and sent and received your messages there. Pyra would blaze a wider trail through the infant genre of Web-based application software: it would serve the burgeoning new class of Web designers and developers, who already understood the power of the new software platform, by providing them with a Web-based program for managing all the information and communications surrounding a project, storing it in one place online that was accessible from anywhere. Ev and Meg knew their product—which they came to call the Pyra App—would succeed because it was the set of tools they'd always needed in their own Web projects and consulting gigs.

In December 1998 they set up shop in the living room of Meg's apartment in the Inner Sunset district, just over a hill from the Haight. The heat didn't work, and when the fog blew straight in from the Pacific, they would shiver in the cold. But there were two desks and a whiteboard, and they were doing exactly what they wanted, and the room soon filled with the crackling of ideas. There were, in fact, so many ideas flying, so many links to pass along and brainstorms to share, that they quickly ran into a problem: How would they coordinate their work? That shouldn't have been so hard; after all, they were just two people working together in a room. Still, email wasn't right. "If I emailed Ev something," Hourihan says, "it was gone." Neither did it make sense to just interrupt each other every time they found a link to share. They couldn't use the

Pyra App because it didn't exist, yet. They decided they needed a website to store and share their random notes to each other.

Williams had recently added a weblog-style section to his personal site, Evhead.com. It was common at the time for webloggers to update their sites by hand, just typing HTML code directly into a file; many of the first generation of webloggers were web designers who could code HTML in their sleep. But Williams was a software developer who thought in terms of tools that automate routine tasks and store text in databases. So he'd written a little script that would automatically add new posts to the Evhead weblog. It couldn't have been simpler: it was just a browser page that showed the Evhead blog on top and, below that, a blank text-entry box with a "save" button underneath it. That box would only show for Ev, logged in as the owner of the weblog. It was like his own private drop box for posts, and it made adding new material really easy—or, as the industry jargon went, *friction-free*.

Williams quickly found that his new posting tool transformed his relationship to his website. "I had an epiphany, I guess," he says. "The site changed from an occasional creative outlet that I would do when I had time, to much more of a linked outlet for my brain. It became a habit. When I saw something interesting on the Web, I had a thought or read a quote I liked—boom! That went into this form and out on this page."

As the living room office began to percolate with Williams and Hourihan's ideas, Ev took a copy of his Evhead weblog script and installed it on Pyra's lone development server. He named it Stuff.Pyra, but they called it just plain Stuff. The two would use this impromptu blog as their shared private bulletin board—a place to post things that could be reviewed at leisure. A crude version of what the corporate world would later call an "intranet," it had the great virtue of being dirt-simple. And it quickly filled up with, well, stuff: links to articles that demonstrated why the world needed the Pyra App, inspirational quotes about startup-company wisdom, insights into product design. It also served more frivolous purposes, like tracking the music playlists in their little office or documenting late-night drinking excursions.

Most startup companies waved ambitious business plans under the noses of venture capitalists to raise investment capital. Pyra was instead self-financed off the proceeds of software-development contract work Williams had lined up with Hewlett-Packard (to build Web applications for the company's internal use). That kept Pyra small but honest. In April 1999, Hourihan and Williams made their first hire—a programmer named Paul Bausch, who'd hung out at Williams's Plexus in the old days and had relocated to the West Coast for proximity to his girlfriend. There was no room in Meg's living room for a third desk, so Pyra moved into a real office—a leaky warehouse basement on Townsend Street that had recently been vacated by a car-parts company. The space came with an unexpected bonus: a speedy T1 Internet connection, left over from a previous upstairs tenant, whose provider never seemed to expect payment. When Bausch came on board, Stuff made it easy for him to catch up fast with Pyra's plans.

Pyra was beginning to to get a bit of buzz on the Web, and in order to stoke interest in their work, Ev and Meg decided they needed to make the company's website livelier. They were already packing tons of information into Stuff, but it was only available inside the office; why not put some of that material on the public site? They could just add a little checkbox next to the posting form, so that each time you wrote a new post, if it was suitable for public distribution, you'd just check the box— and a script would copy the post over from the for-staff-only Stuff server to the public Pyra server. Bausch, who had already converted his own website to a weblog using scripts he'd written himself, quickly whipped up the code, and in late May 1999, much Stuff began flowing from inside the Pyra office out onto the Web via the new weblog, Pyralerts.

The company was getting ready to release an incomplete "beta" version of the Pyra App that summer. But it had already dawned on everyone that there was something fun and useful and alive about what they were doing with Stuff and Pyralerts. "We thought, other people might like something like this," Hourihan says.

Like so many toilers in the Bay Area Web industry, Ev, Meg, and Paul sometimes went to the the Friday rooftop cocktail hours held by the dot-com trade journal *The Industry Standard*. "The idea was that we'd network," Bausch remembers. "But instead we'd always just sort of huddle in a corner and drink." At one such huddle at a party in June, Williams suggested that they could take the script they were using to post Pyralerts and turn it into a product.

Bausch dismissed the idea. "That's too simple. It's so easy. It's just a hack, it's no big deal."

Williams recalls, "We laughed it off. We knew that other people would use it and love it. But it wasn't anything! There was nothing there!" There was certainly no visible means by which such a product could be financially justified—no business model. That worried Meg. She had been taking on the brunt of the Hewlett-Packard contract work that was paying everyone's salaries. ("You're a better consultant than I am," Ev told her. "You're so much better at managing the clients.") She was as excited as everyone else about the appeal of a Stuff-style tool, but she was wary of anything that would distract Pyra from getting a real, revenue-generating product out the door. Ev agreed, but he didn't give up on the idea. Just in case, in June he registered the domain name Blogger.com.

In the middle of the summer, the company released the beta version of the Pyra App. It won some nods of approval and some links, but didn't take the Web world by storm. Ev and Meg realized they'd need to work to drum up interest and attention. Maybe they could use the idea of a Stuff product—this new thing Ev was calling Blogger—as a stalking horse for the Pyra App. What if they presented it as a small "module" that would fit into the larger Pyra product? Make it a free, easy-to-use tool that would be irresistible to Web geeks, who could then be sold on the richer, full Pyra experience?

Ev was torn. He remembered that it was lack of focus—too many ideas, not enough follow-through—that had cost him his first company back in Nebraska. He knew they had to be careful. But he also knew that if they could get Blogger going, it would surely take off.

Trivial as its actual technical details were, the little script they'd written accomplished something important: it cleared the obstacles from the path between brain and Web page. Surely other users would get the same charge from it that he and his colleagues had.

Pyra's Townsend Street office sat at the edge of San Francisco's South of Market neighborhood. In 1999 the wide streets of this warehouse district teemed with young Web-company employees. But if you walked beyond Townsend you'd hit the CalTrain station, and a decrepit trailer park, and then a shallow channel of stagnant Bay water. The inlet was spanned by a pair of old iron drawbridges flanking China Basin Landing, a sprawling, decommissioned freight terminal that had been converted into offices. Over the next few years a new baseball stadium and a giant biotech-focused office park would transform the neighborhood. But then it was a forlorn part of town. My company, Salon, rented space in the China Basin building for a while, and I remember looking out the window one day at the bridge below to see some cops dredging the channel for a corpse.

If you'd looked out that same window one afternoon in the middle of August 1999, you'd have seen a short-haired woman pacing across the bridge, furious and biting back tears. It was Meg Hourihan, trying to decide whether to quit her company.

Meg had just returned from a week's vacation back east with her family. When she got in to the office, Ev excitedly pulled her over to show her what he and Paul had concocted while she was gone. They'd built Blogger and launched it as a separate product. It had only taken a few days to rewrite their scripts. Now anyone could come to Blogger.com, sign up for free, and use it to power a blog. The neat thing was, you could use it—in fact, you *had* to use it—with your existing website and domain name. Write in one place, publish at another—you'd create and organize all your posts via Blogger, and it would publish them for you at your existing home on the Web. This twist ensured that the tool would appeal to the Web's early adopters, people who'd long been updating their personal sites and would never consider giving up their existing Web addresses, but just might appreciate the help Blogger provided.

Meg was not excited at all. In fact she felt betrayed. She'd left for a few days and her colleagues had gone off and "just did whatever the hell they wanted—like two little boys." Ev told her he thought they'd agreed on moving forward with the idea before she'd left; she didn't think they'd decided anything. She stalked out of the office, and tried to walk off her anger.

Finally she returned and pulled Ev aside and told him that something had to give. Pyra now had two separate products, but there were still only three of them on the payroll. She was burned out working nights and weekends on the Hewlett-Packard contracts while he and Paul got to do the "fun stuff."

There were raised voices, and tears. But when it was over they agreed it was time to try to raise some money for Pyra and hire some more people.

In some ways it was an opportune time to try to begin building a business around weblogs. In mid-1999 there was a mini-boom in weblog services: it was one of those moments when the same good idea seemed to occur roughly simultaneously to different people in different places working almost entirely in ignorance of one another.

In Seattle, a freshman programming prodigy at the University of Washington named Brad Fitzpatrick had built a little application to publish weblog-style journal entries. He and his roommate began using it in April 1999 to post frequent short notes to each other. "Now you'll be able to know exactly what I'm doing and when I'm doing it," the roommate's first post promised (or threatened). Fitzpatrick's program, which he called LiveJournal, began growing quickly, first across his campus and then, in 2000, more widely, becoming a favorite for Web users looking for a community of diarists. LiveJournal boasted a number of features, including friend lists, that foreshadowed the social-networking boom of MySpace and Facebook. But compared with the nascent weblog world, its population skewed heavily to college students. And because LiveJournal users didn't link out much, the service remained something of an island unto itself on the Web. (Xanga, a LiveJournal-like service that developed along a similar path, also launched in 1999, though it did not adopt a blog-style format until 2000.)

There were two other early entrants in the weblog boom, Groksoup and Pitas. In May 1999, Paul Kedrosky had converted his personal weblog at Groksoup.com into a service that offered a free weblog to anyone who signed up. Kedrosky, a stock analyst who was teaching business strategy at the University of British Columbia and fooling around on the side with programming projects, had grown bored with his own weblogging and thought it would be more interesting to make a tool for other people. And in July, shortly before Pyra launched Blogger, a self-taught programmer in Toronto named Andrew Smales had opened the doors to Pitas.com—another site that let anyone start a weblog for free. Unlike the original Blogger, neither of these services required you to have your own web address and server space already; they'd provide you with your own site on the Groksoup or Pitas server.

Pitas—named after the Middle Eastern pocket bread, not the acronym for "pain in the ass"—was a shoestring solo operation; Smales followed up in November with Diaryland, a similar site targeted at online diarists. Both were modest successes. But neither captured the imagination of the novelty-hungry technology press, which was busy counting dotcom millionnaires, or the interest of prominent webloggers, who already had their own sites, thank you. Smales says he never figured out how to market Pitas and Diaryland or turn them into something beyond the homegrown services he'd built. "I'm just a bad business guy," he says. Similarly, though Groksoup grew to support a few thousand users, it was primarily a hobby and its technology was sometimes flaky; when hackers trashed the site in 2001, Kedrosky abruptly shut it down.

Blogger was different: it steadily gained traction. It touched a nerve with the tribe of Web design specialists and software tinkerers who had embraced weblogging early. Ev and Meg and Paul, who each had a blog already, belonged to the tribe themselves, and they'd built something specially for its members. In November 1999, Pyra released an upgraded version of Blogger that solved some problems and added new features. By March of 2000, when the Pyra team showed up at the South by Southwest conference in Austin, Texas, they were the toast of the indie-hip crowd there. Ev was becoming something of an iconic spokesman for the blog world; with his unruly shock of dark hair, and a head and arms that somehow looked just a little bit oversized for the rest of his body, he had an off-center charm. Though he could be laconic in person, listeners felt they knew him well already—they'd met him on his blog.

It would have been impossible for Blogger to achieve this kind of success without triggering some sort of backlash. As excitement over blogging trickled out into the media, the skeptics' corner broke out in a chorus of jeers, exemplified by a piece Greg Knauss published on Michael Sippey's site in November 1999, under the headline "My Ass is a Weblog":

> Weblogs are a 'revolution.' They're 'journalism.' They're 'art.' They're, again and again, the next New Thing. To which the only possible response can be: come on, people. . . . How can you not boggle at the level of self-delusion, of self-infatuation, it takes to declare that . . . the concept will be alive and well a decade from now? That weblog readership will increase a hundredfold in that time?

Whenever a phenomenon expands from an in-crowd to a mass following, the old-timers are likely to feel alienated—as with obscure alternative bands whose original fans get turned off once their music starts selling. As Williams later said, "It's much easier to feel like you're tuned in to something exciting when just a few insiders are doing it than when it's done by 50,000 tech-savvy teens and their not-so-tech-savvy grandmas." Some of the original link-based weblog pioneers from 1998 felt that the Blogger-based blogs were an entirely different species from the genre they loved. Instead of filtering the rest of the Web, the newcomers were often just posting random thoughts or notes about what was happening in their lives. In this view, Blogger was diluting the very identity of the weblog pursuit: it was blurring the line between weblogs and online diaries, a line that had never been visible to anyone except the most hardcore webloggers.

Rebecca Blood, in her weblog history essay, suggested that this change was a by-product of Blogger's simple interface, which didn't require each post to come with a link to something. But Williams felt that Blogger shouldn't dictate any particular format to its users. He just wanted to give them an elegant tool and see what they did with it. Some of the unhappiest Blogger critics wanted to try to establish a distinction between the terms *weblog* (for the link-oriented sites) and *blog* (for the Blogger-based newbies). That effort was, of course, futile, like trying to preserve the hyphen in *email*. The flood of new converts to blogging would inevitably drown the abstruse doctrinal disputes of its earliest acolytes.

Blogger's success brought technical growing pains. The Blogger server, as if uncannily conscious of the attention turned on it, chose the weekend of South by Southwest for a high-profile crash. The developers were constantly patching their code and rebooting their machines to try to keep up with the influx of new users. In February 2000, Wired News took note of what it called a "huge surge in popularity" for weblogs, whose numbers were growing at "an unprecedented rate." At the start of the year, Blogger had about 2,300 registered user accounts; not all were actively posting to blogs, of course, but there were still an impressive number of people beginning to use the software. On April 14 the official Blogger news page took note of the arrival of the thousandth new user added to its public list of active blogs. At the time, when weblogs were still understood as handcrafted, labor-intensive personal projects, that seemed astronomical.

In February, Pyra had closed its investment deal, making good on the plan Ev and Meg had agreed on. They'd succeeded in raising a half a million dollars from a handful of what would now be called angel investors—a laughably small amount at a time of runaway speculation in the Internet industry. These backers included Tim O'Reilly, the technology publisher Ev had once worked for; Jerry Michalski, a technology pundit who'd been serving as an informal adviser to Pyra; and Meg's parents. At Advance.Net, a corporate arm of Conde Nast, a former news exec turned Web enthusiast named Jeff Jarvis had been turned on to Blogger, and his firm kicked in some money, too.

The checks were finally in the bank that April—just as the dotcom-driven stock bubble hit its final peak and began losing altitude. The good news was, the company finally had some cash—and used it to bring on a handful of new employees. The bad news was, it was now trying to build a business in the face of a financial downdraft whose duration and force would prove far greater than anyone then imagined.

In theory, Pyra was still working on both the big, original Pyra App and Blogger. The new investors hadn't told the company to scrap either of them. But Ev and Meg increasingly felt that it was time to hunker down and focus on a single product. Meg saw it as a *Sophie's Choice*-style dilemma; choosing one over the other felt to them almost like abandoning a child. In fact, however, the decision was never in much doubt. People still had a hard time just understanding what the ambitious Pyra App was supposed to do. It had no "elevator pitch"—no concise, easy-to-grasp explanation of its purpose. Blogger, on the other hand, was easy to get, and it kept growing faster. On a good day you could spy the long exponential growth curve on which it was embarking. Yes, it still lacked a business plan, but there were some obvious ways to think about making money with it. Advertising might grow increasingly harder to sell as the business climate worsened, but surely Blogger could offer dedicated users extra services via for-pay "pro" plans. Overall, it looked easier to bolt a business plan onto an existing service that had no revenue but lots of actual users than to keep trying to dragoon users for an unfinished product with a clear business plan.

So the Pyra App was left fallow. The company stopped talking about it, and an expanded team turned its attention to improving Blogger. Derek Powazek—a web-design veteran who had once worked at Hotwired, handcoding Dave Winer's columns—joined as design director. He gave Blogger the striking logo that it has kept to this day, a lopsided white B against an orange-red background. Matt Haughey came on to serve as a sort of technical intermediary between Powazek and Paul Bausch, who was handling the heart of the Blogger code, along with another developer, Matt Hamer. Everyone understood that what they were building was not only a service for bloggers but a community as well—and both Powazek and Haughey had their own experiences in that area. Powazek's Fray.com was a pioneering personal storytelling site filled with users' contributions, and Haughey had started an influential community blog called Metafilter in mid-1999. When Haughey moved from Los Angeles to San Francisco to join Pyra, he packed the Metafilter server into his trunk and carted it up I-5 to its new home on Pyra's fast T1 line.

That summer was a heady time for the Blogger team, even as the industry's clouds darkened. Having successfully met the needs of Web insiders and benefited from the buzz they generated, Blogger was now in a position to widen its appeal. In September, Pyra Labs unveiled Blogspot, its version of a hosted blog service. Now you no longer needed your own domain and Web hosting account to set up a Blogger blog; you could just create a free account at Blogspot and be publishing in under a minute. Blogspot caught Blogger up to competitors like Pitas and Groksoup and Dave Winer's EditThisPage.com and Weblogs.com—the two free sites that Userland opened up at the end of 1999 to show off what its new Manila software could do. With Blogspot, Blogger wedded the simplicity of its one box and one button interface to the free and easy model of hosted blogging services. The combination proved irresistible to non-geeks, who might have found the Userland system harder to grasp, and who might never have heard of Pitas or Groksoup.

To longtime Blogger users with their own domains, Blogspot looked like a downmarket neighborhood. But it was perfect for novices, and it kicked Blogger's sign-up rate into overdrive. It also ratcheted up the strain on its technical infrastructure. Slowdowns were rampant, outages became more frequent, and each time the server choked, there were more users to complain.

Not long after Blogspot launched, Meg Hourihan took a look at the company's books and saw that they only had enough money for a few months' more payroll. They had a product people loved and an impressive rate of new sign-ups, but not much to show in the way of revenue. They'd begun work on a for-pay Blogger Pro service, but it wasn't ready; they didn't want to take on paying customers until they'd stabilized the technology and could promise better service with fewer crashes. They had dreams of a new project they called "star-blog" or "asterisk-blog" ("*blog"— in computer code the asterisk means, roughly, "anything can go here"); they'd registered lots of domain names for it, like "babyblog.com" and "momblog.com" and "foodblog.com." The idea was to build new communities of blogs around specific subject areas that advertisers might be interested in. But the company lacked the time or money to execute the plan.

Pyra Labs had plenty of ideas. What it needed was cash. But trying to raise money in the fall of 2000 was an entirely different matter from raising money the previous winter. The full scope of the bust may not yet have been evident, but investors had seen their own portfolios plummet, and they eyed Internet investments with a newly narrowed gaze. Mostly what they wanted to see was dollars flowing in. Pyra didn't have any. Blogger was free because it originally was meant to help sell the Pyra App, which would have targeted paying business customers. (Winer's hosted services, similarly, were free because they were intended to help market Manila.) Starting to charge people for something they'd previously gotten for free seemed suicidal, particularly with free alternatives in the market.

That fall, Ev began scrambling to raise more money. But he kept hitting brick walls. At the time, lots of failing consumer-oriented Web companies were making last-ditch efforts to survive by offering "enterprise" products—that is, retooling their software to try to appeal to big businesses and organizations that theoretically might still pay cash. Should Blogger try to "go enterprise"? The debate went back and forth. As outright investment looked decreasingly likely, Williams began hunting around for partnership and acquisition deals instead. At least one such deal came close to fruition—an acquisition of Pyra Labs by a company called Moreover, which specialized in content syndication. (One of its founders was Nick Denton, the entrepreneur who would later found the Gawker Media blog publishing network.) Neither Meg nor Ev was thrilled by the Moreover offer, but it would have saved the Blogger team's jobs, at least. Meg wanted to make it happen; Ev was opposed, but eventually gave in—because, he said, he didn't want to be the "asshole" responsible for unemploying his friends. At the last minute, however, Moreover's board backed away.

Meanwhile, the Pyra Labs bank balance was ebbing, time was short, and tempers grew shorter. Ev and Meg had always had a tempestuous relationship; long afterwards friends would ask, what had they been thinking, starting a company together after they'd dated? Now they were having daily shouting matches, often in front of the rest of the team. Both Paul Bausch and Matt Haughey remember thinking, "Oh, Mom and Dad are fighting again."

The two would sit down each morning and Meg would tell Ev where they stood: "Today we have $80,000." "I ran a payroll. Now we have $60,000." They started skipping their own paychecks and running up credit-card balances to keep paying everyone else. Meg began to suspect that maybe Ev didn't really know *how* to raise money—it had all fallen so easily into their laps the first time around. Or maybe he wasn't working the phones or pounding the pavement hard enough. Why was he hanging out in the office when he should have been camping out on potential investors' doorsteps? "I'd come in in the morning, she recalls, "and he'd have slept on the sofa, he'd have worked through the night on some cool new thing for Blogger. And I'd say what the fuck? Now you're exhausted and asleep and you can't go through your email 'cause you were up all night coding—*and we still don't have any money!*"

Ironically, from the outside it looked like things couldn't be better for Blogger. Its growth was mind-boggling—it topped 100,000 accounts soon after the new year of 2001. And a *New Yorker* reporter named Rebecca Mead showed up on the doorstep to hang out and write a piece about blogging. But even these upsides had downsides. The *New Yorker* article was published in November 2000 as "You've Got Blog" (a reference to America Online's then-ubiquitous "you've got mail" message). It turned out to be a charming but slight piece focusing mostly on the burgeoning romance between Meg and Jason Kottke, a Web designer and widely known weblog pioneer. As for all those new registrations, they were a blessing, but Blogger simply couldn't keep up. It crashed regularly, and even when it was up, it often ran painfully slowly. All of Blogspot's thousands of blogs were hosted on a single crappy old HP desktop computer, and it was a basket case. In the midst of the financial implosion, the company turned to its users and asked for donations to buy a new box. They poured in; the "Server Fund Drive" took in $12,000. That was enough for *two* new boxes—but didn't help stave off the company's impending doom.

In mid-January 2001 the founders made final desperate efforts to close some sort of deal; they laid off all their employees, but everyone hung around, unpaid, still hoping for rescue. Toward the end of January, after the last of the potential acquisition deals fell through, Meg went to Ev and said that since he'd failed to raise money to save the company, she should take over as CEO and give it a try. He told her he wanted to remain the boss. When they started Pyra they'd split ownership sixty-forty in Ev's favor, so that pretty much settled things. Meg told Ev that was it: she was leaving. Then she strode to the center of the office, told everyone, and walked out. The rest of the employees told Ev that they weren't sticking around either.

On January 31, Ev posted a long message on his personal blog under the headline "And Then There Was One." It was a pained and forthright notice.

> We are out of money, and I have lost my team. . . . It
> really breaks my heart to see the group of awesome
> people that I was so damn proud of having assembled

break apart, feeling beaten and with dreams unrealized. As the CEO of this company, I, of course, hold myself largely responsible.

Pyra had been a company of bloggers, so of course, in the days that followed, nearly everyone involved posted their own postmortems. Matt Haughey lamented their youthful lack of business smarts:

> It seems stupid now, but when you make web pages and web applications, you get this weird sense of god-like power. You can make the sun rise and the sun set, you can kill someone's application with a single blow, you can create whole new worlds in which thousands dwell. So certainly, when it comes to making money, your swelled, I-can-code-anything head figures it can do the business aspects too, right?

> Wrong. Designers are great at designing things, coders are great at coding things, and while everyone is off doing their best at what they're good at, a business person can be trusted to kick ass on the business things. It's definitely hard to find a business person with any idea of what the coders and designers are doing, but I kinda wish we looked harder in the beginning and left them to handle the icky parts we weren't all that great at.

Paul Bausch wrote about what had been so special to him about Blogger:

> I loved Blogger more than Pyra [the "app"] from the beginning. I would speak softly to Blogger when no one was around, "Don't worry, I won't let them put ads on you." or "I won't let them sell you," I would reassure. There was something just as magical about Blogger as

there was with Stuff. It was connecting us with people. And connecting people with people.

And Meg wrote about her pain:

> On January 16th, every employee at Pyra was officially laid off. Every employee agreed to receive one final pay check. And every employee agreed to continue to come to the office every day, to continue to work with no guarantee of payment, all because of the faith we had in what we'd built and in the team we'd assembled. After I sat with each person . . . I went into the office bathroom and I burst into tears. And when I got home, I got into my bed and cried and cried and cried. . . .

> There are only so many sleepless nights where one can lay in bed at 3 watching the clock tick tock till 8. There are only so many days to slog the same path, battle the same unwinnable arguments, endure the same pains and heartaches.

> And then the days run out, either because you die, or you decide enough is enough. Because you decide this is no way to live. . . .

> On Monday I resigned from the company I co-founded.

> I'm still crying and crying and crying.

In the lore of Silicon Valley, startup companies frequently arrive at a critical moment when the world has abandoned them, the money has run out, and the doughty entrepreneur faces a perilous choice: Is it simply all over, time to cut the losses, pack it in, and move on to the next thing? Or is it worth persevering, hanging on to the original vision, fighting to survive long enough for the world to catch up and catch on?

By most objective standards, Evan Williams should have folded Blogger's tent in February 2001. The company was not quite dead, but it was not exactly alive, either: it was a kind of corporate zombie. It had no cash in the bank; it had legions of customers, but virtually no way to collect money from them. But Williams saw no reason not to try to keep Blogger running all by himself. Partly it was pride and a steadfast belief that blogging really was going to matter. Partly it was a sense of obligation to the legions of Blogger users who'd stood by the company through all its server woes, and who'd kicked in donations when asked. And partly it was just Williams's temperament. As he wrote in his "And Then There Was One" post, in words that sounded either disingenuous or delusional: "I'm optimistic. (I'm always optimistic.) And I have many, many ideas. (I always have many ideas.)"

The very public departure of the original team meant that the entire technology industry knew just how close Blogger had come to shutting down. Williams's inbox filled with best wishes, commiserations, and offers of help. One of them was from Dan Bricklin, a legendary software-industry figure known 'for having invented the spreadsheet in the early days of the personal computer. Bricklin now headed a company called Trellix that produced tools for publishing websites. He had first heard about Blogger by reading about it on Dave Winer's Scripting News. A veteran of plenty of startup-company crises himself, he empathized with Williams and suggested a meeting. "As a believer in weblogging, and an admirer of the product, I didn't like the idea of Blogger being lost in the dotcom crash," Bricklin later wrote. Over a sushi dinner, the two men drew up the outline of a licensing deal that would let Trellix offer Blogger's tools to its customers in exchange for a modest infusion of cash ($40,000) into Blogger's empty coffer.

The Trellix contract, along with a trickle of other, smaller deals through the rest of the year, gave Williams some breathing room. But Blogger still lived a touch-and-go existence. Its expenses had dropped from a $50,000-a-month burn rate to a few thousand in rent and technical costs for bandwidth and such; still, even that modest budget wasn't easy to meet. Eventually Williams had to shut down the office entirely and move the servers into his apartment. He remembers this period as an emotional rollercoaster: "I don't know how I'm going to pay the rent, and I can't figure that out because the server's not running, and I have to stay up all night, trying to figure out Linux, and being hacked, and then fix that. I was always thinking, by tomorrow or next week, then I'm not going to be hanging by my fingernails anymore. And usually that wasn't true."

Some of Williams's headaches were the result of the sort of dispute that almost always accompanies the failure (or, in this case, near failure) of a company. The implosion of Pyra had left behind a pool of bitterness and anger against Ev. Later, Meg and Paul and some of the others would express their admiration for the way Williams's lonely vigils over the server saved Blogger's life; right now they were still mad. A straight bankruptcy might have been cleaner, but here there was still a company to wrangle over. Questions about back pay for the former employees had never been settled, and Meg still sat on the Pyra board. She hired a lawyer, and that meant Ev had legal bills to pay, too.

Still, through all the personal and financial turmoil, one constant held: Blogger kept acquiring new users. The Web industry bust and accompanying general economic downturn had left many people with a lot of time on their hands. It cost nothing to start your own blog. Despite the hard times, broadband Internet access was finally becoming a reality for a significant portion of the population, both in the United States and overseas, where Blogger and Blogspot were drawing large numbers of users. And because blogging was one of the only things on the Web that was new and growing, it began attracting more media coverage. In May 2001 *The Industry Standard* magazine profiled Williams in a piece titled "The Idealist" that celebrated his, and Blogger's, survival. The magazine itself went under three months later.

As it turned out, the summer of 2001 marked the nadir for Williams and Blogger, and things began turning around as the year progressed. The 9/11 attacks pushed many of the surviving Web industry companies into even deeper trouble by squelching a small recovery in the online advertising market. But the tragedy sent even more users Blogger's way, as people flocked to the service to share their anger and grief, their insights and fears. At the start of 2002, Williams was finally ready to unveil the long-gestating Blogger Pro service, which provided some additional features for a modest fee (thirty-five dollar a year). There was also a little money coming in from a service that let Blogspot users pay to have the ads removed from their sites (which weren't bringing in much revenue anyway). And there was a deal to set up a version of Blogger for a Brazilian media company.

Blogger had clawed its way back from the brink of death to become a real business, with an expanding pool of customers and enviably low overhead. That meant Williams was, at last, able to begin rebuilding a company around the product. He already had a business partner in Jason Shellen—who'd started providing informal help during Pyra's death-spiral, and who took an increasingly active role in business development as the company came back to life. Now Williams could also hire a couple of additional technical people.

Things were clearly on an upswing for Blogger, and as 2002 advanced, Williams and Shellen began talking about the future. They now had around 700,000 user accounts; how could they catapult the service to 10 million, or even 100 million? That would be harder to do on their own than with partners. When they sought advice from their investor Tim O'Reilly and his colleagues, O'Reilly asked them which companies they'd want to work with. Shellen recalls, "We said there are three companies we really like: Apple, Amazon, and Google. They said, 'We know people at all those companies.' "

O'Reilly's people made the introductions, and in October a Google corporate development manager named Jeremy Wenokur invited Williams and Shellen to a meeting at Google's Mountain View, California, offices.

They didn't know what to expect. Google was a search company. What could it want with Blogger? Certainly, Williams admired Google. It had built a smart, successful business on the ruins of the dotcom era; its search engine, which ranked Web pages based on the quantity and authority of pages that linked to them, had become an indispensable tool for the whole universe of Web users; and it now harbored the grand ambition of "organizing the world's information" using what looked increasingly like a vast, globally distributed supercomputer. Williams and Shellen prepared for the meeting the way people at small companies always have when people at big companies come calling: they brainstormed ways that Blogger and Google might "work together."

But it turned out the Google people didn't want to talk about working together. They wanted to buy Blogger outright.

At that time, Google had no history of acquiring other companies. Ev wasn't sure exactly why Google was interested. "There were all these theories that everyone suddenly came up with, and we were making them up ourselves, because we didn't really know," he recalls. One popular speculation among bloggers was based on an idea that the writer Steven Johnson called "the Blogger Effect" in a 2002 article: "The bloggers are helping Google learn what pages should be connected to other pages. . . . They are helping Google transform the Web from a disorganized mess into a more coherent universe of useful data." Business analysts looked at Google's purchase of Blogger and saw the consummation of Johnson's theory. *Aha!* they said. *Those Google geniuses just added some IQ points to the giant brain they're assembling.*

Williams says he doesn't think Google's management was looking that far ahead: "I think, really, that it just occurred to them, 'We can now buy things, and we should start acquiring small teams. It'll cost us a trivial amount of stock to do this deal, and we like the spirit of it.'"

As Shellen recalls it, "They thought maybe we would just rub off on Google a little bit, with that productive entrepreneurial spirit which they say they like." Later, when the Blogger team met for the first time with Google's co-founders, Sergey Brin and Larry Page, Shellen says, the

Google founders sounded concerned that another big Web company like Microsoft or Yahoo might buy Blogger and then "firewall" it—cut it off from the rest of the Internet in a way that would harm both Google and the Web itself.

Within a few months, getting bought by Google would become the dream of every startup entrepreneur in the industry, but Williams thought carefully before saying yes. Things were finally going well for Blogger, and he cherished his independence. Working inside a big company was not his recipe for contentment. And, for a change, Pyra wasn't desperate—they had another offer of a more traditional venture capital investment on the table.

In retrospect, of course, swapping Pyra/Blogger for Google's pre-IPO stock was an offer no sane businessperson would have turned down. But it wasn't the money that persuaded Williams and Shellen to accept Google, both say. It was instead the likelihood that Google could take Blogger, and blogging, to a scale of millions more effectively than they could on their own. Google would be the catapult they'd sought.

The deal was announced in February 2003. Williams was now a wealthy man—on paper, at least. (Terms of the deal have never been made public, and following the 2004 IPO, Google stock was worth far more than it would have been valued at the time of the acquisition.) The original investors and a few of the original team—including Meg Hourihan and Paul Bausch—also profited from the sale. Early on, Hourihan had defined herself as a "Web person" rather than a stock-hungry dot-commer; now she found herself with her own little slice of Web wealth. But most of the Pyra employees hadn't worked long enough to be able to claim any of their stock options.

Williams joined Google as Blogger's steward. The acquisition meant a drastic shift in the product's focus: the idea of collecting some revenue from Blogger Pro accounts, which had kept the company afloat when it was independent, suddenly made no sense at all. At Google, "our initiative was just to focus on growth," Williams recalls. "Growth meant going mainstream. We were irrelevant to Google unless we were huge."

By that time a turnabout had happened in the blogging marketplace anyway. Blogger, which had begun its life by capturing the imagination of technically adept Web geeks, had lost that crowd to a new generation of blogging tools—most popularly Movable Type, and later Wordpress— that offered serious bloggers more features and tweakability. Blogger, meanwhile, had become the blog tool for Everyman: the way to start your blog when you didn't even want to know about the technical stuff. Under Google's wing, it gave up on charging for service and concentrated on adding new features. That positioned it to take its already exponential growth curve—from three thousand accounts in early 2000, to 100,000 a year later, to over a million (with maybe a quarter of those actively updating blogs) at the time of the Google deal—to new levels.

But Google didn't have any other big plans to integrate Blogger or, as some unfounded rumors occasionally had it, to favor the pages Blogger users created in its search results. Having acquired Blogger, the company did not seem in any great hurry to do much more with it than "let it thrive in our benevolent environment of goodness," as Williams put it.

That was good for Blogger and its users, who could count on Google's legendary systems expertise to keep the service from slowing down or crashing. But a large corporation wasn't a good environment for Williams. What he loved was starting new things. He'd told himself he'd give Google at least a year; he lasted a bit more than a year and a half. When Google went public in August 2004, his stock became tradable— and immensely valuable. He left in October, and immediately began work on his next company.

When Evan Williams refused to accept Blogger's demise and holed up at home with his beloved product until it was safe to go out again, he took a calculated gamble—and won, spectacularly. Not every tale of startup perseverance has such a fairy-tale ending. Much more often, such last-

ditch efforts lead to dead ends when the marketplace simply moves on or
the credit-card debt gets too high to bear.

Ultimately, though, it wasn't the pot of Google gold Williams won
that made the Blogger story so influential for the future of the Web
industry. It was Williams's demonstration of how little you actually
needed, in the post-dotcom era, to run a booming Web service. Alone in
his apartment—and at least some of the time in his pajamas—Williams
had been able not only to keep Blogger alive but to keep it growing, and
then to hand it off to a new owner. Offices were nice; so were regular
paychecks and benefits and all the other accoutrements of a "real" business. But you didn't actually need any of them to build something significant on the Web.

Williams established the template for a whole new wave of Web
companies that would start as a trickle right about the time Google
acquired Blogger and end as the flood that became known as Web 2.0.
Companies didn't have to raise millions or spend millions to achieve
something valuable; they could be built around an idea and sustained
without any of the trappings usually associated with going concerns. As
blogging began spreading beyond the technology industry, its new
acolytes carried the seeds of this ethos into other fields. Maybe you could
start a new publication without rounding up big money. Maybe your
political organization or your marketing consultancy didn't have to
invest in a lease or fancy signage. In this way, blogging became not only a
mode of expression but a way of thinking about guerrilla-style organization-
building.

Blogger's success made blogging a household word. "Weblogs My
Ass" indeed! Today, Greg Knauss calls his cynical essay dismissing the
blog movement "profoundly, spectacularly, epically wrong": "I bought
into not buying into the hype," he says. "I never, ever would have imagined that all the most grandiose dreams of the biggest blog promoters
would be too small to describe what happened."

By bringing blogging to a mass market, Blogger validated the idealism shared by so many of the pioneer webloggers, from Justin Hall to Dave Winer and beyond—the belief that one day millions of people would pour their writing onto the Web, if the software developers and designers and Web companies would just give them good simple tools and then get out of the way. The key, it turned out, lay in ruthless simplification of the path between a thought in your head and a posting on the Web.

That sort of simplicity is hard to achieve and hard to preserve. Over the years, Blogger, like its competition, gradually added new features (like post headlines and RSS feeds and categories or tags) that are useful in themselves but that collectively turn writing a post into a much more ambitious undertaking. In the meantime, Williams has gone back to basics: his latest company, Twitter, allows people to share updates, as with a blog; but each post, or "tweet," is limited to 140 characters.

In a talk at a 2007 conference, Williams argued that starting with tight constraints can help new Web services win users and grow fast. He'd seen that play out with Blogger at a scale few businesspeople ever get the chance to experience. There are reminders of that achievement wherever you look today. The Web is now full of blogs written by and catering to the sort of ambitious kid Evan Williams once was—packed with tips and war stories for those who dream of starting their own companies, but don't know the right people or understand how to get started. At the start of Williams's career, he'd tried to sell CD-ROMs to Nebraska football fans, but they didn't have the right equipment to play the discs, and he lost his shirt. Today, if you Google "Husker football," you find a long list of blogs that will provide you with as much information about the topic as you could ever need.

Chapter 5

THE RISE OF POLITICAL BLOGGING

JOSH MARSHALL

As the sun came up on the morning of November 8, 2000, Americans awoke to the disturbing realization that their presidential election, held with such ritual predictability the previous day, was not over. The contest hung on a few hundred disputed Florida votes, and no one could yet say whether Bush or Gore would be the next president—or even when or how a decision would be made. This threw everyone off. Editors and producers withdrew overly hasty calls on the outcomes of tight races and watched their carefully choreographed coverage plans disintegrate. News addicts felt simultaneously mesmerized by the drama and paralyzed by the uncertainty. Conscientious citizens wondered how their voting system had fallen into such disrepair. It was as if the entire political universe had fallen through a wormhole into a dimension where time had stopped.

As the vote counting devolved into lawsuits and accusations, the news media experienced a kind of meltdown. The explosion of rumors flummoxed slow-moving print publications, which inevitably fell behind the news cycle. And the avalanche of details taxed the broadcast outlets, which weren't well suited to a mathematical inquest into a disputed election. If you wanted to keep up with the madness in Florida, you had to turn to the Web. There you could find mountains of detail about the Florida county vote tallies and the legal maneuvering. You could feast on all the news flashes and questionable gossip you wanted. And you could listen to what vocal, informed partisans in both political camps had to say about the unfolding battle.

In Washington, D.C., a young journalist named Joshua Micah Marshall felt he had some things to say, too. He'd been working as a junior editor at *The American Prospect*—a wonkish, low-circulation policy magazine, like *The New Republic*, only more predictably liberal. But he found himself frustrated by the *Prospect*'s slant—he was more sympathetic to the moderation of the Clinton/Gore camp than his bosses were, and he chafed under what sometimes felt like an editorial party line. He was also more eager than they were to experiment with new forms of online reporting and writing. As a history grad student at Brown, Marshall had earned some money on the side by designing websites. He knew the rudiments of Web publishing, and already had a personal site with a bio and links to his articles in the *Prospect*, *The New Republic*, Slate, and Salon. He'd seen a couple of weblogs that focused on political news, and had toyed with the notion of starting one himself; all it would take, he knew, was to pick a name, design a template, and start writing. Now was the time: the Florida story was irresistible.

On November 13, 2000, less than a week after election night, Marshall published the first post at a new blog he called Talking Points Memo. (The name was an obscure in-joke reference to a long-forgotten detail from the Monica Lewinsky saga.) TPM kicked off with a post about the background of a lawyer who was arguing on Bush's behalf in the Florida recount—Theodore Olson, who'd participated in the anti-Clinton Whitewater witch hunt, and who would later become Bush's solicitor general. That first week, Marshall offered praise for the Gore campaign's call for a statewide recount; second-guessed how Bush adviser Karl Rove had deployed his resources in the final week before the election; and provided nervous updates on the seesawing legal maneuvering that seemed likely to determine the election's outcome. The tone was knowledgeable, casual, and more than a bit partisan. The content was similar to what you might hear in a newsroom, or anywhere else that political junkies were trading nuggets of news and spinning scenarios.

If you read Talking Points Memo that week, you might have thought, *Here's a smart writer who has found a nice way of emptying his notebook of all the stuff he can't fit into his longer articles.* It was respectable but hardly revolutionary. There was little indication that within a few short years its posts would help drive a Senate majority leader from his position, derail the central item on a president's legislative agenda, and force the resignation of a U.S. attorney general. Nor was there much sign, as Marshall began posting, that his improvisations would lead the Web in mapping out new methods for investigative journalism and collaboration between bloggers and their readers.

Within a few years political blogging would become a surging tide, first from the right, then from the left. And the image of the blogger as a cross between kibitzer, reporter, activist, and gadfly would become burned into the popular imagination. In this efflorescence of political blogging, Marshall wasn't the most popular or the best known. What set him apart was his restless creativity in exploring the new shapes for political journalism that blogging made possible.

There weren't too many models for Marshall's new project at the time. The Drudge Report had inspired a number of political sites, but they were more headline aggregators than blogs. Political debate online clustered around a handful of discussion forums and email newsletters. But many of the most popular of these sites—like MediaWhoresOnline on the left or FreeRepublic.com on the right—carried a disagreeable odor; they teemed with aggressively partisan true believers, and were neither interested in nor effective at reaching beyond the faithful. Meanwhile, the weblog world was still almost exclusively a realm for Web geeks, a place for amateur enthusiasts with a techie streak, not for professional journalists who already had outlets for their writing. Exceptions to this rule were rare enough that you could count them.

One of the few was Dan Gillmor, a columnist for the *San Jose Mercury News* who covered Silicon Valley. In October 1999 he had taken up a suggestion from Dave Winer and started his own blog as an experiment. Years before, when he'd begun writing about technology for the people who were creating it, he had an insight: the people who read his columns generally grasped the complexities and subtleties of the industry better than he did. It wasn't that Gillmor was an idiot; far from it. Rather, he had the humility—a trait not always widely distributed in the American newsroom—to accept that, as he pithily put it, "my readers know more than I do." For years he had included his email address at the bottom of his columns, opening a channel through which his readers could send him ideas, tips, corrections, and the occasional flame; the new blog, part of the *Mercury News* site, opened that channel wider and moved his work from what he called "lecture mode" to more of a conversation. He started posting items that said: Hey, I'm working on this or that story. Here's what I think I know. Am I onto something? Am I wrong? Am I right?

Gillmor's posts made waves in the insular realm of weblogs and among the tech journalists who followed them. But in his own newsroom and in the wider world, they barely registered. "There was hardly any curiosity about it at all," he remembers. "I think almost no one at the *Mercury* even knew it was there." Far from inspiring a flood of imitations by other journalists, Gillmor's blog remained an oddball experiment. News executives in 1999 were too busy trying to figure out how to grab their slice of Web wealth, while also feasting on ad revenue from dotcom companies, to pay much attention to the blog fringe. (Though today you can read the postings of many early bloggers all the way back to their beginnings, Gillmor's blog has been entirely effaced from the Web: too many technology-platform transitions, website redesigns, and changes of editorial direction removed the old pages from the *Mercury News*'s archives without a trace. You can't even find them in the Internet Archive, a repository of snapshots of the Web in past times, because the newspaper blocked the archive from copying its material. On the Web, it turns out, if you want to preserve your work for posterity, you're better off taking care of it yourself than relying on your employer.)

Gillmor was a professional a little too far ahead of his time. The first experienced journalists outside of the technology press to take up blogging weren't, like him, mainstream bylines with institutional backing; they were outsiders of one sort or another, who cherished the freedom from editorial fiat, embraced the conversational hurly-burly online and viewed their blogs for the most part as after-work fun—even, in some cases, as a kind of professional slumming. The first to gain any sort of following or mainstream notice was Mickey Kaus, a Harvard Law School–trained journalist who had authored a book on welfare reform policy and worked for *Newsweek* and *The New Republic*, but never settled in to a long-term gig. Kaus had written a short-lived column of brief items for Slate, the Microsoft-backed online magazine, at the onset of the Monica Lewinsky scandal. But his deal with Slate was an on-again, off-again thing. In June 1999, during one of the "off" phases, Kaus started posting commentaries two or three times a week at a new personal website he called Kausfiles. In September he expanded Kausfiles with the Hit Parade, a sidebar filled with short items. "I didn't know it was a blog," he recalls. "We didn't call it a blog. I was like everybody else—I thought I was inventing this format where the new thing goes on the top and it gets pushed down."

Kaus's independence was provisional; over time, Kausfiles would get swallowed up by Slate, which paid Kaus and gave his work an online home, but never edited his posts. Ostensibly a liberal, Kaus had a dyspeptic style and a contrarian temperament, and in the increasingly bitter partisan divides of the day—from the Clinton impeachment to the Florida recount debacle—he seemed almost perversely eager to infuriate left-leaning readers who came to his site expecting to have their preconceptions confirmed.

If Kaus was the sort of liberal who enjoyed riling his fellow liberals, Andrew Sullivan was a similarly unorthodox figure on the right. A gay, British-born writer and editor who'd taken the helm of *The New Republic* in 1991, while still in his twenties, and then had moved on to a freelance career, Sullivan began blogging in the fall of 2000, just a few weeks before Marshall. With the aid of a friend, Robert Cameron, who ran a Web design firm, Sullivan had set out to build a personal website as a home for his columns. But he knew nothing of Web technology, and each time he needed to post something new, he had to get Cameron to do it. One day Cameron called him up and told him about Blogger: Use it, Cameron said, and you won't have to bother me anymore.

Once he started using Blogger to streamline the reposting of his print columns, Sullivan realized he could use it to post original material as well. In a scrolling window on the home page of his personal site, under a banner that read "Daily Dish," he started penning brief comments in the vein of the short-item columns he'd sometimes written for *The New Republic*. He quickly found the format irresistible and addictive. And as readers began responding to him, he made the same discovery that Dan Gillmor had: the value of what was flowing into his inbox was incalculable. As he later wrote:

> With only a few hundred readers, a few started writing back. They picked up on my interests, and sent me links, ideas, and materials to add to the blog. Before long, around half the material on my site was suggested by readers. Sometimes, these readers knew far more about any subject than I could. I remember trying to fathom some of the complexities of the Florida election nightmare when I got an email from a Florida politics professor explaining every detail imaginable. If I'd been simply reporting the story in the traditional way, I'd have never found this font of information. As it was, I found myself scooping major news outlets on arcane electoral details

about chads and voting machines. Peer-to-peer journalism, I realized, had a huge advantage over old-style journalism. It could marshal the knowledge and resources of
thousands, rather than the certitudes of the few.

Sullivan was a journalism pro with a blue-chip pedigree and a high
public profile. But his online venture remained an eccentric outlier. In
late 2000, when Josh Marshall launched Talking Points Memo, the field
of political blogging remained as sparse as the world of technology blogging had been three years before. There were only a handful of participants, scattered across the political spectrum: Bob Somerby, a comedian,
former teacher, and *Baltimore Sun* columnist, had been posting liberal
commentary at his Daily Howler since 1998, and was gradually shifting
to a more bloglike format. Libertarian intellectual Virginia Postrel, who
had set up a website to promote a book in 1999, added a blog called The
Scene in December 2000. In August 2001 a mildly conservative law professor at the University of Tennessee named Glenn Reynolds started up a
blog at Instapundit.com and almost immediately began producing a torrent of brief, chatty posts. Something was building here, slowly. But to
hear it, you had to cup your ear and listen hard.

The terrorist attacks of September 11, 2001, turned up the volume
overnight: they galvanized the nascent political-blogging scene into a
frenzy of posting and linking, and drove a horde of newcomers into its
ranks. In basements and home offices around the nation, people ached to
raise their voices in outrage and grief, to ask questions and look for
answers. Many also found themselves unsatisfied by what they were hearing on TV and reading in the press. For those who felt this discontent
most acutely, the new blogs beckoned, and if you found one, it meant you
found links to many others. A decent number of these new blog readers
soon hied themselves to Blogspot and became blog writers themselves.

The loudest and most numerous of these new voices were outspokenly conservative. These blogging newcomers had little patience for Josh Marshall's measured, liberal-leaning observations on Talking Points Memo. Andrew Sullivan's caustic rhetoric from the right was more their style. Most of all, they rallied around Reynolds's Instapundit blog. Conservative publications already had bloglike Web features—like the daily "Best of the Web" at the *Wall Street Journal*'s Opinion Journal site, or the Corner at the National Review Online. But Instapundit's Reynolds provided a quirkier and more personal window on the growing conservative-blog universe—he was mainstream-conservative in some areas, like foreign policy, but more of a libertarian on social issues (he was against gun control but for same-sex marriage). Influential as his views were, his blogging style was even more infectious: he was generous with his links and indefatigable with his posts.

A week after 9/11, a writer in Los Angeles named Matt Welch started a blog and, filled with the zeal of the moment, christened it Warblog. Welch had labored in the trenches of the liberal press for years, at outfits like WorkingForChange.com, "marinating in the deeper wells of blue-state journalism," as he puts it today. Now he found himself enraged by what he saw as the "woefully inappropriate" commentary on the *Los Angeles Times* op-ed page and other outlets, articles that "basically responded to these attacks by calling the U.S. a terrorist state."

"Starting a blog," Welch says, "was a chance to stand up to people I'd walked among for fifteen years and yell 'ENOUGH!'"

Welch opened his blog with a post that declared "Welcome to War. . . . I, for one, advocate a Global War to abolish terrorism." His "warblog" label rapidly became associated with the entire weblog Class of 9/11. This new generation of "warbloggers" was angry, proud, and intoxicated with the potential of their new medium. They wrote with awe about the brave new Web world they felt they were discovering, and with disdain for the tired old media world they were leaving behind—a world they would eventually label dismissively as "the MSM" (for "mainstream media"). They discovered, as if for the first time, the power of linking, to one another and to original source material. They reveled in their freedom from authority and paraded what they saw as their dissent from liberal norms. Some may have been dimly aware that they were not, in fact, the first to experience this power and freedom, but in the urgency of the moment it didn't seem to matter. The cause they were enrolling in felt so overpoweringly important to them that it obliterated any obligation to the past. Just as al-Qaeda's attacks had reset the needle of world history, their blogs started the Web calendar anew at Year Zero.

Welch, a writer who yearned to transcend what he saw as the tawdry partisanship of Democrat and Republican, felt that the shock of 9/11 had "laid a linebacker-style hit on many people's political views (including my own, to a degree), opening them up to formerly incompatible or simply unknown ideas and thinkers." He praised his warblogger colleagues for sharing "a yen for critical thinking, a sense of humor that actually translates into people laughing out loud, a willingness to engage (and encourage) readers, a hostility to the Culture War and other artifacts of the professionalized left-right split of the 1990s . . . a readiness to admit error [and] a sense of collegial yet brutal peer review."

Indeed, though the new blogs congregated most heavily on the right, they were not limited to any one part of the political spectrum—and that spectrum itself was suddenly in flux, as the shock of the attacks shook up habitual stances. Jeff Jarvis, the Newhouse/Advance executive who'd invested in Pyra/Blogger, was on the last PATH train into the World Trade Center when the planes hit. "I was a block away from the South Tower when it came down," he remembers. "I was one of those guys you saw who was covered in the dust of destruction." Jarvis stayed around to report, and wrote up an account for the Newhouse wire service. He had begun reading blogs, but never thought he'd want to write one himself. Instantly, that changed: "The next day, I had more to say. It was as simple as that. I wanted an outlet. I thought, 'I'll blog for a few weeks.'"

Jarvis described himself as a former liberal pacifist transformed by 9/11 into an avid warblogger; he named his new blog WarLog: World War III. "There's an old joke that a conservative is a liberal who has been mugged," he would say. In a similar trajectory, Charles Johnson, a successful jazz guitarist and Los Angeles–based Web developer who described himself as "center-liberal" before 9/11, had begun a casual blog called Little Green Footballs for his company at the start of 2001; after 9/11 it became a hive of belligerent conservatism.

The warbloggers were academics and military people, journalists and programmers; most were American, but they found kindred voices abroad—among them an Australian journalist named Tim Blair. The warblog circle expanded quickly as participants shared their impatience with liberal efforts to understand grievances in the Muslim world; they cheered President Bush, derided his critics, and contributed to a national mood of self-righteousness that would come into full flower in the run-up to the invasion of Iraq.

Meanwhile, the old-school bloggers eyed the ferment on the right with disbelief. They'd invented or refined the tools that made the warblogs possible; they'd always hoped to see the blog world expand in new directions. But this? In January 2002, Metafilter's Matt Haughey posted to Jesse James Garrett's weblogs mailing list:

> The "war bloggers" are like 1998 all over again. . . . they're heavily link-driven, they appear to be done by 30 or 40 people that point at many of the same stories, the same links, etc. They point at each other a good deal, and whenever articles about them pop up, they mention the same ones and then those guys mention the articles and the rest of the circle continues to pat each other on the back.

> . . . is this the rite of passage all webloggers have to go through? Do we have to wait for them to come out on the other side to realize how pointless some of that stuff is? Is this like the longboard stage of surfing (or how 16-year-olds get their license and drive fast?) where you praise the

veterans and point to others and try to get on people's
link lists and madly read your favorites and take links from
them and read your referrer stats?

. . . It's almost like history is doomed to repeat itself.

Rebecca Blood would later codify this behavior in what she dubbed
"Blood's Law of Weblog History": "The year you discovered weblogs
and/or started your own is 'The Year Blogs Exploded.'" Anil Dash, a New
York–based Web entrepreneur who'd been blogging since July 1999,
offered a corollary: "The first blog you read is the one that invented the
medium."

The warbloggers' heyday was brief. The idea that their advent might
usher in a new, less partisan, more intellectually open era of political dialogue on the Web had about as much longevity as the parallel dream that
9/11 meant an end to low-road politics, the death of irony, and the evaporation of our collective interest in the sex lives of celebrities.

In an article a few years later titled "Farewell to Warblogging," Welch
described his disgust with the inbred close-mindedness he saw rampant
in the warblog movement. The bloggers who'd raised a banner against
media bias and error now routinely ignored fact-based arguments when
those arguments conflicted with positions dear to their camp. He
lamented the brevity of the disruptive post-9/11 moment he'd cherished: "For a few months there it was possible for readers and writers
alike to feel the unfamiliar slap of collisions with worlds they'd previously sealed off from themselves. You couldn't predict what anyone
would say, especially yourself."

The left hadn't disappeared. In the immediate aftermath of 9/11, few
American voices on the Web questioned the wisdom of invading
Afghanistan, toppling the Taliban, and going after Osama bin Laden. But

once the Bush administration's determination to expand its "war on ter-ror" became clear, and the White House began beating the war drums against Saddam Hussein's Iraq, the warbloggers began to find that they had company online. The same tools that had so readily served the anger of bloggers who championed the Bush administration's policies right after 9/11 could just as easily serve the anger of bloggers who questioned them.

The year 2002 saw the emergence of a new, energized liberal blog-ging community—the core of what would later be dubbed the Demo-cratic party's "netroots." An anonymous activist who called himself Atrios (he revealed himself in 2004 as Duncan Black, a Philadelphia economist) started his blog, called Eschaton, in April; he'd written for the old Media-WhoresOnline forum and had a sharp tongue and an ear for the quick sarcastic rejoinder. At roughly the same time, a sometime day trader named Jerome Armstrong took a website he'd set up a year before called MyDD—it originally stood for "My Due Diligence" and featured stock tips and market analysis—and began posting there about politics. (Arm-strong rechristened it as "My Direct Democracy.") A month later, a scrappy, ambitious fan of MyDD who went by the handle "Kos"—it was an army nickname, short for Markos Moulitsas Zuniga—launched his own blog, which he called Daily Kos.

The new progressive bloggers criticized the TV news channels and the newspapers as vocally from the left side of the fence as the warblog-gers had from the right. At the top of some of Armstrong's pages you could find an epigraph: "Don't hate the media—become the media." But Atrios, Kos, and the legions they would inspire were after bigger quarry: they shared the sharp-elbowed assertiveness of the warbloggers, but added a new element—a tight focus on the tactics of the political game. Their sites may have been outlets for self-expression and experiments in media-making, but all that was secondary. Bloggers had only posted about the political scene; the thing was to change it—to beat Republi-cans. As Kos put it, "One of my biggest pet peeves is the way this whole blogging thing is being held up as some sort of end in itself—some sort of magic wand. And it's just not true. Blogs are a tool, an instrument, nothing more."

In the beginning, the goal of direct political influence remained remote. In 2002 the chief impact of the new liberal blogs could be seen in two more-indirect areas. First, they challenged their counterparts on the right, who had felt as though they ruled the online roost since 9/11. Then they established a record of information and argument in opposition to the case the Bush administration was making throughout the summer and fall for the invasion of Iraq. At the time, this dissent was barely audible over the loud chorus of pro-war voices. It won little credence in the media, evoked snorts of derision from the right, and seemed to have no impact on the choice of most of the Democratic Party's leaders to support the rush to war. Only later, as the disastrous aftermath of the invasion unfolded, did the war critics earn a new hearing; their record of skepticism came to seem valuably prophetic.

In truth, although both the warbloggers and their counterparts on the left were quick to proclaim the populist power of their new, networked soapboxes, neither side could get the world to pay much attention. TV and print journalists still perceived anything taking place online as belonging to a separate world. Blogs might be amusing, but bloggers were only talking to one another. Their work had little substance and less consequence.

The first inkling that this view might need some adjustment came with the story of how Republican Senate majority leader Trent Lott lost his post in December 2002. The story also brought Josh Marshall a rush of new readers and attention—the first of many. Marshall's centrist-liberal tendencies had sidelined him during the warblogger ascendancy. But he never fit comfortably among the nascent activists on the Democratic left, either: unlike many of them, he had offered guarded support for the idea of a U.S. invasion of Iraq to topple Saddam Hussein, though he changed his mind as the inadequacy of the Bush administration's evidence became clear.

Many successful political bloggers simply echoed their readers' prejudices back to them. Marshall built his following along a more old-fashioned, and also more difficult, road: by seizing a handful of key stories, adding original reporting and judicious commentary to them, and making them his own.

Strom Thurmond, the very senior Republican senator from South Carolina, was being feted for his hundredth birthday at a Senate office building on Thursday, December 5, 2002. Lott, the senator from Mississippi, went to the podium before this friendly crowd of around five hundred, which included Thurmond's family, and offered his colleague the following praise: "When Strom Thurmond ran for president, we voted for him. We're proud of it. And if the rest of the country had followed our lead, we wouldn't have had all these problems over all these years either."

The event was swarming with reporters. At least some of them must have heard Lott's reference to Thurmond's 1948 Dixiecrat run for president against Harry Truman—a campaign that carried only a handful of states, including Lott's Mississippi—and caught its apparent endorsement of Thurmond's platform of segregation and opposition to civil rights legislation. But only one journalist on the scene, an ABC reporter, actually chose to highlight Lott's comment. It made it into a single newscast that night, and also got turned into a brief Friday-morning item in the Note, ABC's popular Web-only daily summary for political news devotees. *Washington Post* writer Thomas Edsall followed up with a short piece, buried on page six of the Saturday edition.

It's not precisely accurate, then, to say that the media *ignored* Lott's remark. It was, rather, treated as a minor tidbit, not a developing story. On the Web, the reaction was considerably more intense. Two leading political Web 'zines, Salon and Slate, both featured brief Lott items on Friday. But it was on a handful of blogs that the story took hold for a longer run.

Both Atrios and Josh Marshall began posting about the story on Friday and kept going through the weekend. Glenn Reynolds picked it up, too, writing, "Trent Lott deserves the shit he's getting from Atrios and Josh Marshall." The criticism from the right was, if anything, more unforgiving, perhaps because conservatives realized how much damage a drawn-out Lott controversy could do to the Republican Party's efforts to clean up its image among black voters. Before long, both Reynolds and Andrew Sullivan were calling on Lott to step down.

In this flurry of blogging, Marshall's Lott posts stood out. After greeting Lott's segregationist nostalgia with a sarcastic jab—"Oh, what could have been!!! Just another example of the hubris now reigning among Capitol Hill Republicans"—Marshall began digging up quotations and documents demonstrating that Lott's remarks fit snugly with his record over a lifetime in politics. "This obviously wasn't some misstatement or hyperbole or slip of the tongue," Marshall wrote. "It's what the guy believes." Some of Marshall's items were based on his own legwork; some were recycled from other sources; some were based on material that came in via email from his readers.

Anyone reading TPM during those few days got a real-time window onto Marshall's reporting process. His work resembled any journalist's—except that, rather than waiting to assemble his finds into a polished final report, he posted them as he confirmed them. Also, of course, he was free to insert his own commentary—unlike newsroom denizens professionally obligated to cordon off news page "fact" from op-ed page "opinion." And the very speed and openness of this process meant that any readers with new information could see that if they took the time to send Marshall a note, there was a good chance he'd make use of it.

The rap against blogs among skeptics was that bloggers never bothered to check their information. That was often true, but not here. For instance, Marshall got a tip from a source that Lott had made a spookily similar statement about Thurmond back in 1980, but he waited to post it until he could confirm it—and ended up being beaten by the *New York Times*, which by then had woken up to the story.

It took the news media five or six days to decide that Lott's segregationist nostalgia was indeed worth some coverage. Once that happened, Lott's demise was swift: two weeks and four increasingly desperate apologies later, he announced he was stepping down as Senate majority leader. John Podhoretz, the conservative columnist, declared that it was the bloggers who'd taken him down: "The Internet's First Scalp," his headline read.

But what had happened was subtler than that. A complex dance had taken place between the big media outlets and the Web—a little egging on; a little competition; a lot of information crossing the professional membrane separating blogs and newsrooms, in both directions. The Lott story, after all, would never have existed if ABC hadn't reported it in the first place; but it would never have brought Lott down without the attention of the bloggers. The bloggers didn't need a flow of "news pegs"—new developments, statements, or reactions—to justify the printing or airing of a new story. What they did, as a detailed case study of the controversy by Harvard's Kennedy School of Government outlined, was to keep the story alive after the uncoordinated yet eerily uniform editorial consensus of the nation's mass media had decided to let it die. The traditional news outlets were slaves to the idea of a "news cycle" that dictated when a story was hot and when it was old news; on a blog, the news cycle was whatever you wanted it to be.

Why hadn't the Washington press corps jumped on the Lott story in the first place? Were the reporters protecting their relationship with a powerful politician? Were they so inured to Lott's Stars-and-Bars sympathies that they just thought (as Larry Sabato of the University of Virginia suggested in the Harvard study), "There he goes again"? Or had they decided ahead of time that the Thurmond event—a birthday party, after all!—called for a light feature article in which this little bit of nastiness simply didn't fit? Whatever the cause, the slow uptake on Lott reinforced the feeling among many bloggers that the mainstream press was missing major stories right under its collective nose.

Marshall's dogged work on the Lott story got him some exposure on

TV and in print. *New York Times* columnist Paul Krugman cited Talking Points Memo as "must reading for the politically curious," in a credit-where-it's-due gesture that at the time was a rarity. All the attention drew new readers to the site.

That was good, because Marshall had been having his doubts about his blog. It was spreading his name and winning praise, but doing nothing to enhance his meager bank balance. That wasn't the most critical issue for him, though: "I was sort of starving regardless," he remembers. "It wasn't like I was turning away assignments because of the blog." Instead, "I was having an ever-present conversation with myself in my head: Was this a good use of my career?" He'd given up on the academic track for the life of the freelance journalist years before, but had always planned to finish his Brown University doctoral dissertation—a study of "the nexus of economic relations and organized violence between Indians and English settlers in mid-seventeenth-century New England." In fall of 2002, he decided that it was time to buckle down, blog a little less, and complete the history paper. Only first there was an election. Then there was the Lott story. And winter and spring brought a looming war with Iraq. At last, on March 18, 2003, on the actual eve of the American attack on Saddam Hussein, Marshall finished the dissertation's final draft.

That must have been a psychological watershed for him, because—though his talent and intelligence were undeniable—he was the sort of writer who often had trouble finishing things. For several years at the start of the decade, he'd been a contributor to Salon, where I was then managing editor. And while there was never any doubt that when Josh Marshall's name turned up on your news budget, you could expect a well-researched and well-argued piece, you would never want to put your money on *when* you might get it. For Marshall, there was always one more source to nail down, one last call to make, one crucial angle to pursue. To be fair, in this he was not very different from many of the best investigative reporters. Still, it was a trait that was bound to cause friction with any organization that had a publishing schedule and deadlines and editors.

Take away the schedule and the deadlines and the editors, as blogging does, and many writers will produce nothing, or produce a mess. But others will flourish. Marshall was one of the latter; the blog turned out to be his ideal form. In his posts, he improvised a mix of journalistic approaches—some opinion, a lot of analysis, a rare digression for a book review or a personal note. He'd mix in chunks of news reporting, but typically only on one or two running stories at a time—stories that he'd explicitly assigned himself to dig deeper into. He was doing what journalists have always done: following leads, connecting the dots, drilling dry holes in the media landscape until one starts to gusher news. But he was doing it in the open, bit by bit, letting his readers follow the process. Conventional-journalism wisdom had it that you couldn't do this because you'd alert subjects and tip off competitors; and there were certainly limits to how far Marshall could go in the direction of pure "transparency." But his approach had one great virtue that trumped all its potential problems: the more he exposed his line of thinking, the easier it was for his readers to add what they knew.

None of the earliest pioneers of political blogging offered visitors to their sites the opportunity to post comments in response to blog posts. Partly this was the fault of the primitive state of publishing technology: whether, like Andrew Sullivan, you were using Blogger, or like Marshall and Kaus, you were publishing by hand-coding basic HTML, there was no easy way in 2000 to allow readers to post their own comments. That gradually changed over the next two years, as new blogging tools arrived with the machinery for commenting built in—most notable was Movable Type, which debuted in October 2001 and automatically appended a small "post a comment" box at the bottom of every post. Matt Haughey's Metafilter had pioneered a simple model for the discussion of blog posts: unlike the geekier format adopted by Slashdot and other tech news sites, which provided "threaded" conversations—ones where each participant could branch the discussion into a sometimes impenetrable thicket of outline-tree branches—Metafilter had simple "linear" discussions, with new comments tacked on to the bottom of a single page. Movable Type made the same choice, and it became the most common style for blog discussions.

But many bloggers still chose not to open the door to comments. Some felt that comments undermined the whole point of the blog as a personal soapbox—the idea, most fiercely articulated by Dave Winer, that your blog was your online castle, a personal space where no one else's voice could drown yours out. Others just thought comments were too much of a bother, and that the real conversation took place across blogs, via linked reactions.

Beginning in 2002, however, comments gradually moved from an add-on offered by some more-adventurous bloggers to a standard feature of the typical blog. And nowhere did the comments play a bigger role than on the new liberal blogs, like Atrios's Eschaton, MyDD, and the booming Daily Kos. These sites began regularly racking up hundreds of comments from vocal followers who were unwilling or unready to begin their own blogs, but were eager to sound off about the many aspects of the Bush administration that enraged them. Visitors thronged to these lengthy discussions in comments and came to expect them; when the blog owners knew they were going to close down for the night or take a rare day off, they took to publishing "open thread" posts—essentially, blank blog posts created explicitly for the purpose of providing a space for comments. *Here*, the blogger in essence told the commenters, *talk amongst yourselves*.

Kos traced the core of his community to a group of avid commenters who'd migrated from site to site over the years. At one point they landed at an early political blog called Political Wire, run by Taegan Goddard. Goddard welcomed the influx of gabby readers but came to feel that their endless bickering was hurting his site, and he shut down the comments. The participants moved over to MyDD, but there the same drama soon repeated. After Armstrong closed off comments at MyDD, they moved on to Daily Kos. Kos, who'd spent several years in the U.S. Army, was prepared with a tough moderation policy—and had no interest in staying on the partisan sidelines. He picked sides in the flame wars, deleting right-wing comments and blocking GOP accounts. As he later explained:

> I had learned my lessons from Political Wire and MyDD's community failures, and immediately shut the door on the Republican commentors who had destroyed the previous sites' communities. I zealously worked to create a "safe zone" for liberal political junkies, despite howls of "censorship" from both liberals and conservatives, and the community grew.

In late 2003, Kos took one more step that cemented his site's preeminence among the new liberal blogs: he switched the software back-end of Daily Kos from Movable Type to a system called Scoop. He made the choice, he later wrote, because of Scoop's advanced moderation features. Scoop also allowed visitors to post "diaries"—their own blogs, basically, that were hosted under the umbrella of Daily Kos. "I actually didn't think anyone would use the diaries," Kos wrote, but his visitors embraced both reading and writing them.

The site's primacy among liberal blogs had grown over time. After the 2002 midterm elections, Jerome Armstrong put MyDD into hibernation; that made Daily Kos even more of a hub for liberals and Democrats looking for a place to gather. And Moulitsas's military service burnished his credibility in wartime, even as his sometimes intemperate posts drew flak (as in 2004, when he wrote "screw them" about the Blackwater contractors whose burned bodies were strung up in Falluja, Iraq). As Kos put it in a 2005 interview, "I was the one war critic, left-wing blogger who was an actual veteran, so it was difficult for people to dismiss me as a pacifist or a bleeding heart or whatever."

The new Scoop software was closer in spirit to a big community site like Slashdot than to the solo approach of most blog tools, and it transformed Daily Kos from a single blog to a blogger hive. The change was fortuitously timed. The hive populated quickly, thanks to a surge of anti-war energy among Kos's followers—they called themselves "Kossacks"—that showed no sign of waning. What 9/11 had been for bloggers on the right, the invasion of Iraq was to those on the left, and the war set off two distinct tidal waves of anger. Front and center, there was widespread disgust with the Bush administration's incompetent management of the war's aftermath, as American casualties mounted in the post–"Mission Accomplished" period and it became evident that, even though Secretary of Defense Donald Rumsfeld insisted he didn't "do quagmires," that was exactly what Iraq was.

But many bloggers were even angrier with the mainstream press than they were with the White House. They felt that the Bush administration's case against Saddam Hussein had been swallowed far too easily by Beltway media insiders and their bosses. As that case fell apart in the months after Saddam's fall, with the failure to find "weapons of mass destruction" and revelations that the White House doctored intelligence findings, lefty bloggers and their readers found themselves experiencing a painful flashback: newspapers finally began piecing together many of the details undermining the administration's war argument, and much of the information they were now assembling had been passed around on progressive blogs *before* the invasion. Just as conservatives often complained of liberal bias in the media, focusing typically on institutions like the *New York Times* and CNN, their counterparts on the left looked at the increasingly powerful Fox News and the *Wall Street Journal* and saw bias to the right. But on Iraq, the liberals saw a wider, systemic media failure: this wasn't just about Ann Coulter raving on Fox; the *New York Times* and *Washington Post* had failed the journalistic credibility test, too.

The conflict between bloggers and professional journalists had been boiled down to a single phrase by Ken Layne, a maverick Web journalist, in 2001. Like many of the warbloggers, Layne nursed a special reserve of bile for British foreign correspondent Robert Fisk, who was viewed as hopelessly anti-American. When Fisk, in a report soon after 9/11, wrote that the pivotal assassination of an Afghan leader shortly before the World Trade Center attacks had been "largely missed" by the world media, Layne cited reports in the *New York Times*, the *Los Angeles Times*, and the BBC to show that the story hadn't been missed at all. Then he crowed, "It's 2001, and we can Fact Check your ass."

The practice of taking a media report apart and arguing with it, line by line, soon became known as "fisking"—at least on the right-wing blogs, beyond which the coinage never spread. But "We can fact-check your ass" was a war cry that people on both sides of the partisan divide could get behind.

If anger with Bush and outrage at the media was what first brought the Kossacks together, along with Kos himself they also harbored a beef with their own political party. The Democratic Party leadership, they felt, had failed to stand up to Bush on issue after issue. Now it had caved on Iraq, authorizing Bush's war out of fear that their opponents might frame them as insufficiently tough on terrorism. Something had to be done, and Kos, who was beginning to see his blog as a mechanism for launching a reform movement within the Democratic Party, knew what to do. He and Armstrong hung out their shingle as political consultants. Their first client was Howard Dean, the former Vermont governor, who was outspoken against the war—and who would win notice as the first major presidential candidate to earn the love, and money, of the "netroots."

Kos and Armstrong didn't turn out to have a big part to play in the Dean candidacy—their consultancy lasted only six months. But their involvement in its early stages helped crystallize the picture of Dean as the first blog-powered presidential contender. That quickly became a media cliché, but it was founded on fact. Dean's candidacy, which rose to prominence in the middle of 2003 and crashed and burned early in the following winter's primary election season, drew its energy from both a rising fury among voters about the Iraq mess and a surge of excitement about the opportunities the Web provided to rethink the basics of political campaigning. Campaigns had been using email for years, and the

Republicans, with their decades-old expertise in assembling targeted direct-mail campaigns, had adapted well to the game of email list management. But the approach crafted by Dean campaign manager Joe Trippi and the Net-savvy kids who joined him was far more innovative: they offered a community of blogs for active "Deaniacs," and— embracing Meetup, a new Web service that helped groups of like-minded people assemble for real-world gatherings—they gave those supporters ways to find one another. Dean's team took seriously the whole notion of a bottom-up campaign, where the supporters could not only give money but exchange ideas with the candidate and with each other. And, more than any other campaign to date, the Dean campaign actually delivered on at least some portion of that uplifting vision.

All this got bloggers excited. But what caught the national media's eye was that Dean's bottom-up populism was also raising significant amounts of cash online. Neither the populism nor the cash put Dean over the top in Iowa, however. After the fact, some analysts speculated that the invasion of the state by young, Web-driven Dean volunteers actually hurt the candidate, getting the locals' backs up. At the same time, the Dean volunteers got their own trial-by-fire lesson in the cruel campaign dynamics of the mass media: a minor moment of bad miking at an election-night-party turned into the infamous soundbite known as the "Dean scream"—a clip in which the candidate fired up his followers with an odd-sounding yowl. The press decided his outburst was insufficiently restrained, and Dean's opponents sat back and chortled.

The Dean campaign had always been a long shot, and its failure set the stage for an even greater Democratic failure in the November election. All the excitement on the Web and in the blogs hadn't seemed to make any difference. Political consultants of the old school felt vindicated; the world wasn't changing so quickly, after all. But in the wake of the 2004 loss, the veterans of Dean's campaign fanned out across the political landscape, seeding the party with their approach. Dean himself took over as the party's national chairman in 2005. One year they were party insurgents; before long they'd become the party establishment.

And no one associated with any of them was likely ever again to dismiss the importance of the political blogs.

Still, for liberal bloggers at the end of 2004, there was no getting around the pain. Their candidate had lost; George W. Bush was still president. In the weeks after Bush's victory, his administration seemed at the peak of its power. Yet, barely a year later, the president's agenda had been stymied, his power stalemated, and his popularity deep-sixed.

Of course, second-term presidents often falter. You could blame the deteriorating situation in Iraq for this turnabout. Certainly, Bush's dreadfully botched response to Hurricane Katrina also played a part. But so, improbably, did Josh Marshall's Talking Points Memo.

After the election, the White House set forth to enact its most ambitious policy initiative ever: an effort to "reform" Social Security by allowing— really, encouraging—citizens to divert a sizable chunk of the payroll taxes that fund the program into private investment accounts. Many Republicans and Democrats alike had long been concerned that Social Security would someday become insolvent, though the timing of such a potential crisis was in dispute. A bipartisan plan to shore up the system in the early 1990s had actually solved the problem once, but President Bush's first-term tax cuts had squandered the surplus that had been set aside to fund future Social Security benefits. In any case, the most conservative Republicans hoped not to fix Social Security but to scrap it—they'd been itching to kill the suspiciously socialistic scheme ever since their nemesis, Franklin D. Roosevelt, created it in the 1930s. But the program had been effective at providing Americans with a baseline level of retirement income, and that made it perennially popular. Previous GOP campaigns to mess with Social Security had proven so painful to the party that the issue had become known as a political "third rail": tampering with it was fatal.

After the 2004 election, however, Bush was feeling invulnerable. Even carrying the burden of an increasingly unpopular war, Republicans had retained control of both the White House and Congress. If the party was ever going to have a chance to dismantle Social Security, this was the moment. "For the first time in six decades, the Social Security battle is one we can win—and in doing so, we can help transform the political and philosophical landscape of the country," wrote Peter Wehner, a deputy to Bush strategist Karl Rove.

A few years later, when the bottom fell out of the stock market in 2008, those American workers who still recalled the Bush plan were probably wiping their foreheads thinking, "Glad we dodged that bullet." But in 2004, in the middle of a bull market, the idea of letting your stockbroker invest your Social Security savings on Wall Street still had some appeal. Fresh from his election victory, Bush announced that his Social Security plan was the centerpiece of his second-term agenda and would be his top priority when Congress reconvened after the holidays. While the administration planned to unleash a full-court press in January, Marshall began hammering on the subject almost immediately. As he wrote, he felt that "abolishing Social Security isn't just any issue. For Democrats, it's an issue of fundamental importance and core values."

> This isn't about financing. It's about whether Americans get to keep Social Security, a program of guaranteed retirement insurance, which unlike the other key elements of a good retirement plan—investments and pensions— cannot be taken away.

The argument around the Social Security issue was important, and complicated. How dire was the crisis, really? Would the entire system melt down in 2018, as the Bush plan's proponents argued? Or were the plan's advocates overstating the imminence of its insolvency and the scale of its long-term problems? Day after day, Marshall patiently explained the subtleties of the statistics, analyzed the assumptions made by each side in the debate, and debunked the GOP claim that their plan aimed to save the program rather than gut it. In the past, he pointed out, some Democrats

had supported adding private accounts on top of the existing Social Security benefit; but Bush was now proposing *replacing* part of Social Security
with the new private accounts. He drew parallels between how the Bush
White House was trying to sell the Social Security "reform" and how it
had tried to drum up support for the invasion of Iraq:

> All the folks who cover the White House are looking for
> WMD2. It'll be one big push of fear-mongering and fibs
> to bum-rush the country into phasing out Social Security.

In both cases, he argued, the administration approach was to scare the
public with a coordinated public relations campaign, then roll out the
attack. Only this time the target wasn't a brutal Arab dictator, but instead
a beloved government program.

There was no better guide to understanding the Social Security
debate than reading TPM in December 2004 and January 2005. As the
Republicans began fine-tuning their campaign, Marshall made comic hay
out of their desperate effort to control the language of the debate. For
years they'd called their plan "privatization" with "private accounts"; but
when they discovered these words didn't poll well, they quickly
switched gears and tried—with only spotty success—to get their own
officials, as well as the journalists who covered the issue, to say "personal
accounts" instead. When the *New York Times* and other media outlets
accepted the White House's line that to use the term "private accounts"
was to take sides, Marshall wrote, "Do journalists really have to genuflect
every time the White House issues a new vocabulary directive?" He
turned the hunt for examples of GOP terminology confusion into a
game with his readers, inviting them to earn points toward free T-shirts
by catching officials out in self-contradiction.

Marshall involved his readers in the heart of his reporting on Social
Security. Early on in his coverage of the story, he started focusing on the
small number of Democrats in Congress who—unlike the great majority

of the party's legislators—had shown some sympathy toward Bush's proposals, or hadn't ruled out supporting some version of them. Republicans controlled Congress and, theoretically, could pass a plan without a single Democratic vote. But Marshall argued that a united Democratic opposition would put pressure on Republicans in Congress who were already a little shaky about touching the "third rail":

> Making the elimination of Social Security a strictly Republican gambit raises the political stakes dramatically. Many Republicans will be far more cautious without bipartisan cover. Democrats must deny them even the thinnest of fig leaves.

On December 16, Marshall asked his readers across the United States to send in information about their legislators' positions on the plan: "Where do your representatives and senators stand on phasing out or keeping Social Security? If you find out from press accounts or by calling up and asking your representative or senator, let us know what you hear."

This was happening on the eve of the holiday season, weeks before the White House was ready to start its publicity campaign, and the responses from at least some politicians contacted by TPM readers suggested that they were caught off balance. As the reports filed in, Marshall would fire off posts. He began maintaining a roster of what he called "The Fainthearted Faction"—wavering Democrats who would be ceremoniously inducted or removed from the ranks depending on their latest statements. Day after day, he'd post who'd been added to the list and who'd fallen off it.

> Stop what you're doing! Spit out your drink!

> Does Sen. Ben Nelson (D) of Nebraska want out of the Faction?

Then he also started tracking a "Conscience Caucus" of Republicans who were defecting from supporting the Bush proposal. Later he added a "Finger in the Wind" category (for "those members who more or less openly state that they are willing to begin phasing out Social Security so long as the president can make it safe for them to do so"). On this single issue, TPM served up a level of detail—and of passion—that no other media outlet could muster.

Bush's plan hit trouble almost immediately. The Fainthearted roster, never much more than a dozen, dwindled, and the Conscience Caucus grew. The president talked up his proposal in the State of the Union speech on February 2 and—even though he had still not offered full details of his plan—hit the road with a sixty-day campaign of town meetings and speeches to try to sell it to the American people. "The bamboozlepalooza begins!" Marshall wrote.

There was always a wide gap between the ambition of Bush's Social Security agenda and the limited enthusiasm for it anywhere beyond hardcore conservative policy analysts. Even as Bush departed to sell his idea, the Republican chairman of the House Ways and Means Committee was labeling it a "dead horse." Nonetheless, Bush's administration— from its birth in the 2000 Florida recount through the passage of its 2001 tax-cut plan to the 2002 Iraq war authorization and on into the 2004 election—had shown a tenacious ability to steamroll its opposition, snatch razor-thin victories against daunting odds, and then claim possession of a broad mandate. That could easily have happened again in 2005 with Social Security.

Instead, the plan foundered. Bush's string of victories was finally over. The more the president and his surrogates campaigned for their plan, the worse it fared in polls, and the colder grew the feet of the Republicans in Congress who would need to push it through; most of their necks would be on the electoral line a lot sooner than the president's. Congress failed to take up the Social Security "reform" before it left town for the summer. When the legislators returned from their recess—amid a storm of national outrage over the mishandling of Hurricane Katrina relief—few

Republicans had the stomach to pick up the Social Security fight again on the president's behalf. The Bush administration had tried, as Marshall put it, to "harness Americans' desire to save Social Security in their own effort to destroy it." But they had failed.

The conflict over Bush's Social Security plan proved to be a genuine turning point—a political Battle of Midway or Gettysburg, a decisive engagement that shifted the momentum of everything that followed. Talking Points Memo was only one player in that fight. But it was arguably the first, the most consistent, and the most effective voice in the swelling chorus of opposition. It was still a modest site, with a self-reported 600,000 monthly visitors—impressive for a one-man operation, but still small potatoes compared with any "real" media outlet. Yet it was influential beyond those numbers because it reached a smart and connected audience of political insiders and reporters as well as news-addicted everyday citizens; and the success of its coverage further deepened that influence, even as the audience contributed to the success of the coverage. In April 2005, Marshall wrote, "It would have been impossible for me to have written most of what I've written on Social Security over the last few months if I didn't have literally thousands of people reading their local papers and letting me know what they're seeing or reporting back from town-hall meetings or giving me the heads-up on things that are about to break on the Hill."

The Social Security story wasn't the first instance in which Marshall mobilized his readers; he'd done something similar twice the previous year. As TPM covered the plan by media conglomerate Sinclair Broadcasting to air a biased show about Senator John Kerry's Swift Boat controversy, Marshall had readers spearhead boycotts of local advertisers. Then he involved readers in covering what he called "The DeLay Rule"—a complex parliamentary effort by House Republicans to change the rules so that majority leader Tom DeLay could hold on to his post even if (as was expected) he was indicted. Marshall urged his readers to contact their representatives and ask how they'd voted in the secret caucus that passed the DeLay Rule; strangely, the GOP representatives were reluctant to tell their constituents where they stood.

But with the Social Security story, Marshall involved his readers in an issue of direct importance to them, on a much larger scale, over a longer span of time, and made it all work. His approach occupied some hitherto unexplored gray area between reporting and activism. As a professional journalist who'd migrated onto the Web, he acknowledged the tension: "I think it was sort of on the edge of my comfort zone," he says. On the other hand, he felt the subject was unique: the soul of the Democratic Party was at stake, and Social Security was worth drawing a line around.

Though he was as ambitious as any political writer might be in wanting to play a part in the national debate, Marshall hadn't set out, the way Kos had, to be a political insider. Yet he'd made his way along a different path toward a significant kind of influence. Beginning in 2005, TPM would expand, adding a handful of paid employees, a group blog, and a new investigative arm called TPM Muckraker. It continued to make its mark on stories like the scandals surrounding the lobbyist Jack Abramoff. Marshall's site led the way in exposing the politicization of Bush's Justice Department under Attorney General Alberto Gonzales, beginning with stories about the firing of a number of U.S. attorneys who had been made to walk the plank to make room for handpicked Bush loyalists in the supposedly nonpartisan department.

Once again Marshall built his stories on his own legwork and the help of readers who fed the site valuable tidbits of local information. When the Justice Department took to releasing "data dumps" of documents requested by Congress, TPM posted them on the Web and invited readers to pitch in and help review the thousands of pages of primary-source material. For his work on the Gonzales story, Marshall won a George Polk Award for Legal Reporting in 2008. The prize seemed to serve double duty, acknowledging both his own work and, more generally, the arrival of the blogging political journalist as a player on the national stage.

Marshall had improvised his way toward a new form of news writing—he described it as an incremental or "iterative" approach of "narrating complex, slowly unfolding stories." In some ways it was more like radio than print. He'd signal an interest in some little event that might have greater significance that hadn't yet been teased out (like, hmm, anyone notice that a number of U.S. attorneys are all resigning at once—wonder what's going on?). Then he'd dig into it, adding a piece of information here, underlining a connection there, thinking out loud about alternative explanations for confusing turns of events, stopping every now and then for a sort of where-we-are-now overview post pulling all the bits together.

The independence of a blog meant that if you were playing Woodward and Bernstein on some new Watergate story, you didn't have to fight your editors each time you wanted to publish a new article with a new piece of the puzzle you were assembling. It wasn't the ideal form for readers who wanted the convenience of a quick summary, but those who could tune in for an extended period were rewarded with a unique perspective on the unfolding of a story over time. If you followed along with Marshall on some issue, you found that you were far ahead of the rest of the press; you could watch—as happened with Social Security or the attorney firings—as the stories made their way up the media food chain, onto front pages and national newscasts.

The original political bloggers set out to satisfy political junkies, and the genre evolved to serve that audience with high-volume, round-the-clock posting and a distant-early-warning system for big news. If you believed the stereotypes, these junkies were outsiders—ordinary citizens beyond the Beltway who just happened to take a strong interest in reading about the affairs of government. But sometimes, in practice, the junkies turned out to be well-connected insiders who wanted to keep ahead of the curve—and who simply rolled their eyes when the blogs would trot out some truculently antiestablishment stance.

The idea of independent muckraking was hardly new; blogs like TPM resembled forebears like *I. F. Stone's Weekly*, the legendary one-man newsletter of investigative journalism. Yet for years, much of the D.C. power set had treated blogs as "here be dragons" territory. Particularly for Washington insiders schooled in an earlier era, the blogs' aggressive blurring of established boundaries—among others, between writer and reader, journalist and activist, editor and publisher—caused confusion, if not consternation.

In 2004, Marshall bumped into one of his idols, the late Arthur Schlesinger Jr., at a cocktail party, and fumblingly attempted to explain the nature of his blog to the eminent Kennedy-administration veteran and liberal historian. "To be polite," Marshall wrote, "Schlesinger's wife asked me to explain to them just what a blog is":

> And though I get this question pretty often, it turns out to be a rather challenging one if the people you're trying to explain it to don't necessarily have a lot of clear web reference points to make sense of what you're saying.
>
> I ended up telling them that it was something like political commentary structured like a personal journal with occasional reporting mixed in.
>
> Now, as I was explaining and watching the looks on everyone's faces it was incrementally becoming clear to me that this was playing rather like saying that something was like a washing machine structured like a rhinoceros with the occasional sandwich thrown in.

Four years later, blogs had become more widely understood inside the Beltway, but no more beloved. John McCain, the Republican candidate in 2008, got along famously with the Washington press corps, but in December 2007, in an aside at a town hall meeting, he quipped, "I hate the bloggers!" Though it was offered lightly, the remark revealed a lasting unease with this upstart class: Who do these people think they are—and who gave them the mike, anyway?

Washington journalists whose work involved prying information from recalcitrant politicians had to play a game with them. At best they were able to smuggle good stories through the corridors of power under the nose of the PR machine; at worst they wound up as patsies, helping plant pre-spun reports in the media bloodstream. Bloggers were anything but immune to being similarly played. In a candid comment to *Texas Monthly* after he left the administration, President Bush's counselor Dan Bartlett explained how the White House exploited sympathetic blogs:

> I mean, talk about a direct IV into the vein of your support. It's a very efficient way to communicate. They regurgitate exactly and put up on their blogs what you said to them. It is something that we've cultivated and have really tried to put quite a bit of focus on.

But most bloggers never got close enough to the centers of power to have their ethics tested. They tended to lob spitballs from a safe distance instead.

As this complex ecosystem of political information evolved, Marshall spent years with one foot on the bloggy Web and the other planted in traditional journalism, and he'd always seemed genuinely torn between the old world and the new. In a 2004 *New York Times Magazine* piece about the rise of political blogging, Matthew Klam wrote: "[Marshall] can't decide between loving the big media, linking to it, hoping they'll pick up on stories, and hating it, despising it, insulting it, trying to convince you, or himself, that it's the worst thing in the world and that it's ruining American democracy." Marshall once told a reporter, "If I had quickly happened into a staff position at *The New Yorker*, I probably wouldn't have done this." Unlike so many of his fellow bloggers, Marshall always recoiled from the messianic zeal of "blog triumphalism," as he called it. Rather than hype the transcendent capacities of the new medium, Marshall stuck to his knitting, building his reputation, credibility, and readership, adding advertising to support TPM, expanding it carefully, hiring interns and a small staff. Though TPM grew steadily and healthily, Marshall resisted the temptation to take outside investment money; he spent only what he made from advertising, and occasionally raised small expansion funds through contributions from readers. In all this, he resembled less a wild-eyed Web visionary touting digital democracy than a small-town businessman keeping a narrow eye and a tight hold on his operation.

Still, as the years passed it became increasingly plain that, for Marshall, the tug of the old journalism world—the prestige byline, the big-bucks-per-word magazine piece—had lost much of its power. One thing Marshall got from blogging that he hadn't found anywhere else was a kind of self-determination. The freelance writing career he had fitfully pursued involved a wearisome and sometimes demeaning routine of pitching ideas to harried assignment editors and navigating pieces through fickle editorial hierarchies. Talking Points Memo liberated him from that routine—and you could sense the giddying energy of that liberation in his inventively improvisational approach to blog-based reporting. As he put it in 2004, "What I backed into, in doing this blog, was freedom."

Chapter 6

BLOGGING FOR BUCKS
ROBERT SCOBLE, NICK DENTON, JASON CALACANIS

In *The Empire of the Air*, the Ken Burns documentary about the early days of radio, a retired broadcaster named Helen Kelley is reminiscing about how her life changed once radio entered it. At one point she recalls with a laugh, "I probably gave up practicing the piano because I didn't have to make my own music anymore."

Dave Winer was watching the film one night, and he found that sequence "pivotal, electrifying." He wrote:

> I said out loud: There it is, that's the moment we're reversing now. It was a mistake to believe that creativity was something you could delegate, no matter how much better they were than you, because it's an important human activity, like breathing, eating, walking, laughing, loving.

For Winer, as for many other idealists on the Web, that moment—the moment broadcasting took over—was like a second Fall. It had brought media consumption to the masses, but restricted media production to a few specialists. There was only so much spectrum, and a finite amount of air time. For everyday people, creating personal media became a fringe activity—the occupation of ham radio nuts and basement mimeographers, the devotees of Super 8 movies and the oddballs who showed up on public-access cable channels.

Many early bloggers felt they were reversing this polarity, turning the broadcast model upside down, restoring the place of media-making in everyday life. Money wasn't in the picture at all—any more than it was for the family that, in the days before radio, sat around the living-room piano to practice a piece of music. Blogging began as a pursuit of amateurs, in the pure meaning of the word: people motivated by love. In the early days there was no alternative—no path to "monetization," no choice of blog advertising network, no revenue from Google text ads. For a long time there simply was no such thing as a "professional blogger." That would be something like an insomniac narcoleptic or a pacifist murderer; the term nonsensically contradicted itself.

To many blogging pioneers, this amateurism was part of the attraction—an essential strength, rather than a flaw to be outgrown. Yet there was a difference between amateur and amateurish; to be unpaid did not necessitate being ignorant. From the start there was never a shortage of people blogging, knowledgeably, *about* their professions. As with so much else on the Internet, the software developers broke the first ground, with Winer's example as inspiration. Blogs turned out to be the perfect format for computer programmers who wanted to ask questions about specific coding problems, make announcements about new releases, or quibble over the finer points of some technical dispute. It was predictable that programmers dedicated to the open-source movement, which rose to prominence in the late nineties, would embrace blogging as a convenient tool for sharing expertise: their methodology depended on open collaboration across the Net. Less predictably, blogging simultaneously took root in the software industry's corporate heart, at Microsoft—the fabulously profitable enterprise that loomed in the open-source programmers' mythology as the Evil Empire.

Microsoft wasn't known as a haven of openness and cooperation. But it was a big place with a lot of smart people. At the turn of the millennium, during the company's bitter antitrust fight with the U.S. Department of Justice, many of those people found it impossible to recognize themselves in the press's portrait of the company. The first programmer at Microsoft to start blogging, Joshua Allen, set himself up with an account on Dave Winer's EditThisPage service in 2000 and started posting under the header "Better Living Through Software: Tales of Life at Microsoft." It was totally informal and unauthorized—a lone call for a parley raised from behind the company's siege walls. Allen explained his intent: "I wanted to say that I am a Microsoft person and you can talk with me." Soon enough, Microsoft-loathing open-source programmers began showing up to quarrel, but so did readers sent via links from Winer and other prominent technology bloggers. The attention was both exciting and problematic: "There was no explicit policy against these things," Allen later wrote, "but people were scared and jumpy. . . . If a co-worker came to you and started a sentence with 'I was reading your blog,' your first thought would be 'Crap! How did he find out about it?!' " As Allen drew attention from outside Microsoft, he also attracted eyes in the company's own legal department, and his superiors began getting email complaints: What in Bill Gates's name was Allen doing? Shouldn't he be fired?

But Microsoft let Allen post, and before long other Microsoft developers were starting blogs, too. Sometimes they echoed the company's public positions; sometimes they expressed their own doubts, and even disagreed with one another. Though these blogs would occasionally become flashpoints for angry online mobs to denounce the monopolist evildoers, more often they inspired visitors to reconsider their broadbrush demonization of a thousands-strong company. Gee, the reader realized, Allen seems like a reasonable enough guy; maybe there's more to Microsoft than I thought.

The Microsoft blogs put human features on a hitherto faceless corporation. Without the formal machinery of a big PR and marketing campaign, they showed outsiders that if you looked closely, this intimidating monolith of a company actually crumbled into a bunch of approachable individuals. This sort of corporate transformation had been predicted, and advocated, in a document titled *The Cluetrain Manifesto* (it started as an online proclamation by a quarter of Web notables in 1999, and became a book the next year). "Markets are conversations," *Cluetrain* announced, as it tacked its own "95 Theses" on the door of the corporate world's church:

> Markets consist of human beings, not demographic sectors.

> Conversations among human beings sound human. They are conducted in a human voice.

> Whether delivering information, opinions, perspectives, dissenting arguments or humorous asides, the human voice is typically open, natural, uncontrived.

> People recognize each other as such from the sound of this voice.

> The Internet is enabling conversations among human beings that were simply not possible in the era of mass media.

Cluetrain told its audience of marketing pros and advertising-agency creatives that the markets-as-conversations train was bearing down on them. It also warned them that the human voice "can't be faked":

> Most corporations . . . only know how to talk in the soothing, humorless monotone of the mission statement, marketing brochure, and your-call-is-important-to-us

busy signal. Same old tone, same old lies. . . . But learning to speak in a human voice is not some trick, nor will
corporations convince us they are human with lip service
about "listening to customers." They will only sound
human when they empower real human beings to speak
on their behalf.

Cluetrain—in both manifesto and book forms—predated the wide
popularity of weblogs; the word *blog* never appears in its text. But its
vision of a teeming global exchange of ideas busting out from behind
institutional barriers was in perfect sync with the conversations that bloggers were beginning to have. Inevitably they helped champion *Cluetrain*,
adopting it as a battle cry against bureaucratic impersonality. It was, for
many, a stark, Manichean conflict, the warm tones of the blogger versus
the bullhorn of The Man. But if you read *Cluetrain* carefully, you understood its argument to be a subtler one. There was, *Cluetrain's* authors
held, no Man at all. Every institution was just a bunch of individual
people, once those individuals had a chance to speak for themselves.

However improbable it was that the Cluetrain's first stop at a large
corporation would be at Microsoft headquarters, the company, far from
shutting down or firing its bloggers, let them be. By spring 2003, about
one hundred Microsoft employees were blogging. Then the company
shifted its position from benign neglect to active embrace: it hired Robert
Scoble, a prolific and well-connected Silicon Valley blogger who had once
worked for Dave Winer's Userland Software. Scoble had cultivated an
extensive network of connections through his blog, called Scobleizer, and
that was what made him attractive to his new employer. But Microsoft
didn't ask him to bring his popular blog in-house. Instead, he kept it going
on his own time. For the company, he spearheaded the development of a
new official video blog called Channel 9, in which he'd wander the
Microsoft campus interviewing developers and managers about their new
projects, bringing the outside world news of goings-on inside the corporate beast. Channel 9 took its name from the audio channel on which

United Airlines lets passengers listen in to the cockpit radio; just as some nervous fliers found comfort in eavesdropping on the pilot-and-tower chatter, so, Microsoft hoped, the tech world's distrust might be soothed by an informal look inside the company's offices.

With a background in both journalism and technology, Scoble was a smart choice for Microsoft. Tirelessly curious and garrulous, he personified the blogger as human network hub. His off-the-cuff writing wasn't for the ages; he was boyishly enthusiastic, sometimes alarmingly innocent. But he was regularly able to disarm critics—he'd admit his faults before others could jump on them.

His blog had played a "major role" in getting him hired, Scoble freely acknowledged; now he had reason to wonder whether it might get him fired. Before he'd even started his new job, Scoble heard from a friend at the company that someone had started a "Scoble dead pool"—wondering how long it would be before he'd write something that would get him in big trouble. "Weblogging is like dancing in a field of land mines," he wrote:

> I find I've had to make friends in the legal profession. Friends in the PR profession. Friends in the journalistic profession.
>
> Will I step on a landmine I didn't see? It's very possible. I guess that's one reason I have 18 readers who come by here every day. "Will Scoble blow up?"

And yet he didn't blow up. Instead he carried his influential Silicon Valley readership along with him into the belly of the Microsoft beast, using his blog and video camera to humanize the company in a way no high-cost public relations campaign could match. Scoble's title ought to be "chief humanizing officer," *The Economist* proposed in 2005. He'd been at Microsoft a year; more than 1,300 of his colleagues were now blogging.

Scoble's success at improving Microsoft's public image came at some cost to his own credibility. He had arrived at Microsoft while the software giant was just beginning to unveil the long-gestating new features of the next version of the Windows operating system, code-named Long-horn. Bill Gates and his lieutenants were promising a whole slew of remarkable innovations in Longhorn, including a snazzy new graphical interface and a radically renovated filesystem. Longhorn was going to revolutionize computing, Microsoft insisted, and no one was more excited about it than Robert Scoble. In a "Corporate Weblog Manifesto" that he'd posted shortly before joining Microsoft, he'd advised bloggers who represented companies to "underpromise and overdeliver." Unfortu-nately, Microsoft was doing precisely the opposite with Longhorn, and Scoble allowed himself to get caught up in the hype, too. For well over a year he talked up the new-and-improved Windows in his posts, linked to every other Microsoft blogger who was singing its praises, and pointed his camera at its developers as they demoed its delights. Then, in August 2004, Microsoft admitted that Longhorn was way behind schedule, and would be gutted of many of its most highly touted innovations so it could finally be delivered. (It became Windows Vista, born in January 2007 and troubled ever since.)

Scoble's own company had cut him off at the knees. It was at moments like these, though, that his forthrightness served him best. "If you screw up, acknowledge it," he'd advised in his manifesto; this time he took his own advice. When the complaints poured in—"Scoble should be earning his pay and telling us why Longhorn still matters," one blogger demanded—he chose candor over defensiveness:

> The thing is that I don't have any credibility left when it comes to Longhorn. Over the last 18 months I got out there and led lots of Longhorn cheers. And now there's a changing of direction.

He knew that his honesty was his main—maybe his only—asset. He'd bartered it, in a sense, by taking Microsoft's paycheck—then struggled to earn it all over again through ostentatious displays of independence. It was a very public high-wire act, balancing the diplomatic language and behavior that corporate survival demanded and the blunt talk that made his blog matter to its readers. Scoble continued to pull this act off until his departure from Microsoft in June 2006.

Although Microsoft's bet on blogging was matched by some other technology companies, outside the tech realm big companies remained ignorant or wary. "Enterprise blogging," or "bizblogging," as it came to be known, was advocated by a relatively small handful of true believers—marketing-world Web geeks and corporate mavericks—and implemented only sporadically in the business world, most often at tech-industry institutions like Sun Microsystems or upstart companies like Southwest Airlines.

But for smaller businesses and independent professionals, the risks were less obvious and the rewards more immediate. One model was to start a blog as a compendium of your accumulated wisdom and war stories. An early exemplar of this approach was Joel on Software—a series of essays delivered informally, blog-style, by a former Microsoft developer named Joel Spolsky, who festooned his technical discourse with recollections from his days in the Israeli army and references to the Yiddish folktales he cherished. These improbably colorful tales from the programming trenches won him a following that grew steadily—and that helped draw customers to the small software-development house he'd founded.

On the Web, what software developers start, other groups soon take up. As blogging became more approachable, it began to be adopted by professionals of all sorts. Naturally, lawyers and economists and anyone else whose specialty involved a passion for contentious debate flocked to blogging. Less predictably, you also started to find blogs written by librarians and educators and even tailors. The champions of blogging for the small-business proprietor liked to point to the example of English Cut, a blog by a Savile Row tailor named Thomas Mahon. Mahon teased his readers with the names of some of his clients (Prince Charles, Bryan Ferry), schooled them in the subtleties of choosing fabric, and patiently explained the difference between "made to measure" (where a preexisting suit template is adjusted to your fit) and the truly personalized, fully hand-tailored "bespoke" suits he sells. In one sense, English Cut was just one big ad for Mahon's services, spread out over blog time and Web space. At the same time, readers got a sense of Mahon's fire for his work and the lore of his craft. And he offered useful inside information on good men's clothing, even for readers who were never going to afford his $4,000 suits.

Spolsky and Mahon and similar bloggers weren't selling ads, and neither could point to direct revenue from their posts. Yet their blogs were benefiting their businesses, helping them reach new customers and stand out from the competition. As the technology columnist Jon Udell observed, "The demonstration of knowledge and expertise over time in a weblog is the modern equivalent of a résumé." Doc Searls—a writer and former marketing exec who co-wrote *The Cluetrain Manifesto* and started blogging in 1999—declared in a 2004 *Newsweek* interview, "If you're into blogs to make money, you're into it for the wrong reasons. Do you ask your back porch what its business plan is?" Searls liked to draw the distinction between making money *with* a blog, directly, the way you might by selling ads, and earning money indirectly *because* of your blog, which spread your reputation and opened doors for you.

The bloggers who'd begun to do the latter enjoyed several advantages: the direct costs were minimal, the field was not yet crowded (Mahon, for instance, could safely assume he was the *only* blogger on Savile Row), and you needed no one's permission or approval to start addressing your potential customers directly. This sort of blogging wasn't really a media business at all, one in which you offer some creative material or "content" to gather a crowd and then sell the attention of that crowd to somebody else. It was more like a kind of low-cost direct marketing—an advertisement for yourself, by yourself.

It wasn't as though nobody had ever thought of "blogging for bucks" before. Andrew Sullivan was probably the first blogger to raise real money by asking his readers for it; as a well-known journalist with an ideologically motivated following on the right, he started out with an advantage, and he reported that his "tip jar" approach brought in $27,000 in 2001—not a full-time wage, but not insignificant, either. The tipping model had other high-profile examples: Josh Marshall kick-started each expansion of Talking Points Memo by raising donations from his readership, and in 2003 a freelance journalist named Chris Allbritton raised about $14,000 from readers to fund a solo reporting expedition into Iraq.

Even at best, however, tipping was a fickle source of revenue. The *Cluetrain*-inspired bloggers might be content to hang out their personal shingles and use their blogs to promote their personal "brands." But there were always other entrepreneurs who looked at blogs and saw a new form of media that was just waiting to be mined for cash. Blogs were attracting readers and press attention; that few yet featured advertising was simply a regrettable oversight. "No man but a blockhead ever wrote, except for money," went Samuel Johnson's bluntly pragmatic credo. It is a line that professional writers have always cherished, and it hung over the whole new blogging enterprise like a taunt.

What was wrong with these bloggers—this army of blockheads? Why was everybody leaving dollars on the table? Something had to be done—and in 2002, Nick Denton decided to do it.

Denton was a British expatriate and ex-journalist who'd made some money during the Internet bubble. He'd covered Silicon Valley for the *Financial Times*, then turned entrepreneur, initially with a company called First Tuesday that sponsored industry mixers, and then with More-over, the news-aggregation firm that almost acquired Pyra/Blogger when it ran out of cash. Reading weblogs, Denton became fascinated with them; then he began occasionally posting to one himself. Adrift in the Web industry's dark post-bubble doldrums, he'd begun to think there might be a business in there, somewhere.

In August 2002 he dipped his toes in the water, and announced a
new blog venture:

> We've been wondering when blogging—rather than
> provide a form of procrastination—will actually make
> anyone a living. . . . But there are still few commercial
> weblog media products. Media products. Notice how
> unwebloggy that sounded. Anyway, Pete Rojas and I
> thought we'd try a little commercial experiment. It's called
> Gizmodo, and it's a vertical blog devoted to superskinny
> laptops, spy cameras, wireless wizardry, and all manner of
> other toys for overgrown boys.
>
> Most importantly, this is a low-risk commercial
> experiment. Most media companies suffer from
> overblown editorial, an ad sales force with padded
> expense accounts, and overly complex publishing systems
> with a team of primadonna sysadmins to maintain it. By
> contrast, Gizmodo will be a couple of hours a day of Pete's
> link-picking skills, some automatically generated
> Amazon.com links, and $150 worth of Movable Type.
> Media has never before been this lean.

Gizmodo pioneered the now widely familiar genre of "gadget blog," and
it was well timed to catch a rising tide of excitement over iPods and digital cameras and fancy cell phones. Its founding author, Pete Rojas, a gan-
gly tech writer with an inexhaustible appetite for geeky minutiae,
gathered a following of the hardest-core early adopters around.

At first Gizmodo's only significant revenue was from links to
Amazon.com that paid referral fees. But Denton didn't lease a newsroom
or pay benefits; the blog's budget was so modest that it didn't take much
for him to view his "little commercial experiment" as a success, and a
green light for more. In December, Denton unveiled blog number two: a

New York–centric gossip site named Gawker, heavily tilted toward the city's media and professional elite, who provided the site with both a target market and target practice. Elizabeth Spiers, a disaffected financial analyst whose blog Denton had taken a shine to, endowed Gawker with the cynical voice that became its trademark, cobbled together from bits and pieces of Suck.com and British tabloids, *Private Eye* and *Spy* magazine. The typical Gawker post had graduated from the David Letterman school of self-conscious irony—the detached tone that said, "I'm better than this crap, and you are, too, and we both know we're wasting our time, but let's hang out here anyway, because there's nothing better to do, is there?" But Web readers were less passive and more fickle than late-night-TV couch potatoes; they had to be won afresh with every click. To succeed with them, Gawker had to wed its ironic detachment to a feverish work ethic and a neurotic love-hate relationship with the people it wrote about. It served up a bitter cocktail of self-loathing cut with self-promotion, and it was impossible to say where one ended and the other began. It became a roaring overnight *succès d'estime* in New York.

Gizmodo, Gawker, and later additions to Denton's lineup established the parameters of a new kind of commercial blogging, in which productivity was at least as important as passion. Denton named his company after Gawker, and readers associated that site's snarky voice with all of his properties, but it wasn't a prerequisite for a successful Denton-owned blog. At another Gawker Media outlet named Lifehacker, for instance, the tone was far warmer. Here it was the subject matter that tied the site to Denton's stable: Lifehacker helped readers get more stuff done, faster—something all of Denton's bloggers had to worry about.

Denton explained his modus operandi to *The Independent* in 2004: "The one common theme is to take an obsession, say a gadget obsession, and feed it—produce more content than the people could ever dream of having or consuming." Where the amateurs who preceded them posted to quench their own obsessions, Denton's growing pool of paid-by-the-post bloggers wrote in order to satisfy the obsessions of their readers. The distinction is subtle—of course Rojas loved gadgets himself—but central. A clear line had separated personal blogging from the media business; the Denton blogs smudged it once and for all. They were blogs *and* "media products." "Professional blog" was an oxymoron no longer.

The bloggers at Gawker Media had quotas to meet—ten, twelve posts per weekday. In theory, both Gizmodo and Gawker were supposed to be part-time gigs, "a couple of hours a day"; in practice, they were all-consuming engagements for their authors. Denton kept his pay scale close to his chest, but in the early days of Gawker, Spiers reportedly earned just $2,000 a month. By 2005 the typical pay for a Gawker Media blogger was rumored to have risen to a still-paltry $2,500 a month, with bonuses for meeting traffic-growth goals. Denton could hardly claim that undervaluing entry-level journalism talent was an innovation; there was a long tradition of paying young writers a pittance in exchange for the opportunity to get published and show their stuff. This was standard procedure among the old alternative weekly newspapers, like the *Village Voice* and the *Boston Phoenix*, and the small politics-and-culture magazines, like *The New Republic* and *Washington Monthly*. Denton could reasonably argue that, hey, at least his bloggers were earning *something*. No blockheads, they.

Denton kept rolling out new additions to the Gawker blog lineup, which over time came to include new blogs dedicated to porn and cars and Hollywood gossip and more. He made another splash in January 2004 with the launch of Wonkette, a Washington-gossip blog created by a former editor of Suck.com named Ana Marie Cox. Cox mocked her Beltway readers over the tawdriness of their social milieu even as she teased them with salacious details their mainstream chroniclers were too prudish to mention. For instance, she turned a spotlight on an anonymous blog named Washingtonienne, in which a young congressional aide detailed her hyperactive sex life (some of it for pay); then she revealed the author's identity (Jessica Cutler, an aide to Senator Mike DeWine). As Gawker had conquered Manhattan, Wonkette quickly won over the capital.

The whole Gawker Media enterprise held a special fascination for journalists, who seemed to be simultaneously mesmerized and repelled by its products. It was as though they could see their future in its mirror, and recoiled, but couldn't resist coming back for more. At Slate, critic Jack Shafer complained that Denton's blogs "handed out rote poundings with a monotonous sadism"—yet admitted to checking Wonkette several times a day. Denton always seemed pleased with criticism as long as it came in the form of coverage that helped bring in new readers. And he dismissed the tut-tutting of journalism traditionalists with a shrug: in the new world of blogging, he said, "Immediacy is more important than accuracy, and humor is more important than accuracy."

Like many startup companies in the technology world, Gawker Media began acquiring customers (or, in its case, readers) well before it had much idea exactly how it would make money. Denton's small personal fortune, and his business's low overhead, gave him some time. But within a year the money picture got a lot clearer.

One reason blogs rarely sold advertising was that they were personal labors of love. But another was that at the very moment their explosive growth began, with Blogger in 2000, the Web advertising market had taken a deep plunge—one that only deepened after 9/11. It still hadn't recovered when Gizmodo and Gawker debuted. But Denton had seen the first Web boom close up and understood that the industry was cyclical; eventually, he knew, the advertisers would come back.

They started to do so between 2002 and 2004, a period that saw two milestones in the commercialization of blogging. The first tentative effort to create an advertising network for blogs was called Blogads, the project of a former journalist and toiler on Wall Street named Henry Copeland. In 2002 Copeland began placing traditional banner ads on bloggers' pages in return for a cut of the revenue. Business was slow at first, but during the 2004 election it saw some real growth as activist organizations and local candidacies took to the relatively low-cost blog advertising channel as an efficient fundraising tool.

Banner ads (the catch-all label for display advertising on the Web) were fine, but they'd been invented back at Hotwired, and were now almost a decade old. They brought money in the door, but they'd never shaken off the sense that they were a foreign import to the online world—a remnant of the machinery of print and broadcast that Web users viewed as at best distraction and at worst pollution. Meanwhile, Google had begun to introduce the world to a different model of online advertising. The search engine had started out as yet another "Look, ma, no business model!" Web service, but in 2000 it began to sell AdWords, "contextually relevant text ads" that would appear (clearly labeled as ads) on its search results pages. Much of the time, if your search was for specific information about a product or a place, the ads were no annoyance at all—sometimes they were even welcome. Other companies had sold text ads before, but Google designed a system that rewarded advertisers for offering the most relevant ads and penalized them for trying to divert the user's attention, so the ads actually got better—more useful and less annoying—over time, and that helped Google turn them into a colossally successful business.

In 2003 Google introduced a new service called AdSense that expanded the program to include independent Web publishers. In return for a cut of the revenue, Google would scan your site and serve up text ads that theoretically had some relationship to a page's contents. The system was hardly perfect: some pages just didn't lend themselves to useful ads, and you could end up with embarrassing juxtapositions, like pitches for massage services next to news stories about prostitution-ring busts. But AdSense represented a sea change in the financial ecology of the Web. Overnight, it transformed any Web page or blog post that previously had zero material worth into something with a potential dollar value, however marginal.

That potential remained largely unfulfilled, or at least underexploited, for the time being. In September 2003, after roughly a year in business, Denton pegged the monthly revenue of his two flagship blogs, Gizmodo and Gawker, at a measly $2,000 per month. His description of his ambition at the time was characteristically modest: "The basic business model is Internet media, circa 1999," he told *New York* magazine. "Put text and pictures up on the Web, read projections of Internet advertising, and, um, dream. I sometimes feel like one of those Japanese soldiers, discovered in the jungle five years after Nagasaki, still fighting the war they never realized had ended."

Still, the buzz around the Gawker Media blogs and the prospect, if not yet the actuality, of ad-driven blog profits brought entrepreneurs, and gold diggers, out of the woodwork. Not everyone was convinced this was a good thing. After all, blogs were, as their enthusiasts kept insisting, a kind of conversation, and nobody likes having conversations interrupted by commercial pitchmen. Too much of old-school Web advertising—with its pop-ups and animated monkeys and crude attempts to fool you into clicking on fake windows—had the reputation of a public nuisance, and blogs had been blissfully free of all that. The marketers weren't champing at the bit, anyway; they'd learned that ads didn't perform well on bulletin boards, discussion forums, and similar spaces, because users, immersed in their conversations, tuned out the ads. In any case, their clients were leery of placing their ads out in the wild on unpredictable pages of unedited "user-generated content." In the business, this was known as "adjacency risk": You didn't want your precious fast-food brand's message to wind up next to some teenager's confession of a bulimia relapse.

One solution to that problem had emerged in the form of "the narrow vertical blog"—the industry's label for a blog that provided regular information on some circumscribed topic that usually had some commercial potential. In 2001 a technology journalist named Glenn Fleishman took his interest in the new wireless Internet technology called Wi-Fi and started a blog devoted to it—including news reporting, product reviews, and useful information for novice users. Before long Fleishman's Wi-Fi Networking News had become a popular destination—it ranked high in Google searches on Wi-Fi topics—and, over time, he found that companies with Wi-Fi hardware and services to sell were eager to buy sponsorships and ad space.

Since Fleishman's approach made eminent sense, other, similar efforts began to sprout: in 2003, for example, Matt Haughey of Metafilter started a blog devoted to TiVo and related "personal video recorder" technologies. The problem for these entrepreneurial solo bloggers was simply one of time: if they kept up the volume of posting their blogs required, they hardly had enough hours in the day to sell ads themselves. And though Google's text ads and ad networks like Blogads could do the job, they weren't yet able to bring in enough revenue to support a writer of the narrow vertical blog as a full-time undertaking. According to Fleishman, his Wi-Fi blog, one of the most successful early examples of such a venture, brought in about $200,000 total from 2003 through 2008—not, he says, "a living wage, but a good hourly wage."

If blogging was going to emerge as a business with healthy ad-based profits, it was clear that publishers would have to do something more than just wait for advertisers to knock on their doors or trickle in from Google. Blogs would have to change. The whole field had to get bigger and faster and tougher. It was a process that Nick Denton had already begun. When his first major competitor entered the ring, the process accelerated.

Jason Calacanis had built the *Silicon Alley Reporter* up during the dot-com bubble from a photocopied newsletter into a successful trade-publishing business. Then, when the bust came, he saw it collapse in a cloud of cutbacks and layoffs. Calacanis renamed and sold what remained of the *Reporter* and looked around for something else to do. Brash but gregarious, he was a tireless networker and unabashed promoter of his enterprises and himself; he'd started his own blog in 2001, and in 2003 he was ready to make his move. He announced the formation, with his business partner Brian Alvey, of a new blog network called Weblogs Inc.

There is an old saying in the venture capital business that you should be glad when someone comes along and copies your idea: if you're not the only one who thinks it can make money, perhaps you're not crazy. Denton's Gawker Media had the "first mover advantage"—it had a head start in building traffic and business relationships. But the arrival of

Calacanis's venture meant you could now talk about a "blog publishing industry" without, entirely, joking.

Weblogs Inc. set out with a plan of starting its own "B2B" blogs. In New Economy patois, B2B meant "business to business," and B2B was ostensibly an easier road to profits than the "B2C" (business to consumer) approach Denton had adopted. Calacanis talked grandly of launching three hundred blogs and building the "Ziff Davis of weblogging," his own trade-publishing empire fashioned after the once-dominant publisher of computer-industry magazines. Like everything else about Weblogs Inc., these plans changed almost as quickly as Calacanis could post. The constant in the enterprise, from day one, was his promise to give bloggers a better deal than Denton. Weblogs Inc. would split revenues with its blog authors; as the business grew, they'd benefit.

The two publishers carried out a very public argument over how to run their companies and how to treat their writers. For observers, it was a real novelty: a publishing war in which the two antagonists debated the finer points of their business models, revenue predictions, and traffic growth in public and in great detail, with a combination of capitalist verve and what-the-hell informality that made for great business theater. The cross-blog sniping was intense, and it all served to win both entrepreneurs even more coverage from the mesmerized mainstream press. Calacanis was the fast-talking, glad-handing blog huckster, scrawling back-of-the-napkin calculations of a rosy future for blog-based businesses, beckoning writers to light out for the new territories and stake out their acres of equity. Denton, in turn, cast himself as the gimlet-eyed skeptic: he was always lowballing the prospects for blog profits, reminding anyone who'd listen how dicey a business it all was, shooting down Calacanis's revenue and traffic numbers and always, always glumly predicting a downturn Real Soon Now.

The sparring started even before Weblogs Inc. had officially launched. In September 2003, rumors swirled that Gawker's Elizabeth Spiers was jumping ship for a gig running a similar gossip blog for *New York* magazine. First, Calacanis advised Spiers that Gawker would one day be worth $10 million, and urged her to forget about the day job at *New York*—instead, he said, she should demand that Denton give her a stake in the company. A little later, Calacanis offered her a version of that sort of deal himself. Denton dismissed his rival's comments as "late 90s enthusiasm":

> Calacanis should hold the hype till the first blog IPO. And, if you're a starving freelance writer-blogger, and a magazine offers real money and benefits: take the deal.

That's what Spiers did a month later when she joined *New York*. But the following March, a similar story unfolded with a different ending. Denton returned from a trip to Brazil to discover that Gizmodo's Peter Rojas had been (as Denton put it) "poached" by his rival to edit a "copycat" site, Engadget. Calacanis had given Rojas what Denton wouldn't: a piece of the company. He told *New York* (which avidly covered the media spat of which it was part): "You can't say 'Work with me for as little as possible; I'll build a valuable brand you won't have a share in.' Nick wants to own all of it, so his writers are leaving."

On his own blog, Denton vented:

> I was, as they say back home, royally shafted. That's just like shafted, only worse. . . . The shafting will be complete, today, with an artfully-placed item in New York Magazine, in which Calacanis boasts of his plans for 500 blogs. Round One to Calacanis. On to Round Two.

> Is there any broader meaning to all this? Well, I have just one tentative conclusion. Blogs are likely to be better for readers than for capitalists. While I love the medium, I've always been skeptical about the value of blogs as businesses. . . .

> Competition between pro blogs may destroy their
> potential for profit, but the struggle will be excellent for
> readers. Gizmodo and Engadget will keep each other
> alert and honest. They'll compete for scoops. . . .
> We'll all check the Sitemeter traffic stats like coked-up
> day-traders. It's the beginning of the nano wars: enjoy
> the show.

In the United States, where most cities were monopoly media markets, it had been decades since readers had witnessed a real newspaper war. In their bloggy little way, Denton and Calacanis were uncorking some of the raw competitive spirits of the publishing industry's youthful heyday, when newspaper proprietors with names like Hearst and Pulitzer would steal one another's talent, seek to out-scoop their rivals, and battle for readers with can-you-top-this escapades.

Denton hired newcomers to replace the stars who'd fled (he was "building brands"; the talent was fungible). And as he predicted, the competition between the rival gadget blogs quickly went ballistic. Those readers who simply couldn't get enough spec-filled reviews of smartphones and worshipful rumor-assessments about top-secret Apple products were in heaven. For the gadget bloggers themselves, it was a mixed picture: they were gratifying their obsessions, but they were also working like dogs. Rojas found himself clocking eighty-hour weeks. "Anyone can start a blog, and anyone can make it grow," he would later say. "But to keep it there? It's fucking hard work, man. I've never worked so hard in my life."

The blog format had always built on a couple of simple promises: Reward visitors with new material frequently and they'll return more often; reward visitors with good links to other sites and they'll make a point of coming back to you. For the pioneering amateur bloggers, these promises had taken a personal and casual form: *Welcome to my table. Hope you enjoy your visit. Feel free to leave if you don't.* For the new pros, the promises took on a more desperate quality: *Faster, blogger! Post, post!*

In this new incarnation of blogging, there was little remnant of the personal motivation that had once defined the form. The pro-bloggers might be free to write in an edgier, more offbeat voice than their old-media counterparts, but they weren't going to go far off-message with posts about their relationships, politics, or pets: their job was to attract a measurably larger set of obsessive-reader eyeballs each month. As Gizmodo and Engadget fought an escalating arms race of rumor-chasing and first looks at new products, with a perpetually expanding arsenal of audio and video auxiliaries, they took blogging to a new level of intensity. Their following of deskbound office workers responded as hoped; they kept hitting "refresh" on their browsers, like laboratory rats tapping a bar to get another hit of some intoxicant. It became an involuntary reflex—for some, a kind of addiction. That made the bloggers their pushers.

In the end, for all the transparency of his self-promotional bluster, Calacanis probably had the best of Denton financially, at least in the short term. In October 2005, after barely two years in business, he sold Weblogs Inc. to America Online for a reported $25 million. The deal established his own fortune; his investors—including dotcom billionaire (and Dallas Mavericks owner) Mark Cuban, who'd become a blogging enthusiast—did well, too. And so did Peter Rojas, whose round-the-clock posting had earned a quick payoff more typical of the go-go software business than of the freelance-writing career. For Rojas, certainly, Calacanis's advice had proven sound: equity was good.

Calacanis had opted for the familiar tech-industry exit strategy of "flipping" your company—feeding it like a prize calf until it was just fat enough to sell to some deep-pocketed "BigCo." As in so many similar acquisitions, though, the price was high: Weblogs Inc. went nowhere under its new ownership, and—after some idle talk about being groomed to become AOL's CEO—Calacanis lasted barely a year there.

Denton, meanwhile, seemed to be playing an entirely different game—one less shaped by Silicon Valley models than by publishing-industry traditions. He appeared to enjoy the role of mini-media baron. He'd periodically reshuffle his editorial teams, taking each new media-gossip-column scuffle in stride, sometimes filling in himself for some blogger he'd just axed. When a blog failed to catch on with readers or advertisers, he'd shutter it unceremoniously and trot out a couple of new replacements. He kept his expenses low, built his business slowly over time, and remained a reliable source of blog-hype-busting quotes. In 2006, during one round of reshuffling, he declared, "There is no doubt that there is a bubble. . . . Better to sober up now, before the end of the party." Yet, for someone who so regularly proclaimed the blog market's imminent crash, he seemed profoundly uninterested in selling high. When *New York Times* columnist David Carr asked him why he didn't follow Calacanis's example and cash out, he answered, "Because it would be too hard to start over. Sites need to be well managed and well designed and even then it is harder and harder to launch a site. The world does not need more blogs. . . . The barrier to entry in Internet media is low. The barrier to success is high."

Denton's management approach—either attentive or meddlesome, depending on which end of the editorial org chart you sat at—showed results over time. By 2007, Gawker Media had grown to roughly one hundred employees and contractors; *New York* magazine guessed it might have $10–12 million in annual profits, though the assumptions behind that number—of a fully sold ad inventory at list prices—were the kind of thing Denton had been snorting at for years. In five years the concept of blogging as a business had grown from a handful of speculative experiments into a thriving, chaotic commercial ecosystem, with Gawker and its competitors at the top of the food chain. Below these high-profile, high-traffic blogs were swarms of smaller pro blogs clustered around different industries and fields—politics, science and the environment, technology, finance and investing, sports, media, advertising, and on and on. These supported themselves typically through a combination of Google text ads and banner or display ads, via Blogads or one of several new sales networks that followed in its path.

The sole proprietors of these smaller blogs usually wore the publisher's and editor's hat on the same head; that ruled out the journalism world's old model of "church and state separation," in which a proverbial Chinese wall kept business interests from dictating coverage. But bloggers often enforced their own rough ethical standards upon one another. The important thing, they generally agreed, was to keep the editorial matter separate from the ads, and to label the ads plainly. There were always going to be gray areas, but the same held true in print—as with the magazine business's practice of "advertorial" inserts.

Disclosure was the bloggers' ethical totem, transparency their mantra. Conflicts of interest were inevitable; if you had one, you should let the world know. This ideology ensured that the 2006 advent of a novel twist on the blog business, from an outfit called PayPerPost, would inspire a hurricane of outrage. The PayPerPost idea was simple: it proposed to pay bloggers under the table to shill for advertisers, handing out cash in return for "sponsored posts" that the sponsors could review ahead of time.

A lot of bloggers had always said they'd welcome any innovation that helped turn their blogs into successful businesses. What infuriated them about PayPerPost was that the company didn't care whether the bloggers revealed the payments or not: if you took the cash, you *could* be transparent about it, but, you know, that was up to you. If PayPerPost succeeded, bloggers fretted, it would cast suspicion on all blogs, whether they were on the take or not, and dissolve the personal bonds so many bloggers felt they'd cemented with their readers. PayPerPost's CEO, Ted Murphy, defended the scheme by analogy to the practice of celebrity endorsements:

> . . . this will be an incredibly powerful tool for advertisers and finally gives bloggers a chance to make a buck for all the benefit they provide to companies. Celebrities get

paid millions to wear products and be seen with their
favorite drink. It's up to the celebs to choose what they
wear and drink and if they are being true to the fans. If
they love the product and they can make a buck at the
same time everyone wins.

After six months of withering criticism and derision, PayPerPost
bowed to the prevailing blog ethic and began requiring that bloggers
reveal when a post had been sponsored (though the company left it up
to the blogger to determine the location and prominence of the disclosure). But the aura of sleaze still clung to the whole operation, and only
deepened over time, as a small community of PayPerPost bloggers began
cross-linking to one another in an effort to drive up their visibility in
searches on Google, which ranks sites based on the number and quality
of inbound links. This pyramid-scheme behavior eventually brought
down the wrath of Google, which penalized a number of PayPerPost-
focused sites by demoting their Google rank to zero, effectively ostraciz-
ing them. PayPerPost cried censorship, but the company got little
sympathy from the leaders of commercial blogging, who felt that the
practice of letting cash dictate the agenda of your posts—even when
fully disclosed—was beyond the pale. Jason Calacanis, hardly allergic to
the profit motive himself, expressed the general detestation: "PayPerPost
versus authentic blogging is like comparing prostitution with making
love to someone you care for deeply. No one with any level of ethics
would get involved with these clowns."

PayPerPost wounded the pride of the new breed of pro-bloggers, who
felt their independence was their prime asset. It had stepped far over
acceptable lines. But within those lines—sometimes just barely—a vast
new bazaar was assembling around the blogging business. At the high
end, little consultancies sprouted, manned by real experts at the fine art
of advancing any website's Google ranking and promoting it among bloggers without rousing their ire. At the low end, the Web began swarming

with the crudest of pitches from blogging con men. Email spam filters became clogged with blog-based come-ons:

> Two new blogs are launched EVERY SECOND! Launch your own cash-generating blog in 5 minutes! Catch the wave! Make money with your own blog! buy the Blog Toolkit.

A kicker below this message appended the age-old seal of quality: "As Seen on National TV." Websites, like one called Bloggingtothebank.com, offered similar promises:

> If You Want The Inside Story On How To Make Thousands Of Dollars Every Month From Blogging Or How To Use Blogs To Drive Thousands Of Targeted Visitors To Your Website For FREE Then Read Every Single Word On This Page Now!

It was easy to view such low-rent material as a mark of debasement. Look at how far blogging had come in just a handful of years—from the original vision of a paradise for unedited self-expression to a breeding ground for get-rich-quick hucksters.

But of course there was much more to blogging than that. It was a breeding ground for *everything*. At some point by mid-decade, it had become clear that if you were starting any sort of publication on the Web, you were going to publish it as a blog. The blog had consumed the old model of the Web, it too had passed the old illusion as of the Web portals and become the default format, the de facto standard not only for link sites and diaries and niche publications but for all Web publishing, whether personal or commercial. Because it cost so little to start a blog, the commercial blogging industry became a petri dish for new experimental businesses. The ones you ended up hearing about were the ones that didn't die in infancy; maybe they'd found some successful new wrinkle on the format, maybe they'd come up with a novel revenue-producing idea, or maybe they'd just been started by people who were well known or well connected or both.

In 2005 a Silicon Valley lawyer named Michael Arrington came seemingly out of nowhere and started a blog called TechCrunch that tracked the ups and downs of the new generation of Internet companies known as Web 2.0. The Web 2.0 phenomenon had grown out of blogging and other online innovations dependent on user contributions, and was now a broad movement of cheap small companies fighting for attention and investment. The petri dish kept getting bigger; TechCrunch was covering it and, simultaneously, swimming in it itself. Arrington had participated in the dotcom bubble, but, failing to strike it rich, had dropped out of the business and hung out on a beach for a year. When he returned, he began researching the industry for his own benefit. But instead of locking his findings away on his hard drive, in the Web 2.0 spirit he posted them to a blog, and quickly attracted a crowd.

TechCrunch took the by-then-common formula for blog success—posting feverishly, breaking small scoops in a specialty field—and added a new element: at his rented home in Atherton, a wealthy Silicon Valley enclave, Arrington began holding backyard barbecues for his readers. The TechCrunch parties became a magnet for startup founders, financiers, and engineers; they downed beers and pitched one another in a frenzy of mutual entrepreneurial back-scratching. Only a couple of dozen people came to Arrington's first party, but, like the user databases of the successful companies he wrote about, attendance grew at a dizzying geometric pace. Unlike the Web's virtual real estate, though, the Arrington house and yard maxed out at around five hundred visitors.

Arrington operated TechCrunch out of his house, too. Arrington, the parties, the office, the house—it was all one big mashup of life and business, editor and publication, trade journal and the industry it covered. The blurring of lines was, as a management consultant might put it, TechCrunch's core competency.

TechCrunch grew exponentially along with Web 2.0 itself. By 2007 Arrington had hired several bloggers and a CEO, started a conference business, and was pulling in about $200,000 a month in revenue. Next to the older generation of Web-based technology-trade publications, like CNET, TechCrunch's coverage was rough around the edges, but it was lively and nimble and full of insider information. It was also less encumbered with the pressure to squeeze revenue from every pixel on the page.

As an industry participant who'd become a kind of journalist, Arrington was disdainful of old-school strictures about conflict of interest, yet he would adamantly defend TechCrunch's integrity, offering his word as a guarantee of probity. When Jason Calacanis floated a rumor that Arrington was selling positive reviews, Arrington indignantly wrote, "I couldn't sleep at night if I did that. Companies that have offered to pay me have never been written about on TechCrunch." But he did invest in startup companies, too, and that raised hackles. Sure, he disclosed his interests; but as his influence grew, critics began to wonder how fair it was for him to play in a startup game that he was also refereeing.

Still, it was Arrington's very immersion in the game that gave him an edge in the tech press's scrum for hot stories. When Google acquired the young Web-video giant YouTube in 2006, he was first to break the news. How'd he get the scoop? "I was online at 2:00 a.m., and a friend told me about it," he told an interviewer.

Despite Robert Scoble's success at Microsoft as a marquee example of corporate blogging, the corporate world remained highly uncomfortable with all manner of blogs. Executives feared that officially sanctioning bloggers was tantamount to handing open mikes to unlawyered, unvetted employees; but they also feared that employees blogging unofficially, on their own time, would fail to toe the company line. Every blogger looked like a potential loose cannon, every post a looming lawsuit. But as blogs became a corporate-communications flavor of the moment, many companies felt obligated to start them anyway, and wound up with wooden, synthetic imitations. There was little point in creating a blog if it read like a reverse-chronological list of press releases; when nobody read these blogs, the company could say, "Well, so much for that—boy, is blogging overrated!" In 2008 the veteran tech pundit Esther Dyson, when asked why the hyperconnected tech elite liked to congregate in person at conferences, said that they "want to hear the unofficial story, rather than the sanitized press releases and corporate blogs that they get online." In too many cases, the blogs that were supposed to be the "unofficial" story and the human face of the corporation had become just another faceless channel for soulless PR.

In a sense, of course, the TechCrunch approach was a bizblogging move, too—just one writ large. Where someone like Robert Scoble would sit inside a large company that employed him and serve readers as a kind of surrogate eyes and ears, Arrington kicked things up a level: he was doing something similar from his perch inside an entire industry. By following the Web 2.0 business via TechCrunch, you got the news and the scoops, and as a bonus you got a taste of Arrington's unvarnished, tempestuous personality. Traditionalists sniffed, but TechCrunch was running away with the market.

What TechCrunch was doing to the technology trade press, other new ventures began trying to accomplish in other realms. Arianna Huffington, the wealthy socialite and former conservative who'd become a familiar face on cable news shows, started her Huffington Post in 2005. Huffington's site was clumsily referred to as "a blog" by its mainstream competition, but it was really a packaged collection of blogs and news reports—a lively, messy hybrid of Daily Kos, Salon or Slate, and the Drudge Report. To jump-start the business, Huffington invited a roster of her friends— Hollywood celebrities, Beltway insiders, and liberal pundits—to start blogging under her tent. Some posted once or twice and wandered off, but some stuck around and added glitz and heft to HuffPost's pages.

The central innovation Huffington brought to her publication was a simple one: though the site was a for-profit business, it did not pay the bloggers who contributed most of its content. This approach, some observers complained, constituted a kind of "digital sharecropping." But the criticism didn't seem to stick, and most of the bloggers who contributed to Huffington seemed more pleased by the volume of traffic her name and brand were sending their way than disgruntled by her failure to provide cash compensation. This tended to infuriate salaried journalists, who found the Huffington Post model an affront to their livelihood. But it was hard to argue with the success of Huffington's formula; after all, no one was putting a gun to her contributors' heads. Felix Salmon, an economics blogger, defended Huffington's approach:

> . . . it's a real positive-sum game. The bloggers get much more in the way of readership on HuffPo than they ever would on their own. That means the "no-name" bloggers have a much greater chance of breaking out and becoming "name" bloggers if they can get HuffPo to publish their thoughts. And as those bloggers increase the volume of content on the HuffPo site, the site itself becomes inceasingly popular and valuable.

Salmon favorably compared the Huffington Post approach to Denton's Gawker Media business model, "where you increase your amount of content by paying people to work incredibly hard." Still, the Gawker model was more familiar, and paid professional blogging was the norm at most of the new blog-based publications that continued to emerge as the 2000s wore on—like the national-politics site Politico, founded by *Washington Post* veterans or GigaOm, a tech-news blog by tech-journalism star Om Malik.

The rise of blogging for pay could be seen as a reasonable and inevitable development—the professionalization that any new medium undergoes.

Meg Hourihan, of Pyra/Blogger, had once argued just that: "Until we create a financial structure to enable the creation and maintenance of professional blogs, we won't see the best, next generation of weblogs," she wrote in 2002. In 2008, Jason Calacanis made the same case: it was only "when we started paying folks" that blogging really started to grow, he said.

But once folks started getting paid, the nature of the blogs they produced changed forever. The gadget-blog war established the inexorable, grueling logic of the commercial blogging industry: more was never quite enough, and now was always a bit late. Over time, this logic pushed commercial blogging to unnatural extremes of both quantity and quality. The result was nothing like the *Cluetrain* concept of the market as a conversation; it was the market in its familiar role as an accelerator of everything it touched. Sites that had set out to give readers a satisfying stream of updates about some obsessive interest turned into overwhelming firehoses of information, as bloggers strove to meet traffic and posting quotas. And the fight to boost page views pushed bloggers to discard whatever standards they might have started out with: tech bloggers would build items around the most trivial news tidbits and product announcements, or they would write lazy "me too" posts, while gossip bloggers bottom-fed with abandon till there was nothing left to chew on but their own spleen.

Some readers, at least, began to notice and recoil. Gawker, which had once charmed the media establishment with its breeziness and cheek, found itself the object of growing revulsion. A detailed essay in the online journal N+1 traced the site's downward spiral of tawdriness and cruelty over the years. The blog backlash crested when *New York* magazine ran a cover story in 2007 headlined "Gawker.com and the Culture of Bile." The article described Denton's employees as an exploited and ill-paid "creative underclass" who fueled their impossibly long hours at the keyboard with stimulants and casual sex.

Denton posted a characteristically saturnine response: "Every age has its own cultural panic, in which uncouth interlopers threaten all that is decent and good, and the media establishment, like a stuffy dowager, strikes them from polite society." Denton still saw his blog enterprise as an insurgency of outsiders revolutionizing a stuffy old order—but he offered no platitudes about quality or sermons about authenticity:

> Internet media can indeed seem, particularly to the gentlemanly and leisurely American magazine business, a Hobbesian environment. The new journalism is solitary, poor, nasty, brutish, and short. For many New York writers, Gawker is a proxy for this harsh and competitive new world, because the gossip site covers the death agonies of Manhattan's old-line media industry, without much respect for the club's cosy rules.

Was Gawker in decline? Did it matter? The question seemed hardly of concern to anyone outside of the narrow confines of Manhattan's media industry. The *New York* piece had declared Gawker's snarky tone to be "the most important stylistic influence on the emerging field of blogging," and called it "the de facto voice of blogs today." But this was patently wrong. The statement betrayed an alarmingly narrow field of vision; it was like a blog-centric version of the old Saul Steinberg *New Yorker* cover, the one in which New York City is portrayed in vital detail, but the world beyond the Hudson River recedes into a barren void. The world of blogs had become far too sprawling and diverse and dynamic to have its tone set by a handful of twentysomething writers in a handful of apartments in Manhattan and Brooklyn.

Gawker's chief influence on blogging was not stylistic but simply economic. Denton had succeeded in transforming the awkward idealistic, not-ready-for-prime-time-marketing blogging movement into something that could turn a profit. He'd also demonstrated the costs of that transformation—costs that many others in the movement of problogging that followed in Gawker's tracks eventually found themselves paying. It looked like a simple matter to take blogging's tools and format—reverse chronology, "wheneverly" updating, casual tone, and reader comments—

and bolt them back onto the chassis of a traditional media business. But the resulting contraptions sometimes proved ungainly, and maybe even unsafe.

In April 2008 a front page *New York Times* headline read, "In Web World of 24/7 Stress, Writers Blog Till They Drop." The article, by Matt Richtel, described blog publications as "digital-era sweatshops" and bloggers as afflicted by "weight loss or gain, sleep disorders, exhaustion and other maladies born of the nonstop strain of producing for a news and information cycle that is as always-on as the Internet." Richtel cited, as a sign of the pressure, the recent deaths of two high-profile bloggers who'd had heart attacks—though he added a sentence of ritual qualification: "To be sure, there is no official diagnosis of death by blogging, and the premature demise of two people obviously does not qualify as an epidemic." The article was alarmingly fuzzy in its attempt to get its arms around the scope of the professional blogging class it described. "Some" bloggers "write for fun," it admitted, but "thousands" write for pay: "It is unclear how many people blog for pay, but there are surely several thousand and maybe even tens of thousands."

Thousands of pros? It might be true—nobody had the numbers. But there were better statistics about the total number of bloggers, most of whom were amateurs. And those numbers all had a lot more zeroes at the end.

For all its hyperbole—"Blogging kills!" mocked a chorus of critical posts—the *Times* article certainly contained a substrate of truth. For many pros, blogging had indeed become a wearying treadmill. Arrington told Richtel that, thanks to TechCrunch, he'd put on thirty pounds and couldn't sleep at night: "At some point, I'll have a nervous breakdown and be admitted to the hospital, or something else will happen. . . . This is not sustainable."

But the article failed to talk about the vastly larger universe of bloggers who never earn or expect a dime, and who therefore never get anywhere near the kind of pressure that someone like Arrington faced. That made it a deeply distorted picture. Generalizing from Arrington's experience was like projecting the stress levels of an Indy 500 competitor onto the general driving population.

That a small number of ambitious, talented, driven bloggers had been able to extend the blog form and push its pedal to the floor was certainly a sign of the form's flexibility and vigor. But whether these red-eyed pros succeeded or failed just didn't matter much to most of the world's bloggers. They were not blogging till they dropped. They weren't staring at Arrington and his ilk, thinking, "Someday that'll be me!" For most of them, posting was a gratifying pastime rather than a grueling ordeal. If it wasn't, they wouldn't do it. They certainly weren't getting rich.

Chapter 7

THE EXPLODING BLOGOSPHERE
BOING BOING

I n 1989, the husband-and-wife team of Mark Frauenfelder and Carla
Sinclair published the first issue of their magazine, *bOING bOING*.
The cover promised "Energized fun . . . Cyberpunk. Brain Toys. Nano-
tech." The name was a sound effect designed to convey "the idea of
bouncing around in a positive energetic way," as Frauenfelder put it.

Frauenfelder had a day job as an engineer. Like a lot of people in their
twenties, he was bored with it and spent his spare time thinking about
doing something else. When *Whole Earth Review*—that West Coast bridge
between the sixties counterculture and the nineties digital revolution—
dedicated a special issue to underground 'zines, he read it, and liked what
he saw, and thought, *Why not me?*

Before the Web became ubiquitous, if you wanted to publish your
ideas and share your discoveries, you had a limited set of options, and
they all involved a lot of bothersome labor. It required a certain sort of
obsessive personality to take the trouble; Frauenfelder seemed to have it.
He designed the whole magazine himself, and ran off a hundred copies on
the Xerox machine at the office where he worked in Boulder, Colorado.

"I was a mechanical engineer who designed one of about a hundred parts. It took months and months to design and test your assigned part," he later explained. "I love 'zines because one person can be responsible for all hundred parts."

bOING bOING was a vehicle for Frauenfelder's eclectic enthusiasms, from sci-fi retro-kitsch art to the cult writings of Robert Anton Wilson to ukuleles. This underground-culture grab bag was tied together by a whimsical, "don't worry, be happy" stance in the face of a potentially frightening future. The 'zine's tag line summed up this sunny disposition with only the tiniest trace of irony: "Brain Candy for Happy Mutants."

Over the next five years, *bOING bOING* would become what passed for a hit in the 'zine underground. It started using higher-quality offset printing, got some wider distribution deals, and worked its circulation up to fifteen thousand or so. It didn't make much money, but it didn't lose much. In 1993, Frauenfelder took a job with *Wired* magazine, and he and Sinclair moved to San Francisco. Over the next couple of years, two of the distributors who were selling *bOING bOING* went bankrupt, owing the couple thousands of dollars. They decided to scale back their publishing effort and sell by mail only. When the Web took off, *bOING bOING* migrated online, becoming an irregular Web 'zine. But Frauenfelder was busy at *Wired*, and he had lost interest in the project; it languished with only infrequent updates.

Two things happened at the start of 2000 to give *bOING bOING* a new life. First, Frauenfelder decided to give up on the eccentric capitalization—henceforth, he'd just write "Boing Boing." More significantly, he turned the site into a blog. He'd been writing freelance articles for *The Industry Standard*, John Battelle's dotcom-era trade weekly, and he'd prepared an in-depth piece about the rise of blogging circa 1999. But the topic was simply "too tiny" for the magazine, in Frauenfelder's words— blogging wasn't a real business, and how could it ever be?—so the story never ran. (*Whole Earth Review* later picked it up.) But Frauenfelder had learned all about blogging, and liked what he'd learned. In January 2000, he turned on Blogger at the Boing Boing website and began posting.

At first the new Boing Boing was a typical one-person blog, an outlet for

Frauenfelder's myriad boyish enthusiasms (Sinclair didn't contribute to the site). He would post about offbeat games, *Mad* magazine, "UFO-themed paintings" by science fiction author Rudy Rucker, or the death of psychedelic guru Terence McKenna. In person, Frauenfelder had an upright shock of hair, a friendly mien, and a slack voice that always sounded a little stunned at the sheer wonderment of whatever he was talking about. It took a little time, but Boing Boing's posts slowly acquired the same tone. The site's new tag line was "A Directory of Wonderful Things." A remnant of an abortive early effort by Frauenfelder to build a sort of Yahoo-style directory or portal to underground resources on the Web, the phrase came to embody the attitude the new Boing Boing had inherited from the old print version: it was underground yet approachable, alternative yet ingenuous.

After about a year of casual posting, in January 2001 Frauenfelder got a scoop of sorts. An inventor named Dean Kamen had a secret project called "Ginger"; the press was desperately stoking speculations that it was going to revolutionize the entire transportation industry. But nobody knew exactly what Ginger was. (We now know it as the Segway.) Poking around through the U.S. Patent Office database online, Frauenfelder found a line drawing of a woman standing on what appeared to be a lawnmower rearing up on its hind legs. He linked to it, commencing a minor news frenzy online. That night there was a story on CNN, and a link to Boing Boing from the CNN website. Traffic went through the roof—from maybe three hundred visits a day to six thousand.

This was fun! Only Frauenfelder was about to take a holiday in Hawaii, and he knew that none of those people would return unless Boing Boing had some fresh posts. So he asked his friend Cory Doctorow to fill in as guest blogger. Doctorow was a Canadian writer with a budding career in science fiction and a passion for the ideal of openness on the Web in all its manifestations—from open-source software to the peer-to-peer file-trading movement exemplified by Napster to the newfound popularity of mashups and remixes that created new art from the bits and pieces of existing works. The open-source software company he'd cofounded, OpenCOLA, had gotten caught in the crossfire of the intellectual-property war between Hollywood and Napster—but not before Frauenfelder had profiled it, along with Doctorow, for *The Industry Standard*. The two became frequent email correspondents, and Doctorow took to bombarding Frauenfelder with suggestions for Boing Boing links.

When Doctorow took the blog's helm for two weeks in early 2001, he ramped up the posting frequency; where Frauenfelder had typically posted once or twice each day, Doctorow would add a half-dozen or a dozen new items. Returning from his vacation, Frauenfelder found that Boing Boing's traffic was soaring. He invited Doctorow to stick around, then continued to carefully expand the site's roster of contributors. A couple of months after Doctorow joined, Frauenfelder brought on a third editor—his old friend David Pescovitz, a science writer and Wired contributor who had worked on the original, paper *bOING bOING* 'zine. A year later saw the addition of Xeni Jardin, a tech-culture journalist and graduate of Jason Calacanis's *Silicon Alley Reporter* operation. The platinum-haired Jardin injected a cyber-couture sheen into Boing Boing's mix; her arrival put an end to the site's boys-only club and completed the quartet that has edited it ever since.

Frauenfelder had learned the same lesson that Nick Denton's employees and the rest of the pro-blogging brigade would later discover: if you want to draw a crowd with a blog, post early and post often. But Boing Boing had no business model at the time, no advertisements and no plans to generate revenue. Like many other popular blogs of that era, it achieved its initial success not as a business but as a pastime for its creators.

Cory Doctorow's first science-fiction novel, *Down and Out in the Magic Kingdom*, published in 2003, is set in the twenty-second century in a "post-scarcity" world, where death and material want have both been vanquished. There's no need for work, or for money to motivate it. But humanity remains a status-conscious species; people still want to know how they're doing compared with others. In place of wealth, there's a new currency for success—a measure of respect earned from one's peers for acts of skill or successful daring or generosity. Doctorow's name for this stuff was "whuffie." Whuffie tracked achievement by esteem rather than cash, intangible reputation rather than material recompense.

Doctorow's readers immediately understood that he was describing a kind of value that already existed in the Web's cross-linked conversations. Links had a sort of whuffie value. So did positive email and comments. Whuffie was close cousin to status in gift-culture, where your standing is based on how much you give away. (In his popular essay "Homesteading the Noosphere," Eric Raymond had described this sort of prestige as the chief goal of open-source software developers.) The Web was seeing steady growth in all sorts of contributions that were not driven by the dollar; whuffie was a pretty good way to think about the motivation underlying any of them. It was also what was fueling Boing Boing itself.

Doctorow laid this out in an article titled "My Blog, My Outboard Brain":

> As a committed infovore, I need to eat roughly six times my weight in information every day or my brain starts to starve and atrophy. I gather information from many sources: print, radio, television, conversation, the Web, RSS feeds, email, chance, and serendipity. I used to bookmark this stuff, but I just ended up with a million bookmarks that I never revisited and could never find anything in. . . .
>
> Blogging gave my knowledge-grazing direction and reward. Writing a blog entry about a useful and/or interesting subject forces me to extract the salient features of the link into a two- or three-sentence elevator pitch to my readers, whose decision to follow a link is predicated on my ability to convey its interestingness to them. This

exercise fixes the subjects in my head the same way that taking notes at a lecture does, putting them in reliable and easily accessible mental registers.

Blogging also provides an incentive to keep blogging. As Boing Boing's hit-counter rises steadily, growing 10-30 percent every month, I get a continuous, low-grade stream of brain-rewards. . . . The more I blog, the more reward I generate: strangers approach me at conferences and tell me how much they liked some particular entry; people whose sites I've pointed to send me grateful email thanking me for bringing their pet projects to the attention of so many people.

Doctorow's brain was now "outboard," so anyone who visited could pick it. If visitors liked what they found, they would pay Doctorow back with their attention and regard—whuffie. He also benefited from a positive-feedback loop, becoming the recipient of more suggestions and ideas and tips from the visiting crowd. Doctorow was already an impressively polymathic guy, but he said blogging was actually making him smarter:

Operating Boing Boing has not only given me a central repository of all of the fruits of my labors in the information fields, but it also has increased the volume and quality of the yield. I know more, find more, and understand better than I ever have, all because of Boing Boing. . . . Being deprived of my blog right now would be akin to suffering extensive brain-damage.

By late 2002 Boing Boing was humming on all outboard-brain cylinders. It embraced novelty and cherished weirdness, yet resisted becoming parochial or obscure. However fringy its content, its authors—all of whom earned a living (or some of it) as freelance writers—offered clean design, clear writing, and concise headlines. Doctorow later attributed the blog's success in part to this commitment to directness: "Every link one follows from Boing Boing, one follows to find out not *what* is at the other end, but more *about* what is at the other end." (This was the exact opposite of the old Suck.com style of linking, where the link often worked obliquely or sarcastically in relation to the text.) Visitors were rewarded with an endless stream of loopy tidbits, linked only by the range of the contributors' interests. Here's a rant about a music piracy lawsuit! Here's a report on the elections in Serbia! Here's a hot-dog roaster designed to look like Cthulhu, H. P. Lovecraft's indescribable monstrosity! Here's a link to a story about people who pull out their own teeth! And every time we show you something truly gross like that, we'll follow it with a psychic palate cleanser—here's some kitschy unicorn art!

The formula worked, and the editors kept refining it, finding new ways to expand the site's reach. Within a couple of years they had won the heart of a certain portion of the Web: Boing Boing was geek central, only without the programming tips. And its editors came to embody a certain type of hip integrity. The music world had a label, "indie cred," for the sense of authenticity you got from a band that had won success independent of a major label contract; on the Web, Boing Boing's bloggers were indie cred personified.

The editors said that Boing Boing was something they did in their spare time, and that was true. Yet that didn't mean they lacked ambition. They wanted to see Boing Boing succeed, to reach more readers with their posts; but they didn't seek readers by the traditional route. Conventional editors started out with an idea of a target audience and strove to assemble content that would appeal to its profile. Boing Boing's editors were more like the curators of a 24/7 exhibit of the "wonderful things"— or weird, or outrageous, or funny things—that had caught their fancy. Then they watched, delighted, as the first trickle of visitors brought their friends, who brought more, until the place was packed.

It was not an approach that anyone schooled in the media mainstream would have chosen. But it beautifully suited the blog format. In the sprawling new blog universe, Boing Boing found itself propelled by links and growth—and oodles of whuffie—to a position of central influence.

"I propose a name for the intellectual cyberspace we bloggers occupy: the Blogosphere." On January 1, 2002, a conservative blogger named William Quick made this declaration, along with a pompous (and puzzling) derivation of the word's root from the Greek *logos*. At first, Quick's "blogosphere" gained currency among his peers in the post-9/11 warblogger crowd. Then it gradually spread into more general use, winning out over equally plausible alternatives—Doctorow, for example, once referred to "the Distributed Republic of Blogistan." "The blogosphere" came to mean the entire global conversation space that the rise of blogs had opened up. (Quick's claim to have invented the term "blogosphere," it turned out, was open to question: Brad Graham, a first-generation blogger, had used the word long before, in a humorous post from 1999. But who was arguing? Actually, a good number of people.)

Before anyone had time to get too comfortable with this coinage, a problem arose: though *blogosphere* itself was a handy word, there was a big problem with that preceding *the*. *The* blogosphere simply didn't exist. There were many blogospheres. The one you saw depended on which little slice of the blog universe you were following. The extensive blogosphere that software developers had built was almost entirely different from the burgeoning political blogosphere. And newer, smaller 'spheres were accumulating beyond these centers of gravity, like aggregations of interstellar dust beginning to coalesce into new galaxies.

Blogging had started out as a refuge for the individualist, the "unedited voice of a person" fixed to a Web address and beholden to none. But by 2002—five years after Jorn Barger introduced the term *weblog*—it was becoming clear that these lone soapboxes existed in increasingly complex and fascinating constellations of interrelationship. Such connections had become easier to make, and to track, thanks to three evolutionary changes in blogging tools, all of which had unpresentable names: permalinks, RSS, and "pinging."

In March 2000, Blogger began to include "permalinks"—a code for each blog post that enabled other websites and bloggers to link back to a specific post. (Previously it had been difficult to do anything other than point to a blog's home page, which would change all the time, foiling any attempt to link to any particular item.) Later the Movable Type platform would expand this concept by giving each individual blog post its own separate Web page as a permanent home with a unique address to which links could point. Most other blogging tools followed suit. This software wrinkle, little noticed at the time, made a huge difference: it meant that the basic unit of writing online would change from the page to the post. Blog posts became the atoms of the Web.

This mattered in all sorts of ways. Blogging had already "liberated the writer from word count," as Meg Hourihan pointed out in a 2002 essay, allowing authors to "blog a short thought that previously would have gone unwritten." The advent of permalinks further transformed the notion of blogs as conversations—something bloggers had long averred, but outsiders frequently couldn't see—from an abstract notion into an everyday reality. As Tom Coates, the pioneering British blogger behind plasticbag.org, wrote, "It was effectively the device that turned weblogs from an ease-of-publishing phenomenon into a conversational mess of overlapping communities." Before, when one blogger linked to some current post on the home page of another, the link had no meaning—it pointed to a page that would be different in a few days, as new posts crowded out the one that had been linked to. With permalinks, in Coates's words, "For the first time it became relatively easy to gesture directly at a highly specific post on someone else's site and talk about it."

The shape of a blog, with its emphasis on "what's new," had always emphasized "now"; permalinks restored some weight to "then"—and each old post came clearly marked with its original date and time. Meanwhile, Google's phenomenal success at making Web search faster and better gave new value to old blog archives. Like blogging itself, Google had grown from tiny origins in 1998 to household familiarity by 2002. Its new ubiquity meant that every permalinked post might continue to serve as a resource for Web users hunting down the specific information it contained.

As the number of new blogs exploded, most readers found themselves constantly stumbling on additional bloggers they wanted to follow. One link led to another; the more blogs you read, the more you wanted to read—up to a point. That point was, typically, when you'd throw up your hands and cry, "Too much!" The voracious "infovores" of the blogosphere sought tools to help them consume more posts in less time. The most important of these was a software standard called RSS, which turned blog posts into a "feed" or stream of data updates that users could subscribe to and then keep up with using a program called an RSS reader, or aggregator.

There is a knotty tale behind RSS, a saga filled with ancient griev-ances and grudges whose origins were never comprehensible to outsiders and are now largely forgotten even by insiders. The topic is beyond a sore spot—it's like a chronically inflamed wound. Mention it at any gathering of Web developers and, more likely than not, people will shake their heads and give you a don't-go-there look. A quick summary might read something like this:

RSS grew out of work by Netscape and by Dave Winer. Netscape sought a software standard that would make it easy to share structured data about Web pages—like "headline," "author," and "summary" for a news article. Winer sought a similar tool for turning news headlines and weblog postings into data that programs could more easily share and manipulate. Some other developers wanted to see the standard built on a more complex foundation called RDF that came out of Tim Berners-Lee's MIT consortium. A series of mailing-list flame wars and hopscotch-ing version releases followed. When the dust cleared, RSS 2.0 became a widely adopted standard supported by most blogging tools.

You'd probably also want to mention that RSS owed much of its early success to Winer's missionary work on its behalf, as he wrote tirelessly about it on Scripting News and kept incorporating it in new products and experimenting with new applications for it. Then you'd still need to go back and explain how some other developers, unhappy with what they saw as the technical limitations of RSS 2.0, came up with an alternative and competing standard called Atom that achieved ends similar to RSS's, but was incompatible with it. And the more you said, the more you'd hear back from partisans in this arcane dispute that your account was really irresponsible because it left out this or that detail.

So maybe "don't go there" was good advice.

RSS stood for "Really Simple Syndication," "RDF Site Summary," or "Rich Site Summary," depending on who you asked. It was always cursed by its technical-sounding name—imagine if the name "World Wide Web" had never existed, and we had to talk about reading stuff "on HTTP." Although RSS was slow to catch on among the wide public, it would eventually form the technical underpinning for most of the websites and services that collected and ranked blog posts and other kinds of timely Web data. And it found speedy and enthusiastic adoption among the most avid bloggers and blog readers. Reading a blog via RSS stripped it of the design and context of the Web page; posts became a long list of plain-text items, and as you scanned the list, the reader would check off items as "read." What you lost in the personality of the material, you gained in sheer efficiency. Without RSS, you'd have to keep visiting the sites of your favorite blogs to see whether they'd added something new since your previous visit; with it, you could just scan the list of subscriptions in your reader and see at a glance who had posted something new.

In building out the infrastructure for RSS, Dave Winer also created what came to be known as a "ping server" at Weblogs.com. Each time a blog added a new post, it could send a message—or "ping"—to this server to notify it of the update. The ping server would wind up with a real-time log of which blogs had new stuff; it could offer a one-stop shop for such information. At first, the Weblogs.com list of recently updated blogs provided a fascinating slice of the blogosphere at any moment. Eventually, as the number of blogs updating mushroomed, it became largely useless for the eyes of human visitors. But it remained a valuable resource to other software programs, which could use it to assemble information about what was happening on blogs *right now*. The ping server was in part just a piece of plumbing that made RSS work more efficiently; but the services it enabled sped up the blogosphere, and made possible all sorts of experiments in pulling together all the blog posts surrounding particular breaking news events.

All these new features of blogging would have been painful for any individual blogger to implement. Fortunately, the blog-publishing tools gradually caught up and took care of them automatically. By 2002, Movable Type was beginning to win the allegiance of many of the most ambitious bloggers, and it put together the set of features that, to this day, are considered the basics. It built permalink pages for each post. It automatically produced an RSS feed from your posts. And each time you added a new post, it would take care of pinging Weblogs.com (and other ping servers that would come along later).

All this meant that blog posts had become something more than just random jottings: they were now *data*. And any time programmers see a pile of interesting data, they will itch to crunch it.

Most likely the first site that tried to mine the collective posts of bloggers for interesting data was Beebo.org's Metalog, operated by Michael Stilwell, an Australian Web developer living in London. Beginning in September 2000, Beebo tracked the link addresses that bloggers most frequently pointed to. (Jorn Barger's Robot Wisdom blog topped the first list, with forty-four links.) The Beebo Metalog was assembled by hand, and as blogging exploded, it simply couldn't keep up; it lasted about a year. In the summer of 2001, two new sites took a more automated approach. Both Blogdex, created by an MIT researcher named Cameron Marlow, and Daypop, a weekend project by a game developer named Dan Chan, crawled a list of blogs to track the most-linked-to Web pages or blog posts. These services were sometimes fuzzily described as "blog search engines," and later came to be called "memetrackers," after Richard Dawkins's name for an infectious (or "viral") concept or idea.

Bloggers found these mirrors of their own obsessions fascinating. But because both projects had little money, limited computing hardware, and imperfect software, they were incomplete and unreliable—they tended to crash and go off-line a lot, often when people wanted them most, during some surge of news excitement that spiked their traffic.

In November 2002, over the Thanksgiving weekend, an entrepreneurial programmer named David Sifry cooked up his own version of a blog tracker, called Technorati. Sifry had been posting to his own blog for a while, and he conceived Technorati as a service for bloggers themselves to get useful information about their work. Technorati was less interested in tracking the popularity of links or memes than in charting the relationships of blogs to one another. It would tell you all about the "cosmos" of other blogs that linked to yours, and—when it worked, for at times it would prove nearly as flaky as its predecessors—it would provide automatic, real-time updates.

It was a lot more convenient than constantly looking at your referrer logs, and it was an instant hit. Technorati began growing as fast as the blogging population it tracked, and before long Sifry had turned it into an expanding company with outside investment. But one feature in particular made Technorati's reputation: the blog-popularity contest known as the Technorati Top 100.

Technorati kept a master list of every blog whose owner registered it—and, because the service was useful, a good proportion of active bloggers did so. Then it tracked all the incoming links each of those blogs received. The links were, in turn, weighted according to "freshness" (how recent?) and "authority" (a Google-style approach that gave extra weight to linkers who had won lots of high-quality incoming links themselves). It crunched the numbers, and spat out a list of the top one hundred blogs.

Technorati's Top 100 wasn't the first effort to rank blogs. In June 2002 a blogger pseudonymously named N.Z. Bear started compiling a list he called the Blog Ecosystem, which grouped bloggers who registered with the site into categories like "Higher Beings," "Playful Primates," and "Adorable Little Rodents" based on their volume of incoming links. But Bear's list, which emerged out of the conservative warblogger community, didn't catch on among the technology bloggers responsible for extending blogging's software standards. The Technorati list did.

That meant blogging now had a leaderboard. The anti-media medium had acquired something like the Nielsen ratings. An ostensibly egalitarian realm now had a fine-grained public hierarchy. Who was up? Who was down? Bloggers found it fun, and irresistible, and more than a little scary. They worried that the Technorati Top 100 would turn them into "link whores," rustling up incoming links to boost their standing. But they couldn't stop clicking on the list.

There had always been lists of blogs, going all the way back to the one Jesse James Garrett sent to Cameron Barrett. For a time after Barrett stopped maintaining his list, the canonical catalog of blogs became Brigitte Eaton's Eatonweb, a hand-maintained list that by early 2000 linked to more than five hundred blogs. As the number of blogs continued to grow, any single central listing of all blogs became a practical impossibility. But most bloggers kept their own partial lists in the form of a blogroll, a list of links to the blogs that they respected and—at least theoretically—read on a regular basis. The first blogrolls served as a convenience for their owners, who could click on them like bookmark lists to make their daily reading rounds. Later, Google and Technorati endowed each blogroll link with external value; the more incoming links, the higher a blog's search or Technorati ranking. "Link love" meant respect. It meant whuffie. And now, with the Technorati Top 100, it meant a higher rank on the charts.

Most bloggers had long understood that they were not all equals. They could see that certain names seemed to reappear on blogroll after blogroll. They knew that when they got a link from a leading blog, like Glenn Reynolds's or Dave Winer's or Meg Hourihan's or Doc Searls's, they would see a sudden influx of newcomers. Many bloggers had started out with the belief—one explicitly or implicitly inculcated by all the promises of early blog evangelists—that all they had to do was post regularly, and they would win an ever-increasing share of readers and links. It was certainly true that rapid geometric growth in the early days of blogging meant there was a steadily growing pie of readers and links for bloggers to feast on. But neither was infinite. And so the advent of the Technorati Top 100 occasioned an eruption of resentment among the vast multitudes of bloggers who did not find their names on its list—and who doubted that they ever would.

The complaint that blogging harbored an elite and impermeable "A-list" had first been floated by a Toronto-based blogger named Joe Clark. When Rebecca Mead's *New Yorker* article about Blogger, Meg Hourihan, and Jason Kottke came out in November 2000, Clark wrote a post "deconstructing" it and decrying the "A-list" for its incestuousness and undeserved prominence:

> Despite no appreciable difference in the "thoughtfulness" of their respective Web criticism, some Webloggers are superstars.
>
> The myth, of course, holds that all bloggers are equal, because we all can set out our wares on the great egalitarian Internet, where the best ideas bubble to the surface. This free-market theory of information has superficial appeal, but reality is rather different.
>
> Jason's commentary is quite good (Meg's less so), but so is the commentary written by literally a dozen other bloggers I read. . . .
>
> Web-design skills cannot account for everything, either. Jason's site, in its various forms, offers a middling level of programming complexity. Yet I can name three other A-list bloggers, and a far greater number digging for coal

> with their bare hands in the caverns of the net, whose
> sites are more complex and better-looking. . . .
>
> Any way you cut it, there is no rational or even pseudo-
> rational explanation for the distribution of fame in the
> blog biz. Fame is like that.

"There is pretty much no way to breach the velvet rope," Clark declared. "If you're not an A-list blogger, you will stay off that list forever."

On the face of it, this last claim, at least, was plainly wrong. Boing Boing was one good counter-example. It wouldn't have made anyone's A list at the time Clark wrote; two years later, it was near the top of everyone's. Similarly, many of the hugely successful pro blogs that started years later, like TechCrunch, managed to break into the top blogging ranks fairly quickly; in fact, most of the top slots of the Technorati 100 today are occupied by blogs that didn't even exist for most of the first half of the decade.

Still, Clark's feeling of being locked out of the insiders' club was powerful and, for some, contagious. Over the next few years it became a commonplace lament among bloggers that there was indeed an A-list, and it was getting increasingly difficult to join. In February 2003, Clay Shirky, a New York University scholar and longtime student of the dynamics of online communities, published an influential essay titled "Power Laws, Weblogs, and Inequality," which offered a theoretical framework to confirm this sense of exclusion. Shirky maintained that the inequalities bloggers carped about could not be laid at the feet of the usual suspects—pioneers betraying their ideals or newcomers diluting some original community spirit. Rather inequality was a fundamental mathematical characteristic of the blogging system, one that would increase in proportion to the amount of diversity and freedom of choice the system provided. "This has nothing to do with moral weakness, selling out, or any other psychological explanation," Shirky wrote. "The very act of choosing, spread widely enough and freely enough, creates a power law distribution."

"Power law" has a grim, realpolitik ring; like the economists' Iron Law of Wages, it sounds cruel and inexorable. In fact, the word "power" here is a mathematical usage, as in "powers of 10," and the name refers to the shape of a distribution curve. We are most familiar with the bell curve, which bulges at the center, where most of the participants fall, and becomes sparse with outliers at both extremes. If you plot the height or weight of a given human population, you end up with a bell curve. But if you plot the distribution of wealth in the United States today, you get something very different—a "power law distribution." (It is also sometimes referred to by the names of two scholars who observed it in different fields, Zipf and Pareto.) The power-law curve takes the form of a steep, rapidly dropping arc, like a skateboard ramp. Shirky explained it crisply: "In any system sorted by rank, the value for the nth position will be $1/n$. For whatever is being ranked—income, links, traffic—the value of second place will be half that of first place, and tenth place will be one-tenth of first place."

In blogging, the power law meant that whoever was number one, by whatever reasonable yardstick you chose (page views, inbound links, daily visitors), was likely to be twice as successful as number two. Number three would be a third as successful. And so on. As the denominators of these fractions increased, of course, the differences between each place diminish (that is, the difference between 1/2 and 1/3 is much greater than the difference between 1/287 and 1/288). That's why you see the flattening out of the power-law curve once it extends beyond the top positions—creating the phenomenon known as the "Long Tail." The Long Tail, popularized by *Wired* editor Chris Anderson, was the populous end of the power-law curve, where you find lots of marginally successful or unsuccessful participants in any market. (And if you had a Long Tail, bloggers joked, you could also have a Fat Head—and maybe even a Big Butt.)

"Inequality occurs in large and unconstrained social systems," Shirky wrote, "for the same reasons stop-and-go traffic occurs on busy roads, not because it is anyone's goal, but because it is a reliable property that emerges from the normal functioning of the system." If you start by assuming "each person has an equal chance of liking each blog," you end up with a flat distribution—everyone's roughly the same.

> But people's choices do affect one another. If we assume that any blog chosen by one user is more likely, by even a fractional amount, to be chosen by another user, the system changes dramatically. Alice, the first user, chooses her blogs unaffected by anyone else, but Bob has a slightly higher chance of liking Alice's blogs than the others. When Bob is done, any blog that both he and Alice like has a higher chance of being picked by Carmen, and so on, with a small number of blogs becoming increasingly likely to be chosen in the future because they were chosen in the past. . . . The thousand-and-first user will not be selecting blogs at random, but will rather be affected, even if unconsciously, by the preference premiums built up in the system previously.

It made no difference *why* people might prefer one blog over another; as long as they expressed any preference at all, Shirky said, the power-law curve would impose its inequity.

For bloggers miffed at what they felt was A-list exclusion, Shirky laid out the bad news: bloggers who stood at the head of the list at any given moment would be way more popular than the rest, and there was not much anyone could do about it. He also observed that "most elements in a power law system are below average, because the curve is so heavily weighted towards the top performers." There is an old joke about Bill Gates walking into a bar and transforming the "average" drinker there into a millionaire; by the same logic, the average performance of a blog would inevitably get skewed by the handful of superstar blogs at the head of the curve, leaving most of the participants in the system below that average—and presumably stewing over the unfairness of it all.

Yet it wasn't unfair at all, Shirky maintained. Blogging—an open, easy-to-enter, anyone-can-play system—was eminently fair. If bloggers at the head of the curve stopped posting, they'd lose their primacy. And a blog's popularity was "a result of the kind of distributed approval it would be hard to fake." In other words, the game was difficult to rig because winning required the participation of large numbers of independent individuals. On top of all that, he said, the concept of a discrete A-list was a fiction, since the power-law curve offered no natural "discontinuity" or break-point, no visible cutoff where you could say, *This is where the unwashed masses end and the A-list begins.*

Shirky's message, though not hopeless, was harsh. "It's not impossible to launch a good new blog and become widely read," he concluded, "but it's harder than it was last year, and it will be harder still next year."

Shirky built his analysis on recent academic research in network theory, and it sparked extensive and rancorous debate. Some bloggers read "Power Laws, Weblogs, and Inequality" as confirmation of their most cynical hunches about the way the blogosphere was rigged against them. Others in the most idealistic echelon of bloggers found Shirky's tone irritatingly Olympian and his pronouncements overconfident, given how new blogging was. Their experience of blogging was inspiring, even life-changing; it felt deeply different from the old broadcast-model world in which a handful of gatekeepers held the keys to fame. To be told that, sorry, the new world was going to be a lot like the old one felt like a miserable come-down. Dave Winer wrote that Shirky simply didn't understand weblogs because he didn't have one himself.

Shirky predicted that blogging would stratify into a top tier of high-traffic, high-profile leaders indistinguishable from non-blog media businesses, a middle rank of "classic" blogs with smaller followings, and a Long Tail of bloggers who were posting conversationally for just a few friends or relatives. In the years since he made these predictions, they have proved largely accurate. Yet there were qualitative aspects to the experience of blogging that the "Power Laws" essay failed to capture. For one thing, the simple fact that there was any sort of Long Tail at all helped blogging continue to feel vastly different to its participants from previous media forms—since TV and radio had no tail whatsoever and print had only a truncated one. Then there was the unusual wrinkle that, in the world of blogs, the A-list big fish and the Long Tail small fry tended to resemble one another far more than in any previous medium: they looked the same, functioned similarly, often used similar software. Hollywood movies and home movies felt like creatures from different planets; you were never going to mistake a high-school newspaper for the *New York Times*. But one blog tended to look a lot like the next in your browser window. There was, too, a sense of freedom of movement, of permeability, in the world of blogs: you probably weren't going to see your little blog vault into the Technorati Top 100, but you could sometimes engage the top bloggers via email or comments, and if you posted something unusual it wasn't impossible to get a link from them. (It was a lot easier than getting on *The Today Show*.)

On the Long Tail of blogging, a vast crowd was getting firsthand experience of the old joke about being "famous for fifteen people." But on the Web, with one link often leading to another, that sort of "microfame" would, on rare and unpredictable occasions, abruptly transmute into the more conventional sort of famous-for-fifteen-minutes celebrity. The dynamics of such moments were richer and stranger—and the instances of them more frequent and commonplace—than had ever been possible before, in any previous media environment. All of this helps explain why the harsh certainties of Shirky's "Power Laws" argument—sound though they were—seemed to have zero deterrent effect on the stream of newcomers flooding the many blogospheres with their enthusiasm and posts. Most of them doubtless knew that the odds of breaking out of the Long Tail were poor, but hoped to do so anyway—blogging as if buying a lottery ticket. Many others simply found their fulfillment through something other than fame. Nearly all of them knew that they'd never see their URL in the Technorati Top 100; few of them seemed to care.

In fact, at the moment Shirky's essay appeared—roughly at the same time that Google was acquiring Blogger and the political blogosphere was debating the Bush administration's rush to invade Iraq—blogging was just beginning a long ride up a geometric growth curve. In March 2003, shortly after the publication of the "Power Laws" essay, Technorati reported tracking 100,000 blogs. By October the number had climbed to 1 million. A year later, in October 2004, the number was 4 million. Another year brought it up to 20 million. By October 2006 the figure had leaped to 67 million. The curve fluctuated a bit, but on average the blogosphere seemed to be doubling in size every five to seven months. These numbers were fueled by the expansion in blogging outside the United States, and they also carried a significant asterisk: something close to half the blogs were "inactive" (which Technorati defined as "not updated within the last three months"). Many had been abandoned by their authors; others were just throwaway blogs—people fooling around with a free service like Blogger, opening up an account to check it out, and then walking away.

Still, the numbers were staggering. As blogging grew, it extended both ends of the power-law curve with it. The Long Tail stretched out, seemingly infinitely, with vast numbers of little-read blogs that mattered a whole lot to their writers' small circle of friends and not much to everyone else. And the handful of "winners" at the top of the curve, like Boing Boing, saw their followings swell to a size that a couple of years before would have been unimaginable.

In April 2004, Mark Frauenfelder posted a note on Boing Boing about the cost of the site's "explosive growth" (to 3.5 million daily visitors a month):

> Our bandwidth bills are going through the roof. If traffic
> continues along the projected curve, maintaining Boing

Boing will become unaffordable. We've been thinking
about what we can do to survive.

The bandwidth bills at the time were roughly $1,000 a month—the
bloggers paid out of their own pockets, split evenly four ways—and
Frauenfelder expected that number to double fairly soon. He announced
that the Boing Boingers had brought in John Battelle, formerly of *Wired*
and the defunct *Industry Standard* and now an enthusiastic blogger in his
own right, to explore "a variety of ways to help us pay the bills." He also
invited suggestions from readers in the comments.

Jason Calacanis posted immediately, urging Boing Boing to join his
new Weblogs Inc. operation. Henry Copeland showed up later and
pitched BlogAds. Other readers suggested rent parties, pledge drives, and
merchandise sales. Some posted tips for cutting bandwidth by tinkering
with the pages' images and HTML code. A few pointed to low-cost hosting providers and said, in effect, "Stop whining."

Battelle did his research and reported to Frauenfelder that if Boing
Boing was going to sell ads, limiting the sales to just covering costs would
be tough: any good ad salesperson would set out to sell a lot more than
$1,000 a month. It seemed that just trying to break even might prove a lot
harder than accepting the likelihood of making good money. So in June,
with Battelle's help, Boing Boing began running "sponsorship"-style advertising, and in following months and years it played around with different
configurations and density of ads on its pages. Meanwhile, Battelle—who
likened the Boing Boing operation to a music group and referred to himself as the "band manager"—got to thinking about applying more widely
the lessons he'd learned with Boing Boing. A year after he began working
with Boing Boing, he started a new company, Federated Media, with the
idea of serving as an ad sales and support network for Boing Boing and
other successful, wide-circulation bloggers who wanted to earn some
money but didn't want to spend their time on business.

By that time, Boing Boing itself was beginning to bring in substantial
revenue. In the course of doing so, some critics complained, it was also

beginning to look awfully commercial. "They're the NASCAR of the weblogging world," wrote Lance Arthur, a veteran Web designer and publisher and early blogger, in a March 2005 post headlined "Boing Boing, Ka-Ching Ka-Ching." Arthur traced the conflict Boing Boing faced between what he called its "good DIY, indie rock, mirrorshade crypto-punk rebel" roots and its new financial success:

> OK, fine. Boing Boing is profitable. Probably very profitable. It's not many sites written "for my friends and my family" that need bookkeepers and reader surveys.
>
> Except it feels sort of wrong, doesn't it? It's got the same indie-Orwell feel that calling their business manager a "band manager" has: We're not corporate! We're rebels! . . .

Arthur discounted Boing Boing's original explanation that the advertising was all about covering costs. "These champions of the purity of the Web, these advocates of transparency" would never accept such a "big, sticky wad of hype" from a run-of-the-mill corporation, he said.

> The thing is, it really is about love. They've been at it for too long for it not to be. Which is exactly why they need to come clean, why they need to explain themselves, to correct the lingering white lies. I don't care how many ads the site has, I don't care how much money they make—I care that the justification for them is so wildly misleading, so ridiculously out of date. So—forgive the term— corporate. So PR.
>
> So not Boing Boing.

Arthur's critique evoked a flurry of links and comments, but if it reflected any larger disaffection with Boing Boing among the site's readership, they didn't show it by abandoning the site. Quite the opposite: as a business, Boing Boing had moved from a niche product to the mainstream. It had ranked near the top of the Technorati Top 100 from early on in the list's existence; in November 2004 it seized the number one spot, and held on to it for the next year or two. (In January 2009 it's at number five.) But throughout this growth, its fringy content remained remarkably consistent. If you compared a paper copy of the old *bOING bOING* 'zine with any week's worth of Boing Boing blog posts, you could see a clear line connecting them. The cries of "sellout!" that the site's advertising evoked were probably inevitable, a predictable milestone in the life cycle of any underground sensation that takes off. But in fact, aside from the advertising, Boing Boing was notable for how very little it changed over the years, how closely it hewed to its original formula.

You can find one explanation for this consistency in something Frauenfelder once said about Boing Boing's growth: "It's kind of impossible for me to conceptualize the fact that there are hundreds of thousands of people reading the posts. I just imagine it to be forty or fifty people. My brain can't accommodate a larger audience than that." Maybe so, but Boing Boing itself could. The blog had achieved an impressive scale, serving millions of readers and selling a respectable volume of advertising—*BusinessWeek* reported it hit around $1 million in revenue in 2007, and Frauenfelder said the number was close to double that in 2008. But the site still had no editorial process or structure. The four editors worked in different cities (Doctorow made his home in London), held no meetings, adhered to no schedule, set almost no policies. They just posted at will. Each of them had hobbyhorses and enthusiasms that readers quickly got to know. If snarkiness was the dominant voice of the big-blog universe, as the media coverage of Nick Denton's successful Gawker enterprises kept saying, no one had bothered to tell Boing Boing: it was full of ardent advocacy for the rights of hackers, file-sharers and mashup artists, and loving links to oddball video clips, handcrafted objects, and geek curiosities. (Anyone for a Higgs Boson plush toy?)

In all this, Boing Boing seemed to have pulled off an adroit trick. It had turned itself into a successful business as a mass-market blog while holding on to what readers had been attracted to when it was small: personality, spontaneity, nonconformity. Its editors won their credibility by reliably providing links that their readers loved (often well ahead of the blogging crowd), and they burnished it by openly correcting their errors (adding updated information and crossing out mistakes with a strike-through line so you didn't have to guess what they'd gotten wrong).

Was this success something that just naturally came to those who stayed true to their cool? Or was it a calculated and adept campaign of integrity management? It could easily have been both. But any way you looked at it, there was no denying Boing Boing's skill at forging a bond with its readership that stayed intact even with the addition of ads and the steady growth in traffic. All of which made the unlikely controversy that suddenly erupted over Boing Boing in the early summer of 2008 so exquisitely ironic.

On June 23, Violet Blue, a San Francisco–based blogger and sex columnist for the *San Francisco Chronicle*, posted the following note:

> It was brought to my attention this weekend that every Boing Boing post (except one) with my name in it is gone. It might have happened a while ago, and no, I have no idea what's going on. How do you even ask someone about something like that? Personally, I never delete posts for any reason so I just think it's really weird.

It turned out that Boing Boing had written quite a bit about Violet Blue over the years; she was a sometime friend of Xeni Jardin's, and the blog had treated her as a member of its very extended family. But now a whole lot of posts were missing from the Boing Boing archive—any that mentioned Violet Blue's name. Blue, who said she and Jardin had once been "really close," declared she didn't know what had sparked the Boing Boing purge.

This raised a decent number of eyebrows in those corners of the tech-culture blogosphere that viewed Boing Boing with veneration. Was it just some bizarre technical glitch? Was there some reasonable rationale to explain the wholesale rewriting of blog history? Was Boing Boing just scrubbing its archive of embarrassing posts? This commonly happened when a site was trying to go commercial and discovered that advertisers were uncomfortable with outré material. But that couldn't be it—Boing Boing had crossed that divide long ago, and items headlined "The Sex Machines Next Door" or "Crocheted Flying Spaghetti Monster Dildo Cozy" hadn't seemed to scare off its sponsors yet.

Whatever the explanation, the situation grew into a widening blog storm precisely because it seemed so wildly out of Boing Boing's character. For days, Jardin and the other Boing Boing editors—some of whom were vacationing at the time—remained silent, further fueling the accelerating rumor mill. After David Sarno, a blogger at the *Los Angeles Times*'s website, wrote about the missing posts, Boing Boing finally offered a partial explanation of the deletions. Jardin had quietly removed the Violet Blue posts (roughly seventy in total) over a year before, the Boing Boing editors confirmed, but they weren't going to say exactly why.

> Violet behaved in a way that made us reconsider whether we wanted to lend her any credibility or associate with her. It's our blog and so we made an editorial decision, like we do every single day. We didn't attempt to silence Violet. We unpublished our own work. There's a big difference between that and censorship.

> We hope you'll respect our choice to keep the reasons behind this private. We do understand the confusion this caused for some, especially since we fight hard for openness and transparency. We were trying to do the right thing quietly and respectfully, without embarrassing the parties involved.

> Clearly, that didn't work out. In attempting to defuse
> drama, we inadvertently ignited more. . . .
>
> Thank you all for caring what happens on Boing Boing. And
> if you think there's more to say, by all means, let's talk.
> We're listening.

The post, far from quelling the controversy, inflamed it instead: Boing Boing's readers took up the invitation to talk with hundreds of impassioned comments. Many readers cheered the editors and told them to ignore the critics ("hooray BB. do what you feel with the page, I'll keep drinking in the wonderfulness"). Others chided Boing Boing for tampering with history, and charged that its use of the verb *unpublish* was doublespeak out of *1984*. (In fact, it is the technical term the Movable Type publishing system uses to distinguish between removing a post from public view—unpublishing it—and deleting it, which permanently scrubs the post from the blog's internal database.) Meanwhile, Sarno sank his teeth into the story with the doggedness of one of Cory Doctorow's campaigns against anti-copying software: "This is a business and a major media outlet, not a page on LiveJournal," he wrote. "There are no transparency exceptions for 'personal issues.'"

By now the Boing Boing editors understood that they had a crisis on their hands. Some fraction of their most devoted readers wasn't buying their non-explanation explanation, and the Web press began generating feverish speculations. A headline in Valleywag, a Gawker Media blog dedicated to tech-world gossip, asked, "Did the Internet's free speech guardians try to hush up a girl-on-girl love affair?" Blue herself provided Valleywag with a photo of the pair embracing. Valleywag repaid that indiscretion by suggesting that Jardin had removed the posts because she realized "she was being used by a groupie."

In the end there was no wider significance to the backstory between Jardin and Blue, and Jardin had flatly stated that she would never publicly discuss it, anyway. "Link love" was not eternal. At one time she'd wanted to point links to Blue; now she didn't. Links from Boing Boing had material value—they directed substantial traffic and boosted Google rank. If Jardin and her colleagues had the right to confer such benefits, they believed they had the right to withdraw them, too. Just as, years before, bloggers alienated by Jorn Barger's comments about Jews had "de-linked" him, Jardin had, for her own private reasons, chosen to disassociate Boing Boing from Violet Blue.

Nonetheless, Boing Boing's response to the controversy had a circle-the-wagons feeling to it. For many readers, Boing Boing had embodied a blogging ideal, inherited from the Cluetrain Manifesto and the open-source world and the long tradition of the hackers who'd built the Internet itself. In accordance with that ideal, it had spoken in informal, conversational, recognizably human voices. Now it had suddenly lapsed into the flat, noncommunicative tones of corporate PR. That couldn't really stand if Boing Boing was going to keep its well-nurtured reputation—its whuffie.

One could point out—and defenders of Boing Boing did—that the blog was, after all, free, and if you didn't like what the editors had done, you could, you know, find something else to read. But love-it-or-leave-it would have mocked Boing Boing's image, and it ill suited Frauenfelder's genial sensibility. A day after the original explanatory post—a day in which Boing Boing readers posted 1,500 comments—Frauenfelder and his colleagues offered a considerably fuller and more open response, this time in conversation with Sarno, who posted excerpts of a conference call.

The editors explained that, really, it was true: they were just four people who posted without ever meeting or planning or coordinating or discussing things. They'd always had a practice of unpublishing posts as a way to avoid duplication when one of them posted a link to some curio only to learn that a colleague had already posted about it weeks before. The Violet Blue matter seemed like just a bigger version of that sort of thing. Jardin hadn't told her colleagues of the deletions at the time. She still felt they were justifiable:

> This is my work, this is my blog. This is not the same
> thing as Wikipedia or the paper of record. It's Boing
> Boing. And I have the right to take these things down
> while I think about whether I want them out there or not.

That made sense—or did it? Mass elimination of published material seemed to violate some primal taboo of Web behavior. Yet putting your finger on exactly why Boing Boing's behavior rankled was tricky. If the ethos of blogging was simply one of self-expression, then it was hard to argue with "it's my blog and I'll delete what I want to." But if you aimed to cultivate a relationship with readers and other bloggers, the stance was likely to trip you up.

In the course of the conversation that Sarno reported, Jardin's colleagues backed her; yet it also sounded as if they were having second thoughts about where they thought Boing Boing belonged on the spectrum between professionalism and informality. David Pescovitz said:

> This is a really basic question that gets at the core of
> people having the capability to tell their own personal
> narrative, and democratization of media: Should you
> have the freedom and the flexibility to do what you want
> with the work you create? And I thought I knew the
> answer to that. Now I'm not sure that I do.

A couple of weeks after the first Boing Boing post addressing the controversy, Jardin posted a second one, titled "Lessons Learned," in which she apologized for not communicating faster and better. The Boing Boingers had initially avoided responding in public because they hoped to avoid "something I feared would become a petty, personal online fight that would violate the privacy of parties involved." But that had plainly backfired. "We screwed up and we're sorry," she wrote. But the posts would remain unpublished, and Boing Boing wasn't going to tamper much with its successful formula: "Boing Boing is still the shared personal blog of multiple editors who work together asynchronously with almost no formal editorial process. That's the way Boing Boing began and I hope it doesn't change too much." The editors did agree that if any of them ever again planned a mass removal of some kind, they'd consult with their colleagues—though the final decision on the disposition of any particular post would continue to rest with its author alone.

To this day Frauenfelder says that he doesn't know why Jardin removed the posts. "I never asked her," he says. "I didn't feel that was my business. I trust her enough to know, if she wants to delete her own posts, she should be able to do that. . . . But it did create this bad perception out there." For her part, Jardin remains adamant about not going public with her reasons for removing the posts. "Sometimes talking about stuff does not make it better," she says. As she explains it, she has chosen to take her lumps in public from dissatisfied Boing Boing readers rather than violate the privacy of a personal relationship.

Boing Boing had grown along with the blogosphere itself. When you looked at one of those charts drawn by the network-theory scholars— the ones that look like star maps, with dots representing blogs and a thicket of lines illustrating links between them—Boing Boing usually sat at the center of the universe, an enviable hub of attention and intercon- nectedness. Today the concept of an A-list of bloggers means different things to different people, but however you define it, the odds are high that Boing Boing will turn up at or near the top. At some point in its growth, Boing Boing had crossed a defining line—in the minds of its readers, if not fully in those of its authors. It was no longer some throw- away website of transient value, where the loss of a bunch of posts was of little consequence, but rather an institution whose behavior was going to face scrutiny and challenge. Its authority was conferred, whuffie-like, by its readers; they could withdraw it as well.

Remarkably, through all this, Boing Boing remained a part-time endeavor for everyone involved. Its creators, as if defiantly uninterested in acknowledging their site's new institutional status, still viewed it as a casual, friends-and-family sort of enterprise. As the Violet Blue affair demonstrated, that works beautifully—until it doesn't.

Even as they turned Boing Boing into a multimillion-dollar business with millions of customers, Frauenfelder and his crew held on to a surprisingly hefty chunk of the freedom that had originally attracted them to blogging. At the same time they were able to retain the trust that accrued to a publication that had stayed true to its fringe-'zine roots. But could they hold on to all of it—the freedom, the trust, the whuffie, and the money—forever? That, it seems fair to predict, will prove an increasingly difficult maneuver.

Chapter 8

THE PERILS OF KEEPING IT REAL
HEATHER ARMSTRONG

In Web parlance, to be "dooced" means to lose your job thanks to your blog. We owe this word to a woman named Heather Armstrong, whose blog is called Dooce. That word was a nickname her coworkers had given her after her tendency to mangle the word "dude" in too-quickly-typed instant messages.

Armstrong was not the first person to lose a job because of something she'd written on the Web. That might well have been Cameron Barrett, of the CamWorld blog, who was fired from a small advertising agency back in 1997 when colleagues found a mildly off-color piece of short fiction he'd posted to his personal website. Still, Armstrong's firing was the incident that gave this lamentable fate a name that has stuck. On the Web, the wage of indiscretion is to get dooced. Many bloggers today know this, and those that don't know are likely to find out.

Armstrong had started a blog in February 2001. Like a good number of her peers in the lower rungs of the Web industry, she sought an outlet for stray creativity and a relief from the dullness of a stifling day job. "What really excited me," she once wrote, "was that I got to design the thing myself, choose its name, code it, write it, and then publish it without anyone else saying, 'The client wants more purple. Make it more purple.' There were no clients."

Armstrong (at the time, her last name was Hamilton) had grown up Mormon in Tennessee, gone to Brigham Young University in Utah, and then moved to Los Angeles to join the booming dotcom economy. She was tall and photogenic, and had a wicked sense of humor along with an unerring eye for detail. Her first post set her blog's beguilingly acrid tone and profane voice. In it, she complained about too much rain in Southern California ("I came here for the fucking sunshine, and I want mine") and then added:

> I just thought of a poem I read about five
> years ago in college:
>> Carnation milk is the best in the land,
>> I sit here with a can in my hand.
>> No tits to pull, no hay to pitch,
>> Just punch a hole in the son of a bitch!

Like many of her fellow bloggers, Armstrong wrote about bands she listened to and TV stars she liked. But she also wished her mother happy birthday by recalling "the three distinct moments that My Mother Turned Demonic" and wrote about her alienation from the religion she was raised in—posting an excerpt from a Mormon elder's advice to young men on masturbation, then adding, "I will be excommunicated from the Mormon church when they find this."

Armstrong found some readers for Dooce among friends and strangers who stumbled on the site and savored her tart jokes and rants. Three months after she started posting, she sent an email to Jason Kottke, whose popular blog she admired. Kottke took a look at Dooce and wrote her back with a warning. As Armstrong recalls it, he said, "'You do know that your family is going to find your website and totally freak out?' And I said, oh no they're not—my mom doesn't even know how to turn on a computer, are you crazy?"

Two days after 9/11, Armstrong posted what she calls "a martini-fueled diatribe against the Mormon church," comparing it to fundamentalist Islam. On the same day, her brother found Dooce and showed it to her parents. "I really naïvely thought I was in this private little world," she later said. "I found out very quickly that was a very stupid, stupid assumption." Armstrong took down the Mormon/Islam piece with a note that read:

> I want to publicly apologize to my family for shocking them and for hurting them. I should have shared with them who I really am, openly and unabashedly. I love them dearly and only meant to celebrate our idiosyncrasies as a family.
>
> Dooce.com, however, will continue to offer up the best in expletive-laden religious and social frustration. This is who I am, just now I will leave my family out of it.

This new circumspection would, over time, help Armstrong repair her family ties. But it did not yet extend to her posts about her job. She'd had to leave one company she liked when it tanked in the downturn, and now she found herself at one she detested—a software company with "a dark office and too many vice presidents." She regularly vented her disgust with the soul-crushing environment in venomously funny reports from the cubicle jungle:

> I hate that one of the 10 vice-presidents in this 30-person company wasn't born with an "indoor" voice, but with a shrill, monotone, speaking-over-a-passing-F16 outdoor voice. And he loves to hear himself speak, even if just to

himself. He loves to use authoritative expressions such as "NO! NO! NO! IT'S LIKE THIS!" and "DUDE, NO! YOU SHOOT IT LIKE THIS!" because, well, he's a VP and must be an authority on something, right? Lately he's been an authority on patently grotesque facial hair patterns.

She knew that references to "The Vice President of Spin" and "That One Co-worker Who Manages To Say Something Stupid Every Time He Opens His Mouth" were unlikely to endear her to her officemates. She just assumed she had what computer privacy experts call "security through obscurity": most likely, the targets of her satire would never see it.

Wrong again. In February 2002 a colleague emailed Dooce's Web address anonymously to every VP in the firm. A couple of weeks later Armstrong got called into her boss's office—the same boss whose Botox injection marks she had been mocking in her posts—and was fired. That day, she wrote:

> I guess I could be bitter. I mean, I defended myself rather studiously, explaining that I had never mentioned the company or any employee by name, and that I had exaggerated several characteristics of the personalities showcased in a few of my posts.
>
> But I really don't feel like I have the right to be all that bitter. I made my bed; I'll lie in it, to quote the inimitable Courtney Love. I understood the risk.

"I started out thinking that I could say anything in my space and that everyone else needed to get over it, including my family and friends," Armstrong wrote much later. "Of course, I ended up alienating my family and losing my job and pissing off my friends, and it took WAY TOO LONG for me to figure out that while there is great power in personal publishing, there is also great danger. My supposed right to say anything

I wanted got me into hot water in so many facets of my life that I finally realized it wasn't worth it."

As Jason Kottke had once counseled her, so Heather Armstrong would later advise other bloggers who read her "About" page:

> I am that girl who lost her job because of her website. . . . My advice to you is BE YE NOT SO STUPID. Never write about work on the internet unless your boss knows and sanctions the fact that YOU ARE WRITING ABOUT WORK ON THE INTERNET.

These days Armstrong's blog is popular, but at the time she was dooced, it was a relatively low-profile operation. Until her firing introduced her name to a wider audience, Armstrong's Dooce was, for all its personality, just one more Web designer's blog, a Long Tail blog—not a media business or a bid for celebrity, just some stuff someone was posting to please herself and maybe show off her writing chops for a small following. Yet neither the casual nature of the posts nor the low profile of their author provided Armstrong with any protection when her blog wrecked her life.

Armstrong got into trouble in part, as she admitted, because she was headstrong and reckless and couldn't imagine getting into trouble. But she was also navigating unfamiliar waters. She'd bought in to the idea— one whose pedigree stretched back to Justin Hall—that the highest calling for a writer online was to say everything, and say it as outrageously and flamboyantly and uninhibitedly as possible. As someone who'd embraced the Web early, she'd been seduced by the notion that you could write that way, and win a crowd's approval, and not have to worry about any of it ever coming back to bite you. It was as if she imagined that, somehow, what happens on the Web stays on the Web. She learned, painfully, that the Web is just another precinct of the real world.

Years later an interviewer asked Armstrong what advice she would offer a novice blogger. She answered, "Ask yourself, who is the one person

you would not want to read what you have just written? And now imagine that person finding your website and reading it. Because it will happen. Are you comfortable with that? If so, carry on. If not, maybe you
should consider keeping a private journal."

Getting dooced turned out to be one of the occupational hazards of
blogging, and Armstrong would soon be joined by a long list of fellow casualties. There was Ellen Simonetti, a flight attendant who got
sacked by Delta Airlines in 2004, apparently because she'd posted
photos of herself in uniform revealing a bit too much leg (though nothing that would put a PG rating at risk). There was senatorial aide
Jessica Cutler, whose salacious tales of Capitol Hill liaisons gained notoriety for her anonymous blog, Washingtonienne, but cost her her job
once Wonkette named her. Two weeks into a new job at Google in early
2005, programmer Mark Jen got fired for violating company policy,
apparently by posting detailed gripes about compensation and employee
meetings.

Maybe employers should have been clearer up front about their policies regarding employee blogs. But in most of these cases, shouldn't the
employees simply have known better? As blog veteran Anil Dash once
put it, "I assert that nobody's ever been fired for blogging. How can you
test this hypothesis? Take a person's words, and guess what would happen if you took the exact same words or ideas and sent them to the public via letter to the editor, streetcorner soapbox, or pony express. Would
they still get you canned?"

Dash was right. Yet there was plainly something about blogging itself
that made it hazardous to employment. Perhaps it lulled people into
thinking that words in a post had a uniquely protected status and could
be cordoned off from the rest of their existence. Or perhaps it tempted
bloggers toward rebelliousness or exhibitionism until they ended up
much farther out on some limb than they ever intended. In their quest to
stay true to an ethos of self-revelation, telling it like it is, keeping it real,
they seemed to keep ending up endangering their livelihood.

In most instances of doocing, the fired bloggers discover a silver lining in their plight in the form of a traffic boost from inbound links and media coverage. Such rubbernecking provides a natural opening for entrepreneurial behavior. But after Heather Armstrong got fired, she didn't feel like cranking up the blogging at all. She found herself in a downward spiral of dejection, and in April 2002, several weeks after she lost her job, she shuttered her blog. "I was unemployed and disgusted with who I'd become," she says. "How did I get to a point where I would do this to my life and do this to other people?" She took a six-month break from Dooce, during which she married Jon Armstrong, a Web developer she'd known since college, and moved with him back to Salt Lake City. "I pulled myself together," she says, "and got my priorities in order."

One day Jon mentioned that if she was still interested in doing a blog, he could install Movable Type for her (Dooce had always been coded by hand). In September 2002 she resumed her blog, reporting to her readers:

> After I quit the website back in April, I took some time to sleep, to play with my dog who is cool, to marry my very cool husband, and to take a necessarily large step back from the brink. During that time I also probably drank too much, but who can blame me after this?

Who indeed? It's easy to imagine someone in Armstrong's shoes simply deciding, *I will never write about my life again.* Alternately, the online fame Armstrong had earned from her firing was something she could easily simply have exploited, turned into a cause celebre, made into her personal brand. Instead, her return to Dooce marked the start of a long but steady evolution as a writer.

"In the beginning I thought, I'm *brash*, you know, and I'm *unfiltered*, I'm *raw*—I can say anything I want to say," she recalls. Now she felt she had to grow out of that. She'd always had a bourbon-and-sarcasm voice that was vibrant and crowd-pleasing; she used it to write about everything from her dog to her depression to her constipation with a frankness that would overwhelm readers if it were any less entertaining. There had to be a way for her to maintain that voice, and hold onto at least some of that openness, without having them wreck her life.

▌

"Be real!" is advice that veteran bloggers often give novices. To blog, they say, is to present the truth about your life or the world as you see it. The earliest bloggers all shared one or another variation on the ideology of self-revelation. If you were blogging at all—whether you were Justin Hall posting about your sex life, Dave Winer narrating the story of your work, or Jorn Barger assembling a mosaic of links that mirrored your obsessions—you were trying to give the world an honest picture of yourself.

In the history of online communication, this aspiration to personal truth has always served as a powerful magnetic pole. But people just beginning to explore the opportunities and boundaries of self-expression online have also felt the tug of an opposite pole: they've understood that the online world allows for all sorts of experiments with mutable identity and alternate personas. In a blog, you can aim to "be real"—but you can also fool around with being fake; you can be yourself, but you can also try out being someone else. Confusingly, bloggers at both ends of this spectrum have presented themselves as bearers of truth. No wonder, then, that the timeline of blog history is studded with so many incidents of blog fraud unmasked and reader confidence betrayed. The record is like that of financial panics or seismic activity: Although you can't predict the exact timing or severity of each recurrence, you can be certain that they will keep coming around.

Kaycee Nicole was a high school basketball star in Kansas who began her blog, Living Colours, in 2000, to chronicle her fight with leukemia. That, at any rate, is what her readers thought. Through her posts and those of her mother, Debbie, they got to know her as a plucky young woman who adopted "The Warrior" as her nickname and whose spirits rose and fell as her illness ebbed and flowed. There were photos of Kaycee on the blog, and she would instant-message with some of her well-wishers, and a handful of her closest online friends had talked with her on the phone. When a notice that she had died appeared on her blog on May 15, 2001, her admirers were heartbroken.

But Kaycee's sudden death was followed by a cremation and memorial service so speedy that none of her online following had a chance to attend. Some of her readers began comparing notes on Metafilter, the community blog where many of them had first discovered her site, and they realized that not a single one of them had ever met Kaycee in person. Then they began to unearth other inconsistencies and warning signs: Where, for instance, was the death notice in the local paper?

Three days after the announcement of Kaycee's passing away, someone on Metafilter started a new discussion about her. Admitting that "this is a really delicate thing here," a user who went by the handle "acidrabbit" asked, "Is it possible that Kaycee did not exist?" One group of Metafilter users played detective (they called themselves the ScoobyDoos) and beat the Web bushes for details that might corroborate her existence or demonstrate her fraudulence. Another group just sat in stunned incomprehension. If Kaycee's story was so moving, how could it be fake? As one wrote, "Do I think Kaycee is real? YES. I have read her blogs many a time, and they are too emotional, too touching, and too compelling NOT to be real." This response was understandable but illogical—as anyone whose eyes have ever watered in the theater, or whose heart has raced at the end of a novel, can attest. Still, Kaycee's devotees had faith in her story and believed that those who questioned it were not only wrong but cruel. Metafilter user burg—actually a writer in Hong Kong named Randall van der Woning, who had set up the blogs for both Kaycee and Debbie—wrote:

STOP! STOP!! STOP!!!

this is deplorable. it's making me sick to my stomach!

i have spoken to kaycee on the phone, as well as her mother,
numerous times. i can assure you kaycee was quite real.

as far as i am concerned, all the cynics can go to hell.

Yet two days of further detective work by Metafilter's ScoobyDoos
brought a conclusive answer: Kaycee was indeed a fabrication. Debbie
Swenson, a Kansas mother, had written all her posts—based, she said, on
a composite of three different cancer victims she'd known. "What I did
was wrong and I apologize for it," Swenson confessed. When *New York
Times* reporter Katie Hafner interviewed her (in person), Swenson said
she'd meant no harm: "The whole idea of an online journal is to write
what you want to write," she said. "I wanted it to be something positive."

Swenson's purpose in inventing Kaycee remains a mystery to this
day, and despite her deception and bad faith, it is hard to think of the
Kaycee Nicole story as a conventional hoax or scam. Swenson didn't rob
anyone; the fleecing was not financial but emotional. Even after the truth
came out, there were some in Kaycee's following who didn't view the
episode with revulsion. One Metafilter comment read, "Sure, it might
not be real. does it really matter? if nothing else, the story of kaycee's
death was a moving experience for some people. which is more than you
can say for a lot of weblogs." Others felt no pity: "So, it's wrong to be
deeply offended that an untold number of people spent several days
mourning and dealing with emotional hell because they'd been tricked
into believing that a girl who never existed died from a long and terrible
terminal illness?"

Whether you saw Kaycee Nicole as a disgraceful trick or as inspired
performance art, Swenson had unquestionably played fast and loose with
the trust Kaycee's readers had generously offered—and left many of
them feeling like suckers. It would be nice to report that the Kaycee
Nicole incident inoculated future Web users from getting similarly taken
in. But in fact Kaycee's example was more like the pioneering work in a
new genre—one in which comely young women open their hearts and

lives online, only to leave the Web fans who try to embrace them clutching empty air. In 2003–4, there was Plain Layne—a popular blogger
whose tales of bisexual exploits turned out to be the creation of a novelist who confessed to having been inspired by the Kaycee saga. In the
summer of 2006, there was lonelygirl15, a teenager named Bree whose
confessional videos enthralled a wide following on YouTube. Bree turned
out to be an actor, yet lonelygirl15 held on to her audience while
smoothly morphing from a meme of mysterious provenance into a more
conventional episodic Web-TV show.

As blogging became popular and accessible, it attracted no end of literary experiments, including original "blog novel" serials and shenanigans
like "Bloggus Caesari—a Weblog by Julius Caesar" ("the original warblogger," with updates from the front in Gaul) or *The Diary of Samuel
Pepys* painstakingly repurposed, entry by entry, into blog form. These
were self-evident stunts. But the blogs of this fictional ilk that excited the
most interest were those that deliberately obscured their nature, playing
hopscotch on the line between art and life, teasing visitors with the possibility of authenticity while reveling in the freedom of fiction.

One reason bloggers were able to play this game was that so many
otherwise run-of-the-mill, Long Tail blogs, real sites by real people, made it
difficult for you to answer the simple question, "Who wrote this?" Of
course, a website can say, "By Stephen King," and you might still wonder, is
it really by Stephen King—*the* Stephen King? Or some other guy also
named Stephen King? Or someone just using his name? But plenty of
blogs didn't have any sort of credit at all. The posts didn't have bylines; the
"about this site" page was blank. The blog wasn't explicitly anonymous—
and the author didn't have any evident reason to hide from anyone—but
the assumption seemed to be that if you were reading the words, you
already knew who was responsible for them. For the growing throngs of
bloggers writing for some narrow circle of friends and family, that assumption was usually correct.

There were, to be sure, circumstances in which blog authors had good
reason to keep their names secret. The whistle-blower, the dissident, or

the disgruntled employee hoping to avoid getting dooced—any of them might seize limited anonymity by blogging under a pseudonym using a free hosted service like Blogger's Blogspot, and post away. (The services had technical information that could help identify their users, but generally they would only divulge it if they faced a demand from the legal system.) The advent of this practice—which soon acquired the label of "anonyblogging"—represented a strange twist on the creed of the early bloggers, so many of whom believed in showing a true self to the Web. Keeping your blog anonymous meant you had less chance to enjoy conversational give-and-take; there was no whuffie to be had, or at least no way to claim it. And while it was easy enough to begin anonyblogging, the difficulty of keeping an identity secret grew in direct proportion with whatever success the blog had in reaching a crowd. The very details that might add verisimilitude to your account of life inside some government agency or corporation could identify you to others there. And the same online detective toolkit the ScoobyDoos of Metafilter used to unmask Kaycee Nicole—assembling a case by comparing notes and search engine results and offline clues—was available to any skilled observer hoping to out an anonyblogger.

These concerns about identity all came to a head during the American invasion of Iraq in 2003—the first large-scale shooting war ever between two nations with active bloggers on both sides who could share real-time notes on their experiences. As the U.S. government massed troops on the borders of Iraq, and American planes began their "shock and awe" bombardment, Americans at home began reading a blog called Where is Raed? Written by an Iraqi in Baghdad who called himself "Salam Pax" (the words for *peace* in Arabic and Latin), Where is Raed? originally took the form of letters addressed to Pax's friend Raed Jarrar, who was studying in Jordan.

The blog began in 2002, chronicling the deteriorating state of life in Baghdad as the U.S. invasion loomed. On December 25, 2002, Pax wrote, "Because of these sudden electricity blackouts, this is the third time I write this post. I keep forgetting the save button." He was outspoken in his disgust with the Saddam regime; here, for instance, was his comment on a mention of Saddam's son Uday in the *New York Times*:

> Everyone except his closest "friends" know that he is a sick monster. He has already driven himself into a dead end before his father did. Families walk out quietly when he enters a restaurant, he is known to send one of his boys to bring him the women sitting at the closest tables to "join" him. People hate him, as much as they fear his father.

But he also held the U.S.-backed opposition-in-exile in low regard, and wrote of it sarcastically:

> The Iraqi "Opposition Groups" have met and made plans for a post-Saddam Iraq. I feel so much more relaxed now. My future is in good hands. Excuse me while I jump around and celebrate this.

And he mocked U.S. press reports of the Bush administration's hope that this opposition could "enhance its credibility without growing too independent":

> man this is way too funny, the way everyone is so blatant about it. at least try to be a bit discreet. No need for that eh?, just a bunch of stupid arabs there, they won't notice the threads moving these puppets

A secular Iraqi writing in English with a mordant sense of humor, Salam Pax gave readers around the world a picture of daily life in wartime Baghdad from Saddam's final days in power through the U.S. bombing and into the chaos following the city's capture. For a few weeks after the invasion the blog displayed no new posts, causing readers to fear

Pax had been arrested or killed; it turned out he'd just been unable to connect to the Net, and once he did, he added posts that he'd composed offline during those difficult weeks.

The Baghdad Blogger, as Pax became known, was an overnight Web sensation—"the Anne Frank of this conflict," as Nick Denton put it, with the crucial difference that his diary was available in real time (and, also, that he survived). But some Western readers wondered: How can we be sure he is who he says he is? Where, really, was Salam Pax? After all, *Where is Raed?* was an anonyblog hosted at Blogspot. (By enabling the Unicode technical standard early on, which allowed the use of non-Roman alphabets, Blogger and Blogspot had become the service of choice for bloggers outside the United States.) As Jason Kottke wrote in a post on March 20, 2003, shortly before Pax stopped posting: "Other than what he tells us, we have no way of knowing if he's actually posting live from Baghdad or is running some elaborate hoax from the middle of Kansas." Paul Boutin, a blogger and tech journalist with a background as a Unix system administrator, tried a little detective work:

> I emailed Salam and asked for proof of his location just before the first attack on Baghdad this morning. "how can i do that?" he emailed back. "you don't expect me to run out in the street and take a picture near something you'll recognize."

Boutin checked the headers on the email he received and found technical evidence that generally confirmed Pax's presence in Iraq. But a couple more months would pass before readers got conclusive confirmation of the blog's authenticity—when journalist-author Peter Maass wrote a piece for Slate describing how he figured out that Salam Pax and the interpreter whom Maass had employed while on assignment in Baghdad were one and the same. Pax—his real name, Salam al-Janabi, eventually came out, too—landed a book deal and wrote a newspaper column in *The Guardian* for a time.

Similar uncertainties were bound to swirl around the bona fides of any eyewitness blog (as they did, for instance, around Baghdad Burning—another Iraqi blog, by the pseudonymous Riverbend). For the most part there was no simple way to know whether any blog you chose to read was what it claimed to be. Each instance posed a new and unique challenge for verification. For example, perhaps you enjoyed reading the Waiter Rant blog, a bitterly amusing chronicle of a restaurant server that for obvious reasons maintained strict anonymity. One of the Waiter's first posts, in April 2004, was titled "Sit the Fuck Down" and began:

> So you want the best table in the house? You are not alone. Everyone in this entitled culture feels they deserve the best tables. Never been here before? Why right this way to table nirvana. Going to order 10 bucks worth of salad? Let me fall over myself while I kick Christy Turlington out of her table. You asshole.

The abundant and pungent details in the blog's tales of lousy tippers and rude customers had the ring of truth. It was hard to imagine someone making up the tale about the pharmaceutical rep's PowerPoint presentation of gynecological disorders ("We had to redirect all the other customers well away from the doctors so they did not upchuck their $30 entrees"). But you couldn't know for sure that you weren't reading some novelist's after-hours prank. Waiter Rant's author eventually got a book deal and came out, after four and a half years in hiding, as New Yorker Steve Dublanica—but he still didn't want to tell the world where he worked.

Dublanica's readers could enjoy his cynical insider's take on the restaurant business without caring much about his identity. But if you were Dublanica's employer, you might feel differently. The same anonymity that enabled a waiter to rant without too much fear of retribution also enraged those who were, or believed they were, the targets of drive-by defamation. One person's whistleblower could easily be another's character assassin.

In November 2005, *Forbes* magazine outlined this problem from the perspective of the businessperson in a piece headlined "Attack of the Blogs." The subhead read, "Weblogs are the prized platform of an online lynch mob spouting liberty but spewing lies, libel and invective." The piece, by Dan Lyons, described blogs as "the ultimate vehicle for brand-bashing, personal attacks, political extremism and smear campaigns," and told stories of companies big and small that had become the targets of rumor-mongering "blog mobs." The businesspeople confounded by this new species of reputational warfare eventually learned that conventional defenses—like lawsuits and PR offensives—were largely ineffective: "Filing a libel lawsuit, the way you would against a newspaper, is like using eighteenth-century battlefield tactics to counter guerrilla warfare," one legal expert told Lyons. For better results, you had to wade into the online fracas yourself, or find some third party to attack your critics, or try to get their Internet provider or hosting service to take down the attacks (today, in the United States, copyright law provides more-efficient weapons to achieve this than libel law).

The *Forbes* piece offered a decidedly one-sided portrait of the evils of blogging. Lyons sounded convinced that this new medium, in which anyone could lob anonymous criticism at corporate leaders with impunity, was a vile thing. So his next move was quite a turnabout: he started an anonymous blog of his own, satirizing one of the technology business's iconic celebrities. Lyons's blog, Fake Steve Jobs, maintained its anonymity for almost a year after its 2006 inception, entertaining readers with a stream-of-consciousness narrative from inside the brain of Apple's notoriously secretive and control-freaky founder. Fake Steve's internal monologues featured a torrent of megalomania and a private vocabulary of insults (anyone in the Microsoft camp was a "microtard," and Microsoft CEO Steve Ballmer was "monkey boy"). Lyons—who'd written fiction as well as financial reporting—was eventually unmasked after an increasingly frenzied media guessing game; he proceeded to turn Fake Steve Jobs into a real book, then commenced blogging for *Forbes* under his real name before hopping to *Newsweek*. For him, certainly, blogging had proven more hospitable than the hotbed of "lies, libel and invective" he'd originally described.

It took years, but marketers and PR professionals gradually started paying attention to blogs, seeing both a giant opportunity for word-of-mouth (or "viral") promotion leveraged by technology and a complex new threat to a company's brand image. In this new landscape of "conversational marketing," as some began calling it, blog comments were at least as important as blog posts in shaping online reputations. But comments sections were even more rife with anonymous sniping. And that presented newcomers to the online arena with a novel and seductive form of temptation: when somebody slammed you or your company, it was easy to make up some spurious pseudonym and impulsively wade in to set the record straight. This gambit came to be known as sockpuppetry, since a blogger who commented on his own post under a pseudonym was in effect holding a conversation with himself, like a puppeteer with a sock over one hand.

Episodes of sockpuppetry would regularly surface in the business world, often in the dingy demimonde of small-cap or penny stocks whose prices were manipulated via planted rumor, but occasionally it reared its head in more-respectable precincts. In 2007, for instance, John Mackey, the CEO of the Whole Foods supermarket chain, admitted to using a pseudonym to post attacks on a competitor on Yahoo's financial message boards. The most egregious instance of sockpuppetry to date, however, involved not a businessperson trying to defend a stock price, but rather a cultural critic trying to protect his own ego.

Lee Siegel had made his reputation writing blistering reviews of books, TV and art; he was something of an intellectual pugilist. But when he started a blog on the website of *The New Republic*, where he worked as an editor, he found himself the uncomfortable target of negative comments from the unwashed Internet masses. It turned out that some of his readers—enough to fill comment threads with potshots—really didn't like his work at all.

Siegel faced the same personal test encountered by everyone who publishes writing on the Internet. It can be brutal to expose yourself to the overwhelming influx—via email or comments—of casual, frequently careless reviews from your own readers. As a result, some writers just don't read their comments. Others come to terms with the flood of feedback by ignoring the childishness and idiocy and paying attention to the considered criticism. After all, you could learn a lot from your readers, as Dan Gillmor and countless other bloggers had discovered, if you could get past the insults, flamers, and "trolls" (as commenters who deliberately and repetitiously tried to provoke fights were called).

But Siegel couldn't get past any of that. He fumed at each challenge to his authority and his opinions. Who were these illiterates, defacing his prose with their inanities and obscenities? He began writing cranky essays about what he called "blogofascism" and focusing his ire on what he saw as the Web's baleful tendency to erase distinctions of quality.

Then one day Siegel found a champion, a supportive commenter who strode into the fray on Siegel's blog and started laying into his critics. The newcomer called himself "Sprezzatura" (after the quality of effortless artfulness described in Castiglione's Renaissance self-help manual, *The Book of the Courtier*). Sprezzatura didn't just defend Siegel; he turned the firehose of insult back on the commenting crowd. When Siegel's pan of Jon Stewart's *The Daily Show* came under fire, for example, Sprezzatura shot back:

> How angry people get when a powerful critic says he doesn't like their favorite show! Like little babies. Such fragile egos. Siegel accuses Stewart of a "pandering puerility" and he gets an onslaught of puerile responses from the insecure herd of independent minds. I'm well within Stewart's target group, and I think he's about as funny as a wet towel in a locker room. Siegel is brave, brilliant and wittier than Stewart will ever be. Take that, you bunch of immature, abusive sheep.

To another critical commenter, Sprezzatura responded, "You're a fraud, and a liar. And a wincingly pretentious writer. You couldn't tie Siegel's shoelaces."

The regulars in Siegel's comment threads thought they detected a familiar note in Sprezzatura's haughty fusillade. They soon began speculating that the commenter might actually be the writer himself, showering fulsome praise upon his own work. The question caught the interest of other bloggers, and the editor of *The New Republic*, Franklin Foer, decided to look into the question. On September 1, 2006, Foer announced he'd determined that Sprezzatura's comments had been "produced with Siegel's participation"—which seemed to be a euphemistic way of confirming that Sprezzatura was indeed Siegel. Saying, "We don't let our writers misrepresent themselves to readers," Foer shut down Siegel's blog and suspended him from further writing for *The New Republic*.

How could Siegel have allowed himself to fall so low? He was a professional critic; was it so hard to accept criticism himself, or to rise to his own defense under his own name? Later he would complain that he was simply goaded by the "thuggish" behavior of his commenters, who were posting schoolyard taunts like "Siegel is a mongoloid retard." (It's difficult to verify such quotations or put them in any kind of context because the discussions are all gone from the Web today—only a handful of excerpts were rescued from browsers and Google's cache.) Sprezzatura's name had connoted nobility and grace, but his unmasking made Siegel look baser and clumsier than the crudest of his commenters. The whole episode wasn't just deceitful, it was undignified, risible. It cast Siegel as a sort of commedia dell'arte villain, a comic schemer whose feeble revenge plot had collapsed into a ludicrous heap of exposed lies.

At first Siegel sounded contrite at his exposure: "I made a dumb mistake, and I'm very sorry I did it," he told *The New York Observer*. "I took the blogosphere's bait, and I stooped to the level of these people who were commenting on my pieces, and I shouldn't have." But remorse quickly turned to wounded anger, and a little over a year later, Siegel vented it in a book-length diatribe against Internet culture titled *Against the Machine*. Rigorous self-examination was surely a critic's obligation under these circumstances. But rather than engage in soul-searching, Siegel devoted little more than a page to the Sprezzatura incident, dismissing it as a "prank" and a "rollicking misadventure": "I decided that since I had fallen through the looking glass into some surreal landscape, I might as well have a little fun, get down in the mud, and give thuggish anonymity a taste of thuggish anonymity."

Siegel had plenty of critical credentials, but he seemed to lack some essential moral ballast. Despite his public humiliation, he couldn't bring himself to admit that, even in the comments on a blog, two wrongs didn't make a right. The Web was heaping all manner of indignities on Siegel's life of the mind, but the one that seemed most responsible for driving him off the rails was the anonymity of the "electronic mob" that assailed him. Yet that anonymity was far from absolute. For instance, one of the commenters whose "thuggish anonymity" most enraged Siegel— the one who pointed out "with 99 percent certainty" that Sprezzatura was likely to be Siegel himself—went by the handle of "jhschwartz." He was, in fact, a lawyer in New York named Joseph H. Schwartz.

Still, although Siegel's antics were justifiably ridiculed by the bloggers whose work he had derided, beneath all his layers of self-regard and defensiveness and hauteur he did have a point. There often seemed to be an inverse relationship between the quantity of anonymity in any given online space and the quality of discourse there. The opportunity to be anonymous was an essential feature of blogging and the Web in general—one that allowed people in vulnerable positions to publicize useful information, and gave the rest of us access to previously undisclosed dimensions of human expression, from the wartime ordeals of a civilian to the dinnertime travails of a waiter. But too much anonymity left the participants in a conversation unmoored from reality and prone to out-of-control spirals of invective and personal abuse. In 2004 the Web comic Penny Arcade summarized this process in a strip titled "The Greater Internet Fuckwad Theory," which displayed the following formula on a blackboard: "Normal person +

anonymity + audience = total fuckwad." Kevin Kelly, the *Wired* magazine cofounder and writer, has likened anonymity online to the role that rare-earth metals play in human physiology:

> These elements are a necessary ingredient in keeping a cell alive, but the amount needed is a mere hard-to-measure trace. In larger doses these heavy metals are some of the most toxic substances known to life. They kill. Anonymity is the same.

This was a reasonably subtle view; more common was the blanket condemnation by Web critics, who treated the anonymity of blog comments as self-evidently dangerous.

Anonymity would indeed be a fatally toxic feature of the Web if we were all Lee Siegels, unable to resist the adolescent temptation to don a mask and smite our persecutors. Fortunately, many grown-up bloggers and participants in Web conversations possess more reliable ethical compasses than Siegel, and have found ways to keep their bearings through the jungle of the Web. Today we can distill lessons in managing the dynamics of online discussions from several decades' worth of experience. For instance, when the author of an article or blog post participates in the comments, the discussion is more likely to stay on track—but only if the author shows self-restraint and knows not to "feed the trolls" by responding heatedly to repeated deliberate provocation. Moderation of comments by the blogger—or, on bigger websites, by a moderator or host—can make all the difference, with reprimands or deletions or bans meted out according to whatever set of rules the site has posted. Over the years, moderators have become increasingly crafty. One ingenious tool, "disemvowelling," was invented by blogger Teresa Nielsen-Hayden, who used it first on her own site and later to patrol the comments at Boing Boing. It involves editing out all the vowels from objectionable comments, then allowing them to stand, amusingly garbling them while neatly sidestepping protests of censorship. But moderation can become a nightmare if it devolves into circular arguments between moderators and participants over interpretation of the rules. (Siegel, echoing the complaint that many a forum troll has lobbed at the hosts, charged that his *New Republic* colleagues failed to live up to their own rules.)

Even better than moderation is the enforcement of conversational norms by the participants themselves, which for a moderator or host demands a skill closer to gardening than police work. Mostly, however, the social tenor of a website is simply going to mirror that of the real-world community from which it draws its participants. The commenters on Gawker are naturally going to outdo one another with displays of the snarkiness that attracted them to the blog in the first place. Similarly, if the writing under discussion is itself polemical and acerbic, like Siegel's, the comments are more likely to be vituperative, too.

If anonymity was a problem, then wouldn't accountability be a solution? In some online spaces, users are encouraged to use their real names voluntarily, and in rarer cases a website will try to verify contributors' identities. Some online services accept the impossibility of requiring real names, but make sure that participants have persistent identities with cumulative reputations—so that, for instance, you may not know the real name of a particular contributor to Wikipedia, the collectively authored online encyclopedia, but you can easily learn about the sum total and history of any contributor's participation in the project. Most of the Web, though, functions under a sort of honor system: use your real name if you like, but it's up to you, and you can join in even if you don't.

As blogs kept expanding their scope and reach over the last half-decade, the free-for-all back-and-forth that filled so many blog comment threads became a frequent target for social critics. Conservative columnists fretted that the Web's "disinhibition effect" was corroding social norms, while liberals worried that hate speech and intolerance had found fertile new ground to infest. But the writers and programmers and entrepreneurs who had actually built the world of blogging didn't seem to share these worries. Most of them had found one way or another to come to terms with the unruliness of comment discussions. Some simply lived with it. A good number of others chose to provide no opportunity to comment on their blogs; if you had something to say, post it on your own blog! Others moderated their comments with an iron hand. The best-known bloggers all seemed content to live with a let-a-hundred-flowers-bloom stance. There need be, and could be, no standard approach to handling comments; let each blogger find the method of shaping the conversation that suited him or her best.

Then, one day in March 2007, someone posted threatening comments on Kathy Sierra's blog—and, overnight, a lot of observers began to doubt the adequacy of their laissez-faire attitude.

Sierra was a game developer and author of programming handbooks who started her blog in December 2004. Titled Creating Passionate Users, it drew on her experience devising an unconventional and successful series of technical books packed with humorous charts and graphics intended to draw in "visual learners." Her posts combined bits and pieces of cognitive science and marketing wisdom. Sierra urged product developers and marketers to stop worrying about what users thought of them or their work, and to focus instead on how their products made users feel about themselves: if your software or service left a user thinking, "I rule!" you had won over a dedicated fan, who would in turn become an advocate for you or your company. Sierra also understood that this product-related passion could cut both ways: one of the first posts on Creating Passionate Users declared, "If some people don't HATE your product, it's mediocre."

A lively and articulate woman with flowing blond hair, Sierra fit few of the stereotypes of the geeky, male-heavy programming world. Creating Passionate Users attracted a passionate crowd of its own, divided between those who were inspired by Sierra's brainy pep talks and those who found them cloying or shallow. The blog's growing following eventually landed it on the Technorati Top 100 list, and since it inspired both fans and haters, it met Sierra's own criterion for success. It would doubtless have remained just another hot tech-marketing blog were it not for the storm that engulfed it in 2007.

On March 27, Sierra had been scheduled to deliver a keynote address at a technology conference. But the day before, she published an anguished post announcing that she was canceling the talk and shutting down her blog.

> I have cancelled all speaking engagements.

> I am afraid to leave my yard.

> I will never feel the same. I will never be the same.

Sierra's post cited a series of threatening posts and comments that had led her to this state. Some were in the comments on her own blog; others were posts and comments on two other group blogs, meankids.org and unclebobism.com. Some were crude verbal comments describing sexual violence; others were photographic, including one that Sierra reproduced—a doctored photo of her in which her open mouth, nose, and part of her face were covered in a red-and-black panty to form a degrading and disturbing, albeit muddled, tableau. (Was it about oral sex? Suffocation, maybe? Who could say for sure?) There was another post with a photo of a noose next to Sierra's head, to which someone had appended the comment "The only thing Kathy has to offer me is that noose in her neck size." There were comments (signed "Rev ED") that made reference to "beating bitches with bats" in violent and obscene language.

The barrage of abuse was scary—and also elusive. It was no simple matter to try to pin down the identity of the authors of the threats and the context of their comments. The "Rev ED" comments, for instance, were disgusting in themselves; but they seemed to be part of some side dialogue among the posters, and not aimed at Sierra herself.

Sierra intended her post in part to sound an alarm and start a discussion, and in part to seek help in identifying whoever was responsible for the threats. She succeeded spectacularly at the former but only partially at the latter. For the comments on her own blog, Sierra would have, at the least, the Internet Protocol address to try to track down the commenter who'd written "fuck off you boring slut . . . i hope someone slits your throat . . ." The comment had been signed "siftee@yahoo.com." In the voluminous comment thread on Sierra's post, full of support and outrage, the participants tracked him down, describing him as a Web designer and "31 year old expat Brit living in Barcelona." Three hours later, in the same comment thread, siftee (or someone claiming to be him—how could you be certain?) posted an apology of sorts:

> sorry kathy, i really meant no harm

Identifying who was responsible for the material on the other two blogs was a tougher problem; both were now offline, taken down by their proprietors. There were several well-known bloggers involved in the sites. One of them, Alan Herrell, was a computing consultant who blogged as "the Head Lemur"; his name seemed to be linked to some of the most vicious comments. But as the story unfolded, he sent out an email saying that his computer and all his accounts had been hacked, and he had no idea who'd been posting under his name. None of the other well-known bloggers at meankids was directly implicated in the threatening posts or comments. (And at least one of them—PR and marketing consultant Jeneane Sessum, who'd been blogging since 2001—was a woman.) Chris Locke was one of the four authors of the Cluetrain Manifesto who'd been composing rants for years under the penname "RageBoy." He'd been known as an instigator of Web satires, but assured Sierra and the world that he was not responsible for any of the attacks on her. Frank Paynter was another well-known blogger who had helped start the meankids blog. The site, he explained, was originally intended as "purposeful anarchy" to "create art and criticism, pointed and insulting satire"—but not to "foster a climate of fear."

Sierra's fear was real. But as at least some of the puzzle pieces fell into place, the nature of the threats came to look more diffuse. "It now seems fairly certain that the images posted on meankids and unclebob-ism were not intended as actual threats," wrote Tim O'Reilly, whose tech-book publishing house had published Sierra's books. "But as long as the perpetrator remains anonymous, there is no way to be sure."

Sierra's post, in any event, focused less on charging the meankids bloggers with threatening her than on protesting their creation of an environment that tolerated the intolerable:

> I do not want to be part of a culture—the Blogosphere— where this is considered acceptable. Where the price for being a blogger is kevlar-coated skin and daughters who are tough enough to not have their "widdy biddy sensibilities offended" when they see their own mother Photoshopped into nothing more than an objectified sexual orifice possibly suffocated as part of some sexual fetish. (And of course all coming on the heels of more explicit threats)

> I do not want to be part of a culture where this is done not by some random person, but by some of the most respected people in the tech blogging world. People linked to by A-listers . . .

> . . . Do not let them get away with calling this "social commentary", "protected speech", or simply "criticism". I would never be for censoring speech—these people can say all the misogynistic, vile, tasteless things they like— but we must preserve that line where words and images become threats of violence.

Sierra's plea elicited an outpouring of support and sympathy on the Web. Robert Scoble—whose wife had also been insulted on the meankids blog—stopped blogging for a week in solidarity. Many who commented on Sierra's plight saw it as a confirmation of a dynamic in online conversation that targeted women. The whole incident demonstrated that "misogyny grows wild on the Web," Salon editor Joan Walsh wrote. Meanwhile, the Sierra imbroglio moved very quickly from the blogs into the offline media. It fueled newspaper articles and columns, and before long Sierra found herself on CNN opposite Chris Locke, having a thoughtful discussion (edited down to mere seconds) of the difficulty of maintaining civility on the Web.

In the wake of the coverage, Tim O'Reilly stepped forward and called for a "Blogger's Code of Conduct" (voluntary, of course). Among the draft provisions were exhortations like "Take responsibility not just for your own words, but for the comments you allow on your blog"; "Label your tolerance level for abusive comments"; "Consider eliminating anonymous comments"; "Ignore the trolls"; "Take the conversation offline, and talk directly, or find an intermediary who can do so"; "If you know someone who is behaving badly, tell them so"; and "Don't say anything online that you wouldn't say in person." This was all eminently good advice, but it seemed highly likely that those bloggers who were most in need of it would be those least likely to take it.

There were, of course, also minority dissenters in the controversy. Some felt that Sierra had overreacted, interpreting nasty but ambiguous words and images as concrete threats to her well-being. Others believed that she had jumped the gun irresponsibly in originally implying that the meankids bloggers were behind the threats, a suggestion that she later mostly withdrew. This position was difficult to express because the attacks on Sierra were so graphic and hostile. Unsurprisingly, Dave Winer was one of the few to spell it out. "I take the side of the mean kids," he wrote, "because no one else is, and I have a soft spot for people who are being attacked by a mob, no matter how pathetic they are."

But there were even harsher reactions to Sierra's situation from the deeper recesses of the Internet, where gamers and humorists had evolved a mostly male subculture whose discourse made meankids.org look like

Sesame Street. The most arresting argument came from a writer named Rich Kyanka, whose website, Something Awful, had been making fun of Web ephemera since 1999.

Kyanka was unimpressed with Sierra's fears and asked, "Can somebody please explain to me how this is news?" He offered this summary of the controversy:

1. Somebody writes a blog.

2. Somebody reads this blog.

3. The person who reads the blog sends the person who writes the blog a message informing them they would be killed.

Am I missing something here? Nobody was murdered. No crimes were committed. The same thing that's been happening on the internet for two decades has happened yet again. The faceless masses make baseless asses of themselves. . . .

Kyanka wrote that he'd been getting death threats for years from disgruntled former participants in his site's forums. He cheerfully ignored his adversaries, and now, he reported, they'd moved on to threatening his two-year-old daughter. He posted the full text of a recent email, whose author—infuriated after Kyanka banned him from the Something Awful forums—said he would fly to Kyanka's hometown in Missouri, molest his little girl, and then "toss her over a bridge."

Next to the reproduced email, Kyanka posted a photo of himself hugging his smiling daughter, as if to say, "Look, nothing happened, I'm not afraid."

In a sense, Kyanka was reaffirming what Heather Armstrong had once believed: that what happens on the Web stays on the Web. People may sound and act crazy online, assuming alternate identities and then uttering outrageous things, but such behavior could be sequestered in its own world—it has no power in our offline reality. For Kyanka, who has paid little apparent price for his years of thumbing his nose at his virtual attackers, this view seems to work. But the same approach cost Armstrong her job. Similarly, Lee Siegel mistakenly thought his incognito sparring with his denigrators could somehow be cordoned off from his day job and kept from sullying his critical gravitas. That didn't work out, either.

By contrast, Kathy Sierra interpreted the hostility aimed at her in deadly earnest. She sent out a Mayday call rather than waiting to see whether the online intimidation was going to manifest itself in real attacks. It is easy to accuse her of overreacting, since, thankfully, she is safe to this day. But it's hard to say she's wrong about how inextricably intertwined the Web and the world are. To hold otherwise, to take Kyanka's gamble, requires a sort of reckless bravado.

By letting us expose our inner selves or masquerade as somebody else, blogs have confronted us with a set of unfamiliar challenges, and most of us are not well prepared to handle them. We hear near-universal praise for bloggers with "authentic voices" who "keep it real," but we find little help in assessing the implications of that advice. What do we mean by "authentic"? With whose reality are we going to keep faith? How is it simultaneously possible for "keeping it real" to mean "document your real life in public" for some bloggers and "make up a story about yourself" for others? How much antisocial behavior are we willing to countenance in authenticity's name? We'll each find our own answers, of course. But perhaps we can make a little progress toward clarity and a shared vocabulary.

In his *Sincerity and Authenticity*, the critic Lionel Trilling drew a careful distinction between these two terms that have often been used interchangeably. To be sincere—a concept that first emerged in the Renaissance—meant, simply, to meet a standard of congruence between one's public face and one's private thoughts. Sincerity, in other words, was the opposite of hypocrisy. To be sincere was to eschew the expedient lies that grease our social machine. Sincerity in moderation creates trust; sincerity taken to extremes creates discord. The literary exemplar of this kind of sincerity—the protagonist of Molière's *Le Misanthrope*, Alceste— chooses in the end to banish himself from society rather than make the compromises necessary to live within it. The Web's most passionate advocates of truth-telling, like Dave Winer, have often flirted with a similar kind of self-imposed ostracism.

In Trilling's account, sincerity came to seem old-fashioned over the centuries, and the Romantic era replaced it with a different ideal. To be authentic was to show the world one's hidden inner life in all its passion and anguish. Authenticity was a sort of sincerity for the age of Nietzsche and Freud. Authentic art abandoned beauty as a yardstick for success; the authentic individual was one unafraid to reveal the chaos inside, to pull demons out of his soul and make them dance. Sincerity had emphasized carrying a personal standard of probity into the corrupt public square, resisting the lies imposed by the group on the individual; authenticity dedicated itself to excavating private torments and confronting the world with their naked reality.

In this distinction we can locate one source of the confusion at the heart of blogging's "keep it real" ethic. The "sincere" blogger (in Trilling's terms) seeks to maintain seamless continuity between a blog self and a "real" or offline self, thereby avoiding hypocrisy and holding a steady face to the world. Here, life and blog are in harmony: *Know me; know my blog.* The "authentic" blogger instead sees a blog as an outlet for the true self that is repressed by the conventions and restrictions of "real" offline existence. Here, life is a charade, and only the blog speaks truth: *You only think you know me; go read my blog!*

Viewing blogging through this lens helps explain how two very different visions of the activity could both end up waving identical banners of fealty to reality while proceeding toward completely different destinations. The sincere blogger's approach to "keeping it real" leads to a hermetic equanimity in the face of criticism; the authentic blogger instead pursues revelatory confrontations or trying on masks. Both styles end up provoking the world, but in one case it is through a refusal to self-censor, and in the other it is through flamboyant exercises in shapeshifting or contrived drama.

To be sure, these concepts are less rigid categories than ends of a spectrum of online behavior. But all across it, large numbers of bloggers exhibit a common trait, a kind of defiant abrasiveness or damn-the-consequences prickliness. So many have shared this characteristic that it has become widely seen as defining the form. To be a blogger, it often seems, is to be spoiling for a fight.

Even blogging's most vigorous promoters will usually admit that blogging and the conversations it enables have regularly devolved into a culture of outrageous extremes, ad hominem attacks, and, yes, in Lee Siegel's phrase, anonymous thuggery. But anonymity is only one of multiple reasons for this descent into rudeness. Also to blame, surely, is another long-understood weakness of online communication: the absence of face-to-face cues like expression, tone of voice, gestures, and eye contact. There are other trapdoors inherent in the social dynamics of the online world: consider, for instance, Warnock's Dilemma. The term describes the peculiar problem of interpreting the lack of response to an online posting. When nobody replies to you in a forum conversation, or with a comment on your post, it could mean that everyone agrees with you. Or it could mean that nobody cares enough about what you said to bother answering. Or maybe it means they think what you said was so stupid they can't even *begin* to rip it apart. Or maybe there's just nobody out there at all. The thing is, silence could mean any of these possibilities, or several of them at once. And you have absolutely no way to tell.

Warnock's Dilemma gives bloggers one reason to express themselves in ways that will get some sort of rise out of readers. "If I poke you hard enough," the thinking is, "maybe you'll let me know you're out there." The aspiration to Trilling-style authenticity adds another incentive for bloggers to get crude or vicious in the name of airing out one's inner demons. Here the inner monologue goes, "The angrier I make other people, the more real I will feel myself, and seem to them."

There's no question that the flamer or the troll will often draw strength from this kind of self-justifying emotional dynamic. But it would be both unfortunate and mistaken to conclude that such bitter isolation represents the inevitable fate of bloggers who set out to show their true selves. There are other stories with more-hopeful outcomes—tales of bloggers who offered the Web touching expressions of vulnerability, and received support and encouragement in return. One of these stories belongs to Heather Armstrong.

Armstrong had resumed blogging at Dooce.com late in 2002, slowly growing an audience, building on the fifteen-minutes-of-fame notoriety of her firing as well as on her deft, bristly humor. When she became pregnant in 2003, she briefly considered giving up the blog again. But writing about the experience proved too valuable for her as a coping mechanism. When she gave birth to a baby girl, Leta, in February 2004, motherhood took Dooce's center stage—but in a decidedly unconventional way, with no accompanying slice of apple pie. Here, for example, is one of Armstrong's new-mom riffs:

> Everything I've ever read about breastfeeding has obviously been written by a man with no tits, because everything says that as long as the baby is in the right position it shouldn't hurt to breastfeed. I am here to tell you that there is no possible way to have an 8-pound creature GUMMING your tender nipple without the slightest bit of discomfort. The only way to describe it to a man is to suggest that he lay out his naked penis on a chopping block, place a manual stapler on the sacred helmet head, and bang in a couple hundred staples. The first two sta-

ples REALLY hurt, but after that it just becomes kinda numb, and by the 88th staple you're like, AREN'T YOU FULL YET?? But then the comparison really fails because a man doesn't have two penises, and after stapling the first boob the baby moves on to the other boob and the happy stapling begins ALL OVER AGAIN.

At times Armstrong wrote with a first-time parent's glow about her newborn's cross-eyed gaze or froggy little feet. But she also fully recorded the grinding exhaustion, the physical ordeal, and the psychological tension of caring for an infant. She continued to write with manic humor and carefully calibrated exhibitionism: she headlined one post about diaper-changing after an unusual meal "A Heartbreaking Work of Super Pooping Genius" ("Jon and I are totally fascinated with the color and texture, as if our baby is some sort of Picasso weaving neon orange and green lumpy creations into her diapers"). But you could see that her efforts to distract herself or cheer herself up by telling funny stories were bringing diminishing returns.

Within a few months of sleeplessness, anxiety, and failed attempts at self-medication—all chronicled on Dooce—it became clear to her and her readers that she was in the throes of a full-blown postpartum depression. On August 26 she wrote:

> The reason you won't be hearing anything from me for several days is because this morning Jon is driving me up to the hospital and I'm going to check into the psychiatric ward. I am very scared that if I don't go ahead and do this that I may experience some sort of nervous breakdown.
>
> . . . I have to get all this shit figured out or I really think I'll hurt myself. I can't believe that I don't feel better. I can't believe that it's been two months and I DON'T FEEL ANY BETTER.

At the hospital, Armstrong received a combination of medications that worked for her. "I felt a difference within two hours," she later wrote:

> And if you ask Jon he will tell you that when he brought
> Leta up to the hospital that afternoon to have lunch, he
> saw *Heather* for the first time in seven months, not that
> awful woman who liked to throw keys at his head. I truly
> believe that my doctor in the hospital saved my life. . . . I
> am a victory for the mental health profession.

There was a positive outcome here, to be sure, but hardly a simple message like "Blogging saved my life!" Blogging had given Armstrong an outlet, not a cure. Still, the outlet was important to her in its own right:

> When people say that they can't believe I'm being so
> open about this I want to ask them WHY NOT? Why
> should there be any shame in getting help for a disease?

Having decided to reveal her ordeal as it unfolded, Armstrong did not find herself jeered by a mob of anonymous thugs or assaulted by hordes of trolls. Instead she was the recipient of a flood of supportive emails. She wrote at the time:

> I feel like a crazed kid at a concert who has, in a moment
> of sheer insanity, jumped off the stage in a grand, sweep-
> ing swan dive. And you people caught me. And here I am
> floating through the crowd on your hands and extended
> arms. Thank you for catching me, Internet.

It was not as though Armstrong had a universally harmonious relation-ship with her readers; she liked to joke about printing out the most obnoxious emails she received, placing the papers in her driveway, and running them over. (She says she has only actually done this once.)

But exposing this moment of naked pain—in a manner that was both sincere and authentic—seemed to silence the peanut gallery and rally the support of a community. Today Armstrong says, "I believe my audience was part of what saved my life."

Dooce emerged from Armstrong's crisis more popular than ever. As traffic grew, she began experimenting with advertising. In its early stages the effort yielded "less than what a part-time fry cook makes at McDonalds," as Armstrong put it. But Dooce's income grew enough to make it a family-supporting enterprise by 2005, with Armstrong's husband quitting his Web-design day job to work full-time on the technical and business sides. Today, Dooce is as successful a company as any personal blog might hope to be, with more than 3 million page views a month and a spot in the Technorati top 100.

Over time, Armstrong's blog also became a leading light in a new movement of "mommybloggers." That tongue-in-cheek name seemed to come with a condescending pat on the head. But it was proudly embraced by its targets and defended thus by Armstrong:

> Some people use that label to belittle the fact that there are women out there writing about their experiences as mothers. How dare they? Who do they think they are? NO ONE WANTS TO HEAR ABOUT YOUR KID, YOU MOMMY BLOGGER! Yeah, that. Turns out lots of people want to hear about your kid. Oh, and did you hear? All this writing about motherhood is bringing people together and changing lives. So you go ahead and wrinkle your nose and dismiss these mommy blogs. And I'm going to sit over here at my laptop and be totally flattered that someone thinks I'm worthy to be among their ranks. Hell yes, I'm a mommy blogger.

Mommyblogging is only one of a whole host of subcultures into which blogging has fragmented as it has expanded: there are not just

crafts bloggers, but whole cadres of knitting bloggers and weaving bloggers; not just foodie bloggers, but beer bloggers and sushi bloggers. There
are legions of diet bloggers and "fat acceptance" bloggers; there are bloggers who will help you overcome anorexia and bulimia—and others
offering tips to keep your eating disorder going. Each subculture has its
own norms of behavior. Unsurprisingly, there's a lot more positive rein-
forcement among mommybloggers than, say, among political or technical bloggers. The support-group vibe can cause some observers to roll
their eyes; on the other hand, support is surely what a lot of mothers desperately need. Yet the world of mommyblogging is not a paradise apart
from the rest of the Web's conflicts. It has its share of rivalries and flame
wars and trolls. Some mommybloggers, like Armstrong, use their real
names, while others blog anonymously to protect themselves from verbal
attack or preserve the privacy of their families. Either way, nearly all of
them are committed to creating a truthful public record of their personal
experience, to whatever extent their sense of privacy, and their skill with
words, allows.

Armstrong describes Dooce as "a memoir being written as it is lived."
Every month since Leta's birth, she has posted a monthly letter to her
daughter. Together these missives form an intimate chronicle of the
child's development—a kind of gift to her offspring that most parents
would be proud to be able to offer. They are also public work, part of a
profit-making enterprise, and that has opened Armstrong to criticism
that she is somehow exploiting Leta or violating her privacy. Every successful autobiographer or memoirist risks such charges. Are they sharing
or selling? Readers will always sniff out the difference: honesty and huck-
sterism both carry traceable scents, even on a website.

Like the very different Boing Boing, Dooce has added more overtly
commercial features over the years (like a daily "style" posting recom-
mending products). Yet it has managed to preserve its following and its
credibility. Armstrong, the original poster child for self-destructive Internet behavior, has also learned how to rein in her indiscretion without
neutering her self-expression. It turns out there are ways to create com-

edy and drama and suspense for your readers that don't involve actually living through hell or alienating everyone in your life. Armstrong's transformation has been a slow one, but today you can't miss how nimbly she treads—stepping gingerly over, under, or around thorny topics that her younger self would have simply charged straight through. Dooce has lost none of its bite or its levity; you're just not always having to cross your fingers for its author's sanity and survival.

Today Armstrong says, "People I meet tell me, 'It's so weird I know everything about you.' No you don't! Ninety-five percent of my life is not blogged about."

Writing about only five percent of your life does not constitute total self-exposure, or even modest self-revelation, in anyone's book. But as Armstrong's balancing act demonstrates, it's nevertheless enough to be honest and captivating. And it has one great advantage over the all-or-nothing credo of blogging's adolescence: it is sustainable.

Part Three

WHAT HAVE BLOGS WROUGHT?

Chapter 9

JOURNALISTS VS. BLOGGERS

I n 2003, friends and strangers started telling John Markoff, the *New York Times*'s senior Silicon Valley correspondent, that he should start a blog. He'd been covering the computer industry since the early 1980s and couldn't get that excited about this latest fad. "I'd seen things come and go in waves," he says today. "The form of expression of participation on the Internet is always changing." When Markoff's friend Joi Ito, a social-media entrepreneur and a veteran blogger in Japan, urged him to take up blogging, he responded tartly, "Oh, I already have a blog. It's at www.nytimes.com. Don't you read it?"

Over the next few years, Markoff trotted out that line whenever he was told, "You oughta be in blogs!" The jibe never failed to elicit an annoyed reaction from true believers in blogging. "I was just being a smart aleck," Markoff admits now. But he was also expressing a genuine puzzlement about the medium that was common among those who made a living by writing.

Blogging just didn't seem like that big a deal. People had been publishing personal writing on the Web for years. Readers had been interacting with writers online for just as long. Magazines and newspapers had always had "reporter's notebooks" and "diaries" and other regular features designed to present short, chatty items. There just wasn't a lot about blogs that was new or worth getting excited about, was there?

This reasonable attitude failed to take one simple change into account: all these experiences and opportunities that were old-hat to professional writers had become available to virtually anyone. Getting your work published used to require jumping many hurdles; now it required next to nothing. This was what excited so many newcomers about blogging. But how could it excite those who already had access to a publishing outlet? Most journalists take their soapboxes for granted; that's why the resentment of the soapbox-less multitude so often blindsides them.

Animus against the press had been a driving force in blogging from the start. Dave Winer wanted to seize his own story, and the technology industry's, back from the media middlemen. Political bloggers of the left and right took fact-checking arms against a sea of error and bias. Everywhere you looked, the litany of grievances against the media was the same: *You don't get it.* Or, *you got it wrong.* Or, *you need to come clean.* It was as though the pent-up pressure of a century's worth of unpublished letters to the editor had suddenly exploded online in a fury of indignation and complaint.

But the media did not, at first, respond in kind. Newspapers and magazines published their first handful of articles about blogging (including Rebecca Mead's *New Yorker* piece) in 1999 and 2000. Written mostly by Web-savvy technology reporters, these pieces noted the arrival of this new Web form with approval or, at worst, amusement. In the *Chicago Tribune*, for instance, Julia Keller wrote that weblogs were her pick for "most promising new genre," and added that she'd found "precious little hype in the weblog world." And in Slate, Rob Walker wrote that though he enjoyed weblogs, they hadn't cut into his reading of "newspapers or 'real' news sites." Some bloggers might rage against the media, but there was no reason for the pros to be alarmed—because, really, how many people actually read blogs? Or would ever?

There was one big hole in this reasoning: these same pros had already fallen hard for this new form themselves. If you peeked at the bookmark lists on the Web browsers in every newsroom in the United States, on any day from late 1999 on, you'd find that a rapidly growing percentage of the journalism profession shared an addiction to a weblog produced by Jim Romenesko called MediaNews. Founded in May 1999 as mediagossip.com and given its more sober name when it got acquired by the Poynter Institute's website a few months later, "Romenesko," as it was universally referred to, served as the journalism profession's virtual water cooler. It was a simple weblog, collecting links each day to stories and columns about the media; Romenesko would also publish a smattering of his email, ranging from arguments about copyediting to disputes about business strategy. And as disaffected or mischievous employees started sending him copies of newsroom memos on sensitive subjects like budget cuts and layoffs, he would repost them verbatim. This made for irresistible reading for anyone in the business.

In other words, the same journalists who were reassuring themselves that they could ignore the anger among bloggers at their profession because "nobody reads blogs" were choosing to get a good chunk of their information about their own field from a blog. Many admitted, when pressed, that they were in fact obsessed with Romenesko—they'd keep returning to the site for updates at idle moments during their workday.

This was perfectly understandable. Journalists love to know things ahead of everyone else. Continually reloading Romenesko meant that the next time your editor mentioned some column to you, you could say, "Oh, yeah, I read that yesterday." The trouble was that so many journalists failed to notice that their own behavior was a harbinger of a much wider shift that was under way in patterns of information consumption online. They couldn't imagine Romenesko as a model for coverage of other fields. The site was too specialized. It was just their profession's inside baseball. And it was all links to material on other sites. In the new vocabulary of online media, it was an "aggregator," not a producer of "original content." In the newsroom culture, aggregation was a low-status activity. Yes, a lot of journalists had bookmarked Romenesko. And getting your story mentioned or linked from his site was usually welcome. But few hankered after Jim Romenesko's job.

It was only slowly that the attitude toward blogging among professional journalists, and the bent of the coverage they gave it, shifted from detached interest to a more active belittlement. This stance changed, not at all coincidentally, at a moment of unprecedented stress in the news industry. In the early 2000s, a long-term slow decline in circulation began to steepen, and profits that had been fattened by dotcom-bubble-fueled advertising began to vanish. At the same time, the professional self-respect of journalists was suffering a series of self-inflicted blows. Jayson Blair's deceits discredited the august *New York Times*; angry readers blamed the entire Washington press corps for swallowing the Bush administration's line on Saddam Hussein's weapons of mass destruction and the urgent need to invade Iraq. Then, at the very moment when newspapers began to eye their websites as a source of revenue that might begin to replace lost profits from the declining "dead trees" edition, editors and reporters found their authority questioned and their work challenged by bloggers.

In their eyes, this self-righteous mob was kicking hardworking journalists when they were already down. Naturally, many reporters and editors responded with hostility. Their brush-offs, tinged with ridicule and contempt, kicked off an interminable debate—Journalists versus Bloggers—that still smolders in many quarters. There was an old saying that advised, "Never pick a fight with someone who buys ink by the barrel." But this was something new: a fight between those who bought ink by the barrel and those who published without any ink at all. That meant there would, practically speaking, be no limits to how long the argument might last. In one lengthy public correspondence between blogger Jeff Jarvis and *New York Times* editor Bill Keller, Keller, apparently exasperated by Jarvis's dogged, detailed replies, distilled his sense of frustration with the open-ended nature of the Journalists-versus-Bloggers dispute: "There seems to be no end to any argument in your world."

Of course, editors are busy people. And one prerogative of an editor has always been the ability to declare, "This argument is at an end." The job of a news editor is to say, "And now this." The news cycle has turned! Time to move on. The trouble was, bloggers were under no obligation to pay attention to such marching orders. If you ran a blog that obsessively tracked the fluctuation of oil prices or the rise and fall of hemlines—or, for that matter, the arguments between bloggers and journalists—then nothing was going to stop you from continuing to post about it. You followed your own news cycle—just as Josh Marshall and his peers did in keeping the Trent Lott story alive after the newspapers and networks had left it behind. This characteristic of blogging became a profound irritant to editors who were accustomed to being able to set the agenda of public dialogue. The bloggers had said their piece, and the editors had responded; couldn't everyone just move along now?

As the volleys flew back and forth between journalists and bloggers, many in the two groups came to treat each other as bitter enemies. But there were at least as many similarities between their respective identities and activities as there were differences. They were more like feuding cousins, squabbling over a family legacy: Who gets to call himself a journalist? Who should readers trust? Which group was meeting democracy's need for reliable public information? If the Web was killing newspapers, could the new medium fill the void?

Journalism was only one of many kinds of writing that bloggers engaged in. But it was the one that attracted the most attention from professional journalists, who, like everyone, saw the opportunities of blogging through the lens of their own experience. When newspapers and TV started covering blogging and introduced it to the majority of the public that hadn't already discovered it on their own, they inevitably shaped its story around their own concerns and fears.

The question "Is blogging journalism?" was not one typically raised from the blogger camp; it was posed overwhelmingly by journalists, who made it the theme of countless columns and the agenda of innumerable journalism-school panel discussions. The answer has always seemed simple and obvious: writing a blog neither qualified nor disqualified you for the "journalist" label. Blogging could be journalism anytime the person writing a blog chose to act like a journalist—recording and reacting to the events of the day, asking questions and seeking answers, checking facts and fixing errors. Similarly, journalists could become bloggers anytime they adopted the format of a blog as a vessel for their work.

These realities tended to be obscured by the tug of group loyalties. *Blogger* and *journalist* ought to have served as simple names for straightforward activities; too often they were used instead as badges of tribal fealty. On the surface, the argument was about accuracy, objectivity, and similar matters of practice; underneath, the conflict was over standing, rights, and respect—matters of identity. Once bloggers began to find a following as sources of information, journalists pointed at them and said, "Who appointed you?" Bloggers wheeled around at journalists and pointed right back, asking, "Well, who appointed *you*?"

Journalism has long straddled the line between craft and profession. On the hurly-burly frontier of the Colonial era and through the nineteenth century, anyone with a printing press—or in the employ of someone with one—could call himself a journalist. Over the last half-century, journalism schools have flourished in the United States, but newsrooms are still full of practitioners who learned on the job instead of in the classroom. The First Amendment's protection of the press from government regulation has prevented the development of any comprehensive accreditation scheme for American journalists. What we have instead are ad-hoc rules for the rationing of scarce resources—primarily, that of access to powerful people and important events. For instance, political reporters who work for major media outfits get press passes to cover presidential trips and press conferences, while small-town papers and bloggers usually don't. So journalists didn't have much of an answer to "Who appointed you?" beyond "My boss."

Most journalists view themselves as quick studies and generalists; part of the job's appeal is that you're always in a position to be learning something new. Good journalism required a variety of skills, from speedy

research and source evaluation to interviewing technique and explanatory storytelling. Certainly, mastery of these skills often gave seasoned
veterans and ace investigative reporters a valuable edge over less-well-
trained competitors. But these skills weren't exactly particle physics. And
now anyone who started a blog had at least the opportunity, if so
inclined, to try to practice them.

That left the legal system in a quandary. It had always used a shortcut
to deal with the troublesome problem of defining who was a journalist: if
your paycheck came from a journalism organization, you were in. Now
that shortcut was being undermined by people like Josh Wolf. Wolf was a
San Francisco–based blogger who recorded videos of an anti-globalization
protest in which a police officer was injured; he spent more than six
months in jail in 2006 for refusing to turn over his tapes to a grand jury
investigation. The court decided Wolf was an activist, or, as a U.S. attorney put it, "simply a person with a video camera who happened to record
some public events." He maintained he was a journalist and as deserving
of First Amendment protection as any other reporter seeking to protect
documents or sources' identities from a prying judiciary: "The notion
that I needed to be under contract by a major media outlet is preposter-
ous," he told the *San Francisco Chronicle*. Organizations like the Reporters
Committee for Freedom of the Press and the Society of Professional
Journalists eventually rallied behind Wolf, and the Newspaper Guild
gave him a press freedom award. (Ironically, he finally won his freedom
through a compromise in which he presented the videos publicly on the
Web rather than turning them over to the court.)

In another "who gets to be a journalist?" controversy, Apple sued a
Harvard freshman named Nicholas Ciarelli in 2005, claiming that his
blog—Think Secret—was publishing trade secrets. The legal questions in
each case were different, but the root issue was the same: Now that anyone could commit acts of journalism, who could claim protection under
laws that privileged a special class of journalists?

The rise of blogging exposed just how porous the line between "journalist" and "non-journalist" really was. Some observers began to use the

term "citizen journalism" to describe the resulting profusion of new forms of amateur reporting and experiments in community-based information-gathering. The label was embraced by journalists and educators like Dan Gillmor and Jay Rosen, a professor at New York University, who defined it thus: "When the people formerly known as the audience employ the press tools they have in their possession to inform one another, that's citizen journalism." Walt Mossberg, the *Wall Street Journal's* popular personal technology columnist, liked to make fun of citizen journalism by likening it to "citizen surgery," and the joke always won him a laugh. But it was a poor analogy. It suggested that journalism was a field like medicine, one that required an elaborate training regime and rigorously policed professional standards. That has never been the case. And if it were, if our lives really did depend on the quality of journalists' work, then in recent years much of the profession lay open to charges of malpractice.

Anger at the American media may have been stoked by a legion of bloggers, but they didn't spark it. It has a long history, encompassing political partisans outraged by the perception of bias, businesspeople unhappy with the difficulty of obtaining coverage for their products, and the general population of all those interview subjects who once spoke to a reporter for an hour but came out with only a three-word quote in the final article (and felt they'd been misquoted). To some, journalists are elitists who look down on the rest of humanity; to others, they are morons who can't get anything right.

Such gripes have always set a baseline for discontent with the media. But in the early 2000s, the level spiked sharply, thanks to the Iraq debate. The Bush administration made its case for an invasion of Iraq— introduced in the spring and summer of 2002, and intensified the following autumn and winter—by blanketing news channels with information about ties between Saddam Hussein and al-Qaeda and imminent threats to the American people from the Iraqi dictator's secret stash of chemical, biological, and nuclear weapons. With just a little bit of effort you could find reasonably abundant counter-evidence in the foreign press, in some small journals, and on specialty websites (like Josh Marshall's). But with rare exceptions, big media outlets in the United States, and the journalists they employed, essentially repeated or reinforced the administration's claims. Reports on Iraq's efforts to acquire weapons of mass destruction by the *New York Times*'s Judith Miller that later proved erroneous attracted the most venom from online critics. But the failure was far more widespread.

· The evaporation of the case for war, once American forces failed to turn up any of those WMDs, discredited not just the Bush administration but the media outlets that had served as its enablers. If journalists' role in a democracy was to make sure that the public and its leaders worked from good information as they weighed life-and-death decisions, then the record of the Iraq war debate represented a system breakdown of imposing proportions. Here's the entire story boiled down to a tongue-in-cheek instant-message exchange posted on the feminist blog Jezebel, between one of its bloggers, Megan Carpentier, and Wonkette founder Ana Marie Cox:

> MEGAN: Like, oh my God, Ana, when are bloggers going to get ethics like real journalists?
>
> ANA MARIE: As soon as we gain enough power to mislead a country into a stupid war.

The judgments American journalists passed on themselves, like this conclusion from a report on a 2008 panel at Harvard's Nieman Foundation, were often as harsh as the attacks of the most livid bloggers: "Covering one of the most important stories of our time—the run-up to war in Iraq—our nation's top reporters and editors blew it. Badly. Their credulous, stenographic recitation of the administration's deeply flawed arguments for war made them de facto accomplices to a war undertaken on false pretenses." A survey of Nieman Fellows gave their profession a grade of "D" for its performance on the Iraq story, in which, as one participant put it, "the national media simply reported what national leaders wanted to do without scrutiny or challenge."

To be sure, the post-Iraq breakdown of trust in the media had a partisan element. Opponents of President Bush and his war naturally felt the betrayal the deepest. Many liberal Democrats already believed the press had helped deliver the White House to George W. Bush in 2000 by relentlessly focusing on trivial blemishes in Al Gore's record; they blamed the media for abandoning its adversarial role. Their view was summarized by blogger Glenn Greenwald: "Propaganda thrives—predominates—in our democracy for many reasons, the principal reason being that we don't have the sort of journalist class devoted to exposing it."

But it wasn't as if everyone on the right was happy with the press. If anything, conservatives' belief in "liberal media bias" was more deeply entrenched than any equivalent belief on the other side of the political spectrum. For many conservatives, the watershed moment for giving up on the media came not during the Iraq debate, but later, during the 2004 election cycle, with the event they came to call "Rathergate." On a *60 Minutes* show that aired September 8, 2004, at the height of that year's political campaign, CBS's iconic anchorman, Dan Rather, presented a story about President George W. Bush's time in the Texas Air National Guard in the early 1970s that seemed to confirm widely circulating rumors that Bush had neglected his service obligations. Rather's story was based on a series of memos that CBS said had been written by Bush's commander at the time.

Bloggers on the right, led by Powerline and Little Green Footballs, immediately painted the *60 Minutes* story as a political hit piece from a network they'd long believed was a den of liberals. Hoping to douse the controversy, CBS posted scans of the disputed memos on its website. Within hours, a poster at the conservative Free Republic forum who called himself "Buckhead" declared they were forgeries: they were typed in a modern, proportionally spaced font and had other typographic flourishes atypical of early-1970s office typewriters. "Buckhead" was hardly a neutral observer, nor did he claim to be; he was an Atlanta lawyer named Harry MacDougald with a Republican Party pedigree who had helped draft an Arkansas Supreme Court petition for the disbarment of President Bill Clinton. His analysis leaped from Free Republic to the conservative blogs to the Drudge Report; Drudge served as a bridge to the rest of the media, which soon swarmed over the story. Probably the most arresting evidence was a simple animated image, created by Charles Johnson of the Little Green Footballs blog, that flipped back and forth between CBS's original memo and a present-day retyping of it using Microsoft Word's default settings. Johnson's image made a dramatic case for Buckhead's speculation that the memo was simply a modern document that had been run through a photocopier multiple times to blur it.

CBS responded the way newsrooms under attack so often have: it stood by its story. The memos had been "thoroughly investigated by independent experts." The venerable network, proud inheritor of the mantle of Edward R. Murrow and Walter Cronkite, didn't need to justify itself to some mob on the Internet waving pitchforks. Former CBS executive Jonathan Klein described the flap in terms that distilled the old guard's disbelief at the upstarts' challenge: "You couldn't have a starker contrast between the multiple layers of checks and balances and a guy sitting in his living room in his pajamas, writing what he thinks."

The trouble was that the guys in pajamas were making more sense than CBS was. CBS stonewalled at first, working from the playbook of a politician engulfed by scandal. Noticeably more determined to protect its reputation than to ascertain the truth, the network resisted suggestions that it launch its own investigation into the documents. In a followup broadcast a week after the first questions arose, Rather said, "If the documents are not what we were led to believe, I'd like to break that story." But it was far too late for that—the Web had already broken it wide open. As more details emerged, a consensus formed, not just on the blogs but among the network's journalistic peers, that CBS had blown it:

The experts CBS relied on hadn't solidly authenticated the memos, and the *60 Minutes* team had made several leaps of trust in sources that could not be justified in retrospect. The rest of Rather's story about George W. Bush's service might well have been accurate, for all we knew; but in recklessly promoting the suspect documents, CBS had damaged its reputation and discredited the entire piece.

One step behind its critics, CBS eventually reached the same conclusion. On September 20, CBS president Andrew Heyward issued a statement admitting that "CBS News cannot prove that the documents are authentic. . . . We should not have used them." Heyward fired the report's producer, Mary Mapes, and several others involved in the story. Rather himself retired six months later—a year earlier than he'd once planned, and under a considerable cloud. In 2007 he sued his former network for $70 million for harming his reputation in the affair.

To this day, Rather and Mapes both maintain that nobody has proven their documents were forgeries. But the vaunted checks-and-balances of the CBS newsroom were supposed to meet a higher standard than that. Surely the story ought to have been nailed down before it aired. Wasn't that what separated the journalists from the bloggers? In defending their story by insisting it has never been 100 percent debunked, Rather and Mapes sound nothing like the model newsroom pro—that eternal skeptic who lives by the motto "If your mother tells you she loves you, check it out." Instead they resemble the caricature of the irresponsible basement-dwelling blogger—who never lets the facts interfere with a dearly held belief.

Anyone can make a factual error or misfire on a big story. CBS's missteps with the Bush documents exposed deeper flaws in its internal processes, the self-regulatory checks-and-balances it proudly brandished as evidence of its superiority to the pajama-clad Web horde. The network had become impermeable to legitimate criticism. When credible external voices raise reasonable questions about a story, a healthy news organization should responsibly evaluate them. CBS reacted instead with what one of its former executives called "insufferable hubris and self-righteousness."

Just as the Iraq story confirmed liberals in their belief that the conservative White House held the media in its thrall, the Rather story confirmed conservatives in their belief that the press promoted a liberal agenda. The newsroom was taking flak from both ends of the political spectrum. That's a situation that actually reassures many newsroom veterans. *Everybody's mad at me*, goes the thinking, *so I must be doing something right!* But there's always another plausible explanation: you could be wrong all around.

It was painful for dedicated journalists to contemplate this possibility, but the more you looked at the field in the middle of the decade of the 2000s, the less confidently you could dismiss it. No matter what your beat was, if you were writing regularly about any topic, you now had to contend with a welter of competing voices on the Web. Some were ill-informed and unlikely to threaten a professional journalist's standing. But many others were experts or self-taught obsessives who were willing to post about their fields around the clock and in far greater depth than any commercial publication would ever provide. It wasn't just fan behavior—*Harry Potter* devotion or *American Idol*-ization—that inspired this sort of blog. You could find heavy hitters in the legal and health professions, technologists and economists, linguists and classical-music archivists, butchers and bakers and somewhere, no doubt, candlestick makers—initiates in every conceivable realm of arcana, publicly displaying their expertise, many hoping to boost their professional reputation or sell stuff, but many others motivated simply by the sheer delight of it. Some of these experts were ensconced in their fields, securely employed in academia or private industry (you couldn't get much more credentialed than U.S. Appeals Court judge Richard Posner, who blogs voluminously); others were self-appointed. In either case, all that mattered was the expertise revealed in their writing. The public nature of the work meant that their credentials were earned and re-earned, post by post.

Many journalists, content in the penumbra of respect and entrée conferred by the institutions that employed them, had complacently

accepted an ex officio basis for their authority. Now they faced discom-
forting challenges to that authority in a new environment where who
you worked for mattered less than how good you were, and how good
you were had become a question anyone could argue. "A passionate amateur almost always beats a bored professional," wrote Chris Anderson
(the professional who edited *Wired* magazine). Here and there, of course,
you could still find passionate professionals, and they were priceless. But
the bored pros found themselves outclassed and outgunned as never
before.

For instance, if you were an American voter mildly interested in the
2008 election, you could follow the ups and downs of the polls the way
you always had, in the brief stories your newspapers and magazines provided and the headlines you heard on TV and radio. But if you were an
American voter who was frantically, unreasonably interested in the
election and its day-to-day, state-by-state poll results, the Web now
fed you as much detail as you could stand. This process had started in
2000, during the overtime-innings election that birthed Talking Points
Memo, and gained real traction in 2004 with the rise of a site called
Electoral-vote.com. Produced by an expatriate American computer scientist living in the Netherlands, Electoral-vote.com aggregated poll
results to provide daily tracking of each state's leaning in the closely
fought Bush-Kerry contest. Similarly, in September 2004, a blog named
Mystery Pollster, by veteran pollster Mark Blumenthal, began providing
in-depth analysis of poll results.

In 2008 the evolutionary process of this sort of site took another
giant leap with the arrival of a blog named Fivethirtyeight.com (after the
total number of U.S. electoral votes). Fivethirtyeight was the brainchild
of Nate Silver—a sports-statistics geek who had helped devise a complex, scenario-based modeling approach to predicting baseball season
outcomes, and who decided, early in 2008, to apply the same methodology to the U.S. election. Fivethirtyeight provided an imposing volume
of data and an impressive range of poll-related commentary, updated
several times daily. Silver was always transparent about his own method-

ology and ever ready to point out the limitations and flaws in other people's numbers. If you wanted a quick-immersion education in the vagaries of political polling, here it was, for free, and entertaining to boot.

Anyone who was reading Fivethirtyeight.com daily during the summer and fall of 2008 was never going to be able to read a daily newspaper's poll stories the same way again. Something similar was happening across the board: in field after field, the new brigades of blog-based specialists were offering devastating, and in many cases unimpeachable, critiques of mainstream media coverage, exposing it as at best shallow and at worst entirely unreliable.

There was nothing new about the "Oh God, they got it wrong again" experiences shared by so many subjects of newspaper articles or journalists' interviews. Dave Winer, for one, had been complaining about them for years; as he put it in 2004: "No matter how diligent Our Good Reporter is, something is lost in translation. This is observable." But until recently, these instances of garbled information or distorted messages took place in isolation: each of us knew of the particulars of shoddy coverage only in our own fields of expertise. Now it was possible to connect all these dots—to piece these dismaying fragments into a comprehensive mural of media mediocrity and error.

Since many bloggers provided both an alternative to the work of journalists and a channel for criticism of that work, it was little wonder that blogs acquired an unsavory reputation among media pros— becoming "synonymous with damp mold and scurrilous invective," in the waggish words of *Vanity Fair* critic James Wolcott, a dedicated blogger himself since 2004. Journalists found many reasons to detest bloggers, but their most consistently irksome trait was their relentlessness. As the *Times*'s Keller had said, they just didn't know when to stop. The world of the newsroom is a world of constrained resources—there are only so many reporters on staff, so many hours in the day, so many column-inches to fill—and editors spend their workdays making choices within those limits. But bloggers lived outside these constraints. They seemed to have all the time in the world to pursue their obsessions. They provided their readers with a feast of minutiae no traditional publication would ever dream of delivering. And they were just beginning to disprove the charge that bloggers only offered opinion or commentary and never pounded the pavement to provide original reporting.

When Scooter Libby, Vice President Dick Cheney's lieutenant, went on trial in January 2007 for his role in the leak of classified information about CIA operative Valerie Plame, among the reporters who descended on the Washington courthouse was a small swarm of bloggers. The controversy was one that liberal bloggers had helped fan in the first place, and their readers were hungry for more than the occasional terse summaries they were going to get from newspapers and broadcast outlets. So Firedoglake, a liberal blog operated by former Hollywood producer Jane Hamsher, sent a half-dozen volunteers to the trial and tag-teamed their coverage. The result was something new: a national event where the best on-the-scene reporting came not from professional press articles but from blog posts by volunteers. As Jay Rosen wrote: "If you wanted to keep up with the trial, and needed something approaching a live transcript, with analytical nuance, legal expertise, courthouse color, and recognizably human voices, Firedoglake was your best bet." A *New York Times* piece on the blog's trial coverage reported what attentive readers already could see: that the mainstream journalists covering the trial were depending on Firedoglake's reports, too.

The Libby trial was, for the moment, an exceptional story. But there was a growing list of topics about which Web-based amateurs were providing more-comprehensive information than the traditional pros. Increasingly, journalists found that when they strayed onto the turf of one of these stories that the blogosphere held dear, they now couldn't get away with the sort of hasty summarizing and overgeneralization that too many of them had long practiced.

Joe Klein, *Time*'s veteran political analyst, discovered this in November 2007, when he wrote some careless sentences about Congress's deliberations on a bill designed to legalize the Bush administration's secret wiretaps. Klein erroneously reported details of the provisions of a

Democratic Party–sponsored version of the bill placing the wiretap program under the supervision of the FISA (Foreign Intelligence Surveillance Act) courts. When blogger Glenn Greenwald—a lawyer with a
hearty appetite for rhetorical trench warfare—began pointing these
mistakes out, Klein responded with a series of increasingly irritated posts
on his own blog at *Time*'s website. It's clear from these pieces that Klein
saw the blogger as a painful distraction—some singleminded animal that
had sunk its teeth into his ankles and would not let go. Couldn't Greenwald see he had other stories to write, press conferences to attend,
speeches to cover? The political beat couldn't be all FISA, all the time!
How could anyone expect him to master every detail of every issue he
covered?

Klein eventually admitted, "I made a mistake by not reporting this
more thoroughly." Then he added a sentence that seemed to encapsulate
the capitulation of the weary professional before the onslaught of the
tireless blogging masses: "I have neither the time nor legal background to
figure out who's right." Later he amended the line, adding the words
"about this minor detail of a bill that will never find its way out of the
Congress." Klein insisted that his errors didn't matter since the Democrats' bill had no future—but they plainly mattered to the throng of commenters on his and Greenwald's posts. And his dismaying admission of
journalistic impotence seemed to cede to his opponents the very ground
of credibility on which his profession was taking its stand.

Like many of his colleagues and peers, Klein found himself writing for a
blog in the latter part of the 2000s because his employer wanted to boost
traffic to its website. Blogs, with their frequent updates and comments
and links, had proven more effective at attracting online readers and
earning search-engine rank than the no-value-added repurposing of
articles from print. As one part of a "throw everything at the wall and see
what sticks" frenzy of Web experimentation, newspapers belatedly began

handing out blogs to the newsroom staff. In 2003 there was only one *New York Times* writer (op-ed columnist Nicholas Kristof) doing anything that might loosely be considered blogging; by 2008 the *Times* published roughly seventy blogs. (Ironically, John Markoff found himself drafted by the *Times* to contribute to a group technology blog. His joke had come true; he really *was* blogging at nytimes.com.)

For these journalists, blogging was typically an added duty—something piled on top of an already groaning pile of work. They were up against competition from self-motivated bloggers whose daunting productivity was fueled by personal obsession rather than institutional edict. Some of the pros embraced their new blog work, reveling in the freedom, the informality, and the lighter or absent editing. But it was little wonder that many others resented blogging: it was making everything about their work harder.

The publishers' new embrace of blogging was less a matter of enthusiasm than of desperation. The decade in which blogging emerged was one in which the entire offline media industry in the United States, and particularly the newspaper business, had gone into a tailspin. Newspaper publishing had been in gentle decline for several decades; circulation numbers were drifting slowly down well before the Web's arrival. Profits fluctuated but mostly depended on the local monopolies that most papers had in their cities. Newspapers made money by bundling a variety of disparate forms of information together—news reports and opinion columns, arts reviews and movie listings, stock prices and sports scores—and then selling that bundle to subscribers and advertisers.

The Web dissolved the threads that held this bundle together. The stock prices and scores and listings no longer needed to fill pages with tiny type; the Web delivered this information in a timelier and more convenient way than paper ever could. Classified ads, too, worked infinitely more efficiently online than in print—and would end up costing advertisers much less, too. As the downhill slide of the industry gathered speed, insiders could no longer pretend that this was anything but a historic, structural transition in the news media. Newspapers were not going to vanish overnight, but their lifespan wasn't going to extend beyond those of the aging people who still read them out of habit.

It was easy to see the inevitability of this from the moment the Web went mainstream in the mid-nineties. (It was a big factor in my own decision in 1995 to forsake a job at the *San Francisco Examiner* for the Web, in the face of incredulous colleagues who clung to their union jobs as if they were tenured chairs.) When Intel chairman Andy Grove told the American Society of Newspaper Editors in April 1999 that they had three years to "adapt or die," the editors' eyes "rolled in 'not this again' circles," according to a *New York Times* account. But as the decade wore on, it was only Grove's number that seemed unduly pessimistic, not his general prediction.

For newspaper publishers, the Web was an attractive new distribution medium in some respects: it would let them reduce costs on trucks and "dead tree" materials. Their hope was that the rising line on their graphs that represented online revenue would cross the falling line representing print revenue before things got too dire—and before they had to scuttle so much of their operation that it couldn't survive. But media companies were having a hard time winning their share of the booming Web advertising market; the online environment favored Google's search-driven advertising over the sort of traditional display advertising that had always fueled media profits. So far, it had proven impossible to match the rich monopoly income of the old publishing model on the still-evolving and far more challenging and competitive Web. Maybe, many analysts (and investors in newspaper stocks) reluctantly began to conclude, that would never happen.

As changes in the news business accelerated, newsroom veterans and their business counterparts kept finding themselves at least a step behind. Newspaper executives realized they had let the portals—big, all-purpose Web services like America Online and Yahoo and MSN—usurp their role as gateways to useful information. The new-media outfits had stolen a march in the 1990s, while their old-media counterparts were still arguing about whether to go online. By 2000, it was already too late to win that fight. So when the dotcom bubble collapsed in 2000–2001, some news organizations tried to impose subscription fees on their Web users. Insiders had long been fretting that newspapers had "given away the store" on the Web (the phrase was used by *Los Angeles Times* business columnist David Lazarus, among many others) by failing to charge for access to their websites. It was "self-inflicted cannibalism," in the words of *New York Times* veteran John Darnton. Now, the argument went, with the Web industry on the ropes and online advertising temporarily depressed, it was time to lower the toll gates and extract a price for the valuable information journalists collected. But with rare exceptions, efforts to require payment for newspaper content on the Web failed, reducing traffic and ad revenue without attracting much new revenue in subscription fees. There was no shortage of information and diversion online; readers simply went elsewhere. They divided their loyalty among an ever-widening set of options, spreading their eyeball time indiscriminately among sites produced by paid professionals and sites created out of obsession or love.

Many journalists eyed the new army of unpaid or underpaid competitors—the contributors at Huffington Post, the citizen journalists, the bloggers, and all the other providers of what media companies called "user-generated content"—with disbelief. Their resentment now went beyond simple puzzlement over why the blockheads were writing for free. Their volunteer rivals, they felt, were more than just suckers; they were tantamount to scabs, undermining secure high-paying jobs by choosing to labor under unfair conditions. ("'Citizen journalist' is just the pretty new construct for 'unpaid freelancer,'" New Orleans–based journalist Kevin Allman complained in a 2007 letter to Romenesko.)

The labor-movement analogy was apt. The entire newspaper industry was entering the sort of vast technology transition that creates genuine labor crises. (While newspapers were first, magazine publishers and broadcast-license owners understood that they were probably next in line.) As online information consumption trended upward, newspaper circulation declines grew steeper, and waves of layoffs, buyouts, and consolidation convulsed the industry. Proud journalists found themselves cast in the role of the handloom weavers of nineteenth-century Britain, rendered unemployable by infernal new machines. Or maybe, as Clay Shirky wrote, they were like monastic scribes idled by the arrival of Gutenberg's press. All these comparisons cast them as victims, and that was exactly how many newspaper employees felt. Thanks to the newsroom ethic of church and state separation—in which the work of newsgathering was kept strictly cordoned off from the business that paid for it—journalists had little professional tradition of scrappy entrepreneurialism. Here and there, newsroom exiles experimented with "hyper-local" blogging, demonstrating how small Web outposts might begin to replace the community coverage so many papers were abandoning. But mostly the newsroom veterans disavowed any responsibility for their economic fate, and sat on the sidelines of the dismemberment of their own industry.

As the decade advanced, the press found its credibility and popularity among the public—its customers—at a low ebb, its financial prospects clouded, and its leaders and employees dispirited. "The news business— our crowd of overexcited people narrating events as they happen—is going out of business," Michael Wolff hyperventilated in *Vanity Fair* in 2008. This environment of perpetual crisis proved hospitable terrain for the flourishing of a new subspecies of journalist: the newsroom curmudgeon.

The curmudgeons were typically but not exclusively newsroom veterans certain that the Web was destroying their profession but unable to propose any practical program to stem the tide of bloggers. They offered up familiar debating points from a now decade-old argument about the nature of news online as if such observations were fresh and urgent. Blogs, the curmudgeons protested, lacked rigorous standards. NPR's distinguished correspondent, Daniel Schorr, cast his lot with them when he wrote, "A person like me who believes in the tradition of a discipline in journalism can only rue the day we've arrived at where we don't need discipline or anything. All you need is a keyboard." Blogging would debase any real journalist's career. Pete Hamill told his journalism students at NYU, "Don't waste your time with blogs." Bloggers—unlike the professionals, with their legalistic newsroom codes—had no ethics; you couldn't trust them. The attributes that made blogs such an appealing alternative to many readers, their informality and personality, made them anathema to the curmudgeons, who saw these traits as betrayals of their ideal of neutrality.

The curmudgeons' arguments all shared a starting point in the tenets of professional journalism as practiced in mid-twentieth-century America: political impartiality; on-the-one-hand-but-on-the-other "balance"; impersonal voice. The whole bundle of "objective" attributes—what Jay Rosen called "the view from nowhere"—was etched into the journalism-school curriculum. These values were held out as timeless verities, but in fact they were of relatively recent vintage. They had been shaped by the specific business needs of the publishing and broadcasting industries. As they consolidated markets and sought to sell advertising that might reach vast agglomerations of consumers, the peddlers of news found they couldn't afford to alienate partisan populations of any stripe; neutrality was a prerequisite for profits. Yet vibrant journalism had existed without the benefit of such values—for example, in the pamphlet culture of late-seventeenth-century and eighteenth-century Britain and Colonial-era America, or in the raucous partisan newspaper competition of the late-nineteenth- and early-twentieth-century urban United States. And vibrant journalism could plausibly survive their demise.

The brigade of curmudgeons behaved like defenders of a faith. They were true believers in belieflessness. And they always won a lot of head-nods wherever journalists gathered. They found support outside their profession, too: as one interviewee put it, in a California public-radio report on the decline of newspapers, "Any idiot with a laptop can post his ramblings. And there's no editor. That's the beauty of a newspaper—

there's an editor!" But the curmudgeons often got their facts wrong, which tended to take the air out of their arguments.

In one widely followed exchange, a journalism professor and Pulitzer Prize winner named Michael Skube took the blogosphere to task in an op-ed piece in the *Los Angeles Times*. What our society desperately needs from journalists, he wrote, is "the patient sifting of fact, the acknowledgment that assertion is not evidence and, as the best writers understand, the depiction of real life"; what we get from bloggers, instead, is endless opinion and commentary. To support his assertion, Skube provided as evidence the names of a number of prominent blogs, including that of Josh Marshall's Talking Points Memo.

As it happened, as Skube published his piece in August 2007, Attorney General Alberto Gonzales was preparing his resignation in the face of a scandal involving the politicization of the U.S. attorneys' offices—a story that had been reported first, and most thoroughly, on Marshall's blog, which had pursued the story by "patiently sifting facts" that the political journalism establishment had chosen to disregard. So for Skube to cite Talking Points Memo was at best a poor choice, and at worst an admission of deep ignorance about the subject on which he was pontificating.

Peeved at seeing his blog knocked for lacking what was in fact one of its proudest attributes, Marshall contacted Skube. First, as Marshall reported the exchange, Skube made the perplexing claim that he had *not* named Marshall in the piece. Then he admitted he had—but explained that it wasn't his problem, because he hadn't written that part of his article: the list of bloggers had been *inserted by an editor!*

"And this is from someone who teaches journalism?" Marshall wrote. "I agree you that the blogosphere needs better bloggers. But, as usual, the need for better critics seems even more acute."

Whatever intelligent points the curmudgeons wished to make, they had a remarkable propensity for undercutting themselves. In April 2008, Buzz Bissinger, a veteran sportswriter, appeared on Bob Costas's HBO talk show opposite Will Leitch, an editor of the Gawker Media sports blog Deadspin. As Costas amiably interviewed Leitch, Bissinger broke in and snapped, "I think you're full of shit." He proceeded to denounce bloggers in blistering terms for their "despicable" writing quality and "abusive" tone. "I think that blogs are dedicated to cruelty, they're dedicated to journalistic dishonesty, they're dedicated to speed," he said. "It really pisses the shit out of me." Bissinger later apologized—apparently figuring out, after the excitement had ended, that the crudity of his own bluster had overshadowed any point he hoped to make about nastiness among bloggers.

The curmudgeons' rhetorical volleys achieved little, partly because of their own misfires, but even more because there was a deep confusion at the heart of their beliefs. These journalists were looking, as those who feel victimized will do, for someone to blame for their displacement. In the nineties, their predecessors had blamed AOL or Yahoo for all that was going wrong in their industry; now they yearned to blame bloggers. But the curmudgeons found it difficult to establish any cause-and-effect relationship between the rise of blogging and the decline of newspapers. In fact, although these two trends emerged simultaneously, each was proceeding under its own steam. If the curmudgeons could somehow have waved a wand and made all the blogs go away, they might have felt better, but their employers would still have been in trouble.

"Is blogging journalism?" was no longer an active controversy for the curmudgeons; to them, the answer was obviously no. The argument they now favored was "Blogging can never replace real journalism!" That question stood at the heart of countless thumbsucking columns by journalism pundits who, in the latter part of the 2000s, seemed to wake up suddenly to the realization that their house was on fire. A 2006 *New Yorker* piece by Columbia Journalism School dean Nicholas Lemann was typical in its conclusion: "None of [Internet journalism] yet rises to the level of a journalistic culture rich enough to compete in a serious way with the old media—to function as a replacement rather than an addendum." That was a defensible position; it was also a straw man. Lemann failed to acknowledge that the overwhelming preponderance of bloggers neither desired to replace journalists nor claimed they could serve as an acceptable substitute. Most bloggers had a visceral understanding that they participated in a complex informational ecosystem, in which their relationship with the traditional media was essentially symbiotic. Maybe they were like the profusion of forest-floor flora, dependent on the environment shaped by the big trees, but also fighting for their own patches of light. Or maybe, as the big institutions began failing, they were like the termites feeding on the fallen media tree trunks.

Ultimately, "can bloggers replace journalists?" was less a question about the unlikely prospect of a wholesale changing of the media guard than a cry from the beleaguered journalists' hearts. Insecure and buffeted by forces outside their control, they hoped to hear the reassuring answer that they were, in fact, irreplaceable. And yet bloggers, for the most part, refused to provide that solace. They might not be trying to steal journalists' jobs, but they weren't going to try to save them, either. The bloggers' indifference to the unfolding turmoil in the journalism business, their unwillingness to view it as a tragedy or civic disaster, appalled the curmudgeons and many of their colleagues. Didn't the bloggers understand what was at risk? Didn't they see the looming Dark Age that would envelop American democracy and culture if the institutions of media collapsed?

Apparently not. It was left to defenders of the journalistic tradition themselves to sketch out the dire consequences of the media meltdown.

Traditionalists offered three arguments to champion journalism's good old ways. First, they asked, without media companies subsidizing it, who would undertake the expensive and politically perilous work of investigative journalism? Next they suggested that the proliferation of online news sources and the multiplicity of partisan blogospheres meant the triumph of the "echo chamber," in which we only learn what we already know about, and only hear those with whom we already agree. Finally, they argued, the collapse of big media would cause the very unity of our culture to disintegrate, leaving us without a central narrative for our national life. Each of these arguments, unlike the most nostalgic carpings of the curmudgeons, was serious and substantive. And each provoked an important debate online.

The future of investigative journalism was indeed in some doubt. That had been true even before the accelerated collapse of the newspaper industry. Investigative reporters typically worked on extended assignment with little guarantee of results. At best they exposed wrongdoing and won prizes; at worst they had nothing to show for months of labor. In civic terms, their work was a high calling, the raison d'être for the institution of independent journalism in a democracy; but in business terms, it was costly to the payroll as well as troublesome for the legal budget, and in hard times it was usually the first thing to get the ax. So it wasn't as if the old media model had the problem of supporting investigative journalism licked. But could the low- or no-profit online world support it at all? Probably not in the traditional manner, with teams of high-paid veteran reporters free to follow their noses for months at a time in search of dirt. That model might now only be possible in the non-profit sector—where ProPublica, a new outfit led largely by exiles from the *Wall Street Journal*, had pitched its tent. Of course, there were other ways to pursue original investigative journalism that might be more suited to the online world. You could see some of them in embryonic form at Talking Points Memo and other lean, enterprising blogs that had begun to find investigative niches for themselves.

The fate of investigative reporting, no matter how vital to the health of the republic, was largely a concern for journalism insiders. The fear that online news consumption might lock us into an echo chamber was an issue with a wider constituency. Critics of the Web like the legal scholar Cass Sunstein and the sociologist Robert Putnam (*Bowling Alone*) had long held that isolation and closed minds were the inevitable by-products of online communication. News consumption was moving from a passive mode, in which editors assembled a batch of newsworthy stories at regular intervals for us, toward an active pursuit, in which we followed only the links that interested us and assembled our own patchquilt of daily news from multiple sources. This led one set of pessimists to worry that we'd gradually lose the experience, much cherished by newspaper lovers, of serendipitously stumbling upon little stories that we didn't know we wanted to read. This initial line of argument quickly dissolved as these critics spent more time online themselves and discovered that the Web, far from banishing serendipity, actually generated an oversupply of fascinating novelties and distractions.

Another, more observant set of pessimists was less easily answered: they suggested that the Web's design meant that it would foster self-reinforcing feedback loops among like-minded people, who would dedicate increasing amounts of their news consumption to reinforcing their existing preconceptions. Call it *homophily*, the psychologist's term for a natural preference for people who are like ourselves; or call it *confirmation bias*, the statistician's term for our tendency to trust information that confirms what we already believe. Whatever you called it, it looked dangerous. Early Web enthusiasts promoted the concept of the Daily Me— the online news source that you could customize to deliver only the information you'd expressed interest in. But the critics recoiled in horror: to them, the Daily Me looked like nothing more than a machine for constructing personal echo chambers. If we each assembled our own news diet instead of consuming what editors chose for us, they feared, we would never eat our informational spinach. We would close our minds to news that contradicted our preconceptions and become isolated in our prejudices.

Before 2000, there was little concrete evidence to suggest that any actual echo chambers could be found on the Web, outside of a handful of partisan discussion forums like FreeRepublic.com. That changed with the rise of political blogging, which gave explicit shape to separate crosslinked worlds on the left and right—visible in the roster of each side's blogrolls, which displayed little overlap. Fans of Daily Kos or Atrios were unlikely to be fans of Power Line or Instapundit, and vice versa. But it was still hard to say that a devotion to either was actually cutting you off from your opponents: bloggers on the left or right still linked across the partisan divide, if only to argue or mock. And even if the Web had intensified the echo in some precincts, it had streamlined the satisfaction of heterodox curiosities, too. It was much easier for a liberal to follow an occasional link to a columnist at *The National Review* than to make the effort to purchase a copy of the magazine—and you didn't have to feel bad about paying cash for something you disagreed with.

Scholars began running numbers on the blogosphere to try to measure whether the echo-chamber effect really existed. In 2005, one widely discussed study—a paper titled "Divided They Blog," by Lada Adamic and Natalie Glance—concluded, unsurprisingly, that there were indeed two well-defined blogospheres, self-sorted ideologically and interacting far more heavily with their own side than across the partisan divide. Adamic and Glance charted the divide via colorful red-versus-blue network diagrams that looked like warring galactic clusters, with each side extending only a handful of tendrils across the void to parley. But which was more notable and new: the existence of the two camps, or the infrequently exercised opportunity for dialogue between them? Profound partisan divides existed long before the Web and blogs. How much did we communicate across them back then? Did bloggers' efforts to reach out today constitute an increase or a decrease in dialogue between ideological opponents? "Divided They Blog" stopped before asking these questions.

Of course we gravitate toward writers we agree with, even as we understand we might learn more by grappling with those we disagree with; this is human nature. According to the echo-chamber argument, the advent of blogging enabled us to overindulge this preference, speeding us down an accelerating spiral into ideological isolation. But a 2007 study of "cross-ideological discussions among political bloggers," by Eszter Hargittai, Jason Gallo, and Matthew Kane, found no evidence to support this picture. Hargittai and her colleagues, like Adamic and Glance, confirmed that bloggers flocked (and linked) along partisan lines—but also found that "bloggers across the political spectrum address each other's writing substantively, both in agreement and disagreement." Most notably, they discovered that the camps' level of isolation from each other did not intensify over time, as the echo-chamber alarmists suggested it would. Bloggers were divided, and their cross-camp dialogue was limited, but their minds did not seem to grow more tightly closed.

As with so many arguments about the media, the echo-chamber advocates often seemed overly eager to scapegoat technology for problems that had deeper roots. Yes, American politics had grown bitterly polarized in the 2000s. But were the angry arguments on the Web the cause of those divisions? More likely, they simply mirrored profound disagreements among the American people about the impeachment of President Clinton, the contested outcome of the 2000 election, the Bush administration's tactics in its war on terror, and the invasion of Iraq. What kind of media environment that accurately represented the political pysche of the American population would *not* bristle with rancor under the pressure of such events?

In 2004, when Howard Dean's Web-driven 2004 campaign for the Democratic presidential nomination collapsed, critics of the Internet couldn't contain their glee. This is what happens, they crowed, when you lock yourselves in an echo chamber with a bunch of hysterical bloggers! The Deaniacs had fed one another's delusions in a feedback loop of unreality, and now they were paying the price. The picture wasn't entirely inaccurate; on the other hand, without the Web, this obscure Vermont governor would never have had any credible shot at the early primary victories that ultimately eluded him. Meanwhile, four years later Barack Obama's outsider campaign followed a similar playbook, honed by experience. This time energies first unleashed online helped to raise a record war chest, inspire masses of new voters, and propel a long-shot candidate—with an unusual name and dark skin, no less—into the White House. Maybe echo chambers could win elections after all! More likely, the whole concept of the echo chamber offered scant insight into the subtle and diverse dynamics of political culture online.

The final argument about the pernicious impact of the Web and blogging on the American polity was a broader take on the echo-chamber idea. Once upon a time, the reasoning went, we all shared a single national conversation. We read our newspapers in the morning, watched the three networks in the evening, and took our cues from them about the topic of the day. Now, alas, the Internet, having enabled each of us to assemble our Daily Me, is depriving us of any kind of "Daily We." Like all notions of a vanished golden age or a lost common culture, this vision was part fairy tale and part nostalgia. We are always going to pine for the media we loved when we were young. (You can bet that, decades from now, an entire generation will look back and yearn for the long-lost common culture of their youth that today's social-networked Web pro-vided.) For all its sentimentality, however, this notion has held a power-ful grip on critics of the Web. They worry that the Web's openness and the fragmentation of blogging set an impossible hurdle for any effort to unify the American story.

A representative expression of this argument can be found in an otherwise astute analysis of the media industry's convulsions by Eric Alterman in a 2008 *New Yorker* piece. Alterman, a liberal journalist who began blogging in 2002, wrote that the culture of the Web and blogging was dragging newspapers into a partisan vortex: "The transformation of newspapers from enterprises devoted to objective reporting to a cluster of communities, each engaged in its own kind of 'news'—and each with its own set of 'truths' upon which to base debate and discussion—will mean the loss of a single national narrative and agreed-upon set of 'facts' by which to conduct our politics."

This "loss of a single national narrative" sounds grievous indeed, until you realize that such unity, if it ever did exist, represented only a short interlude in U.S. history. Alterman admits that nineteenth-century America was "dominated by brazenly partisan newspapers." The rise of broadcast journalism and the mid-twentieth-century consolidation of newspapers did concentrate a mass audience for news by forsaking parti-sanship for the neutral "view from nowhere." But if we look at what is probably the high-water mark of such concentration and the putative heyday of the "single national narrative"—the 1960s—we do not find a halcyon era of comity; instead, the decade was marked by a level of partisan conflict and outright violence that makes the 2000s look like a civics class. If Walter Cronkite was in fact able to set the nation's agenda, he couldn't stop its political polarization. The tumultuous record of the twentieth century, in fact, shows no correlation at all between the concentration of media authority pushing a "single national narrative" and the flourishing of a civil public-sphere debate. The world has always been messier than it looks in sentimental hindsight.

For outsiders listening in as journalists marshaled all these arguments, it was hard not to sense some amount of special pleading. Journalists were hardly neutral parties to the controversies they were addressing; they could not take the "view from nowhere" when their own livelihoods and authority were at stake. To the extent that a "single national narrative" was disintegrating under the pressure of millions of disparate narratives teeming on the Web—and this was, plainly, an oversimplification—it was the journalists who'd lost influence, and everyone else who had gained.

At this point in the argument, whatever side you find yourself favoring, I invite you to pause, climb up a nearby hill, and take a longer gaze down on this rhetorical battlefield. If you have tried to follow the action over the last half-decade, you have had a couple of choices: you could just attend to the traditional media's periodic check-ins on these unfolding controversies, reading the occasional op-ed piece or news-magazine summary. But you would barely scratch the surface of the issues. Or you could dive into the profusion of posts in which the debate has actually taken place. Pursue links into the thickets of new blogs dedicated to the topic, with names like Recovering Journalist, News After Newspapers, and Reflections of a Newsosaur, started by concerned journalists, laid-off journalists, aspiring journalists, and ex-journalists. Follow the broadsides by professors and industry analysts, distinguished editors and young-turk reporters, all scratching their heads trying to figure out how to salvage their vocation from the technological whirlwind.

If you care about the fate of journalism and its role in democracy and culture, this second choice turns out to be the only satisfying option. And when you realize that, you also realize that the debate is over: you have just resolved it. In this controversy, as in most others today, to ignore bloggers is to miss the entire event. Whatever the drawbacks and limitations of blogging, it serves, today, as our culture's indispensable public square. Rather than one tidy "unifying narrative," it provides a noisy arena, open to everyone, for the collective working out of old conflicts and new ideas. As the profession of journalism tries to rescue itself from the wreckage of print and rethink its digital future, this is where its most knowledgeable practitioners and most creative students are doing their hardest thinking.

Chapter 10

WHEN EVERYONE HAS A BLOG

One of the most important things you learn from the Internet is that there is no "them" out there. It's just an awful lot of "us."

—Douglas Adams (1999)

Tim Berners-Lee and Marc Andreessen are the two people most responsible for creating the Web as we know it today. Both had imagined the Web as a vast collective repository for human information and expression, and each had helped standardize the reverse-chronological format that blogging popularized. But for a long time, neither published his own blog.

Berners-Lee finally started one in December 2005. He applauded the blogging movement for its fulfillment of his early vision of the Web as "a space in which anyone could be creative, to which anyone could contribute." But he admitted that, for his own part, he'd never seen the need to blog. The announcement of his new blog, hosted at MIT as part of the larger Semantic Web project he'd been spearheading for years, garnered hundreds of comments from visitors grateful to Berners-Lee for his invention of the building blocks of the Web. But the blog never seemed that important to him—he has posted only a dozen times in three years, mostly on recondite technical issues.

Andreessen had long viewed blogs with polite skepticism; when a reporter asked him in 2003 whether he had one, he answered, "No, I have a day job. I don't have the time or ego need." But when he did start blogging, in June 2007, he took to it with the alacrity of a convert, posting at length about the inner workings of Silicon Valley, the nature of the venture capital industry, and his own philosophy of business and technology. As he got into it, he began to sound giddy with excitement at the possibilities. Five weeks into posting, he wrote:

> I should have started doing this years and years ago.

> Anyone who says blogs are not widely read is incorrect. I have been absolutely amazed at the range and diversity of the people who have been reading this blog, and so quickly.

> It is crystal clear to me now that at least in industries where lots of people are online, blogging is the single best way to communicate and interact.

It has taken blogging roughly a decade to evolve from the pursuit of a handful of enthusiasts on the fringes of the technology industry into the dominant media form online. Whatever it is you are aiming to do or express on the Web today, the odds are good that you, like Berners-Lee and Andreessen, will end up doing it, wholly or in part, using a blog. Whatever information you seek, or debate you follow, or distraction you crave, the odds are equally high that your destination will be a blog of one kind or another.

This outcome looks inevitable only in hindsight. And even today the result still sometimes inspires a double-take: Wait a second, you mean there's a blog about *that*?

On one recent evening, I found myself hitting a wall as I prepared a recipe from a favorite Chinese cookbook. It called for an ingredient, a particular type of dried preserved mustard green from Sichuan province called *ya cai*. But I had no idea whether what I'd picked up at the local Asian grocery—desiccated brown shreds packaged in cellophane labeled "dried marinated mustard"—was the genuine *ya cai* article. The cookbook was no help. Even Wikipedia, that grand collaborative compendium of volunteered human knowledge, offered only scant guidance. But Google pointed me to an American food blogger, the anonymous Kitchen Chick, who'd been cooking her way through the same cookbook and had posted hundreds of words on the intricacies of identifying and purchasing preserved Chinese vegetables—not only how to identify *ya cai* by the Chinese characters, but how to tell it apart from the closely related *zha cai* (made from mustard stems rather than leaves) or *suan cai* (pickled mustard in a jar).

Whatever your particular *ya cai* may be, there is probably a blogger somewhere who has discoursed on it. If for some reason there is not, you can always take on the job yourself, recording your findings and opening a channel for readers to contribute their knowledge and correct your goofs. This inclusive process has populated the Web haphazardly but luxuriantly, like the wind seeding a wild meadow.

The common explanation for this proliferation attributes it to the low cost and simplicity of blogging—what economists call a "low barrier to market entry." We might also call it a low barrier to obsession indulgence. If you care deeply about some topic, no matter how obscure, and you'd like to talk about it, an empty blog awaits you. In this way, blogging has enabled the sharing of a wealth of knowledge that was hitherto private or limited to small groups. It has, in effect, widened the lens through which we can see one another's passions and quirks.

Consider the "Blog" of "Unnecessary" Quotation Marks, an improbable, dryly amusing compendium of photos of signs that inappropriately overuse quotation marks:

Mexican "Food"

or

"Parents" You Are Responsible For your "Childrens" Safety

Bethany Keeley, a grad student in Athens, Georgia, started the "Blog"—
picking up from a family in-joke—to entertain herself. She composes
peevishly funny comments following each instance of quotation-mark
abuse, gently mocking the perpetrators, who aimed to emphasize the
words between the quotes but actually implied some doubt or irony. At
the beginning Keeley posted her own finds, but before long she began
receiving choice submissions from readers on the lookout for camera-
ready punctuational excess. She won a modicum of Web celebrity and
traffic as word, and links, spread. Her site now includes a Frequently
Asked Questions page, where you'll find this reply to a reader's comment:

> *This blog is a waste of time. . . .*
>
> Answer: What's a bigger waste of time? Blogging about
> something you find amusing, or telling a blogger how
> dumb or boring her blog is? I can't believe people are
> interested in it either, I'm just doing this for fun.

Individually, blogs like "Unnecessary" Quotation Marks are mere
diversions. Collectively, they are jaw-dropping. Their range is stunningly
wider than the spectrum of subject matter we are familiar with from the
media of the past—from the extremities of trivial inconsequentiality
(like the goofily captioned cat photos of "I Can Has Cheezburger?") to
analyses of urgent global problems like climate change. Surveying such a
range makes it easy to narrow our gaze selectively, tipping the scale in
the direction of our personal temperament. Do we see desolation or ferment? Is the blog glass half empty or half full?

In the press, the half-empty view has dominated. Media portraits of
blogging have collected an inventory of dismissals and jeers aimed at
policing the boundary between blogs and "real" writing. If you wanted to
point out the shortcomings of the Web's new population of writers, and
you were able to do so cogently or bitingly, you could count on legions of

journalists to echo and amplify your critique. Here, for instance, is one that is nearly perfect in its combination of vivid imagery and disdain: "The Internet is like one of those garbage dumps outside of Bombay. There are people, most unfortunately, crawling all over it, and maybe they find a bit of aluminum, or perhaps something they can sell. But mainly it's garbage."

Computer-science pioneer Joseph Weizenbaum made this remark in 1999 to a *New York Times* reporter. Weizenbaum was famous for a number of reasons. In 1966 he'd created the Eliza chatterbot—a simple program that did a remarkable job of impersonating a human in conversation, mostly by lobbing anything users said back to them in the form of a question. Then, appalled at how easily he'd fooled people and how readily they seemed willing to trust a machine, he wrote one of the great humanist takedowns of technology, *Computer Power and Human Reason*. When Weizenbaum died in 2007, nearly every obituary quoted his putdown of the Internet.

The trouble was, the quotation was incomplete. After the story quoting him appeared, Weizenbaum wrote a letter to the editor. He affirmed the quotation's accuracy but noted that he'd gone on to say, "There are gold mines and pearls in there that a person trained to design good questions can find." That cast his judgment in a very different light.

Weizenbaum viewed our interactions with machines as fundamentally impoverished. Based on his experience of how simple it was to dupe Eliza's users, he feared that human beings would surrender their autonomy without a fight. He saw the Web as an encounter between individual people and a vast, disorderly junkpile of data. For a computer scientist in 1999, that might well have been a sensible view—Google had barely begun helping us navigate the Web's proliferating information. But within a few years many of us had arrived at a very different understanding of the Web. Most of the words we encountered online weren't being generated or organized by machine; what we found on the other side of the screen was other people, typing away. The machine was just making it possible for us to connect with them.

Most of the people who depicted the Web as a garbage dump were not nearly as careful as Weizenbaum had been about qualifying their dismissals. From Michael Hiltzik's 1997 declaration that the Web had already become a "vast wasteland" to media critic Michael Wolff's description of the Web a decade later as "millions of morons . . . sharing their drivel," media arbiters gazed out at the Web that self-publishing was shaping and saw trash in all directions. Pet photos and videos of Mentos-and-Coke explosions hardly constituted a revolution in self-expression. A depressingly high percentage of the "users" generating "content" could barely spell or write a coherent sentence. These critics didn't mind that their objections cast them in an antidemocratic light, as "royalists"—a label impulsively applied by *This American Life* creator Ira Glass during a discussion of the value of reader comments on newspaper websites. They saw themselves as upholders of an embattled tradition of quality.

In one sense, they were right. It is hard to wander the Web or a blog's links for too long without stepping in something foul. As on any crowded city street, you need to watch where you walk. But the critics' big picture was hopelessly skewed. They weren't wrong about the abundance of trash on the Web, but they somehow forgot how much garbage had choked its predecessors. Blogging was merely recapitulating the trashiness of every previous media form. Sure, celebrity gossip outdrew economic policy debates online—but it had long done so in print and on the air as well. Each year the industries built on cranking out media products—Hollywood, the book-publishing industry, broadcast TV and cable—had a surfeit of flops and only a few hits, and there didn't seem to be any dependable correlation between quality, however you defined it, and mass appeal. About all that these industries could promise was that each of their products met certain minimal technical standards of picture quality or proofreading care or factual accuracy (and even that, for the struggling news business, seemed ever more difficult to achieve).

Bloggers encountering the perennial complaint about low standards often pointed to Sturgeon's Law, a principle propounded by science-fiction writer Theodore Sturgeon to defend his genre against a previous generation's elitist critique. Sure, Sturgeon said, 90 percent of science fiction is crap. That's because 90 percent of *everything* is crap. Who could argue with that?

In 2002, Salon.com, the publication that employed me, was barely scraping along through the aftermath of the dotcom collapse and the post-9/11 economic downturn. There weren't too many signs of life in the online industry. But, like many others who hadn't given up on the Web, I was voraciously reading blogs. They were islands of creative energy in a torpid sea of red ink.

We had no money to do anything new at Salon, but I thought that an experiment in blogging might be cheap enough to try anyway—and might teach us something. Salon had a multitude of smart, articulate readers. Some of them might jump at the chance to publish their own writing in affiliation, however vague, with our site. And some might benefit from the chance to have that writing read by a community of other bloggers convened under the Salon logo.

The one rule for any new idea at our company, in those cash-strapped days, was that any proposed undertaking had to offer the prospect of an immediate influx of revenue. Blogger already let anyone start a blog for free; that was a wonderful thing, but ruled it out as a partner for us. (At that market bottom, ad revenue had vanished, too, so we couldn't expect to "monetize" these blog pages that way, and the bloggers couldn't, either.) But Userland, Dave Winer's company, had recently rolled out its Radio Userland software with a forty-dollar price tag. Radio provided an innovative combination of blog publishing tools and an RSS reader (or aggregator) that let you follow other people's posts. At that time, Winer was in the middle of handing Userland off to other people to run—he'd had heart surgery and was rethinking his life. But I was able to cut a quick deal with the new management: Userland and Salon would partner on a new blog service; Userland would run the servers, and Salon would provide the users and manage the community; we'd split the forty-dollars-per-blogger revenue.

I never thought Salon Blogs would bring in a lot of money, and it underperformed even my modest expectations. We were hobbled by disarray at Userland, which eventually stopped further development work on its Radio software, and by our own lack of resources (beyond my own spare time) to support or promote the service. After an initial influx of a few hundred enthusiastic early adopters, the signups slowed to a trickle and stayed there. But if Salon Blogs was insignificant in business terms, it provided eye-opening evidence of blogging's still largely untapped human potential. When we started, I had worried that we were already too late. Maybe blogs had peaked. I'd been following them for years, from their earliest incarnations; now it seemed possible that everyone who had anything to say already had a blog.

I shouldn't have worried. It didn't take long for a constellation of spores to land on our blog program's petri dish and start growing into fascinating exotic shapes. Gordon Atkinson, a small-town Texas minister, started posting anonymously, at first, as Real Live Preacher, telling moving stories about the colorful characters in his community and his inner conflicts between doubt and faith. A young woman in Queens named Julie Powell set out to relieve the drudgery of her office job by cooking her way through every recipe in Julia Child's text on classic French cuisine and chronicling the results on her blog. (Her tale became first a book and eventually a movie starring Meryl Streep.) An activist named Dave Pollard provided daily suggestions on "How to Save the World." And an anonymous blogger who called himself The Raven offered a dyspeptic daily news analysis that rivaled anything we were offering from Salon's paid staff.

These examples are vivid to me, years later, off the top of my head, not because they all broke news or met consistently high literary standards, but because each had such a distinctive voice. Not every participant was equally memorable, but in the thousand-plus sustained blogs that constituted the program's total population over several years you

WHEN EVERYONE HAS A BLOG309

could find a little bit of everything: political blogs, of course, but also science blogs and humor blogs and just plain weird blogs, including one filled with photos of mannequins and another titled Fried Green Al-Qaedas. Participants could follow one another via a page that listed the most recently updated blogs and the blogs that had seen the most trafffic during the past day. It was not "the blogosphere" but *a* blogosphere, composed of people who read each other, cheered each other on, and occasionally sniped at each other.

That Salon's readership was full of articulate eccentrics brimming with ideas certainly helped us off to a fast start. But our experience paralleled what was happening all over the Web as blog communities sprouted across the landscape. That process has never ceased, and it accelerated with the advent of what amounted to a software arms race among a new generation of blog tool companies.

Movable Type had been the program of choice for experienced or ambitious bloggers since 2001, and had led the way in establishing the set of features bloggers had come to consider essential. The program's creators, the husband-and-wife team of Ben and Mena Trott, had been Blogger users who chafed at Blogger's limitations and itched to do more with their own blogs. In 2002 they started a company, Six Apart, around Movable Type, and soon began offering blog hosting for a small fee through a service called TypePad. Movable Type itself had never been open-source software, but the Trotts had given it away for free. In 2004, as Six Apart began to get serious about seeking profitability it announced a set of fees for commercial use of Movable Type (the program remained free for personal use). The move was hardly unreasonable, but its announcement wasn't handled smoothly, and a storm of consternation ensued. The Web developers and bloggers who congregated at Metafilter angrily posted, "Movable Type RIP."

Those bloggers who decided to seek an alternative found one in

Wordpress, an open-source program whose development, beginning in 2003, was led by a nineteen-year-old programmer named Matt Mullenweg. Mullenweg welcomed the Movable Type refugees and jumped at the opportunity to expand Wordpress's base of users and team of developers. At first, Wordpress couldn't match Movable Type, feature for feature; but the bloggers who flocked to it preferred the open-source model, in which the code was a public resource, to the private-property approach. If Six Apart went out of business, Movable Type's future would be in jeopardy, whereas an open-source program like Wordpress could always be maintained and fixed as long as there were programmers who cared enough to work on it. Over time, the differences between these two dominant blog platforms began to get whittled away: today, Movable Type is a fully open-source program, too, and Six Apart earns revenue through managing installations of its software for big customers and by hosting the blogs of advanced users. Meanwhile, although Wordpress continues to be free and open-source, Mullenweg has built a company around it that hosts a multitude of free blogs (4.9 million as I write this) and makes money selling add-on services to those bloggers and commercial clients.

The rise of Six Apart and Wordpress—alongside Blogger, their original inspiration, now Google-owned—made it progressively easier for anyone to start a new blog and do more with it afterwards. The same years saw the evolution of a different but related set of software tools (like the open-source Drupal package) designed to help anyone start and manage whole groups of affiliated blogs, as we had done at Salon. You could now create a blogosphere of your own with little more effort than it took to start a single blog; all you needed was some server space, a little software know-how, and a posse of people to participate. Meanwhile, other new services grew in a symbiotic relationship with the growing blog population, making it ever easier to incorporate other kinds of media, such as audio and video, into your blog, and to post directly from the growing proliferation of mobile devices, like cell-phone cameras and smartphones. One of the reasons YouTube spread so quickly as a distribution hub for snippets of Web video was that its founders made it easy for bloggers to embed individual videos directly in the stream of their posts. From a technically demanding undertaking that required detailed knowledge of compression formats, bandwidth limits, and other arcana, video blogging became painless almost overnight.

All these developments together fueled the phenomenal growth in sheer numbers that blogging continued to experience as the first decade of the 2000s wore on. A March 2008 study by Universal McCann found that 184 million people worldwide had started a blog, with 26.4 million in the United States—roughly one out of ten of the adult population. Among eighteen-to-thirty-four-year-old Americans, 20 percent published blogs. And 77 percent of active Internet users worldwide read blogs. Technorati's most recent report on the blogosphere, from September 2008, reports 133 million total blogs indexed by the service since 2002. Only some fraction of those are still active—7.4 million of those blogs had posts within the four months previous to the survey—but that's still enough bloggers to produce close to a million posts a day. The numbers are controversial for the usual reasons (questions over methodology, disagreements about definitions, and so on). Even counted conservatively, they are staggering—particularly when you consider that, a decade before, the word *blog* did not exist, and you could count the total number of weblogs on your fingers and toes.

In surveying blogging, numbers matter, but only as a starting point. Blogs are, after all, notable for enabling the expression of individuality. If we view them only in the aggregate, we miss the most important details in the picture they collectively paint. You can tell me there are millions of blogs, and I can nod my head. But that isn't the same as hearing about any tiny fraction of them in their unpredictable particularity.

Knowing that politicians and business leaders are now blogging is one thing. Knowing that Iranian president Mahmoud Ahmadinejad has a blog, and so does the billionaire investor Carl Icahn, is quite another. (Icahn has kept up a steady stream of posts on the economic situation; Ahmadinejad hasn't posted since late 2007, when he wrote about feeling torn between spending his fifteen-minutes-a-week blog time writing new posts or keeping up with his readers' comments.)

It is one thing to understand that people are blogging about the real-estate meltdown in the United States. It is another to follow the Iamfacingforeclosure.com blog, by Casey Serin, a "24-year-old would-be real estate mogul" (in his words) who borrowed too much money and then posted about his plight, sparing no detail and earning the contempt of a crowd of critics rubbernecking at the wreckage of his life (prompting CNET to ask whether he was "the world's most hated blogger").

It is one thing to be aware, in general, that bloggers can expose wrongdoing in their communities. It is another to read about Peter Kenney of Yarmouth, Massachusetts, a carpenter in his sixties blogging as The Great Gadfly, who was responsible for posting a series of scoops detailing fraud by the leader of a Native American tribe seeking to open a casino.

It is one thing to know that bloggers can set themselves up as "citizen journalists." It is another to discover that one of the best sources of information in the United States about regional conflicts in Yemen is Jane Novak, a New Jersey stay-at-home mother of two. Novak started her blog in 2004 to rally support for a persecuted Yemeni journalist, and just kept going.

It is one thing to hear in the abstract about "milbloggers" in Iraq, legions of Americans in uniform on tours of duty posting about their frustrations and small triumphs, their fears and doubts. It is quite another to read the blog of Andrew Olmsted, a U.S. Army major who started posting in October 2001 and was killed in January 2008, near Sadiyah, Iraq. A proud soldier who enjoyed mixing it up with both ends of the political spectrum, Olmsted had plenty of blogging friends, and he'd given one of them—the liberal blogger at Obsidian Wings who writes under the pen name Hilzoy—a "last post" to publish in the event of his death, full of mordant jokes and quotations from *Babylon 5*:

> As with many bloggers, I have a disgustingly large ego, and
> so I just couldn't bear the thought of not being able to

have the last word if the need arose. . . . I'm dead, but if you're reading this, you're not, so take a moment to enjoy that happy fact. . . . Believe it or not, one of the things I will miss most is not being able to blog any longer. The ability to put my thoughts on (virtual) paper and put them where people can read and respond to them has been marvelous, even if most people who have read my writings haven't agreed with them. If there is any hope for the long term success of democracy, it will be if people agree to listen to and try to understand their political opponents rather than simply seeking to crush them. . . .

While you're free to think whatever you like about my life and death, if you think I wasted my life, I'll tell you you're wrong. We're all going to die of something. I died doing a job I loved. When your time comes, I hope you are as fortunate as I was.

Once you begin to apprehend blogs in this manner, you may start to feel a little uncomfortable about applying Sturgeon's Law to them. At some point, saying that "ninety percent of blogs are crap" begins to feel misanthropically close to saying "ninety percent of people are crap."

Blogging has hardly presented a perfect mirror of humanity, but it keeps expanding in a more representative direction. In the United States today, it is no longer as male-dominated as it once was, nor skewed as heavily to the white population. As Internet access has become a household standard, the demographics of blogging have more closely conformed to those of the general population, with only the high end of the age spectrum lagging behind. (Even there, you will find a thriving world of "elderblogging" if you look for it.) Outside of the United States, although the picture varies more widely, the trends toward broadening participation in blogging are similar. Japan and South Korea, Brazil and Iran, Italy and India all have their own sprawling blogospheres; by one count China alone had 47 million blogs in 2008, including what is almost certainly the world's most popular blog, that of actor-director Xu Jinglei. These national blogging movements are shaped to an extent by the local technical and legal regimes, but they share a set of essential characteristics: the ease of entry; the blurring of boundaries between professional and recreational, public and private; the opportunity to route around informational roadblocks (like gatekeepers or censorship). A separate book could easily be devoted to each of these national blog movements' stories.

Blogging is now globally ubiquitous. It is one of the central drivers of "the largest expansion in expressive capability in the history of the human race" (in Clay Shirky's words). There is, inevitably, disagreement over whether this expansion is a blessing or a calamity. At one extreme, we find idealists like blogger Doc Searls, who sees the Web as a realization of a Whitmanesque democratic vision:

> I believe what we have with the Web today is as close to a utopia as humans have ever built, or ever could build. If the stars shone through the clouds but once in a lifetime, Emerson said, their beauty would be legend. Incredibly, we have made those stars, and a firmament in which they can shine. And they are ourselves.

At the other extreme, we find the dismissive voices from the trash-heap chorus, like the anonymous wag who posted the following text at the address "internetisshit.org":

> Give an infinite number of monkeys typewriters and they'll produce the works of Shakespeare. Unfortunately, I feel like I'm reading all the books where they didn't.

The success of blogging at a scale of millions has ensured that voices at each end of this spectrum, and at every point in between, will always find a wealth of supporting examples for their cases. That success also keeps opening new fronts in the old arguments over the nature of the Web's influence. The Journalists-versus-Bloggers conflict centered on issues of accuracy and professional standing; now, increasingly, the larger debate focuses on matters of quality and psychological impact. The question has shifted from how blogging is changing the world to how it is changing us.

Doris Lessing established the theme in her Nobel Award acceptance speech in 2007:

> We are in a fragmenting culture, where our certainties of even a few decades ago are questioned and where it is common for young men and women, who have had years of education, to know nothing of the world, to have read nothing, knowing only some speciality or other, for instance, computers.
>
> What has happened to us is an amazing invention—computers and the internet and TV. It is a revolution. This is not the first revolution the human race has dealt with. The printing revolution, which did not take place in a matter of a few decades, but took much longer, transformed our minds and ways of thinking. A foolhardy lot, we accepted it all, as we always do, never asked, What is going to happen to us now, with this invention of print? In the same way, we never thought to ask, How will our lives, our way of thinking, be changed by this internet, which has seduced a whole generation with its inanities so that even quite reasonable people will confess that once they are hooked, it is hard to cut free, and they may find a whole day has passed in blogging etc.

Lessing's observations have a wearying familiarity: "Our culture is fragmenting" and "the young know nothing" are perennial complaints, commonplace a century ago. Nonetheless, her exhortation that we remain conscious of the changes under way is worth heeding, even more so for those of us who are immersed in the "inanities" of "blogging etc." than for those who—like, apparently, Lessing herself—have remained unsullied by them.

Those who worry that blogging is changing our lives for the worse have generally shared a set of recurring concerns. There is the fear that blogging overvalues novelty at the expense of the timeless. There is the fear that blogging breaks everything into small bits and erodes our capacity for big thoughts. And there is the fear that, by increasing the sum of human expression, blogging diminishes the impact of any particular instance of human expression. Each of these concerns is worth a close look.

There can be no argument that the blog format gives "now" the pride of place; novelty leads, and the past recedes into a string of "older posts" links and archives pages. But it is a mistake to think that blogs therefore discard the past. Most bloggers, in fact, are far more assiduous than the proprietors of other kinds of websites about preserving their outdated material. They know their own back-catalog well, and link back into it to support a point, to explain a reference, or just to highlight something that tickles them. With the permalink convention, modern blog software turns each post into a landing page for arrivals from other blogs or Google searches; these destinations may grow more obscure with age, but they do not vanish. For the great mass of bloggers who would never have jotted down their thoughts in the first place if they didn't have a blog, their posts represent the opposite of oblivion: they are a personal archive that can serve as a bulwark against forgetfulness.

Of course, it's reasonable to suspect that a medium organized by reverse chronology may not be the place to turn for the virtues of the timeless. On the other hand, bloggers attend to philosophical discourse as well as pop-cultural ephemera; they document private traumas as well as public controversies. They have sought faith and spurned it, chronicled awful illnesses and mourned unimaginable losses. Blogging turns out to have an extensive reserve capacity for timelessness, much of it still untapped.

What about the fear that blogging, a short-form medium, will turn us into short-form thinkers? This turns out to be only the latest in a long line of culture scares—alarms that accompany the arrival of every new communications medium. Television and movies would privilege visual thinking over abstract reasoning! Radio and the telephone would destroy literacy as we know it! Even writing once had its skeptics: in the *Phaedrus*, as Richard Powers reminds us, Socrates "uncorks at length about how writing damages memory, obscures authority and even alters meaning." (Ironically, Powers goes on, we only know about the warning "through Plato's suspect transcript.")

Leading the current round of this hand-wringing is Nicholas Carr, the business writer and critic, who maintains that too much time spent reading small chunks of text on the Web will crimp our brains. Carr has been building a thoughtful case against blogging since 2005—mostly on his own blog. Making virtuoso use of a medium he can't stop detesting, he is, you might say, a self-hating blogger.

Carr has argued that the blog-ridden Web will "reprogram" our brains and "change the nature of human intelligence":

> Contemplative Man, the fellow who came to understand
> the world sentence by sentence, paragraph by paragraph,
> is a goner. He's being succeeded by Flickering Man, the
> fellow who darts from link to link, conjuring the world
> out of continually refreshed arrays of isolate pixels,
> shadows of shadows. The linearity of reason is blurring
> into the nonlinearity of impression; after five centuries
> of wakefulness, we're lapsing into a dream state.

It is a mesmerizing image, and as I read it I linger on it, and take up its implicit invitation to weigh whether it matches my experience. But then

I shake my head; it doesn't. I still read sentence by sentence, paragraph by paragraph—books, articles, and blogs, too. I'm not Flickering Man, and though I know a few people who might be, I suspect they'd be flickering even in a world without any Web. Kevin Kelly, on his own blog, pricked Carr's fanciful bubble with a pragmatist's point:

> Is the ocean of short writing the Web has generated due to our minds getting dumber and incapable of paying attention to long articles, as Carr worries, or is it because we finally have a new vehicle and market place for loads of short things, whereas in the past short was unprofitable to produce in such quantity? I doubt the former and suspect the latter is the better explanation.

It will surely be worth the time of psychologists and cognitive specialists in coming years to explore Carr's thesis. Maybe consuming blog-post-sized texts really will reduce our attention spans and addict us to "snack culture." Maybe blogging is the ultimate embodiment of the "context of no context" that George W. S. Trow once identified in television's "Now, this!" structure. But right now all we have to go on is anecdotal evidence and self-awareness, and that remains, at worst, inconclusive. If you have read this far in this book, then you seem to have retained a good portion of your ability to read long-form prose; and if you've persevered to this point, you may even feel that I have not entirely lost the ability to write it—even after a decade of reading blogs and writing posts.

The final fear about blogging—that the sheer quantity of contributions renders any individual piece of writing insignificant—is the most elusive; rarely stated directly, it instead hovers on the margins of many conversations about the Web. It is, at root, a species of professional insecurity. You will not hear this concern from the great majority of bloggers, who are excited that they have any opportunity at all to place their words on a platform that can, though rarely does, reach a multitude. It is rather an expression of the vertigo felt by any writer—whether journalist, scholar, or novelist—confronted by the Web's oversupply of verbiage. Like a child contemplating one of those "You are here" charts that places our little speck of earthly dust in its dwarfing cosmic context, the writer is going to be awed, but also cowed: Where does that leave me?

Most writers today grew up in a world where the ability to publish was a hard-won privilege, and, once won, guaranteed at least some attention on its basis alone. That world is rapidly fading. On the Web, publishing has become an abundant, effectively limitless resource. Clay Shirky has laid out the consequences for us: When publishing was scarce, we filtered first, making choices based on relevance or quality before committing words to our limited stock of paper, our costly fleet of trucks, our scarce radio and TV frequencies. The Web inverts this sequence. We publish, then filter. Say everything first; ask questions later.

Putting the questions off is different from not asking them at all. Which piece of writing is telling the truth, and which is trying to manipulate you? Which is going to make you laugh, and which will move you? Which will help you save your job or raise your child? Which will best guide you to the movie you'll enjoy this weekend, or tell you what happened at the baseball game you couldn't watch?

The mechanisms for filtering blog posts—and for fishing out "the good stuff" from everything the Web enables us to churn out in such prodigious quantities—are still in the "let's try stuff out" stage. Traffic information is the simplest filter: What pages and posts had the most readers? But it is a crude, lagging indicator—it merely tells you the results of everyone else's filtration. Google (and Technorati) take a more predictive approach by filtering based on the quantity and quality of inbound links. Many of us still place the highest value of all on the kind of human filtering that the early webloggers pioneered, people using their blogs or bookmarking services like Delicious or other tools to point to some link and say, *Here's a pearl on the trash heap*. On today's Web you'll find an endless variety of experimental hybrid filters: from communities like Digg that turn editing into a collective endeavor, with participants voting stories up and down, to sites like Techmeme that are "edited" by software programs prowling a human-curated list of blogs to track the rise and fall of interest in particular stories. These filters all have their failings, but they are also evolving rapidly. In their restless mutations, we can catch a glimpse of the potential power and efficiency of future mechanisms for finding whatever we might consider to be "the good stuff."

Is it harder to achieve significance, to be heard, in this world than in the filter-then-publish world that preceded it? That depends on who you ask. The blogger struggling to achieve enough "link love" from peers and A-listers to earn a higher Google Rank or land a story on Techmeme may feel frustrated. But at least his words are out there for the fifteen people to whom he's famous. I don't think we're likely to consider him worse off than the writer of a previous generation who could only toss a manuscript over a publisher's transom and pray that the intern would actually read it (and didn't have a hangover).

The dynamics of this new world continue to confound those who made their names in the old one. Consider the perspective of Barry Diller. In media-corporation suites, Diller, the veteran TV executive who has cut a restless swath through the cable and Internet industries, is seen as something of a techno-visionary; his 1994 adoption of a Mac Powerbook and discovery of email merited a flattering *New Yorker* profile that attempted to portray him as a geek. (In his circles, I guess he was.) Diller has spent the last several years assembling and running the Web conglomerate InterActiveCorp, but his worldview remains heavily shaped by his Hollywood background. "Self-publishing by someone of average talent is not very interesting," he told *The Economist* in 2006. "Talent is the new limited resource." At a technology conference that year, he declared, "There's just not that much talent in the world, and talent almost always outs."

Diller's view echoes that of many a complacent media executive, along with that of avowedly elitist polemics like Andrew Keen's *The Cult of the Amateur*. According to this perspective, talent is a resource of fixed supply. The existing institutions of the publishing and broadcast world are already doing an efficient and thorough job of finding all that talent and giving it a platform. And all this other stuff that's spewing forth from the Web's profusion of blogs and podcasts and videos? It's just dross that obscures the real talent's output.

Beyond the obvious arrogance, this view misreads and underestimates the Web in several ways. It's a mistake to think of human creativity as a kind of limited natural resource, like an ore waiting for society to mine; it is more like a gene that will turn on given the right cues. Diller and his ilk envision the Web simply as a new distribution channel for the same old stuff, and human expression as a static commodity, uninfluenced by the medium that bears it or the social environment in which it emerges. Their view values each bit of expression based on marketplace worth and potential breadth of appeal, but ignores any worth the expression may have to the person who made it. Most narrow-mindedly of all, they assume that yesterday's filtering methods will remain reliable and sufficient tomorrow, no matter how radically the environment changes around them.

This is a recipe for failure. Yet, despite these flaws, despite its condescension and its inflexibility, Diller's attitude remains widespread among media company leaders. They are rightly afraid that it will be harder for them to work the same way and maintain the same profits in the new media world; but they are deluded in believing they have any choice in the matter. Already, today's Web has evolved well beyond the familiar shape of Diller's picture. It is expanding the opportunity to manifest talent even as it is exploding the agreed-upon structures for rewarding the works that talent creates. These changes are wreaking havoc with the music industry, whose youthful customers have moved into the new world faster than the companies that sell to them. The same crisis is now beginning to engulf television, movies, book publishing—everywhere that physical goods can be replaced by digital files, and anywhere that the old gatekeeping model of talent recognition can be eroded by the demotic currents of the publish-everything Web.

Diller and his species of executive have always excelled at finding rare talents that can, at their best, enchant a mass market. But this very success has blinded them to the different, more diffuse sort of talent present among the Web's millions of contributors. Of course talent isn't universal, nor is it evenly distributed. But there is far more of it in the world than Diller's blinkered vision allows. On the Web it can reveal itself in a far wider range of ways, and far more people will have a chance to cultivate it. It will never be perceived in a uniform way; you and I will recognize it in very different places and judge it in very different ways. But it is surely there—and, fortunately, denigrating it will not make it go away.

Because the Web comes to us on a screen, it has been easy to misapprehend it as the next phase in the evolution of television. The advent of blogging looked to some observers like the latest mutation of reality TV, which dissects the lives of ordinary people on a mass stage. But there's one defining difference: on a reality show, only a few people get the opportunity to participate, and those who win the chance remain at the mercy of the show's producers. In articles that explore how blogging can turn lives inside out, rendering the private public, references abound to *The Truman Show*—a 1998 movie about a man who discovers his life is an elaborately staged TV program. Truman Burbank, that movie's protagonist, is a victim, practically a prisoner, with no choice in his performance. Bloggers, on the other hand, are volunteers; they may have little power over whom they reach, but they have unprecedented control over what they say and whether to keep saying it. No one can vote you off the island of your own blog.

We talk too much about television as an antecedent to the Web, and not enough about the telephone. When the telephone arrived in American homes and businesses in the late nineteenth and early twentieth centuries, there was some uncertainty over how people would use it and how using it would change their lives. Some social critics worried that the telephone's insistent intrusions would undermine the status of the home as a refuge from the world's pressures. Others feared that the phone would erode the shared public space of our communities and disengage us from social life. Telephone conversations were neither private nor trusted. Party lines and operators meant conversations were likely to be overheard; con artists took advantage of the new technology to prey on the naïve.

Today the telephone has become our most trusted and confidential form of everyday communication. If we don't want a conversation to leave electronic tracks, we pick up the phone instead of sending an email. Businesses that want to verify our identities will call us and speak to us. At a time when we are just beginning to grapple with how to use the Web, the telephone offers comfort and familiarity. It is the Web, now, that poses threatening new questions about privacy and anonymity, and the telephone that reassures with the warmth of the human voice and the intimacy of real-time connection.

In *America Calling: A Social History of the Telephone to 1940*, the sociologist Claude S. Fischer argues that our customary mode of discussing new technologies leads us astray by casting the technology as the protagonist and the human user as a victim. We should not inquire into the telephone's "impacts" or "effects," Fischer writes: "That is the wrong language, a mechanical language that implies that human actions are impelled by external forces when they are really the outcomes of actors making purposeful choices under constraints."

This is good advice for Web critics, too. Like the telephone before it, the Web will be defined by the choices people make as they use it, constrained by—but not determined by—the nature of the technology. The most significant choice we have been making, collectively, ever since the popularization of Internet access in the mid-1990s, has been to favor two-way interpersonal communication over the passive reception of broadcast-style messages. Big-media efforts to use the Net for the delivery of old-fashioned one-way products have regularly failed or underperformed. Social uses of our time online—email, instant messaging and chat, blogging, Facebook-style networking—far outstrip time spent in passive consumption of commercial media. In other words, businesspeople have consistently overestimated the Web's similarities to television and underestimated its kinship to the telephone.

One reason blogs have flourished is that they sit comfortably at this divide between communication types: they partake of some of the characteristics of each, in proportions that vary depending on the style of the individual blogger. Some blogs are simply vehicles for conversation among friends. Some are exclusively public discourse. But many take advantage of blogs' potential to cross back and forth over this line. A post meant originally for a small circle of friends may "go viral" and catch the attention of millions; a broadside post from a public figure may spark a back-and-forth exchange in the comments. This mutability can be breathtakingly powerful; it can also be treacherous. Either way, whenever we observe an instance of it, we sense we are witnessing something that could only occur in this form, via this medium—something uniquely bloggish.

Once we acknowledge that the Web inherits at least as much from the telephone as from the television, complaints about the "problem" of the Web's abundance appear in a different light. In a 2007 article, James McGrath Morris, a journalism historian, wrote, "There is a point when there are simply too many blogs. With 30 million blogs today, we may well have reached that point." He was not the first, nor the last, to raise the "too many blogs!" alarm. In November 2008, *Time*'s Michael Kinsley wrote, "How many blogs does the world need? There is already blog gridlock." The question, echoing a legion of similar skeptics, sounds reasonable at first. But what if he'd written, "How many telephone calls does the world need"? Did someone tell Kinsley that *he* needed to read all those blogs? If they keep multiplying, whose party are they spoiling?

Most blogs are read only "by the writer and his mother," says Sreenath Sreenivasan, a professor at the Columbia School of Journalism. If he is right—and no doubt, in some cases, he is—does that make them worthless? If blogging's only accomplishment was that it got more people to phone home to mom, Web-style, why would anyone object? The sheer volume of blogs evokes a peevish resentment among some observers, as if the outpouring represented a personal affront. How dare all these people presume on our attention! Do they really think that anyone is listening to them?

It is certainly possible to blog into a void—to post and post and never get a visitor or a comment. But it's unlikely many of us would persist with such unrewarding labors. Most blogs have some sort of audience, however tiny—moms and beyond. Where do these readers come from? More often than not, they are other bloggers. Observers steeped in the values of the broadcast world identify this as a failure: *Look, the only people who care what you're doing are already in your club!* But in fact, as they say in the software industry, this reciprocity is not a bug at all—it's a feature.

People who have no experience blogging often fail to understand the essentially social nature of the activity. Blogging is convivial. Bloggers commonly blog in groups, whether formally (as with our Salon bloggers) or simply through the haphazard accretion of casual connections. In these groups, what you contribute is obviously important; but so is where you choose to place your attention. Reading is as much a part of blogging as writing; listening is as important as speaking. This is what so many bloggers mean when they claim that "blogging is a conversation": not that each post sparks a vigorous exchange of comments, but that every post exists in a context of post-and-response that stretches across some patch of the Web, link by link, blog to blog.

In *The First Word*, her book about the origins of language, Christine Kenneally describes the scene when two apes trained in sign language first encountered each other: "What resulted was a sign-shouting match; neither ape was willing to listen." Anyone who's ever witnessed a dead-end flame war online knows the feeling.

For communication of any stripe to take place, listening must somehow be involved. Knowing how to listen is no less essential in keeping a blog than in any other encounter with other people. For bloggers, listening takes many forms, including following other bloggers (or subscribing to their feeds), reading comments, and checking the referrers to find inbound links. When all these channels are open, a blogger can feel embedded in a buzzing hive of attention and support and argument. Of course, that means that if the channels close, the author can feel abandoned, betrayed.

Bloggers, most of them solo bootstrappers of their own stream of self-expression, are the most autonomous writers the world has yet seen—the least dependent on others to publish their words. (This is a central difference between the individualist blog and the collective wiki—the other Web-native writing form that achieved popular success this decade. On a blog, you alone can edit your words; on the typical wiki, anyone with an account can change anything.) At the same time, of all the species of writer, bloggers are the least insulated from their audience, most vulnerable to the ebb and flow of attention and response. They are both alone and in a crowd. Their solitude can inspire self-indulgent ranting; their sociability can tempt them into self-serving pandering. But every now and then they manage to hold their balance in this paradoxical position for an extended, exhilarating spell.

"Each blog," James Wolcott wrote in 2002, "is like a blinking neuron in the circuitry of an emerging, chatterbox superbrain." This striking image cuts two ways. It's alluring to think you might be participating in a grand barn-raising for species-wide consciousness via the Web. It's creepy, too: What if doing so costs you some part of your separate identity—what Nicholas Carr calls a "loss of selfness," a feeling of "slowly being emptied," a sense that "we are beginning to blur at the edges"?

That is certainly a possibility. Any act of public expression, of "putting everything out there"—your political arguments or your creative work or your personal story—is a gamble. We offer something to the world; we cross our fingers that our contributions won't simply be ignored or derided or misappropriated. Sometimes we're surprised at how much we get back, and sometimes we feel used.

Either way, we are going to keep at it. Whatever the outcome of each of our individual bets, we can now see that collectively they constitute something unprecedented in human history: a new kind of public sphere, at once ephemeral and timeless, sharing the characteristics of conversation and deliberation. Blogging allows us to think out loud together. Now that we have begun, it's impossible to imagine stopping.

Chapter 11

FRAGMENTS FOR THE FUTURE

When a thing is new, people say, "It is not true." Later, when its truth becomes obvious, they say, "It is not important." Finally, when its importance cannot be denied, they say, "Anyway, it is not new."

—attributed on the Web to William James (1896), as found on Evan Williams's home page, 1998

On July 11, 2008, Jason Calacanis posted that he was "retiring" from blogging. "After five years," he wrote, "I'm not sure I know any other way of being but the blog, but at some point you have to hang it up. I know that I have made the right decision for me and my family. I am very proud of the success that we have had in blogging and I leave the game with few regrets."

Calacanis's tongue-in-cheek adoption of the clichés of the star-athlete press conference left many readers wondering whether the announcement was a ruse or joke. But he seemed to mean it.

> I'm going to try and build a deeper relationship with fewer people—try to get back to my roots. . . . I'm looking for something more acoustic, something more authentic and something more private. Blogging is simply too big, too impersonal, and lacks the intimacy that drew me to it. The "a-list" pressure, the TechMeme leader-

> board debates, and constant accusations of link-baiting
> are now too much of a distraction. . . . Today the blogo-
> sphere is so charged, so polarized, and so filled with
> haters hating that it's simply not worth it. I'd rather watch
> from the sidelines and be involved in a smaller, more
> personal, conversation.

What form would that "deeper relationship" and "more personal conversation" take? Calacanis said that henceforth he would post his
thoughts on the tech industry to a private email list. In other words, the
2008 edition of Jason Calacanis was going to look a lot like Dave Winer
circa 1995.

At first Calacanis had said he would limit his list to 750 subscribers
("more than enough people to have a conversation with"). Cynics dismissed this exclusivity as a gambit to draw a crowd. By November 2008,
Calacanis had added more than ten thousand subscribers to the list, so
the cynics were probably right. He'd also begun posting many of his
mailing-list essays to his semi-dormant blog ("so I don't have to respond
to hundreds of emails asking for a copy").

Still, Calacanis's once-active high-traffic blog was now effectively
shuttered. Blogging, he wrote, had become a drag. Maybe Calacanis truly
was sick of the pro-blogging rat race—a race he'd helped invent back in
the days of the Engadget/Gizmodo war. Maybe he felt that blogging had
gone so mainstream that it no longer befitted the edgy profile of a tech-
industry innovator. Or maybe the retirement was just the latest ploy in a
long career of crafty and effective publicity stunts.

Whatever the motivation, Calacanis's announcement set off a wave
of obituaries for blogging. In *Wired* magazine, Paul Boutin warned off
prospective bloggers and advised active ones to "pull the plug." Why?
Blogs are "so 2004":

> The blogosphere, once a freshwater oasis of folksy self-
> expression and clever thought, has been flooded by a

tsunami of paid bilge. Cut-rate journalists and underground marketing campaigns now drown out the authentic voices of amateur wordsmiths. It's almost impossible
to get noticed, except by hecklers.

Inevitably, any report of the death of blogging was a form of link-bait—
something bloggers wouldn't be able to resist criticizing, thereby increasing attention and traffic to the article. Whether Boutin really believed
blogging had run its course or whether he was just trolling for links—or
both—his piece fairly represented a wider feeling of exhaustion in one
particular blogosphere: the tech-oriented bloggers who'd opened shop in
the early days of the Web 2.0 boom and built a new pro-blogging industry out of caffeine and scraps of code. Some had been true believers
in the transformative powers of the Web; others were part of "a gentrifying wagon train of carpetbaggers, speculators, and confidence men," as
the blogger Merlin Mann memorably described them in a 2008 post
that crystallized his own disillusionment with this scene. Many of them
were now, like Mann, reconsidering the value of a community that
seemed to reward quantity over quality and promote speed over substance. The pro-bloggers' "diet comprised mostly of fake-connectedness,
make-believe insight, and unedited first drafts of everything" was, Mann
lamented, "making us small."

Mann took this discontent as a prod to rethink his approach to blogging, and recommitted himself to a more contemplative style. But the
more common response was to declare, with Boutin, that blogging was
"over." Such a conclusion was probably inevitable in a crowd of novelty-
addicted early adopters. But in reaching it, these bloggers made the same
self-centered error that previous groups of blogging burnouts had fallen
into: they thought that the fizzling out of their own scene's energies
meant the extinction of blogging itself.

In truth, bloggers had been "hanging it up" for almost as long as
they'd been cranking it out. Jesse James Garrett was probably the first
high-profile blogger to retire from the fray: in November 1999 he got a

new job that left him with less time to post. He also concluded that he'd learned what he'd set out to learn through his weblog, anyway. So Garrett moved on just as the rest of the world was beginning to discover what blogging was. Each subsequent wave of bloggers left its share of casualties and retirees; in 2004, Wired News posted a representative story headlined "Bloggers Suffer Burnout," marking a cyclical ebb of the energies unleashed in the aftermath of 9/11. Some retirees simply shuttered their blogs quietly; others slammed the door on their way out—like Matt Welch, who denounced the warbloggers whose name he'd coined and with whom he'd originally taken up.

Every group of bloggers progresses through its own natural life cycle: childish excitement, teenage angst, midlife crisis, elderly fatigue. In a 2005 post titled "The Blog Cycle," Anil Dash, an early blogger who became the first employee at Six Apart, anatomized the gestational phases that most blog communities pass through as they recapitulate the formative experiences of their predecessors: from asking "what is blogging" to claiming "our community invented blogging!" to recycling the old Blogging-versus-Journalism debate through all the other common discussions that seem to arise whenever bloggers begin to see themselves as a distinct group. Far from complaining that the repetition of these conversations was a problem to be solved, Dash suggested that they were inevitable milestones on the path of each community's development.

Was blogging really "over" in 2008? Certainly, the year's financial meltdown and ensuing advertising recession threatened the entrepreneurial dreams of the tech world's pro-bloggers, and some of them were reaching the end of their road. But for every burnout choosing to move on, there still seemed to be plenty of newcomers ready to move in.

Blogging was in no danger of vanishing. Like all hot new developments in the Web world, however, it couldn't stay hot and new forever. As long as blogs were unfamiliar, they benefited from waves of media attention. The first proposal of marriage on a blog—and the first divorce! Look—bloggers are finding real jobs through their blogs! And over here, bloggers are getting book deals! The flow of such firsts provided reporters with a steady stream of easy stories for a while. But at some point—roughly around 2006—blogging began to become yesterday's story for those mainstream journalists who walked the Web beat. That meant it was time to start covering something else.

The latest hot and new Web phenomenon—collectively identified as "social networking"—centered on sites like MySpace and Facebook. The Web already had professional and personal networking sites, like LinkedIn and Friendster, that allowed you to assemble rosters of contacts and then follow their online doings. MySpace and Facebook took this "add a friend" approach and combined it with some of the personal pub-lishing aspects of traditional blogging. MySpace, founded in 2003 and acquired by Rupert Murdoch's News Corporation in 2005, allowed teenagers, bands, and their fans to build homes on the Web that were part blogs and part old-fashioned "home pages" with personal profile information, all linked together across a network of friends chosen by each user. Facebook, which was founded in 2004 at Harvard and spread first across the college-age population, adopted a similar structure to MySpace, but applied a more sober design and hid your postings from non-friends. When Facebook dropped the college-affiliation requirement and opened up free membership to any adult in 2006, it rapidly expanded to become a sort of alternate Internet-within-the-Internet, like a reincarnation of the old America Online in hipper garb.

If blogging was personal publishing with a little telephone-style interaction mixed in, Facebook (like similar services) inverted the ratio: it offered something more like telephone chatter infused with just a few of publishing's traits. For a new generation of Web users it became the default mode of online communication among friends, a place to share personal news and pictures, keep up with schoolmates after graduation, and—to the horror of a more decorous older generation—gawk at photos from a previous night's drunken revels.

MySpace, Facebook, and their imitators made it easier than ever to post more and more of your life to the Web, so it was time for another round of perennial fretting over the dangers of technologically induced narcissism. Bloggers coined a new term—*the narcissystem*—to describe the self-referential thickets of personal information the new Web services invited users to upload. There was, of course, a chicken-and-egg problem here: Was Facebook actually inculcating narcissism in a new generation, or was a generation of narcissists embracing Facebook as an up-to-the-minute looking glass? The handful of studies of this question to date have not come close to resolving it.

Some amount of narcissistic behavior seems to come with the territory of youth, of course. But what worried adults may have missed as they wrung their hands was that Facebook's users did not seem to take it nearly as seriously as they did. They saw it less as a place to discover one's self than as a stage for entertaining their friends. Alice Mathias, a recent college graduate, tried to school her elders in a 2007 *New York Times* op-ed piece that described Facebook as a kind of "online community theater": "It's all comedy: making one another laugh matters more than providing useful updates about ourselves, which is why entirely phony profiles were all the rage before the grown-ups signed in."

Social networking was a genre of theater that kept getting enhanced with new special effects, as the programmers who built the new services embroidered them with additional features. One novel feature Facebook introduced was the status update—a brief posting for your profile page stating what you were doing at that moment. Twitter, a new service that emerged from Evan Williams's company in 2006, invited users to share very similar status updates from the Web as well as from cell phones and mobile devices. Twitter users posted 140-character statements— "tweets"—about what they had just done, where they were, or what they were reading; they posted links and jokes and attenuated rants, too. Each user chose his own set of friends to "follow," similar to subscribing to an RSS feed; the friends' messages appeared in a reverse-chronological stream in a browser window or on a mobile device screen. Unlike Facebook's status updates, Tweets were public by default—each had its own unique Web address.

In a lot of ways, Twitter was like blogging, only shorter. The 140-character limit was unforgiving, like a hook-wielding vaudeville emcee waiting to cut off any act that ran over; but it provided some guarantee that keeping up with your friends would not take over your life. Twitter, along with the many copycat services that emerged as its popularity among the tech-blogging crowd soared in 2007, came to be dubbed "microblogging." Maintaining a traditional blog, even casually, required some time and thought; trading brief messages with friends on the new social networks required little more than a few spare seconds. Blogging, which had once been the quick-and-dirty method for publishing a thought to the Web, now began to look like a lumbering old beast next to its lithe offspring.

This was the other part of Paul Boutin's "blogging is dead" argument, and it was one that a considerable number of bloggers took to heart. Jason Kottke—one of the original link-bloggers from the late nineties who had turned his blog into a successful personal business without much altering his eclectic posting style—wrote in 2008: "Blogging as I would define it is passé. These days people are writing for online magazines like Gawker or Tumblring or Twittering or Facebooking or doing a million other things on the Web." Kottke was not alone in sensing that newer pursuits were eclipsing blogging. "I don't think there will be that many blogs around in ten years," predicted Bruce Sterling, the science-fiction writer, in a 2007 talk at the South by Southwest conference. This dismissal carried echoes of Greg Knauss's colossally mistaken forecast, in his "My Ass is a Weblog" column from 1999, that blogging wouldn't survive the decade. But Sterling's suggestion of blogging's obsolescence mirrored a new wave of self-doubt among a significant portion of the longtime blogging population.

Could the whole decade-long explosion of blogging have been a mere fad—the transitory adolescence of a Web destined to grow up? Rebecca Mead's 2000 *New Yorker* piece about Blogger and Meg Hourihan and Kottke had referred to blogging as "the CB radio of the Dave Eggers generation." Nicholas Carr, meanwhile, compared the blogosphere to the flourishing of ham radio in the early days of broadcasting. It had taken roughly two decades for "social production" of radio to be absorbed into "corporate production," Carr observed. Now, he maintained, with only the slightest hint of regret, the same thing was happening somewhat more quickly to bloggers, as the amateurs got pushed to the periphery by the pros.

Historically, the succession of media forms and technologies follows a predictable pattern: every innovation arrives with a fanfare announcing that it will replace its predecessor. But when the dust settles, the newcomer almost always winds up having redefined that predecessor rather than eliminated it. Radio did not kill off the telegraph. (Although it is now, finally, dead—Western Union shut down telegram service in 2006— it was the Internet that delivered the final blow.) Television killed off neither radio nor the newspaper. The cinema failed to kill live theater. Home video did not shutter the movie theaters. The Web may be wreaking havoc on the newspaper industry, but it is unlikely to wipe out all publishing on paper in the near future.

Similarly, as people have flocked to Facebook and MySpace and Twitter, they will not stop posting to or reading blogs—but their patterns of blogging will change. The social networks turn out to be an easier and more efficient channel for casual messages intended for a handful of friends. If what you want to tell the world requires only 140 characters, you may well choose to say it on Twitter instead of in a blog post. As a result, some unquantifiable portion of the world's blogging has already started to change, to become a little more deliberate, a little less telephonic in nature.

But there is scant sign of mass abandonment of the form. There's likely to be a long future in which a great number of people who wish to communicate online find the unique characteristics of a blog irresistible. Next to the traditions and constraints of older media on paper or the airwaves, blogging tends to look anarchic and ephemeral and superficial. But next to the crowd-driven networking on Facebook or the stream of Twitter snippets, blogs appear far more substantial and free-standing and powerful. A blog lets you define yourself, whereas on a social network you are more likely to be defined by others. Sure, blog readers can write comments—but the blogger can delete the comments, or disemvowel them, or turn them off entirely. Sure, a blog is dependent on the links you point outward and those that others point in; but it has its own independent existence in a way that no amount of messaging and chat and interaction on a social networking site can match. A blog is not necessarily better than a Facebook profile, nor is it worse; it is, simply, different.

So, while there is no question that the energy that has poured into Facebook and its ilk in the latter part of the 2000s has drawn some of the excitement and media attention that bloggers formerly took for granted, it is also true that the rise of the social networks clarifies exactly what characteristics made blogging last. They are the same traits that once excited its earliest pioneers. A blog lets you raise your voice without asking anyone's permission, and no one is in a position to tell you to shut up. It is, as the journalism scholar Jay Rosen puts it, "a little First Amendment machine," an engine of free speech operating powerfully at a fulcrum-point between individual autonomy and the pressures of the group. Blogging uniquely straddles the acts of writing and reading; it can be private and public, solitary and gregarious, in ratios that each practitioner sets for himself. It is hardly the only way to project yourself onto the Web, and today it is no longer the easiest way. But it remains the most interesting way. Nothing else so richly combines the invitation to speak your mind with the opportunity to mix it up with other minds.

The celebrated principle of Moore's Law—the prediction of a steady doubling in the capabilities of microchips—has driven the growth of the personal computer industry and the Internet for decades now. In 2008, Facebook's young founder, Mark Zuckerberg, offered a similar prediction for the social Web: the amount of information people share online, he said, would double each year. His point wasn't so much that current

Web-sharers would keep finding more nooks and crannies of their lives to expose, but rather that the Web would steadily absorb more material from the still-vast majority of human beings who weren't yet sharing much at all. Either way, Zuckerberg's Law, as the statement was quickly (and mockingly) christened, pointed toward a future of impossible-to-imagine volumes of digital self-chronicling. Nicholas Carr snorted: "Shall no fart pass without a tweet?"

The prospect of an exponential growth in the sharing of lives was a discouraging new twist on the by-now familiar problem of information overload. Computers are efficient at processing enormous mountains of data, but our minds aren't, and the day has only twenty-four hours. The Web's vastness had already blown many people's information-processing circuits; blogging only aggravated the problem. We were "drowning in yak," as the critic Mark Dery put it. Blogs that filtered the Web helped tame this onslaught, but now many readers were seeing them as part of the problem. How could anyone possibly read more posts, view more photos, watch more videos, follow more friends? Might the Web, like an algae-choked pond, face a Malthusian crisis—a kind of die-off in sharing, where the oversupply of personal media caused people to quail and stop paying attention, removing any incentive to share in the first place?

Such a crisis looks unlikely. It has never occurred before, even through successive waves of alarmism over information overload, each one touted as equally dire, each seeming to push us finally over some tipping point of intolerability. We tend to view our era's cognitive onslaught as uniquely unmanageable, but the long view on this subject is instructive. Working forward from a historical baseline of the Renaissance and a sort of "big bang" with the Gutenberg press, we find our species experiencing an expanding universe of information as a consistent condition of its existence. Within our lifetimes, each new technical transformation of the media landscape has inspired its own diagnosis of an overload crisis. Round-the-clock broadcast radio and television seemed impossibly abundant to the generations that first experienced them. Then cable doubled down, with first dozens and later hundreds of channels to choose from—a paralysis-inducing cornucopia of video options. Before the public had ever heard of the Internet and the Web, thoughtful books by social critics like Richard Saul Wurman (*Information Anxiety*), Neil Postman, and Bill McKibben (*The Age of Missing Information*) warned of the consequences of a glutted information diet. Here is Postman, in a 1990 talk on "Informing Ourselves to Death":

> What started out as a liberating stream has turned into a deluge of chaos. If I may take my own country as an example, here is what we are faced with: In America, there are 260,000 billboards; 11,520 newspapers; 11,556 periodicals; 27,000 video outlets for renting tapes; 362 million TV sets; and over 400 million radios. There are 40,000 new book titles published every year (300,000 worldwide) and every day in America 41 million photographs are taken, and just for the record, over 60 billion pieces of advertising junk mail come into our mailboxes every year. Everything from telegraphy and photography in the nineteenth century to the silicon chip in the twentieth has amplified the din of information, until matters have reached such proportions today that for the average person, information no longer has any relation to the solution of problems.

All that, before we even had Cool Site of the Day to distract us! If the deluge was already so intense in a pre-Web world, surely our overload indicators would have melted down somewhere around the millennium. Instead, we find that, even as the amount of actual information continues to pile higher and wider, the alarms sounded by critics have held steady at an elevated, but bearable, level. In the early days of the Web, long before the spread of blogging and social-network sharing, we were already being alerted to the dangers of "data smog" (from the title of David Shenk's 1997 book). The arrival of blogging on the scene, and later the rise of the social networks, inspired new waves of anxiety over the sheer volume of media material human beings were producing.

Information, it seems, is *always* overwhelming us. The crisis is permanent, which makes one wonder whether it is a crisis at all. As Clay Shirky has argued, perhaps it's time to stop thinking of "information overload" as a problem we must solve and start accepting it as a fact we can accommodate.

Even then, to be sure, accommodation is neither simple nor easy. The technologies that enable us to produce information have always seemed to outpace those that help us consume, interpret, or use it. The story of RSS is an illustrative case. The opportunity to subscribe to a list of bloggers whose work you wanted to follow seemed like a perfect solution to the problem of blog indigestion. Instead, users took it as an invitation to load themselves up with an unmanageable influx of reading material. Each day they found their RSS reader confronting them with an intimidating message: You have even more unread messages today than you had yesterday. You will *never* catch up. *Kill yourself now!* Dave Winer, who'd done more than anyone else to popularize RSS, urged users to stop treating RSS feeds like a pile of incoming email—with each message representing a task you had to deal with—but rather as a "river of news." Your feeds gave you a flow of interesting stuff; you could dip into the stream at will, and drop out of it as needed. In a video that briefly made the tech-blogosphere rounds in 2007, Robert Scoble cheerily explained how he keeps up with more than six hundred feeds—and showed exactly how the river-of-news approach works. But few heeded the advice. RSS has never won the wide popularity among general users that it might have. A lot of people saw it as less an answer to information overload than an instrument of self-torture.

The growth of blogging posed an undeniable problem for those who had gotten swept up in its early excitement. At a certain point you had to cut off your blogroll or RSS subscription list, or you'd never have time to do anything besides read blogs. Even those who limited themselves to friends or colleagues found the choices difficult if they were in a blog-rich field, like the Web industry or politics. Just as some in the business world had taken to declaring "email bankruptcy" and starting afresh with an empty inbox, some overwhelmed blog readers decided to stop trying to catch up with their backlog. In 2005, David Weinberger—an author of the Cluetrain Manifesto and early proponent of blogging—posted a piece titled "No, I'm not keeping up with your blog":

> The truth is, I probably haven't read your blog in weeks. Months maybe. And I don't expect you to have read mine.
>
> I don't want to lie any more. I don't want to feel guilty any more. So let me tell you flat out: There are too many blogs I like and too many people I like to make "keeping up" a reasonable expectation. . . . I will read your blog on occasion, either because I've been thinking of you or because something reminded me of you. . . . But I hereby release you from thinking I expect you to keep up with my blog, and I preemptively release myself from your expectations.
>
> Otherwise reading each other's blogs will become a joyless duty. And we're too good friends to do that to each other.

Weinberger didn't explicitly renounce blogging itself, or reading blogs. He was just admitting what a lot of blog addicts had learned: the burden of "keeping up" had grown too great. Anyone for whom "keeping up" was either an aspiration or an obligation was eventually going to burn out.

Yet this spreading realization did not seem to dampen the enthusiasm of newcomers starting up blogs, nor did the volume of postings crater. Individuals continue to find their way through the dense thicket of blogging options. The "too many blogs" argument is heard most often either from professional journalists, who have a job-security beef with all that competition, or from people who have never put sustained effort into reading any particular handful of blogs. That there are more "good blogs" to read than any one enthusiast can keep up with is a good sort of problem to have. For the great majority of bloggers and their readers, the profusion of blogs has presented no more discouragement than the profusion of offerings the publishing industry tempts us with today. In the United States alone, you can find hundreds of thousands of new books each year—276,000 in 2007, according to one industry tracker. Every now and then someone raises a gripe about this flood, but mostly we celebrate it as a sign of our culture's fecund health. Imagine the wailing over the death of literacy, the gnashing of teeth over civilization's imminent collapse, should this number plummet! Yet it is a given, and no mark of shame, that each of us will never actually read more than a tiny sliver of this output. That there are more books—even good books—published each year than any of us could possibly read is simply not a crisis.

Is overload, then, a problem only for those who feel some obligation to "keep up"? Or is the multitude of choices itself a problem, even if we don't feel compelled to avail ourselves of more than a handful? That is the diagnosis provided by the popular work of the psychologist Barry Schwartz, author of *The Paradox of Choice*. According to Schwartz's theory, the dizzying abundance of options in the many blogospheres ought to have driven us around the bend by now. Schwartz argues that Western society's "dogma" emphasizing individual freedom through the maximization of choice provides us with neither satisfaction nor happiness; it "produces paralysis rather than liberation." Confronted by too many options, we freeze up.

Schwartz's analysis comes in handy when we want to understand the behavior of, say, a consumer facing a grocery shelf loaded with dozens of barely differentiated toothpaste selections. The "paradox of choice" also might make sense applied to the problem of information-gathering: If we have a specific question in mind—like "How does a rocket engine work?" or "What time does that movie play?"—we would like to find the best answer most efficiently, without wading through thousands of options. (Google has built its success by meeting this need.)

But blogging has always had a different purpose. The decision to follow someone's blog isn't like looking something up in a telephone directory or encyclopedia; it's more like picking a book to read. It's an advance grant of some of our attention to someone who we think will use it well, or whose life or work we want to follow. In other words, it's more akin to choosing a friend than to buying toothpaste.

We all start with a certain facility in making social choices, thanks to our genetic inheritance from thousands of years of evolution, along with direct experience in various schools of hard knocks—beginning with that interpersonal boot camp, the playground. There are billions of other people on the planet, yet we know that in our lives we will most likely meet only a few thousand, befriend maybe dozens or hundreds, and bond closely with only a handful. The difference in scale between the potential set of friends in the global population and the actual group each of us will have in any lifetime is barely comprehensible. Yet we don't experience a vertigo of choice overload; we don't despair and become hermits. Instead, each of us makes reasonable decisions according to whatever ratio of planning and happenstance suits our temperament. We let the interplay of choice and chance unfold; we meet people intentionally or randomly, and we end up with some number of friends and acquaintances.

If you ask most bloggers and blog readers who they follow and how they made their choices, they will describe a process that is remarkably similar. They are not paralyzed by choice. They pick as they go along, based on personal ties ("that's my sister-in-law's blog, she writes about her business") and recommendations ("Jim sent me a link to this great blog about microbreweries") and serendipity ("last night I followed a link on a whim and stumbled on a crazy story about this family's cross-country trip"). They make changes over time, adding and subtracting people just as a circle of friends will change over time. They find such a process natural—because it is.

In the annals of media, blogging's rise has been speedy. In the space of a decade, the popular spread of a new technology, the Web, enabled a new form of communication, a hybrid of traditional publishing and casual electronic messaging; and that form won quick favor among numbers larger than only a handful of its early enthusiasts ever imagined.

Speed increases resistance. In much of the story that this book tells, blogging itself has appeared as a rebel upstart, a disruptive innovation. It could not help inciting a defensive and frequently angry reaction from many writers and readers who saw, correctly, that the new form was changing their relationship in unpredictable ways. But the fears that blogging represented the latest nail in the coffin of literate culture overlooked some obvious evidence to the contrary. Before the advent of the Web, the gravest threat to that culture was widely understood to be television—the original "vast wasteland." During TV's first flush of popularity, its critics worried that it would entirely eclipse the culture of reading that had served as our society's intellectual and moral backbone for centuries. Ray Bradbury, the octogenarian fabulist, recently reminded readers that he'd intended his famous 1953 novel *Fahrenheit 451* (which envisioned a future America that burned books and outlawed reading) less as a tract against McCarthyism and totalitarian mind-control, as the tale is usually taken, than as a warning that broadcast television would wreck America by transforming us from a nation of individual readers into an undifferentiated mass of passive viewers.

Bradbury wasn't alone; he was just ahead of the curve. By the 1960s and 1970s, everyone was afraid: TV would homogenize our communities, brainwash our kids, and rot our brains. And it did! Yet somehow we survived. Now we are grappling with a new cultural force that, unlike TV—a medium created by a handful of people for mass consumption—is a mass medium created by the mass itself. Despite the radical differences between the two media regimes, the new complaints that the Web, along with its blog spawn, is leveling our culture sound nearly identical to the

charges once aimed at TV. It is as though there were a collective immuno-
logical reflex at work, a social antibody to protect familiar media forms
and reject new ones; it responds to each new invader with the same critical defenses, whether they fit or not.

As a result, the critics have somehow failed to notice a central fact
that you can be certain has not escaped the attention of a single TV executive: the numbers show, pretty consistently, that much of the time
Americans are spending blogging and posting comments and photos and
videos is time taken away from watching television, not from reading
books or otherwise enlightening ourselves. At the very worst, then, we're
trading in one species of mind-rot for another. More likely, this shift in
attention and energy from broadcast to the Web represents a real change
in behavior—a renaissance of personal literacy and social participation
that sustains the democratic promise the Web's pioneers first envisioned.
In this new world, bloggers have a role to play that is precisely opposite
the one in which critics have cast them. Far from wrecking culture, they
will help preserve it.

In the early days of the Web it was commonly agreed, not only by
critics but by many technophiles, that "people wouldn't read online." The
Web was good for scanning snippets, not for reading long articles. There
was some truth to this, but over time, each of the objections to reading
on the Web has evaporated. On most broadband connections, lengthy
pages don't take long to download anymore. Scrolling down a page, it
turns out, is not an advanced skill. Carrying a laptop—or a new e-book
reader—is no more difficult than carrying a hardcover book, and far easier than hauling around three or four. The oldest line in this litany—"You
can't read online in the bathtub!"—may still hold true (although iPhones
and Blackberries have begun to overcome this limitation). But the need
for waterproof bathing distractions hasn't been enough to stem the flight
of readers from paper to digital formats.

Today it's obvious that people *do* read on the Web, both blog posts
and long articles, willingly and in ever-increasing volume. More people
are passing pieces of writing to one another than ever before in human

history. Certainly, there's a lot of "wtf OMG! ck this out" in this torrent of text; there's also an ocean of philosophical musing and political debate and private confession. Readers shunning the telegraphic chat and seeking the substantial discourse will find themselves following a lot of blogs. As new, faster, and ever more casual forms of online communication capture our fancy, they are helping us see blogging's virtues in clearer relief.

For all the novelty surrounding it, the act of blogging is fundamentally literary. A blogger selects some information or experience, shapes it into words and sentences, and hoists it into public view. Linking may change some aspects of reading, and comment threads and permalinks and RSS feeds may dot the screen, but at heart blogging is a species of writing, in the direct line of descent from the Rosetta Stone through Shakespeare to *The New Yorker* (and the *Weekly World News*). Although a blog lives for today, in the moment, more than most other literary forms, its record is intended for the future as well. That is why so many bloggers obsessively maintain their archives, painstakingly reformatting older entries to survive each transition from one publishing system to the next.

Will today's blogs survive long enough to matter to future generations? Most of us are intensely aware of the fragility of digital data: a life savings of information can vanish with the theft of a laptop or the crash of an unbacked-up hard disk. Many early blogs have disappeared from the Web, leaving little or no trace. If you run your own blog software, your writing is unlikely to survive you; if you rely on a Web-based service like Blogger, TypePad, or Wordpress.com, your words' fate is bound up with those companies' welfare. Words on the Web, we rightly fear, are ephemeral.

On the other hand, data on the Internet has a remarkably enduring half-life. Copying bits is what computers do—they are, as Cory Doctorow says, "copying machines." Copies of most material that has been posted online since the late 1990s exist in some form somewhere—a lot of it at the nonprofit Internet Archive—unless the author blocked it from being copied (and even then, some of it survives). "Lots of copies keeps stuff safe" is a mantra among digital archivists. Once a document has been widely dispersed on the Internet, it is difficult to suppress, even when you try, and have the legal right to do so.

Paper fades; bits get deleted. Libraries burn; disks crash. Whatever the medium, permanence is out of reach. No matter: bloggers might hope to be read by children or even grandchildren, but few dream of immortality for their words. They write to amuse themselves or vent a frustration or record some significant moment; they seek to inform their friends or impress their peers or leave a message in a bottle for some reader as yet unknown. To do so, they rely on an ancient technology that remains mysterious and powerful. As the novelist William Gibson once put it, "I make black marks on a white surface and someone else in another location looks at them and interprets them and sees a spaceship or whatever. It's magic. . . . It's very old magic, but it's very thorough." Whether the surface is paper or screen, the magic functions identically, passing thoughts, ideas, and experiences from person to person acoss time.

They do not, however, pass in a raw state. They are distilled. To write anything, even a casual blog post, one must choose what to say, and what to leave out. The canvas of a Web page only seems boundless; the writer's time is limited, the reader's more so. The Web has made it possible for us to write more, to distill more and consume more, and the result, skeptics sniff, is a dim tide of amateurism and mediocrity. But blogging's critics have been so incensed over the ways in which blogging differs from the literary past that they have missed the ways in which it carries literary values into the future.

While cultural mandarins and displaced journalists have trained their withering fire on the renegades of blogging, they have been mostly oblivious to a far more radical transformation of media that is beginning to materialize on the horizon. Today, cheap video cameras, wireless networking, and low-cost mass storage are becoming ubiquitous. As a steadily growing band of futurists predicts, this infrastructure will make it possible for people to record, store, and share chunks of their lives effortlessly, and at a level of detail unimaginable today. In this future, eventually, everything that you see, hear, and read—every conversation you have, every meal you eat, every Web page or TV show you take in—may be automatically recorded for future reference.

Already, some brave (or foolhardy) souls are beginning to explore these scenarios. "Lifeloggers" record personal data—photos, videos, text documents, anything that can be reduced to bits—for their own private use, and sometimes as a legacy for descendants. Gordon Bell, a veteran computer scientist and Microsoft researcher, has been using himself as a guinea pig for one such lifelogging project for nearly a decade. "Lifecasters" do the same thing, but also open up the feeds of their experience for others on the Web to follow.

Enthusiasts for lifelogging envision it as endowing us with "outboard brains" (in Cory Doctorow's old phrase for his blog), cognitive crutches that relieve our overloaded "wetware" memories of the need to try to store too much detail. Personal-productivity coaches like David Allen (*Getting Things Done*) have long preached the value of offloading mental detail to recording systems, freeing our brains for more creative and important work. Kevin Kelly takes an optimistic view of the personal-data packrat future:

> What value can there be in saving every email, every web page EVER, every keystroke? . . . While the value of ubiquitous monitoring seems nil at first, data streams of trivial actions are often the streams that become most valuable later on. Your night-to-night sleep patterns are worthless right now, but they might form an incredibly valuable baseline in the future if some emerging illness were to disturb them.

Charlie Stross, the science-fiction writer, sees a boon for future historians:

> This century we're going to learn a lesson about what it means to be unable to forget anything. What I can be

fairly sure of is that our descendants' relationship with their history is going to be very different from our own, because they will be able to see it with a level of depth and clarity that nobody has ever experienced before.

For years, bloggers have been castigated for capturing quotidian thoughts and events that ought to have been left unrecorded and unpublished. The status updates of Facebook and Twitter are driving us even deeper into thickets of ephemera. Yet neither can compare to the blanket self-chronicling that now beckons in the projects of lifeloggers and lifecasters. Whatever their ultimate value or futility, these prosthetic memories make the practice of blogging, with its patient word-by-word recording of items and incidents of interest, look hidebound and quaint by comparison. Bloggers record selectively, whereas the lifelogger's "record" light is on by default. The idea is to save everything now and worry about organizing it—or letting software organize it—later. This approach is easier, less labor-intensive than actually choosing, editing, and filtering as you go along; you just flip the switch and put it out of your mind, as the words and images of your life get vacuumed up. The promise of a sort of permanent record of our existence for very little effort is a tantalizing one.

But forgetting how to forget has its drawbacks, too. Skeptics, along with lifeloggers themselves, wonder about the social and personal consequences of the fully recorded life. As Gordon Bell once put it, "Fifty years from now, do you want to know that, gee, I visited a porn site today?" There are subtler pitfalls as well. As danah boyd, a researcher in social networking, asks, "Imagine that you had to face every uncomfortable dating situation ever for the rest of your life, every awkward disconnect, every terrible blind date, every painfully unpleasant interaction. Would you ever date again?"

Anyone who has read the stories of Jorge Luis Borges will recall his sad tale of "Funes the Memorious," about a young man whose memory behaves similarly to a lifelogger's recording apparatus, but who finds his prodigal recall more torment than comfort. There is another image from Borges (from his piece "Of Exactitude in Science") that's even more useful in thinking about lifelogging: the concept of a map so detailed that it is as large as the territory it describes.

> The College of Cartographers evolved a Map of the Empire that was of the same Scale as the Empire and that coincided with it point for point. Less attentive to the Study of Cartography, succeeding Generations came to judge a map of such Magnitude cumbersome, and, not without Irreverence, they abandoned it to the Rigours of sun and Rain.

When every moment is preserved, who will have world enough and time to explore the voluminous record? Of course we can rely on technology to do the filtering for us, and no doubt the tools for searching and organizing even such vast troves of data will continue to improve. But enabling you to find someone's phone number or even recall someone's face is one thing; finding the pieces of memory that fit together to tell a story is quite another. And in the end, that's what we want and need to remember about our lives, and the lives of others: not factual details but meaningful stories.

Narratives—stories with beginnings, middles, and ends; stories in which something important changes; stories that "have a point"—are the format for our long term memories. We can't necessarily name the date or exact location of something that happened in our families two decades ago, but we do recall "the time that" this happened to us, or one of our siblings did that. Over the years our minds perform for us the work of boiling down the raw material of memory into the thicker stuff of a story. But it is the same work that any piece of personal writing accomplishes, and that personal blogging does, too. A post is a shared memory—one that, unlike the raw footage of lifelogging, has been transmuted into a more useful and compelling form.

Even the blogger who posts as an expert rather than an autobiographer, or who simply compiles annotated links on a topic, is performing a service of a similar nature. Of course anyone can use Google to find a link. Google is like a lifelog; everything is there for you to rummage through. But what about when you don't have a specific question in mind, but you just want to learn about a subject—Social Security, maybe, or custom tailoring? In those cases, a good blogger on the topic serves as an expert friend and narrator. Readers today or in the future who wish to understand the story of Social Security privatization in 2005 will find no more useful account than the one provided by Josh Marshall's posts from that era; readers who want to learn about the nature of specialty "bespoke" tailoring in modern times will find the whole story on Thomas Mahon's blog. The blogger who culls links on a subject is telling a story, too. If you want to understand what happened in the tech industry at the height of the dotcom boom, you can get one opinionated, rich overview simply by reading through the Scripting News archives from that era. And if you want to understand the explosion of geek culture over the past decade, the collected posts of Boing Boing tell the tale.

Skeptics often disparage the value of the record that blogs provide by pointing to their fragmentary nature. Reading blogs is like being "beaten to death with croutons," as Bruce Sterling once put it. But this dismissal of blogging on the basis of its unit of composition suffers from its own kind of forest-for-the-trees blindness. Blogs are composed of fragments, but a good blog's fragments are not simply random chunks. What every decent blog offers is a point of view. As the futurist Paul Saffo wrote in 1994, before either the Web or blogging had entered the popular consciousness, "In a world of hyperabundant content, point of view will become the scarcest of resources."

A blog's posts, then, are little pieces, but on a good blog they are created according to an individual vision, and they are assembled for a reason. They are not just broken shards; they are fragments that, in T. S. Eliot's celebrated phrase from *The Waste Land*, we have "shored against our ruins." Eliot was a collector of fragments himself: he assembled his poem out of broken tiles of verbiage plucked from classical mythology, Elizabethan verse, and Sanskrit texts, then helpfully (or self-mockingly) provided his own footnotes to the lot. These fragments were bits of cultural flotsam, rescued from the ruins of an unimaginably devastating war. A century later, we have seen ruin upon further ruin, and fragments are now the familiar shape of everything culture has left.

In the face of such a legacy, to hold the poor blogger responsible for the crack-up of old forms and verities seems simply ignorant. Bloggers did not smash culture apart in the first place, and many are doing the patient work of picking up its remnants, tapping on them, figuring out which might still be useful or diverting.

Hostile observers have always painted bloggers as barbarians thronging before the gates of a besieged culture. This picture has been embraced by some bloggers themselves, who have fancied the rough garb of the invader and relished the license to pillage. But it has always been a fantasy. Bloggers are writers who sit down to type character after character, word upon word, day by day, steadily constructing, out of their fragments, little edifices of memory and public record. In this activity they resemble not the hordes outside the gates of a city, but rather the studious scribes within. Individually they are stewards of their own experience; together they are curators of our collective history. Their work may be less polished and professional than that of many of their predecessors. But they are more passionate, more numerous, and more inclusive — and therefore more likely to succeed in saving what matters.

TWILIGHT OF THE CYNICS

n 1974, having a computer in your basement was like having a robot in your garage or a UFO on your back lawn: you got visitors.

That year, a refrigerator-sized Digital Equipment PDP-4 had landed in my classmate Matthew Diller's Queens home through the extravagant largesse of his family's friend, a young man named Ray Kurzweil. Kurzweil (who would go on to a storied career as an inventor and futurist) had previously given Diller a toy computer kit as a holiday present and helped him build it. But the result was, he declared, a piece of junk, and he took the gift back, promising to replace it with something better.

Months later the budding computer entrepreneur reappeared in front of my friend's house with a trailer full of equipment. The PDP-4 required a room of its own; the Dillers stashed it by the laundry.

Under Kurzweil's eye, Diller struggled to write a checkers program for the machine. I couldn't get excited about that. But something else about the system had snagged my interest.

The PDP-4 ate its programs from long ribbons of yellow paper tape with rows of punched holes. The yard-high teletype that sat by the computer would spit these tapes out as you typed; you'd rip them off, roll them up, and then feed them to the computer's processor. But the teletype could also read its own tapes back and, like a player piano repeating a piece of music, retype their contents—computer programs or any kind of text—on its scrolling paper. In other words, you could, if you chose, bypass the brain of this rare digital machine and dragoon the hulk into service as a printing press.

My friends and I were plotting to start our own magazine to host games of postal Diplomacy. Diplomacy is a board game that requires seven players to start and many hours to finish. Neither of these was ever easy to find. So devotees had started playing the game by mail, with moves published every three weeks or so. This eased the procurement of a minyan, but prolonged the game to an epic two years.

Most Diplomacy 'zines were published by mimeograph or ditto. We didn't have the hardware for that yet—we were fifteen-year-olds. But now, miraculously, we had a computer to help us publish.

It is hard, today, after a decade and a half of Web history, to remember how much effort kids, and adults, used to put into publishing their words. At the time, I took the trouble for granted. I sat down at Diller's teletype in his dim basement and cautiously pecked out a paper tape. (Corrections were impossible.) Then I ran it back through the machine, over and over, patiently hovering to make sure the frail punchtape didn't rip, until we had our fifty-copy print run.

I didn't care that the result was smudgy, crude, ill-formatted in upper-case-only characters. It delighted me.

I became infatuated with the Web in the summer of 1994, early in its story, but I can't claim any great prescience as a technofuturist. I just loved publishing, and when I looked at the microchip marvels of personal computers and the engineering wonders of the Internet that linked them together, I saw merely a bigger, better teletype or mimeograph machine. Still, that was fun enough. I abandoned my newspaper career and dove headfirst into the new medium with my friends and colleagues at Salon.

I'd been publishing little periodicals all my life, and it was obvious to me how to publish one on the Web. You needed a cover page, a table of contents, and article pages. Links were intriguing but hardly revolutionary. What was great about the Web was that you no longer needed a newspaper's presses and trucks. You didn't even need the old-school 'zine publisher's drums of mimeo ink, reams of paper, staples, and stamps—the *stuff* of publishing. Atoms were middlemen, and we were cutting them out. Publishing on the Web seemed about as close as we were likely to get in this life to a Vulcan mind-meld. Between your words and your readers, there was no *matter* left—just pure thought.

This was roughly true, as far as it went. But my picture of what one could and should do as a Web publisher turned out to be limited by all the things I already knew about publishing. There was so much more that was important about the Web, and the people who discovered those things were outsiders or kids unencumbered by any experience of "how it's done," or eccentrics and dreamers uninhibited by an awareness of what couldn't be done.

Dave Winer visited us at Salon in 1999 and told me that we should give every one of our reporters a weblog. I'd met him on a few occasions and had been reading Scripting News for a while, and didn't immediately dismiss the idea as a pipe dream. But at the time we were too busy replicating the processes (and high costs) of a traditional newsroom on the Web to listen to him. To us, as to so many others, it was hard to see the significance of blogging amid the onslaught of Web-based innovations clamoring for our attention. This business of short, link-laden bits of text piled up on a page looked trivial.

That word runs through the story of blogging, from its earliest days to the present, like a dismissive refrain. Evan Williams's Blogger team worried that their little product was too trivial a hack to be worth turning into a product. In an introduction to Mark Frauenfelder's article on blogging that he was publishing in *Whole Earth Review* in 2000, Kevin

Kelly wrote, "It is hard to tell whether this is a trivial exploitation of this technology, or profound." As blogging began to be embraced by a wider spectrum of users, the charge began to be leveled by critics in the media, who expressed their disdain for the sheer triviality of the contents of these newfangled personal publishing projects.

I think we now have the answer to Kelly's question. This is not only because of blogging's popularity; it is certainly possible for a pursuit to be embraced by millions of people and yet still remain trivial. Blogging has earned its claim to significance, not simply in the scale it achieved, but in the way it helped the Web fulfill its original vision as a network for pooling human knowledge and understanding. Among many other roles, blogging has served as a laboratory in which a multitude of writers have experimented with the myriad possibilities of online self-expression. Whatever form that expression takes in the future, and whether or not we still call it blogging a decade from now, these experiments have left a trove of valuable results.

We now know at least a little more about what happens when we try to say everything. For the individual, this impulse begins with a rage for self-revelation and nearly always ends in a crack-up of some kind. Writing in public requires the drawing of boundaries around parts of one's life—not so much for propriety but because some sphere of privacy is a prerequisite for any kind of mature personal life. For the group, the opportunity to say everything has a more benign outcome: a welter of human engagement on an unprecedented scale, resulting in a broad dispersal of ideas and stories and debates.

In one of his comic monologues, Spalding Gray tells the story of how he once lost a role in a TV drama. Gray recalls the director explaining the problem: "He could always see something that he could only describe as *thinking* pass over my face every time I made a move." And that was inexcusable. TV, the dominant medium of the era that we are now leaving, has its virtues, but it is remarkably inhospitable to thought. The Web, by contrast, welcomes it, inviting the marshaling of arguments, the assembly (or linkage) of supporting data, the exchange of challenge and response.

I began my writing career as a theater and movie critic. Sometimes, after a curtain or a screening, people would ask me what I thought of what we'd just seen. And much of the time I'd draw a blank. "I don't know," I'd mutter. "I haven't written my piece yet." Writing for public consumption is not a simple matter of typing up polished views or ideas that already exist; the difficult act of writing precipitates the even more difficult act of thinking. The opportunity to write has always been available to anyone with an education, but until very recently the opportunity to publish one's writing has been rare and prized. By making that opportunity nearly universal, blogging has changed something fundamental in our culture. Writing in public lets you discover what you really think by attempting to set your thoughts in prose and "putting your views at risk" (Christopher Lasch's phrase) in front of strangers. Now anyone who wants a taste of this experience can have it. Not everyone will avail themselves of it, but some portion of those who do will come away with a better knowledge of their own minds.

Trying to pin down what you actually think by writing it out sometimes has a salutary side effect: you discover that your mind has changed. The last decade of blogging has provided some extraordinary spectacles of thoughtful people changing their views in real time. The most eminent case is that of Andrew Sullivan. A longtime maverick conservative who endorsed George W. Bush in 2000 and cheer-led Bush's bellicose response to 9/11 and the invasion of Iraq, Sullivan later found himself disgusted by the Bush administration's condoning of torture, its record at Guantanamo and Abu Ghraib, and its incompetence in the Iraq aftermath and the Hurricane Katrina fiasco. Over the course of several years, post by post, he crossed the political divide, and by 2008 he was vigorously supporting Barack Obama. He admitted that his public about-face "wasn't pretty at times," but he stood by all his contradictions, explaining his evolution whenever challenged.

Public figures commonly handle a change of position by hiding or denying any inconsistency. Leaders today face inscrutably complex problems that demand flexible responses, yet mainstream political norms enforce a rigidity on their views; even the most rational shift in the face of changing circumstances can trigger the attack-ad charge of flip-flop. Bloggers often join in this crude haranguing. Sullivan offers an opposite model: deny nothing; chronicle the change in your views; take the reader along on your journey. This model is likely to be seen more widely in coming decades, as many more participants in the public realm arrive on the scene dragging long strings of blog posts behind them.

And if you are not a public figure, why might you bother to chronicle the twists and turns of your political views, the ups and downs of your personal life? There is, as we have seen, the value in learning your own mind. There is also the simple value in making connection with those who happen upon your posts. Putting it this way sounds almost unbearably mundane, like a self-help pep talk; it's the sort of observation that hardbitten media types meet with the back of a callused hand. *What sort of person needs to turn to the Internet to make human connections?* they will sniff, as they fire off clichés about online communication being a poor substitute for in-person engagement.

These clichés are true enough. But they have become clichés because they keep getting repeated—even as we keep ignoring them. For some wide population of bloggers, there is ample reason to keep writing about a troubled marriage or a cancer diagnosis or a death in the family, regardless of how many ethical dilemmas must be traversed, or how trivial or amateurish their labors are judged. Maybe their writing provides some diversion or insight or solace. Maybe it leaves them feeling a little less lonely. Surely an activity able to accomplish that ought to be granted an exemption from condescension.

The story I have traced in this book encompasses a long-running argument between idealists and cynics over the value and import of blogging. During the fifteen years that I've covered the rise of the Web, I've watched this debate seesaw endlessly, as the idealists breathlessly champion the new medium's excitement and potential, and the cynics irritatedly snort at its shortcomings and tawdry excesses.

Except at the peaks of the business cycle, when bubble-borne profits incited crazy dreams even among the conventionally minded, the jaded dismissals have usually had the edge. I have heard, over and over again, that the traits that first excited me about the Web—its openness, variety, unpredictability, and freedom—were doomed in the long run, that such manifestations of a wild youth would evaporate once maturity set in. Business models would coalesce, the pros would elbow the gifted amateurs aside, and the media world would return to its natural course, in which a few people decide what information most people receive. This strange new medium that didn't seem to resemble its predecessors at all would settle down and end up looking very much like them.

This was the chorus early on in the mid-1990s, when the introduction of Web advertising and e-commerce first suggested the Web could be a business as well as a hobby. It was heard again at the height of the dotcom bubble, when the venture-capital investors and IPOs turned the Web into a hall of mirrored greed. Again it rang out during the bust, when media companies felt they could safely dismiss the teeming online rabble and return to calling the shots. And it was heard again through the mid-2000s, as a new boom attracted another wave of gold-diggers determined to monetize eyeballs and page-views. To those who cherished the Web for what it already was, rather than for how much money it might make or for what it might be turned into, the message each time was the same: *Enjoy it now—it won't last.*

I found myself asking, each time, whether the cynics were right. The years I'd spent working as a critic had imbued me with my own skeptical streak. But I was spending much of my time on the Web, and everything I experienced there told me that the idealists and the amateurs grasped what worked there much better than the cynics and the pros. Simple beat busy. Personal beat corporate. Links beat walls and gates. For years I'd wondered whether the cynical diagnosis, which offered itself as the wisdom of experience, might actually represent the resentment of a dying order. Finally I concluded that it did.

Blogging looked inconsequential and sounded ridiculous, yet it turned out to matter, while a parade of overhyped Web ventures devised by people who ostensibly knew what they were doing fizzled into oblivion. (If names like Time Warner's Pathfinder or Disney's Go.com no longer mean anything to you, that proves my point.) This pattern shows no sign of petering out.

The anarchic, energetic Web I fell in love with fifteen years ago has indeed lasted. It continues to provide people of meager credentials and little means with a home for their idiosyncratic ideas and unlikely innovations. Their ideas will continue to flow in a profusion of unpredictable courses. And their innovations will continue to bear names that make you feel slightly silly when you say them—as the word *blog* once did.

Sneering at all these creations remains a tempting option—one that is even warranted on occasion. Thoughtful skepticism always has its place. But the Web's outpouring of human expression deserves a more exuberant response, too. It should delight us.

AUTHOR'S NOTE AND ACKNOWLEDGMENTS

Though I have aimed for accuracy, I can make no claim to completeness. The pioneers and innovators whose stories this book tells would have a place in any chronicle of the rise of blogging. But the other examples I have included could easily have been replaced by many equally relevant and worthy alternatives. I tried to select stories from blogging's recent past that might not have been told fully already elsewhere and that seemed to have something to teach us. But there are many blogospheres; each contains a multitude of fascinating stories; any book can hoist only a handful into the light.

These pages traverse roughly fifteen years of the Web's development, and in the best of all worlds all of that history would be laid out in front of us in a beautiful and functioning network of links. Some of it still is. (You can find a full duplicate of the book's endnotes online, and properly linked, at http://www.sayeverything.com.) But much of this record, par-ticularly from the 1990s, is already plagued by link rot and page decay.

In tracking down some of the fugitive older stories, I have relied on the extraordinary collection of the Internet Archive. The Archive's repository of old pages represents a precious communal resource whose value will only grow with time. I am grateful for it, and for the foresight of its founder, Brewster Kahle, who started taking snapshots of the Web long before people realized they were going to want them.

I haven't counted the people who sat for extended interviews, shared old files and other information with me, or simply helped me confirm some wayward fact via telephone or email. But they number well into the hundreds, and I am thankful for every minute of their time.

I was lucky to have thoughtful friends and colleagues review the manuscript: Josh Kornbluth (a sharp copy editor still!), Andrew Leonard, Jay Rosen, Dan Gillmor, Matt Haughey, Ducky Sherwood, and Mike Pence.

I must thank Stuart Krichevsky, my sage agent (and also his colleagues Shana Cohen and Kathryne Wick); my sterling editors Rachel Klayman, who championed and guided this project, and Lucinda Bartley, who edited each page with a sharp eye; my ace publicist, Penny Simon; and the rest of the team at Crown: Patty Berg, Stephanie Chan, Tina Constable, Maria Elias, Kevin Garcia, Kyle Kolker, Donna Passannante, Annsley Rosner, Patty Shaw, and Jay Sones.

Thanks to my sons, Jack and Matthew, for putting up with my extended work hours over the past year; to my parents, Jeanne and Coleman Rosenberg, for their encouragement and support; and, always, to my wife and first reader, Dayna Macy, to whom this book is dedicated, with love and gratitude for her acumen and her esprit.

INTRODUCTION

1 *"Something very terrible just happened"* James Marino's posts are at http://
www.broadwaystars.com/news/2001_09_09_starchive.shtml#5625730.

4 AP's 8:55 AM report: http://www.interactivepublishing.net/september/browse
.php?time=2001-09-11-9#.

4 Metafilter's 8:58 AM report: http://www.metafilter.com/10034/.

4 *"at these times there's two types"* Justin Hall's 9/11 post is at http://www
.links.net/daze/01/09/attack.html.

4 Evan Williams's page aggregating Blogger posts from 9/11 is at http://web.archive
.org/web/20010921091048/www.blogger.com/news_archive.pyra.

5 *"I see this as an opportunity"* Dave Winer's 9/11 posts are at http://www
.scripting.com/2001/09/11.html.

6 *In September 2001, conventional wisdom* E.g., "Web content is dead as an
independent business," John Motavalli, *Bamboozled at the Revolution: How Big Media
Lost Billions in the Battle for the Internet* (Viking, 2002), p. 302.

6 *study of media consumption on and after 9/11* The Pew Internet & American Life
Project studied Americans' media use at several intervals after the attacks. The one-
year-later report at http://www.pewinternet.org/report_display.asp?r=69 is the most
comprehensive.

7 *"Only through the human stories"* Nick Denton in *The Guardian*, at http://web
.archive.org/web/20010021005058/www.guardian.co.uk/Archive/Article/0,1277,
420088,00.html.

7 *"When the Maine was sunk"* David Weinberger, JOHO, Sept. 27, 2001, at
http://www.hyperorg.com/backissues/joho-sep27-01.html#news.

7 *blogging had "come of age"* In CNET, at http://www.news.com/2010-1071-81560
.html?legacy=cnet.

9 A version of Tim Berners-Lee's W3 Servers page can be found at http://www.w3
.org/History/19921103-hypertext/hypertext/DataSources/WWW/Servers.html.
Note that this represents the page as of Nov. 3, 1992. In correspondence via email,

Berners-Lee recalled that the top portion of the page's list was organized in a reverse chronology, with the newest additions added to the top, though none are dated.

10 *"everybody should be using the Web"* This and following quotations taken from author interview with Andreessen, Feb. 29, 2008.

10 NCSA *What's New page* http://web.archive.org/web/20020623141952/http://wp.netscape.com/home/whatsnew/whats_new_0693.html.

10 *The top of the page would display first* Joshua Quittner and Michelle Slatalla, *Speeding the Net: The Inside Story of Netscape and How It Challenged Microsoft* (Atlantic Monthly Press, 1998), p. 126.

11 *"The initial WorldWideWeb program opened"* Tim Berners-Lee, *Weaving the Web: The Original Design and Ultimate Destiny of the World Wide Web by Its Inventor* (HarperSanFrancisco, 1999), p. 157.

12 *"By many measures . . . the Web reached"* Michael Hiltzik in the *Los Angeles Times*, Aug. 13, 1997, reposted by CNN Interactive at http://www.cnn.com/TECH/9708/13/web.substance.lat/index.html.

12 *most of the Web was "crap"* Michael Kinsley, quoted by Howard Kurtz in the *Washington Post*, "Kinsley Tabs Over to On-Line Magazine for Microsoft," Nov. 7, 1995.

12 *"The first time you go on the Web"* Michael Kinsley, interviewed in Folio magazine, Feb 1, 1997, at http://findarticles.com/p/articles/mi_m3065/is_n2_v26/ai_19077993.

CHAPTER 1
PUTTING EVERYTHING OUT THERE

18 *"It's so much fun . . . putting everything out there"* Justin Hall on camera in *Home Page*, 1998 documentary film by Doug Block.

18 *"I really enjoy urinating"* http://www.links.net/daze/05/01/02/whew.html.

18 *"smart, motivated gal"* http:// www.links.net/daze/05/01/02/meet_an_angel.html.

18 *In their place was a little search box* You can trace the changes on Hall's home page via the snapshots captured by the Internet Archive at http://web.archive.org/web/*/http://links.net.

18 *Dark Night* video: http://www.links.net/daze/05/01/14/dark_night_flick.html.

20 *"raised by a series of nannies"* http://www.links.net/vita/.

20 *"It wasn't just a bunch of fifteen-year-olds"* This and following quotations not otherwise sourced are from interviews with the author conducted in 2008.

20 *"a map to the buried treasures"* John Markoff's Dec. 8, 1993, *New York Times* article about the new World Wide Web is at http://query.nytimes.com/gst/fullpage.html?res=9F0CE1D6113FF93BA35751C1A965958260&sec=&spon=&pagewanted=all.

21 Justin Hall's first Web page is at http://web.archive.org/web/19980128021607/links.net/vita/web/start/original.html.

21   *"Ranjit's HTTP playground"* http://web.archive.org/web/19990203094324/http://www.moonmilk.com/playground.html.

22   *"lunch server"* http://www.moonmilk.com/previous/miscellany/lunch.html. Bhatnagar, in an interview with the author, says he got the idea from another Internet user named Sho Kuwamoto, who'd offered his lunch information each day via his ".plan" file—a sort of personal-bio dossier that early Internet users creatively repurposed. "It was a fun tiny bit of personal information, like a proto Twitter," Bhatnagar says.

23   *"Either the guy was such a brazen suckup"* Howard Rheingold tells the story of his meeting Hall at http://www.well.com/~hlr/jam/justin/justin.html.

24   *"the era of public-access Internet has come to an end"* Louis Rossetto's quote is in Gary Wolf, *Wired: A Romance* (Random House, 2003), p. 113.

26   *"Prodigious Personal Publishing Potential"* http://www.links.net/webpub/.

26   *"we abide by the principle which dictates"* Suck's manifesto is reprinted in Joey Anuff and Ana Marie Cox, eds., *Suck: Worst-case Scenarios in Media, Culture, Advertising, and the Internet* (Wired, 1997), page viii. Matt Sharkey wrote a thorough history of Suck.com at http://www.keepgoing.org/issue20_giant/the_big_fish.html.

27   *"probably the folks in the room"* http://www.links.net/vita/hw/third.html.

27   *"daily thoughts, a useful notion"* http://www.links.net/daze/96/01/10/.

28   Cyborganic Jeff Goodell wrote a profile of Cyborganic and its creators, titled "The Webheads on Ramona Street," in *Rolling Stone*, Nov. 30, 1995.

29   *"am I afraid that my 5 year old nephew"* http://www.justin.org/law/cda/protect.html.

31   *"There was always a German camera crew"* Author interview with Gary Wolf, May 12, 2008.

32   A famous magazine cover Widely quoted on the Web in this form and credited to a magazine titled *Sniffin Glue*, the original is reprinted in Jon Savage, *England's Dreaming* (St. Martin's, 1992), p. 280, and is actually from the Dec. 1976 issue of *Sideburns*. The exact text here reads: "This is a chord. This is another. This is a third. NOW FORM A BAND."

33   *"The Wyrd of Wired"* http://www.links.net/vita/swat/course/histlang/wyrd.html.

35   *"You know how cats' dicks swell up"* http://www.links.net/vita/corp/catdick/.

35   *"hordes of voyeurs discovered legions of exhibitionists"* Wolf, *Wired*, p. 138.

36   *"What does everyone think of Justin?"* This anecdote is from the *Home Page* documentary.

36   *"neither one of my parents"* Hall onscreen in *Home Page*.

37   *"NewD irections"* . . . *"If everyone was to tell"* http://www.links.net/share/speak/ndn/pubpower.html.

39   *"You can't tell whether he's kidding"* Author interview with Howard Rheingold, April 15, 2008.

39   *"TIME TO GET A LIFE"* *San Francisco Chronicle*, Feb. 20, 2005, at http://www.sfgate.com/cgi-bin/article.cgi?file=/c/a/2005/02/20/MNGBKBEJO01.DTL.

40 *"Something deep in me was being fed"* Hall's post is at http://www.links.net/ daze/05/01/07/wordless.html. Subsequent comments are at http://www.links.net/ daze/05/01/07/wordless-comments.html.

42 *"Everyone has a website"* Author interview with Merci Hammon via email.

CHAPTER 2
THE UNEDITED VOICE OF A PERSON

46 *He sent Canter's invitation* The first DaveNet message is at http://www.scripting .com/davenet/1994/10/07/marccantersingsagain.html. The complete DaveNet archive is at http://www.scripting.com/davenet/index.html.

47 *"Bill Gates vs. the Internet"* DaveNet essay at http://www.scripting.com/davenet /1994/10/18/billgatesvstheinternet.html. Gates's response: DaveNet essay at http:// www.scripting.com/davenet/1994/10/27/replyfrombillgates.html.

48 John Seabrook's "Email from Bill": *The New Yorker*, Jan. 10, 1994, http://www .booknoise.net/johnseabrook/stories/technology/email/index.html.

50 *"Ask any expert who's been interviewed"* Dave Winer, April 16, 2004, posting on the BloggerCon site at http://www.bloggercon.org/2004/04/16.

50 The San Francisco Free Press is archived at http://www.well.com/conf/media/SF_ Free_Press/.

50 *"When I first understood how the Web worked"* This and other direct quotations are from a series of author interviews with Dave Winer in 2008.

51 *"Billions of Websites"* DaveNet essay at http://www.scripting.com/davenet/ 1995/02/18/billionsofwebsites.html.

52 *"We make shitty software"* DaveNet essay at http://www.scripting.com/davenet/ 1995/09/03/wemakeshittysoftware.html.

52 *"A Tough Customer"* DaveNet essay at http://www.scripting.com/davenet/1995/ 02/12/atoughcustomer.html.

55 *Winer sat in a crowd of the industry elite* Winer's account of the Ellison encounter is at http://www.scripting.com/davenet/1996/10/24/QueSeraSera.html. Other details confirmed in author email interview with Stewart Alsop.

55 *"All my life, I've placed the highest value"* Winer's first column for Hotwired is at http://web.archive.org/web/20010610045754/hotwired.lycos.com/davenet/95/ 29/index4a.html.

56 *Newsweek*'s 1995 list of the fifty "Most Influential People to Watch in Cyberspace" is at http://www.newsweek.com/id/106555.

56 *"I'm zooooooooming!"* Suck's DaveNet parody is at http://web.archive.org/ web/20040226210138/suck.com/daily/1996/01/12/.

57 *"I'm right, therefore you're wrong"* Winer's "flame-reduction suggestion" column from Hotwired is at http://web.archive.org/web/20010609040625/hotwired.lycos .com/davenet/96/16/index4a.html.

58 The 24 Hours of Democracy project is archived at http://www.scripting.com/ twentyFour/.

59 The "news page" for the 24 Hours of Democracy project is at http://www.scripting .com/twentyfour/news.html.

59 Earliest archives of Frontier News & Updates page are listed at http://web.archive .org/web/19970415002457/http://www.scripting.com/frontier/admin/oldNews Pages/default.html. The earliest entry, from April 27, 1996, is at http://web.archive .org/web/19970219204546/www.scripting.com/frontier/admin/oldNewsPages/ archives96/jun.html.

59 *Winer changed the name*   The first page labeled Scripting News, from February 1997, is at http://web.archive.org/web/19970721193700/www.scripting.com/ frontier/admin/oldNewsPages/archives97/feb.html.

60 *"Your website has finally started to make sense"*   Eric Sink's email is at http://www.scripting.com/mail/mail981228.html.

63 *"Almost all the other elements can be missing"*   Dave Winer, "What makes a weblog a weblog?"   May   23,   2003,   at   http://blogs.law.harvard.edu/whatmakes aweblogaweblog.html.

65 Third Voice debate: Rogers Cadenhead's first message is at http://lists.userland .com/userLandDiscussArchive/msg011525.html. "If any Third Voice users are tuned in": http://static.userland.com/userLandDiscussArchive/msg011532.html.

65 *"I would certainly object"*   http://lists.userland.com/userLandDiscussArchive/ msg011537.html.

66 *"So much for my theory"*   http://static.userland.com/userLandDiscussArchive/ msg012301.html.

67 *"I'm still spending a lot of time"*   Winer shuts down Userland discussion group, at http://static.userland.com/userLandDiscussArchive/msg021856.html.

67 *"I admire his intellect"*   Greg Knauss, author email interview, May 2008.

67 Winerlog is archived at http://web.archive.org/web/20010221070007/winerlog .editthispage.com/2000/03/02.

68 *one incident, in May 2000*   http://web.archive.org/web/20010124201300/http: //flounder.editthispage.com/discuss/msgReader$177. Also discussed on Metafilter at http://www.metafilter.com/1580/.

69 *"He should get an iPhone"*   http://twitter.com/davewiner/statuses/137599502? Winer's comment responds to http://pulver.blog.pulver.com/archives/007193 .html

69 *"People aren't supposed to listen"*   http://www.scripting.com/2007/07.html

70 Video of Jason Calacanis at Gnomedex is at http://www.youtube.com/watch ?v=C4iTTKF2bkg.

71 *"I hate speeches that are ads"*   http://www.scripting.com/2007/08/10.html.

71 *"What perplexes me is why Dave"*   http://calacanis.com/2007/08/11/on-getting-winered/.

71 *"I wish I hadn't done it"* http://www.scripting.com/stories/2007/08/13/apologies ToCalacanis.html.

71 *"Today I got a brief note"* http://www.scripting.com/stories/2007/08/16/aSacredLine .html.

72 *"A sure way to become a former friend"* http://www.scripting.com/stories/2007/ 08/17/friendshipAndBlogging.html.

CHAPTER 3
THEY SHALL KNOW YOU THROUGH YOUR LINKS

75 *"It feels to me like we've got"* William Gibson interview at http://www.salon.com/ weekly/gibson2961014.html.

76 *"worked on self-discovery"* Jorn Barger, "My background in AI," http://web .archive.org/web/20060314214425/www.robotwisdom.com/ai/jbai.html.

76 *"Joyce modestly bragged"* This and subsequent otherwise unattributed quotes are from author email interview with Barger, March 2008.

76 *"do psychology scientifically"* From "Portrait of the Blogger as a Young Man," Julian Dibbell's profile of Barger in Feed, May 3, 2000, at http://www.juliandibbell.com/ texts/feed_blogger.html.

76 *"Literature . . . is descriptive psychology"* From Barger's profile on Epinions, at http://web.archive.org/web/20060623120148/www.epinions.com/user-jorn.

76 *building a file of index cards* A full account of Barger's AI ideas can be found beginning at http://web.archive.org/web/20060314212941/www.robotwisdom.com/ ai/index.html.

76 *"Anti-Math"* Details at http://web.archive.org/web/20060314202426/http://www .robotwisdom.com/ai/antimath.html and http://web.archive.org/web/2006031423 3535/www.robotwisdom.com/ai/antimath1.html.

77 *"If you enumerate"* http://web.archive.org/web/20060314214315/www.robot wisdom.com/ai/ilsmemoir.html.

77 *"a new paradigm for the social sciences"* From "Solace," at http://web.archive .org/web/20060314212952/www.robotwisdom.com/solace/index.html.

78 Barger and Roger Schank: http://web.archive.org/web/20060314214315/www.robot wisdom.com/ai/ilsmemoir.html.

78 Barger's history on Usenet: http://web.archive.org/web/20060314204152/www .robotwisdom.com/jorn/internet.html.

78 *a "lightning-rod for a-holes"* From a "wikipedia template" of autobiographical information Barger posted in 2007, at http://robotwisdom2.blogspot.com/2007/ 08/jorn-barger-wikipedia-template.html.

78 *"By that point . . . the Web had grown into"* From "The Human Behind Robot Wisdom," 1999 interview with Barger, at http://www.webword.com/interviews/ barger.html.

78   *"finding good stuff and arranging it"* . . . *"At first I didn't intend"*   Author's email interview with Barger.

80   *"It was a way for me to play"*   Author interview with Michael Sippey, April 2008.

80   The earliest extant entry on the Obvious Filter from May 28, 1997, is at http://web.archive.org/web/19971015050716/theobvious.com/filter/filter0597.html.

80   *That didn't stop several media outlets*   "Blogs turn 10—who's the father?", CNET, March 20, 2007, at http://news.com.com/In+search+of+the+creator+of+the+first+blog/2100-1025_3-6168681.html; "Happy Blogiversary," *Wall Street Journal*, July 14, 2007, at http://online.wsj.com/article/SB118436667045766268.html.

80   Steve Bogart's NowThis.com is at http://nowthis.com/oldsite/ and http://nowthis.com/oldsite/archive/. The earliest archives for Harold Stusnick's Offhand Remarks are available from 1999 at http://web.archive.org/web/20000818154140/www.offhand.com/archive/index.html.   Howard   Rheingold's earliest "What's New and Rheingoldian?" page is at http://www.well.com/~hlr/oldnew1.html.

82   *"I try to make it my ethic"*   From Dibbell's "Portrait of the Blogger as a Young Man."

83   Matt Drudge as "the Walter Cronkite of his era" from Mark Halperin and John Harris, *The Way to Win: Taking the White House in 2008* (Random House, 2006).

83   *"the most powerful journalist in America"*   Pat Buchanan on MSNBC's *Scarborough Country*, Oct. 17, 2006, transcript at http://www.msnbc.msn.com/id/15317544/.

83   Philip Weiss's *New York* profile of Drudge is at http://nymag.com/news/media/36617/.

84–85   Drudge's income: Richard Pachter's 2003 profile of Drudge for the *Miami Herald* at http://www.wordsonwords.com/reviews/Drudge903.html included Drudge's estimate of $1.2 million revenue at that time.

85   *Jesse James Garrett was working*   Author interview with Garrett, April 2008.

86   Barrett's blogroll: http://web.archive.org/web/19990128075502/http://www.cambarrett.com/.

86   *Barrett was teaching an introductory Web class*   Author interview with Barrett, March 2008.

89   Rebecca Blood's history of weblogs essay: http://www.rebeccablood.net/essays/weblog_history.html. Blood's observation of discovering her true interests through blogging is also drawn from the same essay. [. . .]

89   Leslie Harpold's "Logrolling" essay from Smug.com: http://web.archive.org/web/19990824022812/http://www.smug.com/29/net.html.

89   Ben Brown's "Open Letter" in Teethmag.com: http://web.archive.org/web/19990921080253/http://www.teethmag.com/showart.pl?pid=50.

92   *"I live on bread and water"*   From Dibbell's "Portrait of the Blogger as a Young Man."

93   *"I have a gigantic psychological block"*   Barger as quoted in Wired News at http://www.wired.com/culture/lifestyle/news/2003/12/61458.

93   Paul Boutin's Wired story: http://www.wired.com/wired/archive/13.07/posts.html?
     pg=6. Boutin's blog corrects the headline: http://paulboutin.weblogger.com/
     2005/07/03/jorn-barger-lost-found-lost-again/.
93   *"libelous fiction"* http://robotwisdom2.blogspot.com/2007/08/jorn-barger-wikipedia-
     template.html.
93   *"He's shy"* Author interview with Andrew Orlowski, June 2008.
93   *On December 26, 1999, he'd posted a link* http://web.archive.org/web/200008
     17182540/http://www.robotwisdom.com/log1999m12b.html.
93   *a writer named Leonard Grossman* http://lgrossman.com/mjnk/mjnk0001.htm.
94   *"Webloggers gamble their reputation"* Barger's post was on Philip Greenspun's
     discussion boards, at http://www.greenspun.com/bboard/q-and-a-fetch-msg.tcl?
     msg_id=002IfK.
95   *"Is Judaism simply a religion"* Barger's link is at http://web.archive.org/
     web/20010118201600/http://www.robotwisdom.com/.
95   *"Are Jews incapable of polite discourse?"* Posted on Philip Greenspun's discussion
     board at http://greenspun.com/bboard/q-and-a-fetch-msg.tcl?msg_id=004ImF.
96   *Barger pinpointed his post about Shahak* http://robotwisdom2.blogspot.com/
     2006/12/my-spiritualesthetic-evolutioneducation.html.

CHAPTER 4
THE BLOGGER CATAPULT

101 *In May 1999, Peter Merholz* Merholz's account of the origins of the term is at
     http://www.peterme.com/archives/00000205.html. The original note in the left-
     hand column is not archived anywhere.
103 *"That seemed like a great idea"* This and subsequent otherwise uncredited quotes
     are from author interview with Williams, August 2007.
104 *Meg Hourihan was her name* This story and all otherwise unattributed material
     about Hourihan is from author interview with Hourihan, March 2008.
105 *"A friend told me this story"* From Meg Hourihan's Megnut blog, April 14, 2000, at
     http://meg.hourihan.com/2000/04/ive-been-thinking-a-lot. .
106 *"New Evidence Suggests"* Evan Williams blog post from November 1998, at
     http://web.archive.org/web/19990911164858/evhead.com/column.asp?id=3.
109 Pyralerts are archived at http://web.archive.org/web/20000523150605/www.pyra
     .com/pyralert_archive.asp.
110 *"The idea was that we'd network"* Author interview with Bausch, April 2008.
110 *the beta version of the Pyra app* Details at http://web.archive.org/web/
     20010212054142/www.pyra.com/1999_08_01_pyralert_archive.asp.
112 *In Seattle, a freshman programming prodigy* LiveJournal details are from Brad
     Fitzpatrick's account of the origins of LiveJournal at http://bradfitz.com/misc/bct/,
     as well as author interview with Fitzpatrick, January 2009.

113 *Paul Kedrosky had converted his personal weblog* Author interview with Paul Kedrosky, July 2008. Kedrosky's brief history of Groksoup is at http://paul.kedrosky .com/archives/2004/08/09/groksoup_and_th.html.

113 *"I'm just a bad business guy"* Author interview with Andrew Smales, July 2008.

114 *"My Ass is a Weblog"* Greg Knauss writing on Michael Sippey's Stating the Obvious, at http://www.theobvious.com/archive.html?112299.

114 *"It's much easier to feel like you're tuned in"* February 2001 interview with Evan Williams at writetheweb.com, http://web.archive.org/web/20011120165654 /http://writetheweb.com/read.php?item=107.

115 *Rebecca Blood . . . suggested* From "Weblogs: A History and Perspective," at http://www.rebeccablood.net/essays/weblog_history.html.

115 *In February 2000, Wired News took note* Leander Kahney's piece is at http:// www.wired.com/culture/lifestyle/news/2000/02/34006.

115 *On April 14 the official Blogger news page* http://web.archive.org/web/ 20011003223424/www.blogger.com/news_archive.pyra?which–2000_04_01_ news_archive.xml.

119 *he didn't want to be the "asshole"* This quotation is from the interview with Williams in *Founders at Work: Stories of Startups' Early Days* (Apress, 2007), p. 118.

119 *Both Paul Bausch and Matt Haughey remember thinking* Author interviews with Bausch and Haughey, April 2008.

120 *"You've Got Blog"* Rebecca Mead's *New Yorker* piece is at http://www.new yorker.com/archive/2000/11/13/2000_11_13_102_TNY_LIBRY_000022068, and also reprinted in *We've Got Blog: How Weblogs Are Changing Our Culture* (Perseus, 2002).

120 *"And Then There Was One"* http://web.archive.org/web/20011214143830/ http://www.evhead.com/longer/2200706_essays.asp.

121 *"It seems stupid now"* Matt Haughey's account of Pyra's shutdown is at http://www.haughey.com/pyra.html.

121 *"I loved Blogger more than Pyra"* Paul Bausch's thoughts on the Pyra shutdown are at http://web.archive.org/web/20010208104656/http://onfocus.com/pyra.asp.

122 *"On January 16th, every employee"* Hourihan's post is at http://web.archive .org/web/20010917033719/http://www.megnut.com/archive.asp?which=2001_ 02_01_archive.inc.

123 *The troll in talking in weblogging* Dan Bricklin's post on the Trellix-Blogger deal is at http://danbricklin.com/log/blogger.htm.

124 "The Idealist," by Alex Lash, *The Industry Standard*, May 28, 2001, at http:// findarticles.com/p/articles/mi_m0HWW/is_21_4/ai_75532465/pg_13/.

125 *"We said there are three companies"* Author interview with Jason Shellen, August 2008. Other details on the Google negotiations are from author email interview with Mark Jacobsen of O'Reilly, December 2008.

126 *Google had no history* Before the Blogger deal, Google had previously bought

Deja News, which maintained an archive of Usenet, but that deal involved acquiring the archive as an asset, not integrating a functioning company with a working team of employees.

126 *"the Blogger Effect"* Steven Johnson's article, "Use the Blog, Luke," is at http://dir.salon.com/story/tech/feature/2002/05/10/blogbrain/index.html.

127 *Terms of the deal have never* It's difficult to calculate how much the deal was worth to Williams even if we knew the terms—for instance, how many Google shares he ended up with. Since Google was a private company at the time, there is no public record of its stock price or total valuation. Even if we knew or could guess what Google might have pegged Pyra's value at in 2003—$25 million was a number bandied about at the time—we don't know how many Google shares that translated into then. Furthermore, we don't know at which point in the meteoric post-IPO climb of Google's stock price Williams might have sold shares, or how many.

128 *from three thousand accounts in early 2000* This figure is drawn from http://www.wired.com/culture/lifestyle/news/2000/02/34006.

128 *100,000 a year later* The number is from "Who's Blogging Now?" *Newsweek*, March 5, 2001, at http://www.newsweek.com/id/80101/page/2.

128 *over a million . . . at the time of the Google deal* http://searchenginewatch .com/showPage.html?page=2161891.

129 *"profoundly, spectacularly, epically wrong"* Knauss, from author email interview, May 2008.

130 *In a talk at a 2007 conference* Williams's talk at the Web 2.0 Conference was covered at http://www.informationweek.com/blog/main/archives/2007/10/live blogging_we_2.html.

γ

CHAPTER 5
THE RISE OF POLITICAL BLOGGING

132 *But he found himself frustrated* Author interview with Josh Marshall, April 2008. Also "The (Josh) Marshall Plan," by David Glenn, *Columbia Journalism Review*, Sept. 2007, at http://www.cjr.org/feature/the_josh_marshall_plan.php ?page=all.

132 *the first post at a new blog* http://www.talkingpointsmemo.com/archives/ week_2000_11_12.php

134 *"There was hardly any curiosity"* Author interview with Dan Gillmor, August 2008.

135 *"I didn't know it was a blog"* Author interview with Mickey Kaus, August 2008.

136 *each time he needed to post something new* Author email interview with Andrew Sullivan, August 2008.

136 *"With only a few hundred readers"* "A Blogger Manifesto," Andrew Sullivan, February 2002, at http://web.archive.org/web/20020329011512/http://www .andrewsullivan.com/print.php?artnum=20020224.

137 Earliest entries from Bob Somerby's Daily Howler: http://www.dailyhowler.com /archives_98.shtml. From Virginia Postrel's The Scene, http://www.dynamist.com /weblog/archives/2000/dec25.html. From Glenn Reynolds' Instapundit, http://www .pajamasmedia.com/instapundit-archive/oldarchives/2001_08_05_instapundit_ archive.html.

138 *"marinating in the deeper wells"* Author email interview with Matt Welch, August 2008.

138 *"Welcome to War"* http://www.mattwelch.com/archives/2001/09/16-week/.

139 *"a linebacker-style hit"* Matt Welch, "Farewell to Warblogging," *Reason*, April 2006, at http://www.reason.com/news/show/33290.html.

139 *"I was a block away from the South Tower"* Author interview with Jeff Jarvis, March 2008.

139 *"a conservative is a liberal who has been mugged"* Jeff Jarvis interview at http://normblog.typepad.com/normblog/2003/12/the_normblog_pr_2.html.

140 Charles Johnson self-description as "center-liberal" is at http://www.israelnational news.com/News/News.aspx/62000.

140 *"The 'war bloggers' are like 1998 all over again"* Private email from Matt Haughey to Jesse James Garrett's weblogs mailing list, January 2002. Used with permission.

141 *"Blood's Law of Weblog History"* Rebecca Blood on Rebecca's Pocket, January 6, 2004, at http://www.rebeccablood.net/archive/2004/01.html.

141 *Anil Dash . . . offered a corollary* From Dash's link blog at http://web.archive .org/web/20040404093501/www.dashes.com/links/archives/20040104.php.

142 Earliest posts for Atrios's Eschaton are at http://www.eschatonblog.com/2002_ 04_14_archive.html. For Jerome Armstrong's MyDD: http://web.archive.org/web/ 20020601100213/www.mydd.com/archives/. For Markos Moulitsas Zuniga's Daily Kos: http://web.archive.org/web/20021115215215/http://www.dailykos.com/archives/ 2002_05.html.

142 *"One of my biggest pet peeves"* Interview with Markos Moulitsas Zuniga in David Kline and Dan Burstein, *Blog! How the Newest Media Revolution Is Changing Politics, Business and Culture* (CDS Books, 2005), p. 48.

144 *A brief Friday-morning item in the Note* http://abcnews.go.com/sections/ politics/DailyNews/TheNote_Dec6.html.

144 *Thomas Edsall followed up* "Lott Decried for Part of Salute to Thurmond," *Washington Post*, Dec. 7, 2002, at http://www.washingtonpost.com/ac2/wp- dyn%3Fpagename=article&contentId=A20730-2002Dec6&notFound=true.

144 *Two leading political Web 'zines* Joe Conason in Salon at http://dir.salon.com

/story/politics/conason/2002/12/09/lott/index.html, Tim Noah in Slate at http://www.slate.com/?id=2075151.

145   *"Trent Lott deserves the shit he's getting"*   Glenn Reynolds at http://www.pajamasmedia.com/instapundit-archive/archives/005985.php.

145   *"Oh, what could have been!!!"*   This and subsequent Marshall quotations on Lott are at http://www.talkingpointsmemo.com/archives/week_2002_12_01.php, and http://www.talkingpointsmemo.com/archives/week_2002_12_08.php.

145   *"he waited to post it until he could confirm it"*   Marshall discusses this at http://www.talkingpointsmemo.com/archives/146816.php.

146   *"The Internet's First Scalp"*   John Podhoretz in the *New York Post*, Dec. 13, 2002, at http://web.archive.org/web/*/http://www.nypost.com/postopinion/oped columnists/51499.htm.

146   *a detailed case study . . . by Harvard's Kennedy School of Government* Archived at http://web.archive.org/web/20040412233307/http://www.ksg.harvard.edu/presspol/Research_Publications/Case_Studies/1731_0.pdf.

147   *"must reading for the politically curious"*   Paul Krugman in the *New York Times*, Dec. 13, 2002, at http://query.nytimes.com/gst/fullpage.html?res=9803E4DE103AF930A25751C1A9649C8B63.

147   *Marshall finished the dissertation's final draft*   http://talkingpointsmemo.com/archives/147013.php.

149   *Kos traced the core of his community*   He tells the story at http://www.dailykos.com/story/2004/8/5/35451/65527/473/42251.

149   *Goddard welcomed the influx*   Author interview with Taegan Goddard, August 2008.

150   *"I had learned my lessons from Political Wire"; "I actually didn't think anyone would use the diaries"*   http://www.dailykos.com/story/2004/8/5/35451/65527/473/42251.

150   *"screw them"*   http://www.dailykos.com/story/2004/4/1/144156/3224.

150   *"I was the one war critic"*   Kos interview in Kline and Burstein, *Blog!*, p. 42.

152   *"It's 2001, and we can Fact Check your ass"*   Ken Layne on his blog, Dec. 9, 2001, at http://web.archive.org/web/20011214072915/http://kenlayne.com/2000/2001_12_09_logarc.html#7775214.

155   *"For the first time in six decades"*   Peter Wehner's memo is quoted at http://msnbc.msn.com/id/6791950/ and http://www.talkingpointsmemo.com/archives/149796.php.

155   *"abolishing Social Security isn't just any issue"*   http://www.talkingpointsmemo.com/archives/149772.php.

155   *"This isn't about financing"*   http://www.talkingpointsmemo.com/archives/004236.php.

156   *"All the folks who cover the White House"*   http://www.talkingpointsmemo.com/archives/150038.php.

156 *"Do journalists really have to genuflect"* http://www.talkingpointsmemo.com/archives/149970.php.

157 *"Making the elimination of Social Security"* http://www.talkingpointsmemo.com/archives/004236.php.

157 *"Where do your representatives and senators stand"* http://www.talkingpointsmemo.com/archives/149700.php.

157 *"Stop what you're doing! Spit out your drink!"* http://www.talkingpointsmemo.com/archives/2005_01_27.php.

158 *"The bamboozlepalooza begins!"* http://www.talkingpointsmemo.com/archives/150018.php.

159 *600,000 monthly visitors* As reported at the time on the site for Blogads, which sold TPM's advertising, at http://web.archive.org/web/20050111043530/http://www.blogads.com/order.

159 *"It would have been impossible for me"* http://www.talkingpointsmemo.com/archives/005312.php.

160 *"the edge of my comfort zone"* Author interview with Marshall, April 2008.

160 Marshall's George Polk Award announced at http://www.brooklyn.liu.edu/polk/press/2007.html.

162 *"Schlesinger's wife asked me to explain"* http://www.talkingpointsmemo.com/archives/147911.php.

162 *"I hate the bloggers!"* Video of John McCain's comment is at http://www.youtube.com/watch?v=6o07p7JyzuY.

163 *"talk about a direct IV"* Dan Bartlett's quotation is from an interview in *Texas Monthly*, Jan. 2008, at http://www.texasmonthly.com/2008-01-01/talks-2.php.

163 *"can't decide between loving the big media"* Mattthew Klam, "Fear and Laptops on the Campaign Trail," *The New York Times Magazine*, Sep. 26, 2004, at http://www.nytimes.com/2004/09/26/magazine/26BLOGS.html.

163 *"If I had quickly happened into a staff position"* Noam Cohen, "Blogger, Sans Pajamas, Rakes Muck and a Prize," *New York Times*, Feb. 25, 2008, at http://www.nytimes.com/2008/02/25/business/media/25marshall.html.

164 *"What I backed into"* Klam, "Fear and Laptops."

CHAPTER 6
BLOGGING FOR BUCKS

165 *"I said out loud: There it is"* Scripting News, March 2, 2007, at http://stories.scripting.com/2007/03/02/empireOfTheAir.html.

167 *"I wanted to say that I am a Microsoft person"* Joshua Allen, quoted in Robert Scoble and Shel Israel, *Naked Conversations: How Blogs Are Changing the Way Businesses Talk with Customers* (John Wiley & Sons, 2006), p. 11.

167 *"There was no explicit policy"* Allen's account of his early blogging is at http://web.archive.org/web/20051018193845/http://www.netcrucible.com/blog/ PermaLink.aspx?guid=c0d3c5c7-ad8b-4120-b827-4bdb802bef0c.

168 *The Cluetrain Manifesto* http://www.cluetrain.com.

169 *By spring 2003, about one hundred Microsoft employees* As reported by Robert Scoble at http://scoble.weblogs.com/2003/04/27.html.

170 *His blog had played a "major role"* http://scoble.weblogs.com/2003/04/15.html.

170 *Scoble dead pool* http://scoble.weblogs.com/2003/05/10.html.

170 *"Weblogging is like dancing in a field of land mines"* http://scoble.weblogs .com/2003/05/31.html.

170 *Scoble's title ought to be "chief humanizing officer"* *The Economist*, Feb. 10, 2005, at http://www.economist.com/people/displayStory.cfm?story_id=3644293.

171 *"Corporate Weblog Manifesto"* http://scoble.weblogs.com/2003/02/26.html.

171 *"The thing is that I don't have any credibility left"* http://scoble.weblogs .com/2004/09/23.html.

172 *Joel on Software* http://www.joelonsoftware.com/.

172 *English Cut* http://www.englishcut.com/.

173 *"The demonstration of knowledge and expertise over time"* Jon Udell's statement is from the 2003 Bloggercon conference at Harvard Law School. Recordings are at http://www.cmsreview.com/Videos/Bloggercon.html. Udell's comment can be found in the audio Tape Five at about the 1 hour 5 minute mark.

173 *"If you're into blogs to make money"* Doc Searls in Steven Levy, "The Alpha Bloggers," *Newsweek*, Dec. 1, 2004, at http://www.newsweek.com/id/55915/page/3.

174 Andrew Sullivan's "tip jar": The $27,000 figure is from Sullivan's Blogger Manifesto at http://web.archive.org/web/20020329011512/http://www.andrewsullivan.com/ print.php?artnum=20020224.

174 *Chris Allbritton raised about $14,000* Documented at http://www.back-to-iraq.com/.

175 *"We've been wondering when blogging"* Nick Denton announced Gizmodo's launch on his blog on Aug. 1, 2002, at http://web.archive.org/web/2002101011 5538/www.nickdenton.org/archives/2002_08_01_archive.htm.

176 *"The one common theme is to take an obsession"* "America's First Blog Mogul," *The Independent*, Nov. 29, 2004, at http://web.archive.org/web/20041204112 228/http://news.independent.co.uk/media/story.jsp?story=587881.

177 *Spiers reportedly earned just $2,000 a month* Steven Levy, "How Can I Sex Up This Blog Business?" *Wired*, June 2004, at http://www.wired.com/wired/archive/ 12.06/blog.html.

177 *By 2005 the typical pay* March 2005 interview with Gawker editor Lockhart Steele at http://www.iwantmedia.com/people/people49.html.

178 *"handed out rote poundings"* Jack Shafer in *Slate*, March 11, 2004, at http:// www.slate.com/id/2096976/.

178 *"Immediacy is more important than accuracy"* Denton's quote is from Julie Bosman, "First with the Scoop, if Not the Truth," *New York Times*, April 18, 2004, at http://query.nytimes.com/gst/fullpage.html?res=9402E6DA123BF93BA25757C0 A9629C8B63&sec=&spon=&pagewanted=all.

179 *a measly $2,000 per month* From Denton's blog, Sept. 12, 2003, at http://web.archive.org/web/20031206095421/www.nickdenton.org/archives/008760.html#008760.

180 *"The basic business model"* Nick Denton, quoted in Simon Dumenco, "Blog, Blog, Blog," *New York*, Nov. 3, 2003, at http://nymag.com/nymetro/news/media/columns/download/n_9457/.

181 *brought in about $200,000 total from 2003 through 2008* Author email interview with Glenn Fleishman, Sept. 2008.

182 *launching three hundred blogs* Daniel Terdiman, "Toward a Weblogging Empire," *Wired News*, Sept. 25, 2003, at http://www.wired.com/news/business/0,1367,60552,00.html.

182 *The cross-blog sniping was intense* E.g., Denton at http://web.archive.org/web/20031206095816/www.nickdenton.org/archives/009038.html#9038; and Calacanis at http://web.archive.org/web/20031120004455/calacanis.weblogsinc.com/.

183 *First, Calacanis advised Spiers* As reported in Terdiman, "Toward a Weblogging Empire."

183 *"Calacanis should hold the hype"* Denton post from Sept. 12, 2003, at http://web.archive.org/web/20031206095421/www.nickdenton.org/archives/008 760.html#008760.

183 *Rojas . . . "poached" by his rival* Denton post from March 8, 2004, at http://web.archive.org/web/20040514030020/www.nickdenton.org/001961.html#1961.

183 *"You can't say 'Work with me for as little as possible'"* Calacanis as quoted in *New York*, "Intelligencer: Gawker's Stalker," March 15, 2004, at http://web.archive.org/web/20040402170359/www.newyorkmetro.com/nymetro/news/people/columns/intelligencer/n_10023/.

183 *"I was, as they say back home, royally shafted"* Denton's post from March 8, 2004, at http://web.archive.org/web/20040514030020/www.nickdenton.org/001961.html#1961.

184 *"Anyone can start a blog"* Rojas in Clive Thompson, "Blogs to Riches," *New York*, Feb. 12, 2006, at http://nymag.com/news/media/15971/.

185 *he sold Weblogs Inc. to America Online* The figure appears in Eryn Brown, "Revenge of the Dotcom Poster Boy," *Wired*, Jan. 2006, at http://www.wired.com/wired/archive/14.01/blogger.html; and in John Heilemann, "Suit 2.0," *New York*, July 3, 2006, at http://nymag.com/news/politics/powergrid/17398/.

186 *"There is no doubt that there is a bubble"* Denton in David Carr, "A Blog Mogul Turns Bearish on Blogs," *New York Times*, July 3, 2006, at http://www.nytimes.com/2006/07/03/technology/03carr.htm.

186 *"Because it would be too hard to start over"* Ibid.

186 *By 2007, Gawker Media had grown . . . $10–12 million in annual profits* Vanessa Grigoriadis, "Everybody Sucks: Gawker and the Rage of the Creative Underclass," *New York*, Oct. 15, 2007, at http://nymag.com/news/features/39319/.

187 *"this will be an incredibly powerful tool"* Ted Murphy in Marshall Kirkpatrick, "PayPerPost.com offers to sell your soul," Techcrunch, June 30, 2006, at http://www.techcrunch.com/2006/06/30/payperpostcom-offers-to-buy-your-soul/.

188 *"PayPerPost versus authentic blogging"* Calacanis quoted in Josh Friedman, "Blogging for Dollars Raises Questions of Online Ethics," *Los Angeles Times*, March 9, 2007, at http://articles.latimes.com/2007/mar/09/business/fi-bloggers9.

190 *Only a couple of dozen people came* The figure and the $200,000-a-month 2007 revenue number are from Fred Vogelstein, "TechCrunch Blogger Michael Arrington Can Generate Buzz . . . and Cash," *Wired*, June 22, 2007, at http://www.wired.com/techbiz/people/magazine/15-07/ff_arrington?currentPage=all.

191 *"I couldn't sleep at night if I did that"* Arrington's post from May 29, 2006, is at http://www.crunchnotes.com/2006/05/29/on-conflicts-of-interest-and-techcrunch/.

191 *"I was online at 2:00 a.m."* Vogelstein, "TechCrunch Blogger Michael Arrington."

192 *they "want to hear the unofficial story"* Esther Dyson in Gordon Crovitz, "Social Networking in the Digital Age," *Wall Street Journal*, June 2, 2008, at http://online.wsj.com/article/SB121236428571036459.html.

193 *"digital sharecropping"* Nicholas Carr used the phrase to describe user-generated content on his blog at http://www.roughtype.com/archives/2007/09/a_cautionary_ta.php and http://www.roughtype.com/archives/2006/12/sharecropping_t.php.

193 *"it's a real positive-sum game"* Felix Salmon's post from Oct. 15, 2007, on Portfolio's website is at http://www.portfolio.com/views/blogs/market-movers/2007/10/15/blogonomics-paying-for-content.

194 *"Until we create a financial structure"* "Blogging for Dollars: Giving Rise to the Professional Blogger," Meg Hourihan's August 2002 column for Oreillynet is at http://web.archive.org/web/20021013182512/www.oreillynet.com/pub/a/javascript/2002/08/12/megnut.html.

194 *"when we started paying folks"* Calacanis posted this to Twitter on June 17, 2008, at http://twitter.com/JasonCalacanis/statuses/837213251.

194 *A detailed essay in the online journal N+1* Carla Blumenkranz, "Gawker 2002–2007," N+1, Dec. 3, 2007, at http://www.nplusonemag.com/gawker-2002-2007.

194 *"Gawker.com and the Culture of Bile"* This was the cover line for Vanessa Grigoriardis's "Everybody Sucks" piece.

194 *"Every age has its own cultural panic"* Denton's post from Oct. 14, 2007, in response to *New York*'s piece is at http://nickdenton.org/5083258/the-long-and-illustrious-history-of-bile.

196 *"In Web World of 24/7 Stress, Writers Blog Till They Drop"* Matt Richtel's *New York Times* piece from April 6, 2008, is at http://www.nytimes.com/2008 /04/06/technology/06sweat.html.

CHAPTER 7
THE EXPLODING BLOGOSPHERE

198 *"the idea of bouncing around"* Author interview with Mark Frauenfelder, September 2008.

198 *"I was a mechanical engineer"* Interview by Chip Rowe with Frauenfelder at http://www.zinebook.com/interv/boing.html.

199 *Whole Earth Review later picked it up* Frauenfelder's piece on blogging appeared in the Winter 2000 edition of *Whole Earth Review* and is available at http://www.kk.org/tools/page52-54.pdf.

200 *Frauenfelder found a line drawing* Boing Boing's posts on Kamen's Segway invention, then known as "IT" or "Ginger," are at http://www.boingboing.net/ 2001/01/07-week/.

201 *Frauenfelder had profiled it . . . for* The Industry Standard Mark Frauenfelder, "Nouveau Niche," *The Industry Standard*, Oct. 23, 2000, at http://web.archive.org /web/20001121145100/www.thestandard.com/article/display/0,1151,19498,00 .html.

201 Down and Out in the Magic Kingdom Doctorow has made his novel freely available in many forms online at http://craphound.com/down/download.php.

202 *"Homesteading the Noosphere"* Eric Raymond's essay is at http://www.catb .org/~esr/writings/cathedral-bazaar/homesteading/.

202 *"As a committed infovore, I need"* Doctorow's "My Blog, My Outboard Brain" essay, from May 31, 2002, is at http://www.oreillynet.com/pub/a/javascript/ 2002/01/01/cory.html.

204 *"Every link one follows from Boing Boing"* From a 2002 email exchange between Justin Hall and Cory Doctorow about styles of blogging, posted at http://www.links.net/webpub/200207-boingboing.html.

205 *"I propose a name for the intellectual cyberspace"* William Quick's Daily Pundit Blog, January 1, 2002, at http://webarchive.org http://www.iw3p.com/DailyPundit/2001_12_30_dailypundit_archive.php.

205 *"the Distributed Republic of Blogistan"* Doctorow's comment reported by Ben Hammersley in "Geeks Go Hack to the Future," *The Guardian*, May 23, 2002, at http://www.guardian.co.uk/technology/2002/may/23/internetnews .onlinesupplement.

205 *Brad Graham . . . had used the word long before* I.e., in Sept. 1999, at http://www.bradlands.com/weblog/1999-09.shtml#September%2010,%201999.

Jason Kottke posted on the matter on June 16, 2002, at http://www.kottke .org/02/06/been-there-done-that-times-a-jillion.

206 *Meg Hourihan pointed out in a 2002 essay* "What We're Doing When We Blog," O'Reilly Web Dev Center, June 13, 2002, at http://www.oreillynet.com/ pub/a/javascript/2002/06/13/megnut.html.

206 *"It was effectively the device"* Tom Coates's post from June 2003 is at http://www.plasticbag.org/archives/2003/06/on_permalinks_and_paradigms/.

209 *Beebo.org's Metalog* An archived version of the Sept. 2000 listing is at http:// beebo.org/metalog/.

212 *Clark wrote a post . . . decrying the "A-list"* Joe Clark's essay "Deconstructing You've Got Blog" is at http://fawny.org/decon-blog.html and reprinted in *We've Got Blog.*

213 *"Power Laws, Weblogs, and Inequality"* Shirky's Feb. 10, 2003, essay is at http://www.shirky.com/writings/powerlaw_weblog.html.

214 *The Long Tail* Anderson's original Long Tail article in *Wired* is at http://www .wired.com/wired/archive/12.10/tail.html. "Fat Head," e.g., http://www.stat.columbia .edu/~cook/movabletype/archives/2006/12/the_long_tail_a.html; "Big Butt," e.g., http://www.buzzmachine.com/2006/02/14/the-big-butt/.

216 *Dave Winer wrote that Shirky simply didn't understand* "Clay, Start a Weblog Now," Scripting News, Feb. 9, 2003, at http://www.scripting.com/2003/02/09 .html#clayStartAWeblogNow.

218 *Technorati reported tracking 100,000 blogs* Sifry's 2004 report is at http://www.sifry.com/alerts/archives/000245.html. The most recent "State of the Blogosphere" numbers from 2008 are at http://technorati.com/blogging/state-of-the-blogosphere/.

218 *"Our bandwidth bills are going through the roof"* Frauenfelder's April 5, 2004, post is at http://www.boingboing.net/2004/04/05/boing-boings-explosi.html.

219 *$1,000 a month* Author interview with Frauenfelder.

219 *Jason Calacanis posted immediately* The comments for Frauenfelder's bandwidth-cost post are at http://www.quicktopic.com/26/H/zs665dYrU48w.

219 *any good ad salesperson* Frauenfelder interview in Michael A. Banks, *Blogging Heroes* (John Wiley & Sons, 2008), p. 95.

220 *"They're the NASCAR of the weblogging world"* Lance Arthur's March 24, 2005, post, "Boing Boing, Ka-Ching Ka-Ching," is at http://www.glassdog .com/archives/2005/03/24/boing_boing_kaching_kaching.html.

221 *"It's kind of impossible for me to conceptualize"* Frauenfelder interview in Banks, *Blogging Heroes,* p. 97.

221 BusinessWeek *reported* July 14, 2007, at http://images.businessweek.com/ss/ 07/07/0714_bloggers/source/2.htm.

222 *"It was brought to my attention this weekend"* Violet Blue's post from June 23,

2008, is at http://www.tinynibbles.com/blogarchives/2008/06/digital-notes-and-errata.html.

223 *After David Sarno . . . wrote about the missing posts* Sarno wrote multiple posts on the controversy, at http://latimesblogs.latimes.com/webscout/2008/06/violet-blue-scr.html; http://latimesblogs.latimes.com/webscout/2008/07/regarding-boing.html; http://latimesblogs.latimes.com/webscout/2008/07/violet-blue-s-1.html; http://latimesblogs.latimes.com/webscout/2008/07/boingboing-and.html; http://latimesblogs.latimes.com/webscout/2008/07/xeni-jardin-and.html; and http://latimesblogs.latimes.com/webscout/2008/07/boingboing-blog.html.

223 *"Violet behaved in a way that made us reconsider"* "That Violet Blue Thing," July 1, 2008, at http://www.boingboing.net/2008/07/01/that-violet-blue-thi.html.

224 *"Did the Internet's free speech guardians"* Valleywag on July 1, 2008, at http://valleywag.com/5021146/did-the-internets-free+speech-guardians-try-to-hush-up-a-girl+on+girl-love-affair.

224 *"she was being used by a groupie"* "How Xeni and Violet's Boing Boing affair went sour," Valleywag, July 2, 2008, at http://valleywag.gawker.com/5021288/how-xeni-and-violets-boing-boing-affair-went-sour.

225 *The editors explained that, really, it was true* David Sarno, "BoingBoing bloggers talk about Violet Blue controversy's implications," *Los Angeles Times* Web Scout blog, July 2, 2008, at http://latimesblogs.latimes.com/webscout/2008/07/boingboing-blog.html.

226 *"This is my work, this is my blog"* "BoingBoing's Xeni Jardin on unpublishing the Violet Blue posts," David Sarno, *Los Angeles Times* Web Scout blog, July 2, 2008, at http://latimesblogs.latimes.com/webscout/2008/07/xeni-jardin-and.html.

226 *"something I feared would become"* "Lessons Learned," Xeni Jardin on Boing Boing, July 18, 2008, at http://www.boingboing.net/2008/07/18/lessons-learned.html.

227 *"Sometimes talking about stuff does not make it better"* Author interview with Xeni Jardin, December 2008.

CHAPTER 8
THE PERILS OF KEEPING IT REAL

229 *"What really excited me"* Heather Armstrong interviewed via email by Rebecca Blood for "Bloggers on Blogging," August 2005, http://www.rebeccablood.net/bloggerson/heatherarmstrong.html.

230 *"I just thought of a poem"* Armstrong's first post, from Feb. 27, 2001, is archived at http://web.archive.org/web/20010406013653/www.dooce.com/march.htm.

230 *"the three distinct moments that My Mother Turned Demonic"* Armstrong's post on April 11, 2001, at http://web.archive.org/web/20010604032828/www.dooce.com/april.htm.

230 *"I will be excommunicated"* Armstrong's post on March 28, 2001, at http://web.archive.org/web/20010406013653/www.dooce.com/march.htm.

230 *As Armstrong recalls it* Author interview with Armstrong, July 2008.

.231 *"I really naïvely thought"* Armstrong quoted in Matt Canham, "Utah blogger makes her life public fodder," *Salt Lake City Tribune*, Oct. 15, 2006, at http://web.archive.org/web/20061022135504/http://www.sltrib.com/ci_4492586.

231 *"I want to publicly apologize"* Armstrong's post from Sept. 27, 2001, is at http://www.dooce.com/archives/daily/09_27_2001.html.

231 *"I hate that one of the 10 vice-presidents"* Armstrong's post from Feb. 12, 2002, is at http://www.dooce.com/archives/daily/02_12_2002.html.

232 *"I guess I could be bitter"* Armstrong's post from Feb. 26, 2002, is at http://www.dooce.com/archives/daily/02_26_2002.html.

232 *"I started out thinking"* From Blood's Armstrong interview at http://www.rebeccablood.net/bloggerson/heatherarmstrong.html.

233 *"I am that girl who lost her job"* http://dooce.com/archives/about/09_03_2002.html.

233 *"Ask yourself, who is the one person"* From Blood's Armstrong interview.

234 *"I assert that nobody's ever been fired"* Anil Dash's post from Feb. 2005 is at http://www.dashes.com/anil/2005/02/dont-poke-the-s.html.

235 *"After I quit the website"* Armstrong's post from Sept. 3, 2002, is at http://www.dooce.com/archives/about/09_03_2002.html.

236 *the online world allows for all sorts of experiments* The primary work on this topic is Sherry Turkle, *Life on the Screen: Identity in the Age of the Internet* (Simon & Schuster, 1995).

237 *"Is it possible that Kaycee did not exist?"* The Metafilter post from May 18, 2001, is at http://www.metafilter.com/comments.mefi/7819.

238 *"The whole idea of an online journal"* Katie Hafner, "A Beautiful Life, an Early Death, a Fraud Exposed," *New York Times*, May 31, 2001, at http://www.nytimes.com/2001/05/31/technology/31HOAX.html.

238 *"So, it's wrong to be deeply offended"* Comment on Metafilter at http://www.metafilter.com/comments.mefi/7841/.

239 *Plain Layne* One account of the story is at http://www.museumofhoaxes.com/hoax/weblog/permalink/plain_layne/.

239 *lonelygirl15* Wired's account from Dec. 2006, at http://www.wired.com/wired/archive/14.12/lonelygirl.html.

239 *"Bloggus Caesari"* http://www.sankey.ca/caesar/.

239 The Diary of Samuel Pepys http://www.pepysdiary.com/.

241 *"Everyone except his closest 'friends'"* Salam Pax's post from Dec. 25, 2002, at http://dear_raed.blogspot.com/2002_12_01_dear_raed_archive.html.

241 *"The Iraqi 'Opposition Groups'"* Salam Pax's post from December 22, 2002, at http://dear_raed.blogspot.com/2002_12_01_dear_raed_archive.html.

242 *"the Anne Frank of this conflict"* Denton's comment on his blog from May 30,

2003, is at http://web.archive.org/web/20030621105647/http://www.nickdenton
.org/archives/005924.html.

242 "Other than what he tells us" Jason Kottke's March 20, 2003, post is at
http://kottke.org/03/03/now-seriously-where-is-raed.

242 "I emailed Salam and asked for proof" Paul Boutin's March 20, 2003, post is at
http://paulboutin.weblogger.com/2003/03/20/.

242 Peter Maass wrote a piece for Slate "Salam Pax Is Real," Slate, June 2, 2003, at
http://slate.msn.com/id/2083847.

243 "So you want the best table in the house?" Waiter Rant's post from April 26, 2004,
at http://waiterrant.net/?m=200404.

243 "We had to redirect all the other customers" http://waiterrant.net/?p=10.

244 "The ultimate vehicle for brand-bashing" "Attack of the Blogs," Dan Lyons, Forbes,
Nov. 14, 2005, at http://www.forbes.com/forbes/2005/1114/128.html.

245 John Mackey David Kesmodel and John R. Wilke, "Whole Foods Is Hot, Wild
Oats a Dud—So Said 'Rahodeb,'" Wall Street Journal, July 12, 2007, at
http://online.wsj.com/article/SB118418782959963745.html.

246 "How angry people get when a powerful critic" Lee Siegel's posts as
Sprezzatura are mostly gone from the Web, but several have been preserved. This
one is from http://www.dailykos.com/story/2006/9/1/22145/38331. Others are at
http://majikthise.typepad.com/majikthise_/2006/09/lee_siegel_is_t.html, and at
http://lefarkins.blogspot.com/2006/09/wanktacular.html.

247 "produced with Siegel's participation" Foer's apology is at http://web.archive
.org/web/20061113135156/http://www.tnr.com/suspended.mhtml.

247 "We don't let our writers misrepresent themselves" Foer is quoted in Sheelah
Kolhatkar, "New Republic Critic Tumbles in Blog-land: My 'Dumb Mistake,'" New
York Observer, Sept. 10, 2006, at http://www.observer.com/node/39374.

248 "I decided that since I had fallen" Lee Siegel, Against the Machine: Being Human in
the Age of the Electronic Mob (Spiegel & Grau, 2008), p. 9.

248 He was, in fact, a lawyer in New York Kolhatkar, "New Republic Critic Tumbles in
Blog-land," http://www.observer.com/node/39374.

248 "The Greater Internet Fuckwad Theory" Penny Arcade comic from March 19,
2004, at http://www.penny-arcade.com/comic/2004/03/19.

249 "These elements are a necessary ingredient" Kevin Kelly's observations on
anonymity are from Edge.org's "World Question Center" from 2006, at http://
www.edge.org/q2006/q06_4.html#kelly.

249 "disemvowelling" Teresa Nielsen-Hayden's first use of this moderation practice
appears to be on her Making Light blog on Nov. 21, 2002, at http://nielsenhayden
.com/makinglight/archives/001551.html#8717.

251 "If some people don't HATE your product" Kathy Sierra's post from Dec. 23,
2004, is at http://headrush.typepad.com/creating_passionate_users/2004/12/if_
some_people_.html.

252 *"I have cancelled all speaking engagements"* Sierra's original post is archived at
http://web.archive.org/web/20070405184438/headrush.typepad.com/
creating_passionate_users/2007/03/as_i_type_this_.html. The most detailed
detective work on the Sierra incident was by blogger Jim Turner at his One by One
Media site, in three parts, at http://www.onebyonemedia.com/the-sierra-saga-part-
1-dissecting-the-creation-of-the-kathy-sierra-blog-storm-4/; http://www.onebyone
media.com/the-sierra-saga-part-2-big-bad-bob-and-the-lull-before-the-kathy-
sierra-blog-storm/; and http://www.onebyonemedia.com/the-sierra-saga-part-3-
who-are-the-real-culprits-in-the-kathy-sierra-saga/. Additional sleuthing by Don
Park is archived at http://web.archive.org/web/20070501185623/http://www
.docuverse.com/blog/donpark/2007/03/27/how-awful.

253 *in part to seek help identifying whoever was responsible* Sierra explained her
intentions at http://headrush.typepad.com/whathappened.html.

253 *"purposeful anarchy"* Frank Paynter's explanation of meankids.org is archived at
http://web.archive.org/web/20070408234926/http://listics.com/20070326984.

254 *"It now seems fairly certain"* Tim O'Reilly's post from March 31, 2007, is at
http://radar.oreilly.com/archives/2007/03/call-for-a-blog-1.html.

255 *"misogyny grows wild on the Web"* Joan Walsh, "Men Who Hate Women on the
Web," Salon, March 31, 2007, at http://www.salon.com/opinion/feature/2007/
03/31/sierra/index.html.

255 *Sierra found herself on CNN* The report is at http://www.youtube.com/
watch?v=UQ6IxYaD774.

255 *"Blogger's Code of Conduct"* In Tim O'Reilly's post of March 31, 2007, at
http://radar.oreilly.com/archives/2007/03/call-for-a-blog-1.html.

255 *"I take the side of the mean kids"* Dave Winer on Scripting News, March 27, 2007,
at http://www.scripting.com/stories/2007/03/27/chorusOfCowardice.html.

256 *"Can somebody please explain to me"* Rich Kyanka's post from April 3, 2007, is
at http://www.somethingawful.com/d/hogosphere/internet-death-threat.php. A
full account of Kyanka and the subculture of "griefers" is in Julian Dibbell,
"Mutilated Furries, Flying Phalluses: Put the Blame on Griefers, the Sociopaths of
the Virtual World," Wired, January 2008, at http://www.wired.com/gaming/
virtualworlds/magazine/16-02/mf_goons?currentPage=all.

259 *Warnock's Dilemma* Explained in "Jargon Watch," Wired, Oct. 2001, at
http://www.wired.com/wired/archive/9.10/mustread.html?pg=7. Also on Mark
Warnock's Warning Knock blog on Sept. 28, 2007, at http://thewarningknock
.blogspot.com/2007/09/warnocks-dilemma.html.

260 *"Everything I've ever read about breastfeeding"* . . . *"A Heartbreaking Work of Super
Pooping Genius"* Heather Armstrong's post from Feb. 9, 2004, at http://
www.dooce.com/archives/daily/02_09_2004.html.

261 *"The reason you won't be hearing anything from me"* Armstrong's "Heather,

interrupted" post of August 26, 2004 is at http://dooce.com/archives/daily/08_26_2004.html

262 *"And if you ask Jon he will tell you"* Armstrong's post "Because I couldn't say it on the phone," from Dec. 13, 2007, is at http://www.dooce.com/2007/12/13/because-i-couldnt-say-it-phone.

262 *"When people say that they can't believe I'm being so open"* . . . *"I feel like a crazed kid at a concert"* Armstrong's post "Unlocked," from Aug. 28, 2004, is at http://www.dooce.com/archives/daily/08_28_2004.html.

263 *"less than what a part-time fry cook makes"* From Rebecca Blood's Bloggers on Blogging interview with Armstrong.

263 *more than 3 million page views a month* Figure is from Federated Media's information page for Dooce at http://www.federatedmedia.net/authors/dooce as of January 2009.

263 *"Some people use that label to belittle"* Armstrong's post on mommyblogging, from May 13, 2008, is at http://www.dooce.com/2008/05/13/didnt-woman-blog-about-al-rokers-nipples.

264 *"a memoir being written as it is lived"* Author interview with Armstrong.

265 *"People I meet tell me, 'It's so weird'"* Heather Armstrong talk at BlogHer conference, San Francisco, July 19, 2008.

CHAPTER 9
JOURNALISTS VS. BLOGGERS

269 *"I'd seen things come and go in waves"* Author interview with John Markoff, Oct. 2008.

270 *"most promising new genre"* Julia Keller, "She Has Seen the Future and It Is— Weblogs," *Chicago Tribune*, Sept. 7, 1999, at http://web.archive.org/web/200008 15223515/http://chicagotribune.com/leisure/tempo/printedition/article/0,2669, SAV-9909070005,FF.html.

270 *Rob Walker wrote that though he enjoyed weblogs* Rob Walker, "The News According to Blogs," Slate, March 7, 2001, at http://www.slate.com/?id=102057.

272 *"There seems to be no end"* Bill Keller's email to Jeff Jarvis, at http://www .buzzmachine.com/archives/cat_dmcs.html.

273 *"The notion that I needed to be under contract"* Demian Bulwa, "Blogger Stays in Prison, Defying Grand Jury Order," *San Francisco Chronicle*, October 16, 2006, at http://www.sfgate.com/cgi-bin/article.cgi?file=/c/a/2006/10/16/MNG7FLQ5 OT1.DTL.

275 *Apple sued a Harvard freshman* Brad Stone, "Apple Rumor Site to Shut Down in Settlement," *New York Times*, Dec. 21, 2007, at http://www.nytimes.com/2007/12/21/technology/21apples.html.

276 *"When the people formerly known as the audience"* "A Most Useful Definition of Citizen Journalism," Jay Rosen's post from July 14, 2008, is at http://journalism.nyu.edu/pubzone/weblogs/pressthink/2008/07/14/a_most_useful_d.html.

277 *a tongue-in-cheek instant-message exchange* http://jezebel.com/5050467/what-julia-allison-john-mccain-have-done-to-journalism.

277 *"Covering one of the most important stories of our time"* Dan Froomkin, "The lessons of our failure," Nieman Watchdog, October 17, 2008, at http://www.niemanwatchdog.org/index.cfm?fuseaction=Showcase.view&showcaseid=0092.

278 *A survey of Nieman Fellows* Barry Sussman, "The press gets a low grade for pre-Iraq war reporting," Nieman Watchdog, September 29, 2008, at http://www.niemanwatchdog.org/index.cfm?fuseaction=background.view&backgroundid=00282.

278 *"Propaganda thrives—predominates—in our democracy"* Glenn Greenwald, "The Mighty, Scary Press Corps," Sept. 6, 2008, at http://www.salon.com/opinion/greenwald/2008/09/06/carney/.

278 *a poster at the conservative Free Republic forum* Buckhead's first comment declaring the documents to be forgeries is at http://www.freerepublic.com/focus/f-news/1210662/posts.

279 *an Atlanta lawyer named Harry MacDougald* Peter Wallsten, "'Buckhead,' Who Said CBS Memos Were Forged, Is a GOP-linked Attorney," *Los Angeles Times*, September 18, 2004, available at http://seattletimes.nwsource.com/html/nationworld/2002039080_buckhead18.html.

279 *a simple animated image* Johnson's image is reproduced on the Wikipedia page about the Rather controversy at http://en.wikipedia.org/wiki/Rathergate.

279 *"You couldn't have a starker contrast"* Jonathan Klein made his statement on Fox News, as widely quoted on the Web, e.g., at http://itre.cis.upenn.edu/~myl/languagelog/archives/001459.html.

280 *"insufferable hubris and self-righteousness"* Van Gordon Sauter, "What's Ailing CBS News? Let's Make a Not-So-Little List," *Los Angeles Times*, January 13, 2005, at http://articles.latimes.com/2005/jan/13/opinion/oe-sauter13.

282 *"A passionate amateur"* Chris Anderson's post from Sept. 16, 2008, is at http://www.longtail.com/the_long_tail/2008/09/a-passionate-am.html.

283 *"No matter how diligent Our Good Reporter is"* Dave Winer, April 16, 2004, at http://www.bloggercon.org/2004/04/16.

283 *"synonymous with damp mold"* James Wolcott, "Critical Condition," *The New Republic*, December 4, 2007, at http://www.tnr.com/politics/story.html?id=69e34cc4-6eb7-4c69-a5a7-24681dfac7c4&p=1.

284 *"If you wanted to keep up with the trial"* Jay Rosen's post from March 9, 2007, is at http://journalism.nyu.edu/pubzone/weblogs/pressthink/2007/03/09/libby_fdl.html.

284 *A New York Times piece on the blog's trial coverage* Scott Shane, "For Bloggers, Libby Trial Is Fun and Fodder," *New York Times*, Feb. 15, 2007, at http://www.nytimes.com/2007/02/15/washington/15bloggers.html.

284 *Klein erroneously reported details* Joe Klein, "The Tone-Deaf Democrats," *Time*, Nov. 21, 2007, at http://www.time.com/time/politics/article/0,8599, 1686509,00.html. His blog posts responding to criticism are at http://swampland .blogs.time.com/2007/11/21/latest_column_22/; and http://swampland.blogs.time .com/2007/11/24/fisa_confusion_and_correction/.

285 *When blogger Glenn Greenwald . . . began pointing these mistakes out* http://www .salon.com/opinion/greenwald/2007/11/21/klein/index.html.

285 *"I have neither the time nor legal background"* Klein's post from Nov. 26, 2008, is at http://swampland.blogs.time.com/2007/11/26/fisa_more_than_you_want_to_kno/.

287 *When Intel chairman Andy Grove told* Felicity Barringer, "Intel's Chairman Tells Newspaper Publishers to Supply More Insight," *New York Times*, April 19, 1999, at http://query.nytimes.com/gst/fullpage.html?res=9B0DE3DC1E3BF93AA25757C0 A96F958260.

288 *"given away the store"* David Lazarus, "Free News Online Will Cost Journalism Dearly," *Los Angeles Times*, December 26, 2007, at http://www.latimes.com/ business/la-fi-lazarus26dec26,1,2276712,full.column.

288 *"self-inflicted cannibalism"* Darnton as quoted in Michael Miner, "Death by a Thousand Cuts," *Chicago Reader*, Nov. 6, 2008, at http://www.chicagoreader .com/features/stories/hottype/081106/.

288 *"'Citizen journalist' is just the pretty new construct"* Oct. 30, 2007, letter to Romenesko at http://www1.poynter.org/forum/view_post.asp?id=12941.

289 *they were like monastic scribes* Clay Shirky, *Here Comes Everybody* (Penguin, 2008).

289 *"The news business—our crowd of overexcited people"* Michael Wolff, "Is This the End of News?" *Vanity Fair*, Oct. 2007, at http://www.vanityfair.com/politics/ features/2007/10/wolff200710?printable=true&currentPage=all.

290 *"A person like me who believes in the tradition"* Daniel Schorr, quoted in Sam McManis, "NPR's Schorr Vital Link to 'Responsible Journalism,'" *Sacramento Bee*, January 15, 2008, at http://web.archive.org/web/20080116115348/http://www .sacbee.com/107/story/634053.html.

290 *Pete Hamill told his journalism students* Hamill spoke on WNYC on June 11, 2007, and is quoted on Jeff Jarvis's blog at http://www.buzzmachine.com/2007/ 06/15/pay-no-attention/.

290 *"Any idiot with a laptop"* Café customer interviewed on KQED's California Report, March 7, 2008, available at http://www.californiareport.org/archive .jsp?date=20080307.

291 *"the patient sifting of fact"* Michael Skube, "Blogs: All the Noise that Fits," *Los Angeles Times*, August 19, 2007, at http://www.latimes.com/news/printedition/ opinion/la-op-skube19aug19,0,1667466.story?coll=la-news-comment.

291 *"And this is from someone who teaches journalism?"* Marshall's retort to Skube is at http://talkingpointsmemo.com/archives/024644.php.

292 *"I think you're full of shit"* Bissinger's April 29, 2008, appearance on Costas's show is viewable at http://deadspin.com/385770/bissinger-vs-leitch.

292 *Bissinger later apologized* "An Interview with Buzz Bissinger," the Big Lead, May 5, 2008, at http://thebiglead.com/?p=5684.

292 *A 2006 New Yorker piece* Nicholas Lemann, "Amateur Hour: Journalism Without Journalists," *The New Yorker*, August 7, 2006, at http://www.newyorker.com/fact/content/articles/060807fa_fact1.

296 *"Divided They Blog"* http://www.blogpulse.com/papers/2005/AdamicGlance BlogWWW.pdf.

296 *a 2007 study of "cross-ideological discussions"* By Eszter Hargittai, Jason Gallo, and Matthew Kane; available at http://www.springerlink.com/content/p7m41t21344130t7/?p=09b1b782b5b246ad943a3d968298dec5&pi=4.

298 *"The transformation of newspapers"* Eric Alterman, "Out of Print: The Death and Life of the American Newspaper," *The New Yorker*, March 31, 2008, at http://www.newyorker.com/reporting/2008/03/31/080331fa_fact_alterman?currentPage=all.

CHAPTER 10
WHEN EVERYONE HAS A BLOG

301 *"One of the most important things"* Douglas Adams, "How to Stop Worrying and Learn to Love the Internet," *Sunday Times* (London), Aug 29, 1999, at http://www.douglasadams.com/dna/19990901-00-a.html.

301 *"a space in which anyone could be creative"* Tim Berners-Lee's first blog post from Dec. 12, 2005, is at http://dig.csail.mit.edu/breadcrumbs/node/38.

301–302 *"No, I have a day job"* Andreessen's comment was in an interview in the *San Jose Mercury News*, unavailable online today, but quoted by Dave Winer at http://archive.scripting.com/2003/03/06#When:8:32:14AM.

302 *"I should have started doing this years and years ago"* Marc Andreessen, "Eleven Lessons Learned About Blogging So Far," July 10, 2007, at http://blog.pmarca.com/2007/07/eleven-lessons.html.

303 *Google pointed me to an American food blogger* Kitchen Chick's post on *ya cai* is at http://www.kitchenchick.com/2007/03/pickled_mustard.html.

303 *the "Blog" of "Unnecessary" Quotation Marks* http://www.unnecessaryquotes.com/

304 *"This blog is a waste of time. . . ."* The FAQ page is at http://quotation-marks.blogspot.com/2007/09/frequently-asked-questions.html.

305 *Computer-science pioneer Joseph Weizenbaum* Katie Hafner, "Between Tech Fans and Naysayers, Scholarly Skeptics," *New York Times*, April 1, 1999,

at http://query.nytimes.com/gst/fullpage.html?res=9907E0D61639F932A35757 C0A96F958260.

305 *Weizenbaum wrote a letter to the editor* New York Times, April 8, 1999, at http://query.nytimes.com/gst/fullpage.html?res=980DE0DA1438F93BA35757C0 A96F958260.

306 *"millions of morons . . . sharing their drivel"* Michael Wolff, "Is This the End of News?" *Vanity Fair*, Oct. 2007, at http://www.vanityfair.com/politics/features/ 2007/10/wolff200710?printable=true&currentPage=all.

306 This American Life *creator Ira Glass* On the Media, July 25, 2006, WNYC, transcript at http://onthemedia.org/transcripts/2008/07/25/03.

308 Salon Blogs: Gordon Atkinson's Real Live Preacher, originally at http://blogs.salon .com/0001772/, now at http://www.reallivepreacher.com/; Julie Powell's Julie/ Julia Project at http://blogs.salon.com/0001399/; Dave Pollard's How to Save the World: http://blogs.salon.com/0002007/; The Raven: http://blogs.salon.com/0001381/.

309 *"Movable Type RIP"* http://www.metafilter.com/33072/Movable-Type-RIP.

311 *A March 2008 study by Universal McCann* Figures are from http://www.media post.com/publications/index.cfm?fuseaction=Articles.showArticleHomePage&art _aid=85025 and also http://technorati.com/blogging/state-of-the-blogosphere/.

311 *Iranian president Mahmoud Ahmadinejad* Ahmadinejad's blog is at http:// www.ahmadinejad.ir/en/.

311 *and so does . . . Carl Icahn* Icahn's blog is at http://www.icahnreport.com/.

312 *"the world's most hated blogger"* Declan McCullagh, "Casey Serin: The world's most hated blogger?" CNET, May 14, 2007, at http://news.com.com/Casey+ Serin+The+worlds+most+hated+blogger/2100-1028-6183383.html.

312 *Peter Kenney of Yarmouth, Massachusetts* "House pest: One Cape Cod blogger is getting the scoops and setting the pace for Massachusetts casino coverage—for better or worse," Adam Reilly, the Phoenix, Sept. 12, 2007, at http://thephoenix .com/article_ektid47296.aspx. Kenney's blog is at http://www.capecodtoday.com/ blogs/index.php/Gadfly.

312 *Jane Novak* Novak's blog is at http://armiesofliberation.com/. The *New York Times* story on Novak, from May 20, 2008, is at http://www.nytimes.com/2008/ 05/20/world/middleeast/20blogger.html?_r=1&ref=nyregion&oref=login.

312 *Andrew Olmsted, a U.S. Army major* Olmsted's blog is at http://andrewolmsted .com/. The final post is at http://andrewolmsted.com/archives/2008/01/final_ post.html.

314 *China alone had 47 million blogs* "CNNIC Releases 2007 Survey Report on China Weblog Market," Dec. 26, 2007, at http://www.cnnic.cn/html/Dir/ 2007/12/27/4954.htm.

314 *"the largest expansion in expressive capability"* Shirky interview by Farhad Manjoo in Salon, March 7, 2008, at http://machinist.salon.com/feature/2008/ 03/07/clay_shirkey/.

314 *"I believe what we have with the Web today"* Doc Searls, "Thanking Our Own Heaven on OneWebDay," Linux Journal, Sept. 18, 2007, at http://www.linux journal.com/node/1000305.

315 *"We are in a fragmenting culture"* Lessing's Nobel lecture is at http://nobel prize.org/nobel_prizes/literature/laureates/2007/lessing-lecture_en.html.

317 *in the* Phaedrus, *as Richard Powers reminds us* Richard Powers, "How to Speak a Book," *New York Times Book Review*, Jan. 7, 2007, at http://www.nytimes.com/2007/01/07/books/review/Powers2.t.html?ref=books.

317 *"Contemplative Man"* Carr's quote is from http://blogs.britannica.com/blog/main/2007/06/from-contemplative-man-to-flickering-man/.

318 *"Is the ocean of short writing"* Kevin Kelly's post from June 11, 2008, is at http://www.kk.org/thetechnium/archives/2008/06/will_we_let_goo.php.

318 *the "context of no context"* George W. S. Trow, *Within the Context of No Context* (Little, Brown, 1981).

319 *When publishing was scarce, we filtered first* Shirky's first exposition of this theme was in his 2002 paper on "Broadcast Institutions, Community Values," at http://www.shirky.com/writings/broadcast_and_community.html.

320 *a flattering* New Yorker *profile* Ken Auletta, "Barry Diller's Search for the Future," *The New Yorker*, Feb. 22, 1993, at kenauletta.com/barrydiller.html.

320 *"Self-publishing by someone of average talent"* "Among the audience," *The Economist*, April 20, 2006, at http://www.economist.com/surveys/displaystory.cfm?story_id=6794156.

320 *"There's just not that much talent"* Barry Diller at the Web 2.0 Conference, Oct. 2005, reported by the author at http://www.wordyard.com/2005/10/06/dillers-tale/.

323 *"That is the wrong language"* Claude S. Fischer, *America Calling: A Social History of the Telephone to 1940* (University of California Press, 1992), pp. 27–28.

324 *Some blogs are simply vehicles for conversation* Clay Shirky draws this distinction in an interview in David Kline and Dan Burstein's *Blog! How the Newest Media Revolution Is Changing Politics, Business and Culture* (CDS Books, 2005), p. 287.

324 *"There is a point when there are simply too many blogs"* James McGrath Morris, "Bloggers' Big News Needs Scaling Down," *Legal Times*, Feb. 28, 2007, at http://web.archive.org/web/20070302171232/http://www.law.com/jsp/legaltechnology/pubArticleLT.jsp?id=1172570589622.

324 *"How many blogs does the world need?"* Michael Kinsley, *Time*, Nov. 20, 2008, at http://www.time.com/time/magazine/article/0,9171,1860888,00.html.

324 *Most blogs are read only "by the writer and his mother"* "Figuring Out Blogs, Podcasting, Wikis and Whatever's Next," Mediabistro, at http://www.mediabistro.com/articles/cache/a9549.asp.

325 *Christine Kenneally describes the scene* The description is from William Grimes's

review of Kenneally's *The First Word* (Penguin, 2008) in the *New York Times*, at http://www.nytimes.com/2007/08/01/books/01grim.html.

326　*"Each blog . . . is like a blinking neuron"*　James Wolcott, "Blog Nation," Business 2.0, May 2002, at http://web.archive.org/web/20020601142409/http://www.business2.com/articles/mag/0,1640,39413,FF.html.

326　*"loss of selfness"*　Nicholas Carr's post is at http://www.roughtype.com/archives/2007/10/vampires_of_the.php.

CHAPTER 11
FRAGMENTS FOR THE FUTURE

328　*"When a thing is new, people say, 'It is not true'"*　Evan Williams's Evhead.com page, Dec. 1998, at http://web.archive.org/web/19981202032238/http://www.evhead.com/. The quote is widely attributed on Web quotation sites to William James, but I have been unable to locate it in this phrasing. It may be a corruption of the following line from James's *Pragmatism*: "First, you know, a new theory is attacked as absurd; then it is admitted to be true, but obvious and insignificant; finally it is seen to be so important that its adversaries claim that they themselves discovered it." This passage can be found on page 198 of the Google Books scan of the book (Longmans, Green and Co., 1907) at http://books.google.com/books?id=xh4QAAAAYAAJ&dq=william+james+pragmatism&pg=PP1&ots=agh4j_RIOZ&source=bn&sig=8meyX-jPiPC5WvOMew-C0uddh1M&hl=en&sa=X&oi=book_result&resnum=4&ct=result.

328　*Jason Calacanis posted that he was "retiring"*　Calacanis's post from July 11, 2008, is at http://calacanis.com/2008/07/11/official-announcement-regarding-my-retirement-from-blogging/.

329　*"The blogosphere, once a freshwater oasis"*　Paul Boutin, "Twitter, Flickr, Facebook Make Blogs Look So 2004," *Wired*, Nov. 2008, at http://www.wired.com/entertainment/theweb/magazine/16-11/st_essay.

330　*"a gentrifying wagon train of carpetbaggers"*　Merlin Mann's post of Sept. 8, 2008, is at http://www.43folders.com/2008/09/08/four-years.

330　*Jesse James Garrett was probably the first*　Author interview with Garrett, April 2008.

331　*"Bloggers Suffer Burnout"*　Daniel Terdiman, Wired News, July 8, 2004, at http://www.wired.com/culture/lifestyle/news/2004/07/64068.

331　*a 2005 post titled "The Blog Cycle"*　Anil Dash's post from March 21, 2005, is at http://www.dashes.com/anil/2005/03/the-blog-cycle.html.

333　*Alice Mathias . . . tried to school her elders*　Alice Mathias, "The Fakebook Generation," Oct. 6, 2007, at http://www.nytimes.com/2007/10/06/opinion/06mathias.html.

334　*"Blogging as I would define it is passé"*　Jason Kottke's post from Aug. 20, 2008, is at http://www.kottke.org/08/08/what-makes-for-a-good-blog.

334   *"I don't think there will be that many blogs around"*   Bruce Sterling at South by
      Southwest, March 13, 2007, audio at http://2007.sxsw.com/blogs/podcasts
      .php/2007/03/14/bruce_sterling_s_sxsw_rant.

335   *It had taken roughly two decades for "social production"*   Nick Carr, "Who killed the
      blogosphere?," post of Nov. 7, 2008, at http://www.roughtype.com/
      archives/2008/11/who_killed_the.php.

336   *"a little First Amendment machine"*   Jay Rosen, "Bloggers vs. Journalists Is Over,"
      Jan. 21, 2005, at http://journalism.nyu.edu/pubzone/weblogs/pressthink/2005/01/
      21/berk_essy.html.

337   *Zuckerberg's Law*   Saul Hansell, "Zuckerberg's Law of Information Sharing," *New
      York Times* Bits Blog, Nov. 6, 2008, at http://bits.blogs.nytimes.com/2008/11/06/
      zuckerbergs-law-of-information-sharing/.

337   *"Shall no fart pass without a tweet?"*   Nick Carr's post of Nov. 8, 2008, is at
      http://www.roughtype.com/archives/2008/11/zuckerbergs_sec.php.

337   *"drowning in yak"*   RU Sirius interview with Mark Dery, Oct. 5, 2007, at
      http://www.10zenmonkeys.com/2007/10/05/is-the-net-good-for-writers/.

338   *"What started out as a liberating stream"*   Neil Postman, "Informing Ourselves to
      Death," 1990, at http://web.archive.org/web/20021215073120/http://www
      .frostbytes.com/~jimf/informing.html.

339   *As Clay Shirky has argued*   Shirky's talk at the Sept. 2008 Web 2.0 Expo NY is at
      http://www.youtube.com/watch?v=LabqeJEOQyI.

339   *Robert Scoble cheerily explained*   The video is at http://www.viddler.com/
      explore/masterlock77/videos/1/.

340   *"No, I'm not keeping up with your blog"*   David Weinberger, June 20, 2005, at
      http://www.hyperorg.com/blogger/mtarchive/004138.html.

341   276,000 new books published in 2007: This statistic, from Bowker, is at
      http://www.bowker.com/index.php/press-releases/526-bowker-reports-us-book-
      production-flat-in-2007.

341   *"produces paralysis rather than liberation"*   Barry Schwartz's talk on the "paradox
      of choice" at the TED conference, Jan. 2007, is at http://www.youtube.com/
      watch?v=VO6XEQIsCoM.

343   *Ray Bradbury . . . recently reminded readers*   Amy E. Boyle Johnston, "Ray
      Bradbury: Fahrenheit 451 Misinterpreted," *LA Weekly*, May 31, 2007, at http://www
      .laweekly.com/news/news/ray-bradbury-fahrenheit-451-misinterpreted/16524/.

345   *"copying machines"*   Interview with Cory Doctorow by Joel Turnipseed guestblog-
      ging at Kottke.org, Nov. 4, 2007, at http://www.kottke.org/07/11/cory-doctorow.

346   *"I make black marks on a white surface"*   Joel Garreau, "Through the Looking
      Glass," interview with William Gibson, *Washington Post*, Sept. 6, 2007, at
      http://www.washingtonpost.com/wp-dyn/content/article/2007/09/05/
      AR2007090502582_3.html.

347   *Gordon Bell, a veteran computer scientist*   Two good portraits of Bell's project are

Alec Wilkinson's in *The New Yorker*, May 28, 2007, at http://www.newyorker .com/reporting/2007/05/28/070528fa_fact_wilkinson; and Clive Thompson's in *Fast Company*, Nov. 2006, at http://www.fastcompany.com/magazine/110/head-for-detail.html.

347   *"What value can there be in saving every email"*   Kevin Kelly's post from Sept. 15, 2008, is at http://www.kk.org/thetechnium/archives/2008/09/everything_too.php.

347   *"This century we're going to learn a lesson"*   Charlie Stross, "Shaping the Future," May 13, 2007, at http://www.antipope.org/charlie/blog-static/2007/05/shaping_the_future.html.

348   *"Fifty years from now"*   From Clive Thompson's *Fast Company* piece about Bell.

348   *"Imagine that you had to face"*   Danah Boyd's post of March 20, 2007, is at http://www.zephoria.org/thoughts/archives/2007/03/20/to_remember_or.html.

349   *"The College of Cartographers"*   This quotation is available at http://www.kyb .tuebingen.mpg.de/bu/people/bs/borges.html.

350   *"beaten to death with croutons"*   Bruce Sterling at South by Southwest, March 13, 2007.

350   *"In a world of hyperabundant content"*   Paul Saffo, "It's the Context, Stupid," *Wired*, March 1994, at http://www.wired.com/wired/archive/2.03/context.html.

EPILOGUE
TWILIGHT OF THE CYNICS

355   *In one of his comic monologues*   Spalding Gray, "Terrors of Pleasure," in *Sex and Death to the Age 14* (Vintage, 1986), p. 236.

356   *"putting your views at risk"*   Christopher Lasch, *The Revolt of the Elites* (Norton, 1996), p. 171.

356   *his public about-face "wasn't pretty at times"*   Sullivan's post from Aug. 14, 2008, is at http://andrewsullivan.theatlantic.com/the_daily_dish/2008/08/after-the-cold.html.

Adamic, Lada, 296
Against the Machine (Siegel), 248
Age of Missing Information, The
    (McKibben), 338
Ahmadinejad, Mahmoud, 311–12
Allbritton, Chris, 174
Allen, Joshua, 167
Allman, Kevin, 288
Altavista, 75, 79
Alterman, Eric, 298
Alvey, Brian, 181
America Calling (Fischer), 323
America Online (AOL), 6, 21, 66, 83,
    120, 185, 287, 292, 332
Anderson, Chris, 214, 282
Andreessen, Marc, 10, 11, 59, 301–2
Anti-Math, 76–77

Anuff, Joey, 25, 26, 27
Apple, 21, 49, 51, 125, 184, 244, 275
Armstrong, Heather, 229–34, 256,
    257, 260–65
Armstrong, Jerome, 142, 149,
    150, 152
Arrington, Michael, 190, 191, 192,
    196–97

Arthur, Lance, 220–21
artificial intelligence, 75, 76, 77
Atrios, 142, 145, 149, 295

Barger, Jorn, 85, 90, 101, 205,
    209, 236
    Anti-Math devised by, 76–77
    literature enjoyed by, 76, 77, 78, 81,
        82, 97
    see also Robot Wisdom WebLog
Barrett, Cameron, 86–87, 211, 229
Bartlett, Dan, 163
Battelle, John, 199, 219
Bausch, Paul, 109–10, 117, 119,
    121–22, 124, 127
    Blogger created by, 111–12, 113–14

Beebo.org, 209
Bell, Gordon, 347, 348
Berners-Lee, Tim, 9, 10, 11, 12, 59,
    207, 301–2
Bhatnagar, Ranjit, 21–22
Bissinger, Buzz, 291–92
Black, Duncan (Atrios), 142, 145, 149,
    295

Block, Doug, 32, 37
Blogads, 178, 181, 187, 219
Blogger, 102, 110, 115, 121–23, 130,
        136, 148, 174, 194, 199, 218,
        240, 242, 307, 309, 310, 334,
        345, 354
    business plan for, 16–17
    Google's deal with, 125–28, 129
    growth of, 6, 119–20
    money problems of, 123–24
    on 9/11, 4–5, 125
    release of, 111–12, 113–14
Blogger Pro, 118, 125
"Blog" of "Unnecessary" Quotation
        Marks, 303–4
blogroll, 86–87
blogs, 7, 11, 64, 70, 90–91, 145, 149,
        162, 196
    advertising on, 178–82, 187–88,
        201, 219–20, 223
    audio and video on, 310–11
    Blood's history of, 89, 115, 141
    Carr's opposition to, 317–18
    coining of term, 76, 79, 101–2, 205
    comments on, 64, 148–49, 217,
        249, 255, 345
    criticisms of, 89–90, 114–15, 129,
        314–22, 334, 346, 351, 357
    echo-chamber effect on, 293,
        294–97, 298
    filtering of posts on, 319–22
    growth of, 13–14, 63, 133–34, 207,
        211–12, 218, 269–70, 302,
        313–15, 339–40, 343, 354–55
    independence of, 161, 326
    as intellectual autobiographies,
        95–97
    Iraq War on, 142, 143, 151, 152,
        174, 218, 240–42, 276–77,
        312–13
    lack of professionals on, 166,
        173–74
    Lessing's opposition to, 315–16
    liberal, 142–43, 149
    links on, 95–96, 115, 207, 209,
        329, 345
    Lott controversy reported on, 143,
        144–46, 273
    "national narrative" argument
        against, 293–94, 297–99
    on 9/11, 1–5, 6–7, 8, 151
    origins of, 79–81
    overwhelming choices of, 338–42
    as professional, 175–78, 182–97,
        219–20
    programs and software for, 63,
        85–86, 111–14, 148, 150–51, 175
    range of, 303, 304, 340–42
    rankings of, 210–12, 220–21, 320
    Rathergate on, 278–81
    retirement of, 330–31
    RSS on, 70, 130, 206, 207–8, 209,
        307, 339, 345
    at Salon.com, 307–9, 310, 325, 354
    sincerity vs. authenticity on, 258–59
    by traditional journalists, 285–86
    see also specific blogs and bloggers
blog search engines, 209
Blogspot, 117, 118, 124, 137, 240, 242
Blood, Rebecca, 88–89, 115, 141
Blue, Violet, 222–28
Blumenthal, Mark, 282
Boing Boing, 198–205, 213, 249, 264,
        350
    deletion of posts from, 222–28
    growth of, 203, 218–19, 221, 228
    revenue of, 219–20, 221
bootstrapping, 52, 72
Borges, Jorge Luis, 348–49
Boston Phoenix, 177
bots, 74–76
Boutin, Paul, 93, 242, 329–30, 334
boyd, danah, 348
Bradbury, Ray, 343
Breitbart, Andrew, 84
Bricklin, Dan, 123
Broadwaystars.com, 1–3, 5
Brown, Ben, 89–90

bulletin-board services (BBSes),
19–20, 63
Burke, Carolyn, 28
Bush, George W., 131, 140, 152, 154,
163, 278, 280, 282, 356
in Social Security debate, 154–59
tax cuts of, 154, 158
Bush administration, 149, 151, 272,
276–77

Cadenhead, Rogers, 65–66
Calacanis, Jason, 188, 191, 194,
201, 219
profits sought by, 183, 184,
185, 188
"retirement" of, 328–29
Weblogs, Inc. and, 181–82, 185, 186
Winer's argument with, 70–72
Cameron, Robert, 136
CamWorld, 86, 87, 88, 229
Carpentier, Megan, 277
Carr, David, 186
Carr, Nicholas, 317–18, 326, 334–35,
337
Chan, Dan, 209
Channel 9, 169–70
Ciarelli, Nicholas, 275
Clark, Joe, 212–13
Clinton, Bill, 83, 132, 279, 297
Cluetrain Manifesto, The, 168–69, 173,
174, 194, 225, 253, 340
CNN, 4, 151, 200, 255
Coates, Tom, 206
Cohen, June, 54
Communications Decency Act (1996),
20, 58
Computer Power and Human Reason
(Weizenbaum), 305
Congress, U.S., 155, 156–57
content management system (CMS),
66–67
Copeland, Henry, 178, 219
Cox, Ana Marie, 177, 277
Creating Passionate Users, 251–52

Cult of the Amateur, The (Keen), 320
Cutler, Jessica, 177, 234
Cyborganic, 28, 37

Daily Kos, 142, 149–50, 152,
192, 295
Daily Me, 295, 298
Dark Night, 18–19, 42, 43, 45
Darnton, John, 288
Dash, Anil, 141, 331
DaveNet, 50–53, 59, 70
bootstrapping on, 52, 72
flame-reduction suggestion on, 58,
64–65, 72
on Hotwired, 54, 55–56, 57–58
on mailing-list flame wars, 57–58
Suck's parody of, 56–57, 67
Dean, Howard, 152, 153, 297
DeLay, Tom, 159–60
Democratic Party, U.S., 139, 142,
143, 152
in Social Security debate, 154,
155–56, 160
Denton, Nick, 7, 8, 119, 174–78,
185–86, 193–95, 201, 242
profits sought by, 174, 177, 179–80,
181, 182, 183–84, 185–86
Dery, Mark, 337
Digital Equipment PDP-4, 352–53
Diller, Barry, 320, 321–22
Diller, Matthew, 352, 353
Doctorow, Cory, 200, 201–3, 204,
224, 345, 347
Dooce, 229–34, 260–65
dotcom boom and bust, 6, 23, 33, 104,
105, 116, 174, 190, 230, 280,
307, 358
Down and Out in the Magic Kingdom
(Doctorow), 201–2
Drudge, Matt, 82–85
Drudge Manifesto, The (Drudge), 84
Drudge Report, 82–85, 133, 192, 279
Dublanica, Steve, 243
Dyson, Esther, 192

Eaton, Brigitte, 211
Economist, 170, 320
EditThisPage.com, 63, 67, 117, 167
Edsall, Thomas, 144
elections, U.S.:
  1998, 28
  2000, 131–33, 135, 136–37, 158, 297
  2004, 153, 158, 178, 282, 297
  2008, 83, 282–83, 297
Electoral-vote.com, 282
Eliot, T. S., 351
Ellison, Larry, 55, 71
email, 46, 189, 324
  political campaigns' use of, 152–53
Empire of the Air, The (documentary),
  165
Engadget, 183, 184, 185, 329
Engelbart, Douglas, 52
English Cut, 172–73
Evhead, 103, 108

Facebook, 13, 43, 112, 324, 332–33,
  334, 335, 336, 348
Fahrenheit 451, 343
Fake Steve Jobs, 244
Finley, Karen, 30
First Amendment, 274, 275, 336
First Word, The (Kenneally), 325
Fischer, Claude S., 323
Fisk, Robert, 151–52
Fitzpatrick, Brad, 112
Fivethirtyeight.com, 282–83
Fleishman, Glenn, 180–81
Florida, 131–32, 135, 136–37, 158
Foer, Franklin, 247
Foreign Intelligence Surveillance Act
  (FISA), 285
Frauenfelder, Mark, 198–99, 200, 201,
  218–19, 225, 227, 228, 354
Fray.com, 87, 117
FreeRepublic.com, 133, 278–79, 295
Frontier NewsPage Suite, 63, 78–79,
  80, 85
Frontier scripting tools, 49, 50, 51,
  59, 61

"Funes the Memorious" (Borges),
  348–49

Gallo, Jason, 296
Garrett, Jesse James, 85–86, 88–89,
  140, 211, 330–31
Gates, Bill, 171, 215
  Winer and, 47–48, 64
Gawker Media, 8, 119, 176, 177–78,
  179, 181, 186, 193–95, 224, 250,
  291, 334
Gibson, William, 75, 346
Gillmor, Dan, 134, 136, 246, 276
Gizmodo, 175, 177, 178, 179, 183,
  184, 185, 329
Glance, Natalie, 296
Goddard, Taegan, 149
Gonzales, Alberto, 160, 291
Google, 42, 70, 179, 181, 186–87,
  188, 206–7, 211, 218, 225, 234,
  247, 287, 303, 305, 310, 316,
  319, 342, 350
  Blogger's deal with, 125–28, 129
  YouTube acquired by, 191
Google Rank, 320
Gore, Al, 131, 132, 278
Graham, Brad, 205
Gray, Spalding, 31, 355
Greenwald, Glenn, 285
Groksoup, 113, 117
Grossman, Leonard, 93–94
Guardian, 7, 242

Hafner, Katie, 238
Hall, Justin, 4, 31, 39, 48, 81, 85, 87,
  97, 130, 233, 236
  appearance of, 17, 29, 32–33
  Dark Night video of, 18–19, 42,
    43, 45
  and father's suicide, 20, 29, 36
  at Hotwired, 23, 24, 25, 33, 37
  public speaking by, 18, 32, 37–39
  self-revelations of, 17, 18, 19, 24,
    25, 30, 34–35, 36–37, 40–43,
    44–45

see also Justin's Links from the Underground
Hamer, Matt, 117
Hammon, Merci, 42–43
Hamsher, Jane, 284
Hargittai, Eszter, 296
Harmon, Amy, 5
Harpold, Leslie, 89
Harvard University, 146, 277–78, 332
Haughey, Matt, 117, 119, 121, 140–41, 148, 181
Herrell, Alan, 253
Hewlett-Packard, 109, 110, 112
Heyward, Andrew, 280
Hiltzik, Michael, 12, 306
Hilzoy, 312–13
Hotwired, 53, 79, 117, 179
    DaveNet pieces published on, 54, 55–56, 57–58
    Hall at, 23, 24, 25, 33, 37
    launching of, 23–24
    Suck.com at, 25–27
Hourihan, Meg, 102, 104–5, 119–20, 122, 124, 194, 206, 211, 212, 334
    Blogger and, 111, 112, 113–14, 127
    see also Megnut; Pyra Labs
HTML, 31–32, 74, 86, 102, 104–5, 108, 146, 219
Huffington, Arianna, 192
Huffington Post, 192–93, 288
Hussein, Saddam, 142, 143, 147, 151, 241, 272, 276–77
hypertext, 24–25, 26

Iamfacingforeclosure.com, 312
IBM, 21, 46–47
I. F. Stone's Weekly, 161–62
Independent, 176
Industry Standard, 110, 124, 199, 201, 219
Information Anxiety (Wurman), 338
Instapundit.com, 137, 138, 295
Institute for the Learning Sciences, 78
Interviewing the Audience, 31

Iraq, 142, 143, 151, 152, 154, 156, 158, 174, 218, 240–42, 276–78, 281, 297, 312–13, 356
Ito, Joi, 269

James, William, 328
Janabi, Salam al-, 240–42
Jardin, Xeni, 201, 222, 223–25, 226, 227
Jarrar, Raed, 240
Jarvis, Jeff, 116–17, 139
Jen, Mark, 234
Jennicam, 82, 86
Jobs, Steve, 10
Johnson, Charles, 140, 279
Johnson, Samuel, 174
Johnson, Steven, 126
Joyce, James, 76, 77, 81, 82
Justice Department, U.S., 160, 167
Justin's Links from the Underground, 17–19, 21, 22, 24, 25, 27–32, 40–43, 74

Kamen, Dean, 200
Kane, Matthew, 296
Katrina, Hurricane, 154, 158, 356
Kaus, Mickey, 135–36, 148
Kedrosky, Paul, 113
Keeley, Bethany, 304
Keen, Andrew, 320
Keller, Julia, 270
Kelley, Helen, 165
Kelly, Kevin, 249, 318, 347, 354–55
Kenneally, Christine, 325
Kenney, Peter, 312
Kerry, John, 150, 202
Kinsley, Michael, 12, 324
Klam, Matthew, 163
Klein, Joe, 284–85
Klein, Jonathan, 279
Knauss, Greg, 67–68, 114, 129, 334
Kottke, Jason, 120, 212, 230, 233, 242, 334
Kristof, Nicholas, 286
Krugman, Paul, 147

Kurzweil, Ray, 352
Kyanka, Rich, 256–57

Lasch, Christopher, 356
Layne, Ken, 151
Lazarus, David, 288
Leitch, Will, 291
Lemann, Nicholas, 292–93
Lessing, Doris, 315–16
Lewinsky, Monica, 82, 83, 84, 135
lifeloggers, 347–49
links.net, *see* Justin's Links from the
    Underground
Little Green Footballs, 140, 278, 279
LiveJournal, 112–13
Locke, Chris, 253, 255
Long Tail, 214, 216–17, 218, 233, 239
Los Angeles Times, 12, 138, 152, 223,
    288, 291
Lott, Trent, 143, 144–46, 273
Lyons, Dan, 244

Maass, Peter, 242
McCain, John, 162–63
MacDougald, Harry, 279
Mackey, John, 245
McKibben, Bill, 338
Mahon, Thomas, 172–73, 350
Malda, Rob, 80
Malik, Om, 193
Manila, 63, 117, 118
Mann, Merlin, 330
Mapes, Mary, 280
Marino, James, 1–3, 5
Markoff, John, 20, 269, 286
Marlow, Cameron, 209
Marshall, Joshua Micah, 132, 136,
    137, 138, 143–44, 145, 147–48,
    155–59, 160, 163–64, 174, 277,
    291, 350
    see also Talking Points Memo
Massie, Alexis, 28, 87
Mathias, Alice, 333
Mead, Rebecca, 120, 212, 270, 334
meankids.org, 252, 253, 254–56

media, traditional, 335
    blogging on, 285–86
    and election of 2000, 131–32
    Web vs., 6–7, 8, 9–10, 38, 91, 132,
        136–37, 138, 141, 145–46, 163,
        166, 269–300, 315
MediaWhoresOnline, 133, 142
Megnut, 105–6
Merholz, Peter, 66, 101, 102
Metafilter, 4, 117, 148, 149, 181, 237,
    238, 240, 309
Michalski, Jerry, 116
Microsoft, 21, 47, 48, 61, 127, 135,
    166, 167–68, 191, 244, 347
    blogging at, 169–72
milbloggers, 312–13
mommyblogging, 263–64
Moore's Law, 336
Moreover, 119, 174
Morris, James McGrath, 324
Mosaic, 10, 20–21
Mossberg, Walt, 276
Moulitsas Zuniga, Markos, 142–43,
    149–50, 152
    in Dean campaign, 152
Movable Type, 128, 148, 149, 150,
    175, 206, 209, 224, 235, 309–10
Mullenweg, Matt, 310
Murdoch, Rupert, 332
Murphy, Ted, 187–88
MyDD, 142, 149, 150
MySpace, 13, 43, 112, 332, 335

Napster, 200, 201
National Center for Supercomputing
    Applications (NCSA) at, 10,
    22, 54
National Endowment for the Arts, 30
National Review Online, 138, 296
Netscape, 10, 11, 26, 61, 207
New Republic, 132, 135, 136, 177,
    245, 247, 248
Newsweek, 56, 82, 135, 173, 244
New York, 83–84, 180, 183, 186, 194,
    195, 241

New Yorker, 48, 212, 270, 292–93, 298, 320, 334
New York Observer, 247
New York Times, 5, 20, 145, 147, 151, 152, 156, 186, 196, 217, 238, 269, 272, 277, 284, 286, 287, 288, 305, 333
New York Times Magazine, 163
Nicole, Kaycee, 236–38, 239, 240
Nielsen-Hayden, Teresa, 249
Novak, Jane, 312
NPR, 289–90

Obama, Barack, 297
Obsidian Wings, 312
Obvious Filter, 80, 85
"Of Exactitude in Science" (Borges), 349
Offhand Remarks, 80–81
Olmsted, Andrew, 312–13
Olson, Theodore, 132
OpenCOLA, 200–201
O'Reilly, Tim, 103–4, 116, 125, 254, 255
Orlowski, Andrew, 93, 95

Paradox of Choice, The (Schwartz), 341
Paynter, Frank, 253
PayPerPost, 187–88
Penny Arcade, 248–49
permalinks, 206, 345
Pescovitz, David, 201, 226
Petersen, Julie, 23
ping server, 208–9
Pitas, 113, 117
Plame, Valerie, 284
Plexus Tech, 105, 109
Podhoretz, John, 146
Political Wire, 149, 150
Politico, 193
Posner, Richard, 281
Postman, Neil, 338
Powazek, Derek, 87, 117
"Power Laws, Weblogs, and Inequality" (Shirky), 213–16, 217–18

Powerline, 278, 295
Powers, Richard, 317
Proxicom, 105, 106
Pulver, Jeff, 69
Putnam, Robert, 294
Pyra App, 107, 108, 109, 110, 116, 118, 121
Pyra Labs, 102, 106–7, 109–11, 117, 194
    Blogger released by, 111–12, 113–14
    investment in, 112, 115–16, 118, 127
    money problems of, 118, 119, 120–21, 122, 123, 124
    Moreover's acquisition of, 119, 174
Pyralerts, 109, 110

Q, 40–41
Quick, William, 205

radio, 165, 217, 317, 335
Radio Userland, 63, 307
"Ranjit's HTTP playground," 21–22
Rathergate, 276–81
Raymond, Eric, 202
Rebecca's Pocket, 88–89
Reporters Committee for Freedom of the Press, 275
Republican Party, U.S., 28, 139, 142, 145, 153, 159
    in Social Security debate, 154, 155, 156
Reynolds, Glenn, 137, 138, 145, 211
Rheingold, Howard, 23–24, 25, 33, 37, 39, 44, 81
Richtel, Matt, 190
Ringley, Jennifer, 62
Robot Wisdom WebLog:
    anti-Israel posts on, 93–95, 97, 225
    eccentricity of, 81–82
    large output on, 91–92
    launching of, 78–79, 80
    links on, 209
    origin of term "weblog" on, 79, 81, 87
    slowdown on, 92–93

Rojas, Pete, 175, 176, 183, 185
Romenesko, Jim, 271–72, 288
Rosen, Jay, 276, 284, 290, 336
Rossetto, Louis, 22, 23–24, 27, 33
Rove, Karl, 132, 155
RSS, 70, 130, 206, 207–8, 209, 307, 339, 345

Sabato, Larry, 146
Saffo, Paul, 350
Salam Pax, 240–42
Salmon, Felix, 193
Salon.com, 6, 26, 91, 94–95, 111, 132, 144, 147, 192, 255, 307–9, 310, 325, 354
San Francisco Chronicle, 39–40, 50, 222, 275
San Francisco Examiner, 49, 50, 287
San Jose Mercury News, 87, 134–35
Sarno, David, 223, 226
Schank, Roger, 78
Schorr, Daniel, 289–90
Schwartz, Barry, 341
Schwartz, Joseph H., 248
Scoble, Robert, 169, 170–72, 191, 192, 254–55, 339
ScoobyDoos, 237, 238, 240
Scoop, 150–51
Scripting News, 5, 59–61, 64, 67, 70–72, 78, 80, 85, 86, 87, 88, 123, 207–8, 354
Seabrook, John, 48
Searls, Doc, 173, 211, 314
Segway, 200
Seitz, Bill, 5
Semantic Web, 301
Senate, U.S., 133
September 11, 2001, terrorist attacks, 1–5, 6–7, 8, 15, 137, 138, 139, 140, 143, 151–52, 231, 307, 331, 356
Serin, Casey, 312
Sessum, Jeneane, 253
Shafer, Jack, 178
Shahak, Israel, 93, 96

Shellen, Jason, 125, 126–27
Shenk, David, 338
Shirky, Clay, 213–16, 217–18, 289, 314, 319, 339
Siegel, Lee, 245–48, 249, 257, 259
Sierra, Kathy, 251–57
Sifry, David, 210
Silicon Alley Reporter, 181, 201
Silver, Nate, 282–83
Simonetti, Ellen, 234
Sincerity and Authenticity (Trilling), 257–58, 259
Sinclair, Carla, 198
Sink, Eric, 60
Sippey, Michael, 79–80, 85, 114
Six Apart, 309–10, 331
60 Minutes, 278–81
Skube, Michael, 291
Slashdot, 87, 148
Slate, 26, 132, 135, 144, 178, 192, 242
Smales, Andrew, 113
social networking sites, 13, 43, 112, 324, 332, 335–37
Social Security, 154–59, 160, 161, 350
Society of Professional Journalists, 275
sockpuppetry, 245–48
Something Awful, 356
Spiers, Elizabeth, 176, 177
Spolsky, Joel, 172, 173
Sprezzatura, 246–48
Spy, 176
Sreenivasan, Sreenath, 324–25
Stating the Obvious, 79–80
Steadman, Carl, 25, 26, 27, 56–57
Sterling, Bruce, 334, 350
Steuer, Jonathan, 23
Stewart, Jon, 246
Stilwell, Michael, 209
Stross, Charlie, 347–48
Stuff.Pyra, 108, 109, 110, 122
Sturgeon's Law, 306–7, 313
Suck.com, 25–27, 56–57, 67, 176, 177, 204
Sullivan, Andrew, 136–38, 145, 148, 173–74, 356–57

Sunstein, Cass, 294
Swarthmore University, 20, 23, 25, 28, 32, 33, 36, 37
Swenson, Debbie, 236, 237–38
Swimming to Cambodia, 31

Talking Points Memo (TPM), 137–38, 146–47, 154, 164, 174, 291, 294
  Lott controversy reported on, 143, 145, 146, 273
  on Social Security debate, 155–59, 160, 350
  on 2000 election, 132–33
TechCrunch, 190–91, 192, 196, 213
Techmeme, 320, 329–30
Technorati, 210, 211, 212, 213, 217, 218, 221, 251, 263, 311, 319
Teethmag.com, 89–90
telephone, 317, 322–23, 324
television, 217, 317, 318, 322, 324, 335, 343–44
Texas Monthly, 163
Third Voice, 65–66
Thurmond, Strom, 144, 146
Time, 284–85, 324
Times (London), 95
Time Warner, 6, 21
TPM Muckraker, 160
Trilling, Lionel, 257–58, 259
Trippi, Joe, 153
Trott, Ben and Mena, 309
Trow, George W. S., 318
Truman Show, The (film), 322
"24 Hours of Democracy," 58–59
Twitter, 130, 333–34, 335, 348
TypePad, 309, 345

Udell, Jon, 173
Usenet, 20, 63, 78
user-generated content, 66, 68
Userland, 49, 61, 169, 307–8
  discussion group of, 65–67

van der Woning, Randall, 237–38
Vanity Fair, 283

Village Voice, 177
Virtual Community, The, 23
virtual storefronts, 10–11
Voog, Ana, 82

Walker, Rob, 270
Wall Street Journal, 138, 151, 276, 294
Walsh, Joan, 255
warbloggers, 8, 138–39, 140–41, 142, 143, 205, 331
WarLog: World War III, 139–40
Warnock's dilemma, 259–60
Washingtonienne, 177, 234
Washington Monthly, 177
Washington Post, 12, 144, 151, 193
Waste Land, The (Eliot), 351
Web 2.0, 190–91, 192
Weblogs.com, 63, 67, 117, 208
Weblogs Inc., 181, 182, 185, 219
Web spiders, 74–76
Wehner, Peter, 155
Weinberger, David, 7, 340
Weiss, Philip, 83–84
Weizenbaum, Joseph, 305–6
Welch, Matt, 138, 141, 331
WELL online forum, 23, 63
Wenokur, Jeremy, 125
Where is Raed?, 240–42
Whole Earth Review, 198, 199, 254–55
whuffie, 202, 203
Wichita Eagle, 32
Wikipedia, 250, 303
Williams, Evan, 4–5, 6, 102–5, 119, 123–24, 125, 328, 333, 354
  Blogger created by, 111–12, 113–14
  Google's deal with, 125–27, 128, 129
  see also Pyra Labs
Winer, Dave, 5, 50, 57, 59, 69, 78–79, 85, 90, 118, 123, 130, 134, 149, 165, 167, 207, 211, 216, 236, 255, 258, 270, 283, 329, 339, 354
  billions of websites predicted by, 51–52, 66
  email list created by, 46–47, 48

Winer, Dave (*cont.*):
  Gates and, 47–48, 64
  as outspoken, 53, 55–56
  truth seeking by, 68–70
  "24 Hours of Democracy" created
    by, 58–59
  in Userland discussion group argu-
    ments, 65–66, 67
  see also DaveNet; Scripting News
Winer, Leon, 5
Winerlog, 67–68
Wired, 22, 23–24, 27, 28, 93, 199,
  201, 214, 219, 249, 282,
  329–30
Wired News, 71, 83, 115, 331
wiretapping, 284–85
Wolcott, James, 283, 326
Wolf, Gary, 33, 35
Wolf, Josh, 275
Wolff, Michael, 289, 306
Wonkette, 177–78, 234, 277
Wordpress, 128, 310, 345
WorkingForChange.com, 138
World Wide Web:
  ads on, 287–88
  anonymity on, 248–50
  creation and early days of, 9,
    10–13, 37

  as garbage dump, 305, 306
  growth of, 74–75
  and isolation, 294–95
  news items on, 6–7, 59
  nudity and pornography on, 22,
    29–30, 34–35
  personal details shared on, 43–45
  as political issue, 28–30
  pre-surfing of, 75–76
  as tool of communication, 12–13,
    48–49, 64
  traditional media vs., 6–7, 8, 9–10,
    38, 91, 132, 136–37, 138, 141,
    145–46, 162, 163, 166, 269–300,
    315
  Winer's optimistic prediction for,
    51–52, 66
  see also blogs; dotcom boom and
    bust
Wurman, Richard Saul, 338

Xu Jinglei, 314

Yahoo, 68, 127, 245, 287, 292
YouTube, 13, 18, 191, 239, 310–11

'zines, 189, 198, 199, 228, 354
Zuckerberg, Mark, 336–37

POINTER TO THE ONLINE POSTSCRIPT

BLOGS IN THE AGE OF TWITTER

For a look at the continued evolution of blogging over the year since I wrote this book, please visit SayEverything.com and follow the link to "Postscript."

A WINDOW INTO THE INFORMATION AGE —AND THE ECCENTRICITIES OF THE HUMAN MIND

Our civilization runs on software. Yet the art of creating it continues to be a dark mystery, even to the experts. To find out why it's so hard to bend computers to our will, Scott Rosenberg spent three years following a team of maverick software developers designing a novel personal information manager meant to challenge market leader Microsoft Outlook. Their story takes us through a maze of abrupt dead ends and exhilarating breakthroughs as they wrestle not only with the abstraction of code, but with the unpredictability of human behavior—especially their own.

DREAMING IN CODE

TWO DOZEN PROGRAMMERS,
THREE YEARS, 4,732 BUGS,
AND ONE QUEST FOR
TRANSCENDENT SOFTWARE
$13.95 PAPERBACK
(CANADA: $15.95)
978-1-4000-8247-6

"Beautifully written, *Dreaming in Code* is a book for anyone interested in the roots of creativity and innovation, for coders and noncoders alike."

—Steven Johnson, author of *Everything Bad Is Good for You*

"The first true successor to Tracy Kidder's *Soul of a New Machine*."

—James Fallows, *The Atlantic Monthly*

ALSO AVAILABLE AS AN EBOOK
AVAILABLE FROM THREE RIVERS PRESS
WHEREVER BOOKS ARE SOLD